the Human Project

FIFTH EDITION

the Human Project

Readings on the Individual, Society, and Culture

FIFTH EDITION

Edited by

Clive Cockerton

Melanie Chaparian

StudyDesk Program by

George Byrnes

Editorial Committee

Ian Baird, Nitin Deckha, John Elias, Kent Enns, Aileen Herman, Chris Irwin, Mary Ellen Kappler, Yvette Munro, Greg Nepean, Ella Ophir, Matthew O'Rourke, William Walcott, Doug Wright, Caleb Yong, and Arthur Younger

Pearson Canada
Toronto

Library and Archives Canada Cataloguing in Publication

The human project : readings on the individual, society and culture / edited by Clive Cockerton, Melanie Chaparian. — 5th ed.

ISBN 978-0-13-205353-2

1. Humanities—Textbooks. I. Cockerton, Clive II, 1943– Chaparian, Melanie, 1958–

AZ221.H85 2010   001.3   C2009-902233-8

ISBN-13: 978-0-13-205353-2
ISBN-10:   0-13-205353-5

Vice President, Editorial Director: Gary Bennett
Editor-in-Chief: Ky Pruesse
Editor, Humanities and Social Sciences: Joel Gladstone
Sponsoring Editor: Carolin Sweig
Marketing Manager: Arthur Gee
Associate Editor: Brian Simons
Production Editor: Kevin Leung
Copy Editor: Tara Tovell
Proofreader: Colleen Ste. Marie
Production Coordinator: Avinash Chandra
Permissions and Photo Research: Amanda Campbell
Composition: Macmillan Publishing Solutions
Art Director: Julia Hall
Cover Design: Miriam Blier
Cover Image: *Merry-Go-Round* by Mark Gertler

1 2 3 4 5   13 12 11 10 09

Printed and bound in the United States of America.

CONTENTS

Introduction for the Student   ix
Preface for the Teacher   xi

THE INDIVIDUAL: REFLECTIONS ON THE SELF   1

Introduction   2
Unpleasantness in Vermont *by Antonio Damasio*   9
From Biology to Biography: A Brief History of the Self
    by Wendy O'Brien   20
What Will My Future Self Think of Me?
    by Mark Kingwell   38
Darwin's God *by Robin Marantz Henig*   41
The Skin We're In *by Tim Adams*   58
Am I Free or Determined? *by Melanie Chaparian*   63

CHANGE AND THE SOCIAL WORLD   71

Introduction   72
The Economics of Social Change
    by George Bragues   76
What the Internet Is Doing to Our Brains:
    Is Google Making Us Stupid? *by Nicholas Carr*   87
Sweet Smiles, Hard Labour *by Madeleine Bunting*   96
Marriage: Then and Now *by Stephanie Coontz*   104
Marriage Is Made in Hell *by Laura Kipnis*   113
Identity Crisis *by Allan Gregg*   116
Can We All Just Get Along? *by Greg Narbey*   126
Diversity versus Solidarity—
    The Progressive Dilemma of 21st-Century Politics
    by Bhikhu Parekh   135

THE INDIVIDUAL AND THE COLLECTIVE: CONFLICT AND COOPERATION   139

Introduction   140
Politics in the Life of the Individual *by Morton Ritts*   145
Soul Force versus Physical Force *by Morton Ritts*   158
By Any Means Necessary to Bring about
   Freedom *by Malcolm X*   162
Non-Violent Resistance
   by Mohandas K. (Mahatma) Gandhi   166
Jihad vs. McWorld *by Benjamin Barber*   170
America and the World: The Twin Towers
   as Metaphor *by Immanuel Wallerstein*   182
The Perils of Obedience *by Stanley Milgram*   199
Never Again? The Problem of Genocide in the
   21st Century *by Chris Irwin*   213

SCIENCE AND THE NATURAL WORLD   229

Introduction   230
Making Sense of the Universe *by Suzanne Senay*   235
Can Science Be Ethical? *by Freeman Dyson*   250
Is Humanity Suicidal? *by Edward O. Wilson*   259
On Global Warming: How to Calculate
   and Live within our Carbon Budget
   by Tim Flannery   268
Science and Religion: A Complicated History
   by Mark Cauchi   278

ARTS AND CULTURE   295

Introduction   296
It's Open. Who Cares? *by David Macfarlane*   298
One More Time: Our Ongoing Dialogue
      with Popular Music *by Ian Baird*   301
Serious Pleasure: The Role of the Arts
      by Clive Cockerton   312
Looking for Beauty *by Clive Cockerton*   318
"Murderers": An Introduction
      by Mary Ellen Kappler   324
Murderers *by Leonard Michaels*   328
Let Me Make This Perfectly Clear
      by Gwendolyn MacEwen   332
The Back Seat of My Mother's Car
      by Julia Copus   333
Reflections on Julia Copus's "The Back Seat
      of My Mother's Car" *by Richard Sanger*   334
This Be the Verse *by Philip Larkin*   335
I Go Back to May 1937 *by Sharon Olds*   336
The Voice You Hear When You Read
      Silently *by Thomas Lux*   337
O Me! O Life! *by Walt Whitman*   338

APPENDIX

StudyDesk   341

Photo Credits   343

INTRODUCTION FOR THE STUDENT

Everyone, it seems, wants to be an individual, to be recognized as a unique and special person. Most people also relish the notion of freedom, the idea that they hold the reins, at least some of the time, in determining the course of their lives. Yet, as desirable as individuality and freedom are, very few of us want to live alone. Indeed, most of us need a community of others if we are to live well and flourish. However, the cost of living in a community is usually some sacrifice (in theory anyway) of our individuality and freedom.

Our family expects us to behave in certain ways, our friends demand a code of behaviour, and all the institutions of society, our schools, businesses, places of worship and government, influence and control our behaviour on many levels. So to live with others is to live with constraint, and yet if we submit to everyone's expectations of us, we run the danger of losing ourselves, our sense of who we are. A natural tension exists in every healthy life and this tension between individual and larger goals doesn't ever finally resolve itself. It is not something you grow out of; it doesn't go away. Just when you're being most dutiful, you can be haunted by the temptation to be wild. Just when you think that indulging your every whim is the answer, the heart responds to a larger call and a need greater than the self.

What do you do with a tension that cannot be resolved, that resists easy answers? You can pretend it doesn't exist and be blown about by the forces of change in an unconscious way. Or you can seek to understand the great tensions and problems of our day and hopefully gain not only awareness, but also some influence on how your life evolves.

The Human Project attempts to grapple with some of the difficult problems that confront everyone, from questions of our basic human nature, to social change, to politics, to technology, and to arts and culture. This is frequently a dark and complex world, and modern students need all the information, all the understanding, and all the light they can get if they are to find their own way in this world. Grappling with these questions will most probably give your grey cells a good workout, and thinking skills can be developed that will be useful in all your courses at college and, even more importantly, in your place of work. The possibility of developing your high-level thinking skills through the study of this text is of real and obvious practical benefit. But along the way, not in every section, but perhaps in some area, we hope you find some personal revelation and acquire some understanding that is unique to you.

PREFACE FOR THE TEACHER

The Human Project is an issues-based reader designed to introduce college students to the Humanities and Social Sciences. It is organized around the fundamental questions asked by a liberal education— questions of personal identity, social change, politics, science and the arts. Students are challenged to grapple with issues that don't have easy answers, to develop the higher level thinking skills that complex questions require, and to acquire a tolerance for the fundamental ambiguities that many of life's basic problems engender. Those who meet this challenge not only become more valuable, flexible and reflective workers and citizens, but, as they start down the path of discovery, they also become wiser and more fully rounded individuals.

Features This text includes a number of features designed to make the book both approachable for students and useful to teachers. The readings present a good balance between commissioned articles, written by experienced college teachers and specifically geared toward the college audience, and previously published articles, written by journalists or academics and geared toward the wider Canadian and international communities. Each unit begins with a number of quotations intended to stimulate interest in, and dialogue about, the readings to follow. The unit introductions, moreover, bring into relief the common themes and implicit agreement or disagreement among the different readings. Throughout the text, marginal definitions are provided for terms, names, places, and events that are essential to the discussion or likely to be unfamiliar to the first-year student. The units are no longer numbered, a revision made to support those teachers who elect to teach the units in a different order than how they appear in the text.

StudyDesk CD-ROM StudyDesk is a computer-based companion guide to the text that runs on the internet browser of any Pentium-level PC or Mac computer with an OS X or Unix operating system. StudyDesk provides a rich bank of supplementary material including point-form summaries of every textbook article, definitions and commentary on over 150 terms and concepts, biographical sketches of over 80 historical figures discussed in the textbook, and a selection of representative works from a number of authors cited in the textbook.

New to the Fifth Edition In the fifth edition of *The Human Project,* we have continued to present multidimensional issues that encourage students to explore different perspectives and compare theoretical views with their own experience. New articles have been included to ensure that current issues are addressed and an array of views represented. While this edition, taken as a whole, has a greater historical perspective than the last one, the overall focus remains on the contemporary relevance of the issues explored.

Each of the five units has been updated. The first unit—"The Individual: Reflections on the Self"—has been enriched with three new readings. Drawing upon lessons learned in the fields of medicine, technology and evolutionary science, Antonio Damasio's "Unpleasantness in Vermont," Mark Kingwell's "What Will My Future Self Think of Me?" and Robin Marantz Henig's "Darwin's God" all serve to complement, and complicate, the existing discussion on issues of personal identity and free will. The second unit—"Change and the Social World"— features a number of new articles that render it more reflective of contemporary issues. In "Is Google Making Us Stupid?" Nicholas Carr explores how our increasing reliance on the internet is affecting our cognitive abilities, while in "Sweet Smiles, Hard Labour" Madeleine Bunting analyzes how today's employers try to manage employees' emotions on the job. Stephanie Coontz surveys developments in the institution of the family over the past two centuries in "Marriage: Then and Now," and Allen Gregg provides a critical, international perspective on the issue of multiculturalism in "Identity Crisis." The third unit—"The Individual and the Collective"—includes three compelling new readings. A speech delivered just a few weeks after the September 11, 2001, attacks on the US, Immanuel Wallerstein's "America and the World: The Twin Towers as Metaphor" adds a decidedly American perspective to the existing discussion of globalization. Stanley Milgram's famous experiment, recounted in "The Perils of Obedience," provides a disturbing insight into the human tendency to uncritically submit to authority. This phenomenon figures largely in "Never Again? The Problem of Genocide in the 21st Century," in which, with great care and sensitivity, Chris Irwin examines, via the example of Rwanda in 1994, how genocide occurs and, moreover, what measures might be taken to minimize its recurrence. The fourth unit—"Science and the Natural World"—features two important new pieces. The topical issue of climate change is examined in Tim Flannery's "Global Warming: How to Calculate and Live within Our Carbon Budget." In "Science and Religion: A Complicated History," Mark Cauchi puts the current debate over evolution and creation in its larger historical and philosophical context to explore the possibility of simultaneously maintaining a belief in both. The fifth unit—"Arts and Culture"—also boasts some compelling new additions. In "It's Open. Who Cares?" David Macfarlane suggests that while we may not be personally interested in all the art that cities offer, we should nonetheless support this variety as it is the ground from which excellence springs. Meanwhile, in "Looking for Beauty," Clive Cockerton explores the emotional impact of experiencing the beautiful, all the while lamenting the infrequency of its occurrence. A different sort of aesthetic experience is offered by Leonard Michaels' short story, "Murderers." This gripping tale of adolescent desire is masterfully introduced by Mary Ellen Kappler in "Murderers: An Introduction." Noteworthy, too, are a number of new poems that complement the existing selections: Gwendolyn MacEwen's "Let Me Make This Perfectly Clear," Julia Copus's "The Back Seat of My Mother's Car"—complete with a thoughtful commentary by Richard Sanger—and Walt Whitman's "O Me! O Life!"

Organization: The readings are drawn from various disciplines, including philosophy, psychology, sociology, anthropology, political theory, natural science, medicine and the arts. They are organized into units that begin with the individual and extend to the social, political, physical and cultural realms where the individual operates. This organization, going from the individual outwards, allows the student to approach the complexities of the world from familiar ground. As already noted, however, teachers may choose to cover the units in a different order. Some, for instance, may begin with the last unit—"Arts and Culture"—and use the concept of narrative as a unifying theme as they explore in turn the "scientific narrative," the "political narrative," etc. Others, to take another example, may begin with the fourth unit—"Science and the

Natural World"—and use the distinction between scientific knowledge and its alternatives to navigate the various units.

Acknowledgments: The editors wish to thank the team that gave their time and effort so generously to the task of creating this new text. Our editorial committee—Ian Baird, Nitin Deckha, John Elias, Kent Enns, Aileen Herman, Chris Irwin, Mary Ellen Kappler, Yvette Munro, Greg Nepean, Ella Ophir, Matthew O'Rourke, William Walcott, Doug Wright, Caleb Yong, and Arthur Younger—made the evolution of this text an object lesson in collaborative effort.

The editors would also like to thank the team at Pearson Education Canada—including sponsoring editor Carolin Sweig; associate editor Brian Simons; production editor Kevin Leung; photo researcher Amanda Campbell; and copy editor Tara Tovell. Special thanks go to our Humber writers—Ian Baird, George Bragues, Mark Cauchi, Chris Irwin, Mary Ellen Kappler, Greg Narbey, Wendy O'Brien, Morton Ritts and Suzanne Senay—all of whom carefully drew from their experiences in the college classroom to compose readings that explore difficult issues in ways that maintain the integrity of the material covered yet also render it accessible and relevant to the college student.

the Human Project

FIFTH EDITION

The Individual:
Reflections on the Self

After all, mind is such an odd predicament for matter to get into. I often marvel how something like hydrogen, the simplest atom, forged in some early chaos of the universe, could lead to us and the gorgeous fever we call consciousness. If a mind is just a few pounds of blood, dream, and electric, how does it manage to contemplate itself, worry about its soul, do time-and-motion studies, admire the shy hooves of a goat, know that it will die, enjoy all the grand and lesser mayhems of the heart? What is mind, that one can be *out of one's?* How can a neuron feel compassion? What is a self? Why did automatic, hand-me-down mammals like our ancestors somehow evolve brains with the ability to consider, imagine, project, compare, abstract, think of the future? If our experience of mind is really just the simmering of an easily alterable chemical stew, then what does it mean to know something, to want something, *to be?* How do you begin with hydrogen and end up with prom dresses, jealousy, chamber music?

Diane Ackerman

Introduction

Toward the Examined Life

You have likely already noticed that the scope of *The Human Project* is quite broad—encompassing issues drawn from the entire spectrum of the liberal arts, including the humanities, social sciences and natural sciences. But unless you are preparing for a career that draws heavily upon one or more of these academic areas, you may have also questioned the value of this textbook and the course for which it is required reading. In other words, you may have asked yourself the question: *Why should I care about all this?*

As you will read later in the third unit, "Whether we care or not, politics matters." The same may be said of all the disciplines introduced in this text: Whether we care or not, developments in psychology, sociology, biology, climatology, art, philosophy—as well as politics—matter. Why? Because they shape the world in which we live, study, love, hate, work, play, buy, parent, socialize, vote, worship, etc. The latest theories in psychology, for example, may very well influence the way teachers teach—via lectures, or group work, or experiential exercises—in our college or university courses as well as in our children's elementary-school and high-school classes. And the conditions in which we work—at the office or at home, full time or part time, long term or by contract—may be significantly affected by the current views of those sociologists, political scientists and economists who study and comment on the business world. Even new ecological findings can profoundly affect our everyday lives as, for instance, we begin to look for more environmentally sustainable methods to support our technology-dependent lifestyles. So to truly understand our world and have some real control over our lives, it is necessary to have a familiarity with the ideas that matter. As the old adage says, "The unexamined life is not worth living." A study of the ideas introduced in this reader is a good beginning for an examination of timely issues in contemporary life. This is precisely why you should care about all this!

And the "this" that we should, must and actually do (although perhaps unwittingly) care about is nothing less than the "human project"—the world as it has been and continues to be constructed, transformed and explained by the accumulated efforts of humankind. This may sound like too lofty a subject of study until we recognize that this "project" is all around us in the everyday world in which we live. A selected survey of the issues presented in *The Human Project* reflects this perspective: Is the "self" nothing more than a naturally occurring, albeit sophisticated, piece of "software" that is haphazardly "designed" and "redesigned" by the rewards and punishments we encounter in our social and natural environments? What might this mean about the personal decisions we make in life? Are big changes in society best understood as the result of countless individual decisions aimed at maximizing personal benefit? What might this imply about the growing incidence of alternative family structures or the increasingly multicultural composition of contemporary society? Is conflict among individuals and violence between nations inevitable? How might this question affect the way federal governments and international coalitions are structured? Do the conclusions of the physical sciences always trump explanations drawn from social science, philosophy, art and religion? How might this influence the working relationship between scientists and others? Do the arts offer nothing more than pleasant entertainment or do they also contain a special kind of serious insight? What impact might this have on the required curriculum not only in elementary schools and high schools but also in professional and technical programs in colleges and universities?

As this list of issues reveals, the human project is—and always has been, and always will be—a work in progress. As such, it can be seen as the largest public works project ever, since every individual, in every society, in every era—including you, in Canada, at the beginning of the 21st century—plays a part in modifying, maintaining and interpreting this project. The part we play as individuals depends on the responses we make to the timely issues of our day. And our responses, in turn, are greatly enhanced by a familiarity with some of the theories proposed by those thinkers who have wrestled with similar, and even different, issues in the past. It is for this reason that *The Human Project* invites us to think through contemporary issues in consultation with works constructed in the near-to-distant past in the fields of psychology, sociology, politics, science, art and philosophy.

Ultimately, all theories about the world—even scientific theories seemingly unconcerned with humanity—make assumptions, if not statements, about human nature. (The very idea that we are capable of transcending our human perspective and understanding the world objectively is itself a bold assumption about human nature.) Thus, we are led to the question of questions: What is human nature? In other words, what makes humans human? Any answer to these questions must account both for the qualities that make us all human as well as the characteristics that make each of us different.

"Know Thyself"

Every man bears the whole stamp of the human condition.

— *Michel de Montaigne, Essays, Bk. II, Ch. 12.*

Since the abstract concept of "human nature" is brought to life in each individual human being, perhaps this is the best place to begin our investigation. In other words, the first step toward the examined life may be to "know thyself." Thus, this first unit in *The Human Project* is entitled "The Individual: Reflections on the Self."

So what is the "individual"? Is it the same as the "self"? And what is the "self"? When you refer to "your*self*," who is the "you" that speaks? Is it the same as your "soul" or "mind"? Clearly, these are important to your understanding of "self" if you take pride in your spirituality or your intellect. But is not your body also essential to your understanding of "self"? It certainly seems so if you take any pride in your physical appearance and abilities. If so, is the significance of the body—in particular, the brain—equal to that of the mind? Contemporary neurology suggests that the brain is essential to all mental processes. That said, what is the relationship between the mental and physical qualities of the individual?

These are but a few of the difficult questions that arise when a serious attempt is made to understand the meaning of our life experience as human beings, as individuals, as minds, as bodies. This quest is even more difficult because our subjective experience may stand in the way of a fully objective self-investigation. But unless we accept the prospect of living the *un*examined life, we are compelled at least to attempt such an investigation.

Fortunately, we can benefit from the previous investigations of others. In "From Biology to Biography: A Brief History of the Self," Wendy O'Brien explores the theories of self proposed by the French philosopher René Descartes (1596–1650), the Austrian psychologist Sigmund Freud (1856–1939), the American psychologist B.F. Skinner (1904–1990) and the German philosopher Friedrich Nietzsche (1844–1900)—as well as the research of the Human Genome Project. In her discussion, O'Brien touches upon three issues fundamental to the study of self: (1) the mind–body problem, (2) the nature–nurture question, and (3) the free will–determinism debate.

The Mind–Body Problem

The mind–body problem stems from the "dualism" proposed by Descartes. This is the theory that human beings consist of two essentially different and distinct "substances": mind—a thinking entity that is purely mental in nature—and body—a physical thing that is completely material in nature.

Although both of these substances are important to human nature, Descartes argues that the mind is not only the more knowable but also the more essential of the two. Most of us find that common sense confirms the Cartesian view of the dualistic self: We tend to think of ourselves as mind—our true, lasting, "inner" self—on the one hand, and body—our less true, changing, "outer" self—on the other. As Tim Adams explains in "The Skin We're In," we nonetheless spend a good deal of time, effort and money on our less essential "outward selves." In contemporary Western culture, for example, people go to great lengths to modify their bodies: they "make up" their faces; they cut, dye, curl, straighten and iron their hair; they pierce and tattoo various parts of their bodies; they diet to slim down their waists; they undergo plastic surgery to attain bigger breasts, smaller thighs and younger faces. The point of all this, Adams suggests, is to make our bodies more accurately reflect the internal selves we believe we are or want to become. In "Unpleasantness in Vermont," however, Antonio Damasio suggests that it may actually be the mind that is a reflection of the body. The famous case of Phineas Gage—who miraculously survived a terrible workplace accident in which a metre-long, 3-centimetre-wide, 6-kilogram iron bar was thrust right through his skull—demonstrates the profound way in which damage to the body (i.e., the brain) can transform the mind (i.e., the seemingly intangible "self") beyond recognition—even when there is no other discernible lasting mental or physical injury.

Whether the body reflects the mind or vice versa, the question itself points to a problem that dualists like Descartes have yet to answer convincingly: How is it possible for a purely mental, non-physical mind to interact with an entirely material, physical body? In other words, is it really possible to move physical objects (including your body) with your (purely mental) mind alone? According to dualism, this is precisely what is involved when you decide, for instance, to take a walk: your (non-physical) mind somehow makes your (non-mental) body move. When put this way, it is less obvious that dualism conforms to common sense.

Of course, Damasio is not the only one who does not agree with Descartes that the mind is distinct from, and more significant than, the body. As O'Brien explains, the scientists involved in the Human Genome Project take a very different approach to the study of human nature; in fact, this impressive research project is limited in scope to a physical investigation of human beings through study of our genetic makeup. This does not mean that geneticists necessarily deny the existence of the mind. But when they propose that personality traits are determined by genetics, they are in effect claiming, like Damasio, that the mind is at most the creation of, and, as such, less essential than, the body.

The Nature–Nurture Question

Behaviourists such as B. F. Skinner skirt the mind–body problem either by ignoring the mind—since it is not an observable entity and, therefore, is not amenable to scientific study—or by simply denying its existence altogether. Nonetheless, behaviourists do have a very clear position on another big issue in the study of human nature: the nature–nurture question. This question asks whether the self is more the result of nature—qualities we are born with, such as genetics or instincts or even innate "drives"—or more the result of nurture—influences stemming from our environment, such as upbringing, schooling, socioeconomic status, culture, etc. Behaviourism is the theory that we are not what we think but rather what we do, i.e., how we behave, and that what we do is determined by rewards and punishments in our environment. But, as O'Brien argues, these environmental influences do not seem to have the lasting effect that behaviourists claim they do.

The Human Genome Project will provide evidence for the nature side of this debate if it does indeed discover that personality traits are determined by genetic makeup. But, as O'Brien notes, our understanding of genetics to date only points to probabilities, not certainties. Environmental factors may ultimately explain why certain genetic dispositions develop into realities while others do not.

Indeed, most if not all serious thinkers acknowledge that both nature and nurture are significant factors in understanding human nature. The field of evolutionary psychology may be particularly instructive on this point. Evolutionary psychologists argue that human beings, like all other species, have evolved into what they are today by natural selection. As discussed in the fourth unit, natural selection is the process by which random variations (i.e., genetic diversity, genetic mutations) within a species become dominant if they help individuals or groups of individuals better adapt to, and therefore survive in, their environment. This applies just as much to the mind as to the body. In "Darwin's God," Robin Marantz Henig explores how evolutionary psychologists try to explain the fact that human societies everywhere—throughout history and across cultures—seem to encompass faith in a transcendent deity. According to this field, religious belief exists either because it has helped humankind adapt to its environment or because it is an "evolutionary byproduct" of another such adaptation. Either way, both nature *and* nurture are essential to this explanation: the *genetic* variations (e.g., the "brain architecture" necessary for belief in God) that lead to evolution of a species are "selected" by the *environment* in which the species lives.

The significance of both nature and nurture is also acknowledged by Sigmund Freud's theory of self: while the *id* consists of irresistible innate instincts, the *superego* contains socially constructed rules and expectations, forcing the *ego* to try to mediate between the two in a realistic way. For Freud, nature (id) has a greater impact on the self than nurture (superego and ego), but both are strong and essential forces in human nature.

The Free Will–Determinism Debate

The id has the stronger hand in Freud's model of the self because it is part of the unconscious mind; after all, it is hard to control something if we are not aware of it. This leads us to the debate over whether or not we are truly free to make choices between alternative courses of action. As summarized by Melanie Chaparian in "Am I Free or Determined?" this issue hinges on the debate between determinists—those who argue that all our actions are caused by forces beyond our control—and libertarians—those who argue that at least some of our actions are the result of our free will.

This debate is informed by our investigation into the nature of self. In other words, our view of the nature of the individual has a direct bearing on our position on free will. If you agree with Freud, for example, that the self is inalterably created by natural and environmental forces over which we have no control, you will have little hope that human beings can exercise true freedom. Or if, alternatively, you are persuaded by the behaviourist thesis that we are unendingly shaped by rewards and punishments in our environment, you will see no trace of free will in human behaviour. If, however, you are convinced by Nietzsche's understanding of the self as a personally styled work of art, you will find the theory of libertarianism not only probable, but likely evident.

Indeed, the American philosopher and psychologist William James (1842–1910) invites us to view both the determinist and the libertarian positions through introspective lenses to discern which makes the most sense of reality as we experience it in our daily lives. He suggests that although objective explanations of reality may be useful at times, they do not successfully account for our subjective experience of our lived lives in which we frequently feel free to make choices and often regret the choices we and others make. A therapist who successfully treats her patients using principles of behaviour modification, for instance, may still find it difficult to convince herself that she, like her patients, is ultimately determined by rewards and punishments over which she has no control. In her everyday life at least, she probably *feels* free as she decides, for instance, what to wear each morning, and she likely *regrets* her choices on occasion when they prove to be less than fitting for the day's activities. A determinist would counter this kind of argument by pointing out that just because something is hard to believe does not mean that it is not true.

In "What Will My Future Self Think of Me?" Mark Kingwell introduces an intriguing question that has great implications for the free will debate: what is the relationship between our "past, present and future selves"? Clearly, we change over time. This becomes more apparent the older we get: the 10-year-old version of you (your past self) is very different from the 20-year-old version of you (your present self), who will, in turn, be even more different from the 50-year-old version of you (your future self). Are all these "selves" the same "person"? There is no doubt that decisions made by your past self have affected your present self and that decisions of your present self will affect your future self. James suggests that any regrets about your past decisions imply that they were freely made, i.e., that you could have decided differently. At the same time, as Kingwell notes, you may not feel that your present self is *responsible* for the actions of your past self, especially if you have become a very different person in the interim. While this consideration complicates the issue, it does not settle it: i.e., it does not necessarily lead to the conclusion that we are determined creatures nor that we can escape the responsibility that comes with free will. Instead, it simply underscores how very important this issue ultimately is.

Unpleasantness in Vermont

Antonio Damasio

Phineas P. Gage

It is the summer of 1848. We are in New England. Phineas P Gage, twenty-five years old, construction foreman, is about to go from riches to rags. A century and a half later his downfall will still be quite meaningful.

Gage works for the Rutland & Burlington Railroad and is in charge of a large group of men, a "gang" as it is called, whose job it is to lay down the new tracks for the railroad's expansion across Vermont. Over the past two weeks the men have worked their way slowly toward the town of Cavendish; they are now at a bank of the Black River. The assignment is anything but easy because of the outcrops of hard rock. Rather than twist and turn the tracks around every escarpment, the strategy is to blast the stone and make way for a straighter and more level path. Gage oversees these tasks and is equal to them in every way. He is five-foot-six and athletic, and his movements are swift and precise. He looks like a young Jimmy Cagney, a Yankee Doodle dandy dancing his tap shoes over ties and tracks, moving with vigor and grace.

In the eyes of his bosses, however, Gage is more than just another able body. They say he is "the most efficient and capable" man in their employ.[1] This is a good thing, because the job takes as much physical prowess as keen concentration, especially when it comes to preparing the detonations. Several steps have to be followed, in orderly fashion. First, a hole must be drilled in the rock. After it is filled about halfway with explosive powder, a fuse must be inserted, and the powder covered with sand. Then the sand must be "tamped in," or pounded with a careful sequence of strokes from an iron rod. Finally, the fuse must be lit. If all goes well, the powder will explode into the rock; the sand is essential, for without its protection the explosion would be directed away from the rock. The shape of the iron and the way it is played are also important. Gage, who has had an iron manufactured to his specifications, is a virtuoso of this thing.

Now for what is going to happen. It is four-thirty on this hot afternoon. Gage has just put powder and fuse in a hole and told the man who is helping him to cover it with sand. Someone calls from behind, and Gage looks away, over his right shoulder, for only an instant. Distracted, and before his man has poured

---

the sand in, Gage begins tamping the powder directly with the iron bar. In no time he strikes fire in the rock, and the charge blows upward in his face.[2]

The explosion is so brutal that the entire gang freezes on their feet. It takes a few seconds to piece together what is going on. The bang is unusual, and the rock is intact. Also unusual is the whistling sound, as of a rocket hurled at the sky. But this is more than fireworks. It is assault and battery. The iron enters Gage's left cheek, pierces the base of the skull, traverses the front of his brain, and exits at high speed through the top of the head. The rod has landed more than a hundred feet away, covered in blood and brains. Phineas Gage has been thrown to the ground. He is stunned, in the afternoon glow, silent but awake. So are we all, helpless spectators.

"Horrible Accident" will be the predictable headline in the Boston *Daily Courier* and *Daily Journal* of September 20, a week later. "Wonderful Accident" will be the strange headline in the *Vermont Mercury* of September 22. "Passage of an Iron Rod through the Head" will be the accurate headline in the *Boston Medical and Surgical Journal*. From the matter-of-factness with which they tell the story, one would think the writers were familiar with Edgar Allan Poe's accounts of the bizarre and the horrific. And perhaps they were, although this is not likely; Poe's gothic tales are not yet popular, and Poe himself will die the next year, unknown and **impecunious**. Perhaps the horrible is just in the air.

Noting how surprised people were that Gage was not killed instantly, the Boston medical article documents that "immediately after the explosion the patient was thrown upon his back"; that shortly thereafter he exhibited "a few convulsive motions of the extremities," and "spoke in a few minutes"; that "his men (with whom he was a great favorite) took him in their arms and carried him to the road, only a few rods distant (a rod is equivalent to 5½ yards, or 16½ feet), and sat him into an ox cart, in which he rode, sitting erect, a full three-quarters of a mile, to the hotel of Mr. Joseph Adams"; and that Gage "got out of the cart himself, with a little assistance from his men."

Let me introduce Mr. Adams. He is the justice of the peace for Cavendish and the owner of the town's hotel and tavern. He is taller than Gage, twice as round, and as solicitous as his Falstaff shape suggests. He approaches Gage, and immediately has someone call for Dr. John Harlow, one of the town physicians. While they wait, I imagine, he says, "Come, come, Mr. Gage, what have we got here?" and, why not, "My, my, what troubles we've seen." He shakes his head in disbelief and leads Gage to the shady part of the hotel porch, which has been described as a "piazza." That makes it sound grand and spacious and open, and perhaps it is grand and spacious, but it is not open; it is just a porch. And there perhaps Mr. Adams is now giving Phineas Gage lemonade, or maybe cold cider.

impecunious

poor

An hour has passed since the explosion. The sun is declining and the heat is more bearable. A younger colleague of Dr. Harlow's, Dr. Edward Williams, is arriving. Years later Dr. Williams will describe the scene: "He at that time was sitting in a chair upon the piazza of Mr. Adams' hotel, in Cavendish. When I drove up, he said, 'Doctor, here is business enough for you.' I first noticed the wound upon the head before I alighted from my carriage, the pulsations of the brain being very distinct; there was also an appearance which, before I examined the head, I could not account for: the top of the head appeared somewhat like an inverted funnel; this was owing, I discovered, to the bone being fractured about the opening for a distance of about two inches in every direction. I ought to have mentioned above that the opening through the skull and **integuments** was not far from one and a half inches in diameter; the edges of this opening were **everted**, and the whole wound appeared as if some wedge-shaped body had passed from below upward. Mr. Gage, during the time I was examining this wound, was relating the manner in which he was injured to the bystanders; he talked so rationally and was so willing to answer questions, that I directed my inquiries to him in preference to the men who were with him at the time of the accident, and who were standing about at this time. Mr. G. then related to me some of the circumstances, as he has since done; and I can safely say that neither at that time nor on any subsequent occasion, save once, did I consider him to be other than perfectly rational. The one time to which I allude was about a **fortnight** after the accident, and then he persisted in calling me John Kirwin; yet he answered all my questions correctly."[3]

The survival is made all the more amazing when one considers the shape and weight of the iron bar. Henry Bigelow, a surgery professor at Harvard, describes the iron so: "The iron which thus traversed the skull weighs thirteen and a quarter pounds. It is three feet seven inches in length, and one and a quarter inches in diameter. The end which entered first is pointed; the taper being seven inches long, and the diameter of the point one quarter of an inch; circumstances to which the patient perhaps owes his life. The iron is unlike any other, and was made by a neighboring blacksmith to please the fancy of the owner."[4] Gage is serious about his trade and its proper tools.

Surviving the explosion with so large a wound to the head, being able to talk and walk and remain coherent immediately afterward—this is all surprising. But just as surprising will be Gage's surviving the inevitable infection that is about to take over his wound. Gage's physician, John Harlow, is well aware of the role of disinfection. He does not have the help of antibiotics, but using what chemicals are available he will clean the wound vigorously and regularly, and place the patient in a **semi-recumbent** position so that drainage will be natural and easy. Gage will develop high fevers and at least one abscess, which Harlow will promptly remove with his scalpel. In the end,

integument
outer covering, skin

everted
turned inside out

fortnight
a period of two weeks

semi-recumbent
semi-reclining

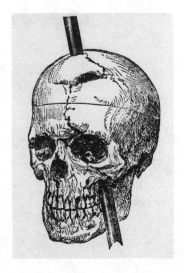

Phineas Gage's skull showing wound site

Gage's youth and strong constitution will overcome the odds against him, assisted, as Harlow will put it, by divine intervention: "I dressed him, God healed him."

Phineas Gage will be pronounced cured in less than two months. Yet this astonishing outcome pales in comparison with the extraordinary turn that Gage's personality is about to undergo. Gage's disposition, his likes and dislikes, his dreams and aspirations are all to change. Gage's body may be alive and well, but there is a new spirit animating it.

Gage Was No Longer Gage

Just what exactly happened we can glean today from the account Dr. Harlow prepared twenty years after the accident.[5] It is a trustworthy text, with an abundance of facts and a minimum of interpretation. It makes sense humanly and neurologically, and from it we can piece together not just Gage but his doctor as well. John Harlow had been a schoolteacher before he entered Jefferson Medical College in Philadelphia, and was only a few years into his medical career when he took care of Gage. The case became his life-consuming interest, and I suspect that it made Harlow want to be a scholar, something that may not have been in his plans when he set up his medical practice in Vermont. Treating Gage successfully and reporting the results to his Boston colleagues may have been the shining hours of his career, and he must have been disturbed by the fact that a real cloud hung over Gage's cure.

Harlow's narrative describes how Gage regained his strength and how his physical recovery was complete. Gage could touch, hear and see, and was not paralyzed of limb or tongue. He had lost vision in his left eye, but his vision was perfect in the right. He walked firmly, used his hands with dexterity, and had no noticeable difficulty with speech or language. And yet, as Harlow recounts, the "equilibrium or balance, so to speak, between his intellectual faculty and animal propensities" had been destroyed. The changes became apparent as soon as the acute phase of brain injury subsided. He was now "fitful, irreverent, indulging at times in the grossest profanity which was not previously his custom, manifesting but little deference for his fellows, impatient of restraint or advice when it conflicts with his desires, at times **pertinaciously** obstinate, yet capricious and vacillating, devising many plans of future operation, which are no sooner arranged than they are abandoned . . . . A child in his intellectual capacity and manifestations, he has the animal passions of a strong man." The foul language was so debased that women were advised not to stay long in his presence, lest their sensibilities be offended. The strongest admonitions from Harlow himself failed to return our survivor to good behaviour.

pertinaciously
stubbornly

These new personality traits contrasted sharply with the "temperate habits" and "considerable energy of character" Phineas Gage was known to have possessed before the accident. He had had "a well balanced mind and was looked upon by those who knew him as a shrewd, smart businessman, very energetic and persistent in executing all his plans of action." There is no doubt that in the context of his job and time, he was successful. So radical was the change in him that friends and acquaintances could hardly recognize the man. They noted sadly that "Gage was no longer Gage." So different a man was he that his employers would not take him back when he returned to work, for they "considered the change in his mind so marked that they could not give him his place again." The problem was not lack of physical ability or skill; it was his new character.

The unraveling continued unabated. No longer able to work as a foreman, Gage took jobs on horse farms. One gathers that he was prone to quit in a capricious fit or be let go because of poor discipline. As Harlow notes, he was good at "always finding something which did not suit him." Then came his career as a circus attraction. Gage was featured at Barnum's Museum in New York City, vaingloriously showing his wounds and the tamping iron. (Harlow states that the iron was a constant companion, and points out Gage's strong attachment to objects and animals, which was new and somewhat out of the ordinary. This trait, what we might call "collector's behaviour," is something I have seen in patients who have suffered injuries like Gage's, as well as in autistic individuals.)

Then far more than now, the circus capitalized on nature's cruelty. The **endocrine** variety included dwarfs, the fattest woman on earth, the tallest man, the fellow with the largest jaw; the neurological variety included youths with elephant skin, victims of **neurofibromatosis**—and now Gage. We can imagine him in such **Fellinian** company, peddling misery for gold.

Four years after the accident, there was another theatrical coup. Gage left for South America. He may have worked on horse farms, and was a some-time stagecoach driver in Santiago and Valparaiso. Little else is known about his expatriate life except that in 1859 his health was deteriorating.

In 1860, Gage returned to the United States to live with his mother and sister, who had since moved to San Francisco. At first he was employed on a farm in Santa Clara, but he did not stay long. In fact, he moved around, occasionally finding work as a laborer in the area. It is clear that he was not an independent person and that he could not secure the type of steady, remunerative job that he had once held. The end of the fall was nearing.

In my mind is a picture of 1860s San Francisco as a bustling place, full of adventurous entrepreneurs engaged in mining, farming, and shipping. That is where we can find Gage's mother and sister, the latter married to a

endocrine
gland malfunctioning

neurofibromatosis
a genetic disorder that can cause multiple birthmarks, skin tumours and, in some cases, bone deformity or cancer

Fellinian
reminiscent of films of Federico Fellini (1920–1993), which often depicted the grotesque and bizarre

prosperous San Francisco merchant (D. D. Shattuck, Esquire), and that is where the old Phineas Gage might have belonged. But that is not where we would find him if we could travel back in time. We would probably find him drinking and brawling in a questionable district, not conversing with the captains of commerce, as astonished as anybody when the fault would slip and the earth would shake threateningly. He had joined the tableau of dispirited people who, as Nathanael West would put it decades later, and a few hundred miles to the south, "had come to California to die."[6]

The meager documents available suggest that Gage developed epileptic fits (seizures). The end came on May 21, 1861, after an illness that lasted little more than a day. Gage had a major convulsion which made him lose consciousness. A series of subsequent convulsions, one coming soon on the heels of another, followed. He never regained consciousness. I believe he was the victim of *status epilepticus*, a condition in which convulsions become nearly continuous and usher in death. He was thirty-eight years old. There was no death notice in the San Francisco newspapers.

Why Phineas Gage?

Why is this sad story worth telling? What is the possible significance of such a bizarre tale? The answer is simple. While other cases of neurological damage that occurred at about the same time revealed that the brain was the foundation for language, perception, and motor function, and generally provided more conclusive details, Gage's story hinted at an amazing fact: Somehow, there were systems in the human brain dedicated more to reasoning than to anything else, and in particular to the personal and social dimension of reasoning. The observance of previously acquired social convention and ethical rules could be lost as a result of brain damage, even when neither basic intellect nor language seemed compromised. Unwittingly, Gage's example indicated that something in the brain was concerned specifically with unique human properties, among them the ability to anticipate the future and plan accordingly within a complex social environment; the sense of responsibility toward the self and others; and the ability to orchestrate one's survival deliberately, at the command of one's free will.

The most striking aspect of this unpleasant story is the discrepancy between the normal personality structure that preceded the accident and the **nefarious** personality traits that surfaced thereafter and seem to have remained for the rest of Gage's life. Gage had once known all he needed to know about making choices conducive to his betterment. He had a sense of personal and social responsibility, reflected in the way he had secured

nefarious
wicked, evil

advancement in his job, cared for the quality of his work, and attracted the admiration of employers and colleagues. He was well adapted in terms of social convention and appears to have been ethical in his dealings. After the accident, he no longer showed respect for social convention; ethics in the broad sense of the term, were violated; the decisions he made did not take into account his best interest, and he was given to invent tales "without any foundation except in his fancy," in Harlow's words. There was no evidence of concern about his future, no sign of forethought.

The alterations in Gage's personality were not subtle. He could not make good choices, and the choices he made were not simply neutral. They were not the reserved or slight decisions of someone whose mind is diminished and who is afraid to act, but were instead actively disadvantageous. One might venture that either his value system was now different, or, if it was still the same, there was no way in which the old values could influence his decisions. No evidence exists to tell us which is true, yet my investigation of patients with brain damage similar to Phineas Gage's convinces me that neither explanation captures what really happens in those circumstances. Some part of the value system remains and can be utilized in abstract terms, but it is unconnected to real-life situations. When the Phineas Gages of this world need to operate in reality, the decision-making process is minimally influenced by old knowledge.

Another important aspect of Gage's story is the discrepancy between the degenerated character and the apparent intactness of the several instruments of mind—attention, perception, memory, language, intelligence. In this type of discrepancy, known in neuropsychology as *dissociation,* one or more performances within a general profile of operations are at odds with the rest. In Gage's case the impaired character was dissociated from the otherwise intact cognition and behavior. In other patients, with lesions elsewhere in the brain, language may be the impaired aspect, while character and all other cognitive aspects remain intact; language is then the "dissociated" ability. Subsequent study of patients similar to Gage has confirmed that his specific dissociation profile occurs consistently.

It must have been hard to believe that the character change would not resolve itself, and at first even Dr. Harlow resisted admitting that the change was permanent. This is understandable, since the most dramatic elements in Gage's story were his very survival, and then his survival without a defect that would more easily meet the eye: paralysis, for example, or a speech defect, or memory loss. Somehow, emphasizing Gage's newly developed social shortcomings smacked of ingratitude to both providence and medicine. By 1868, however, Dr. Harlow was ready to acknowledge the full extent of his patient's personality change.

Gage's survival was duly noted, but with the caution reserved for freakish phenomena. The significance of his behavioral changes was largely lost. There were good reasons for this neglect. Even in the small world of brain science at the time, two camps were beginning to form. One held that psychological functions such as language or memory could never be traced to a particular region of the brain. If one had to accept, reluctantly, that the brain did produce the mind, it did so as a whole and not as a collection of parts with special functions. The other camp held that, on the contrary, the brain did have specialized parts and those parts generated separate mind functions. The rift between the two camps was not merely indicative of the infancy of brain research; the argument endured for another century and, to a certain extent, is still with us today.

Whatever scientific debate Phineas Gage's story elicited, it focused on the issue of localizing language and movement in the brain. The debate never turned to the connection between impaired social conduct and frontal lobe damage. I am reminded here of a saying of Warren McCulloch's: "When I point, look where I point, not at my finger." (McCulloch, a legendary neuro-psychologist and a pioneer in the field that would become computational neuroscience, was also a poet and a prophet. This saying was usually part of a prophecy.) Few looked to where Gage was unwittingly pointing. It is of course difficult to imagine anybody in Gage's day with the knowledge *and* the courage to look in the proper direction. It was acceptable that the brain sectors whose damage would have caused Gage's heart to stop pumping and his lungs to stop breathing had not been touched by the iron rod. It was also acceptable that the brain sectors which control wakefulness were far from the iron's course and were thus spared. It was even acceptable that the injury did not render Gage unconscious for a long period. (The event anticipated what is current knowledge from studies of head injuries: The style of the injury is a critical variable. A severe blow to the head, even if no bone is broken and no weapon penetrates the brain, can cause a major disruption of wakefulness for a long time; the forces unleashed by the blow disorganize brain function profoundly. A penetrating injury in which the forces are concentrated on a narrow and steady path, rather than dissipate and accelerate the brain against the skull, may cause dysfunction only where brain tissue is actually destroyed, and thus spare brain function elsewhere.) But to understand Gage's behavioral change would have meant believing that normal social conduct required a particular corresponding brain region, and this concept was far more unthinkable than its equivalent for movement, the senses, or even language.

Gage's case was used, in fact, by those who did not believe that mind functions could be linked to specific brain areas. They took a cursory view of the medical evidence and claimed that if such a wound as Gage's could fail to produce paralysis or speech impairments, then it was obvious that neither motor control nor language could be traced to the relatively small brain regions that neurologists had identified as motor and language centres. They argued—in complete error—as we shall see—that Gage's wound directly damaged those centres.[7]

The British physiologist David Ferrier was one of the few to take the trouble to analyze the findings with competence and wisdom.[8] Ferrier's knowledge of other cases of brain lesion with behavioral changes, as well as his own pioneering experiments on electrical stimulation and **ablation** of the cerebral cortex in animals, had placed him in a unique position to appreciate Harlow's findings. He concluded that the wound spared motor and language "centers," that it did damage the part of the brain he himself had called the prefrontal cortex, and that such damage might be related to Gage's peculiar change in personality, to which Ferrier referred, picturesquely, as "mental degradation."

ablation
surgical removal

. . . .

A Landmark by Hindsight

There is no question that Gage's personality change was caused by a circumscribed brain lesion in a specific site. But that explanation would not be apparent until two decades after the accident, and it became vaguely acceptable only in this century. For a long time, most everybody, John Harlow included, believed that "the portion of the brain traversed, was, for several reasons, the best fitted of any part of the cerebral substance to sustain the injury"[9]: in other words, a part of the brain that did nothing much and was thus expendable. But nothing could be further from the truth, as Harlow himself realized. He wrote in 1868 that Gage's mental recovery "was only partial, his intellectual faculties being decidedly impaired, but not totally lost; nothing like dementia, but they were enfeebled in their manifestations, his mental operations being perfect in kind, but not in degree or quantity." The unintentional message in Gage's case was that observing social convention, behaving ethically, and making decisions advantageous to one's survival and progress require knowledge of rules and strategies *and* the integrity of specific brain systems. The problem with this message was that it lacked the evidence required to make it understandable and definitive. Instead the message became a mystery and came down to us as the "enigma" of frontal lobe function. Gage posed more questions than he gave answers.

To begin with, all we knew about Gage's brain lesion was that it was probably in the frontal lobe. That is a bit like saying that Chicago is probably in the United States—accurate but not very specific or helpful. Granted that the damage was likely to involve the frontal lobe, where exactly was it within that region? The left lobe? The right? Both? Somewhere else too? . . . .

Then there was the nature of Gage's character defect. How did the abnormality develop? The primary cause, sure enough, was a hole in the head, but that just tells why the defect arose, not how. Might a hole anywhere in the frontal lobe have the same result? Whatever the answer, by what plausible means can destruction of a brain region change personality? If there are specific regions in the frontal lobe, what are they made of, and how do they operate in an intact brain? Are they some kind of "centre" for social behavior? Are they modules selected in evolution, filled with problem-solving **algorithms** ready to tell us how to reason and make decisions? How do these modules, if that is what they are, interact with the environment during development to permit normal reasoning and decision making? Or are there in fact no such modules?

algorithm

precise method for solving a particular type of problem

What were the mechanisms behind Gage's failure at decision making? It might be that the knowledge required to reason through a problem was destroyed or rendered inaccessible, so that he no longer could decide appropriately. It is possible also that the requisite knowledge remained intact and accessible but the strategies for reasoning were compromised. If this was the case, which reasoning steps were missing? More to the point, which steps are there for those who are allegedly normal? And if we are fortunate enough to glean the nature of some of these steps, what are their neural underpinnings?

Intriguing as all of these questions are, they may not be as important as those which surround Gage's status as a human being. May he be described as having free will? Did he have a sense of right and wrong, or was he the victim of his new brain design, such that his decisions were imposed upon him and inevitable? Was he responsible for his acts? If we rule that he was not, does this tell us something about responsibility in more general terms? There are many Gages around us, people whose fall from social grace is disturbingly similar. Some have brain damage consequent to brain tumours, or head injury, or other neurological disease. Yet some have had no overt neurological disease and they still behave like Gage, for reasons having nothing to do with their brains or with the society into which they were born. We need to understand the nature of these human beings whose actions can be destructive to themselves and to others, if we are to solve humanely the problems they pose. Neither incarceration nor the death penalty—among the responses that society currently offers for those individuals—contribute to our understanding or solve the problem. In fact, we should take the question further and inquire about our own responsibility when we "normal" individuals slip into the irrationality that marked Phineas Gage's great fall.

Gage lost something uniquely human, the ability to plan his future as a social being. How aware was he of this loss? Might he be described as self-conscious in the same sense that you and I are? Is it fair to say that his soul was diminished, or that he had lost his soul? And if so, what would Descartes have thought had he known about Gage and had he had the knowledge of neurobiology we now have? Would he have inquired about Gage's pineal gland?

Notes

[1] J. M. Harlow (1868). Recovery from the passage of an iron bar through the head, *Publications of the Massachusetts Medical Society*, 2:327–47; and (1848–49). Passage of an iron rod through the head, *Boston Medical and Surgical Journal*, 39:389.

[2] See note 1 above.

[3] E. Williams, cited in H. J. Bigelow (1850). Dr. Harlow's case of recovery from the passage of an iron bar through the head, *American Journal of the Medical Sciences*, 19:13–22.

[4] See note 3 above (Bigelow).

[5] See note 1 above (1868).

[6] N. West (1939). *The Day of the Locust*. Chapter 1.

[7] Exemplifying this attitude is E. Dupuy (1873). *Examen de quelques points de la physiologie du cerveau*. Paris: Delahaye.

[8] D. Ferrier (1878). The Goulstonian Lectures on the localization of cerebral disease, *British Medical Journal*, 1:399–447.

[9] See note 1 above (1868).

From Biology to Biography: A Brief History of the Self

Wendy O'Brien

What do you mean when you say: "I'm so sorry, I'm just not myself today"? Do you mean that somehow you have inadvertently deviated from your essential being? If you aren't yourself, then who or what have you become? When you sit back and think about it for a minute, this simple phrase, one you hear people use all the time, raises important questions about the nature of identity. Who or what is this self that we refer to, this presence that provides continuity and perspective to our experience? Many great minds such as Descartes, Freud, Skinner and Nietzsche have asked themselves similar questions; while they have all contributed to our understanding of the self, they would also acknowledge that even after careful reflection and analysis there still remain many unanswered questions about the nature of personal identity.

René Descartes

The modern search to understand the self has its origin in the writings of the 17th-century philosopher René Descartes. Descartes was writing during the scientific revolution, a time of great hope and belief in the possibility of progress. It was, as well, a time marked by insecurity, as science began to challenge existing theories about the natural world and, consequently, called into question long-held beliefs about human beings—about their innate qualities and characteristics, their place in nature and their relationship to God.

In raising these questions, the new science dispelled many myths about the natural world and challenged many traditional beliefs about humanity. Most importantly, it also changed the way people thought. No longer could they rely on authority figures to explain how the world worked and how they should act. People were left on their own to discover for themselves the answers to these questions. Reason replaced faith as the source of knowledge and humankind was forever changed as a result. While many of his contemporaries, including Galileo, were busy applying the principles of science to the natural world, Descartes used these principles to study human beings. His methodology consisted of four basic rules:

René Descartes

This article was written for *The Human Project*. Used by permission.

1. Do not accept any statement as true without evidence.

2. Divide every problem into its simplest parts.

3. Start with what is simple and build your way up to more complex ideas.

4. Be thorough: carefully record and analyze data in order to ensure that nothing is left out.

Why try to study human beings from a scientific perspective rather than accept the teachings of the church or rely upon tradition? As noted earlier, Descartes lived through a time when it seemed that the whole world was being turned upon its head. In this regard, perhaps he had a lot in common with people today living at the dawn of the 21st century. Even if you are as young as 20 or 25, you know how many things have changed throughout your lifetime. And with the current advances in science and technology, you know that things aren't likely to slow down any time soon. Descartes responded to change by trying to find one thing, just one thing that he could hold onto, one thing that he could know was true and would always be so. If he could find one thing that he could know for certain, then maybe he could make sense of the changes that were taking place.

In order to accomplish this goal, Descartes adopted the method of "radical doubt." For a claim to be true, for it to be certain, it had to be literally beyond doubt. So he began doubting everything that he had once taken for granted as true. He began by doubting the teachings of authority. Descartes was a rebel in his time. He dared to ask if politicians, religious leaders, teachers and other experts could be relied on to tell the truth. He quickly realized that while authorities often knew a lot about one thing, they tended to extend their claims beyond the area of their expertise.

Well, if you can't rely on others to tell you what is true, surely you can rely on your own experiences, your own sense perceptions, to provide you with knowledge. As you sit reading this, you see the words on the page. You feel the textbook in your hands. You smell the coffee that sits in the cup beside you. Given what your senses tell you, you can claim that these things— the book and the cup—are real. Or can you? You only have to think for a minute about how even great food can taste flavourless when you have a cold or how you can feel chilly even when you have a high fever to understand why Descartes concluded that even your own experiences cannot be trusted to lead you to the truth.

Moreover, how do you know that you aren't dreaming that you are reading this page? Haven't you ever had a dream that was so "real" that you thought that you had really lived it? If you have, then you can understand Descartes's point. How can you prove that what you are experiencing now isn't the same sort of a dream? Descartes questioned whether everything that you have known to date is part of a long and elaborate dream and, thus, he put into question all those things that you readily take for granted as real.

But even if the claims of authorities, the knowledge gained from sense perceptions and our assumptions about what is real are all possibly false, certainly such abstract truths as mathematical formulas must be true. It seems that 2+2 has always been, and will always be, 4. But how do you know that this is the right answer? What if there is some supreme being who, rather than being benevolent as portrayed in many religious teachings, is, in fact, an evil demon? What if he/she/it gets his/her/its kicks out of playing mind games with you and has indeed tricked you into believing that 2+2 is 4 when in reality it is 27?

True, this argument may seem far-fetched; however, if you have seen the movie *The Matrix*, you have a good idea of what Descartes had in mind here. In this film, robotic bugs have tricked human beings into believing that their everyday lives are real. The humans think that they live in New York City, that they work, that they socialize and that they fall in love, when, in fact, they are living inside of pods, having their energy sucked out of them to fuel a complex computer system known as the Matrix. How can you prove that even the most obvious truths aren't, in fact, illusions? Can you conclusively put aside any and all doubt that Descartes's evil demon or the Matrix may be real? If even the smallest doubt remains in your mind, you are left to conclude that you can't even be certain of the most basic mathematical equations.

At this point, it may seem like Descartes's search for one thing to believe in, for one thing that he could know for certain, had failed: there was nothing in the world that he could unquestioningly accept as true. Quite to the contrary, however, Descartes was on the verge of discovering the foundation on which he was to base all knowledge. For it was at this point that he realized that there *was* one thing that he could know for certain. In order to be sitting there doubting everything that exists, there was one thing that he was unable to doubt: he couldn't doubt that he was doubting, for if he doubted that he was doubting, he would nonetheless be doubting. (Don't worry if this sounds confusing the first time you read it. Read the sentence over a few times. Now sit back and doubt whether the book in front of you is real. Now doubt that you are doubting that the book is real. It is impossible, for in doubting that you are doubting you are still doubting.) But proving the existence of doubting alone didn't make much sense to Descartes. How can doubting exist on its own? This was impossible. Indeed, in order for there to be doubting, there must be some thing that is doing the doubting.

What is this thing that, according to the logic of the argument, you can know is true? Descartes concluded that it is the self. But what is the self? For Descartes it was "a thing that thinks"—a thing that understands, affirms, knows, imagines and doubts. In other words, the self is synonymous with what many of us would describe as the mind. This means that the minute you begin to doubt that you exist, you prove your own existence—for to doubt your existence is to think and, thus, to affirm the reality of the self. "*Cogito ergo sum,*" Descartes concluded: "I think, therefore I am."

In making this claim, Descartes made the self the grounding concept of modern philosophy. The one thing that you can know for certain, the one thing that will provide a foundation for the knowledge that you gain about the world, about other people, about the existence of God, is your knowledge of the self. But in making this claim, Descartes really only began his investigation of identity. For, while he had proven the existence of the mind, he found himself with a new problem.

Recall that the method of radical doubt led Descartes to question the **veracity** of information gained through the body. In discrediting the body as a source of knowledge and locating the self in the mind, Descartes advocated a form of "dualism." According to this theory, you are composed of two different substances: mind and body. The mind has an immaterial and internal existence that only it can know. It is not available for public scrutiny. It cannot be located in space nor is it divisible. The body, on the other hand, exists in space and therefore is divisible. You can clearly distinguish between its various parts, for example, your hand, your finger and your thumb. Moreover, the body exists in the external world and, as such, is open to public appraisal. For Descartes, it was critical to distance the mind from the body in such a manner, as this ensured that the uncertainty associated with bodily perceptions would not infect the perfect knowledge that we could have of the mind.

Descartes's descriptions of the mind and the body seem fairly accurate. You don't experience yourself as a disembodied, dislocated and lonely mind. When you talk about your "self," you are referring to your body too. Descartes himself seemed to recognize this fact when he defined the self as a "*thing* that thinks." But how is this possible? How can the self be two such different kinds of things, different substances, at one and the same time?

Descartes resolved this dilemma by acknowledging the existence of the body but giving it a secondary role. The mind was the "pilot of the vessel." It controlled and directed the body. Indeed, this is the view that many of us continue to hold regarding the self. How many times have you heard someone say that looks aren't everything and that what really matters is what kind of person an individual is? In doing so, they are claiming, along with

veracity
truth

Descartes, that when push comes to shove, the body really isn't all that important. It is the mind that makes you who you are.

But this account of the self has raised as many questions as it has provided answers. Can you be so certain that the self exists as Descartes described it? Descartes thought that it was impossible to disprove the existence of the self, but you might counter that it isn't all that clear that there is an essential self inside of you directing and guiding your actions. How many times have you been asked "what are you thinking?" and your response has been "I dunno"? It seems like the mind may not be easy to access after all. Indeed, it may be one of the hardest things to know. Think of how difficult it is sometimes to know what you are thinking, what you are feeling or what is motivating your actions. Further, the mind and the body are not isolated aspects of the self. Somehow they manage to work together to create your identity. Consider, for example, how the body affects the mind just as the mind affects the body. If you have ever drunk too much alcohol or have been with someone who is drunk, you have first- or at least second-hand experience of how powerful this influence can be. It is not so clear who or what is the "pilot of the vessel."

Sigmund Freud

Sigmund Freud

Questions such as these convinced Sigmund Freud that there is more to the self than his predecessors had appreciated. Theories that grounded the self in the thinking mind seemed to him too simplistic. They attempted to make the self a thing that is in control and relatively easy to understand. Listening to people describe their experiences, however, Freud realized that the self was mysterious, messy and complicated. More specifically, the mind seemed to be divided against itself—pulled and pushed in different directions by unknown forces.

Consider, for example, what could happen when you attempt to do something as simple as buying a pair of shoes. Suppose you get to the shoe department and immediately notice that the sales clerk is cute. You remind yourself that you are there to buy shoes, not to look for a date. You begin looking through the displays. You find the perfect pair. They look good on you. The only thing is that they cost about three times more than you had planned to spend. There are other shoes more in keeping with your budget, but, well, they just aren't *those* shoes. As you are standing there still checking out the clerk, a debate rages on in your head: "Buy them." "Don't buy them." "Buy them." "Go for a walk and think about it." "Buy them." "No, don't."

How often do such conversations take place in your head? Sometimes they may concern shoes, while at other times they might be about whether to ask that certain someone out or merely what to watch on television. It seems that you are often divided against yourself. Why? Why can't you be clear and decisive? Why is it so hard to make decisions about even the simplest things? What is it that pulls and pushes you in so many directions? Freud abandoned Descartes's project of trying to find one thing to believe in and, instead, in attempting to be more true to our lived experiences, he tried to explain why the self seems uncertain of everything—including its own workings.

The self, as described by Freud, could be compared to an iceberg. If you saw *Titanic*, you know that the ice formations that you see looming above the water compose only a small portion of the complete size of an iceberg. The same holds true for human beings. A large part of the self, for Freud, is an intricate web of conflicting desires and dictates of which you remain virtually unaware. His goal was to chart this unknown territory, to provide a map of the psyche. His analysis divided the self into three parts: the id, the superego and the ego.

Go back to the shoe example. Why do you want the expensive shoes? Is it really because they are comfortable, or do you have some ulterior motive? Why shoes, of all things? To answer these questions, Freud would suggest that you have to explore your id. This part of the self is housed in your unconscious—that mysterious part of yourself of which you are unaware but which, nonetheless, has a powerful effect on everything that you do, say, feel and think. The id contains two instincts—thanatos and eros—that constantly nag at you, wanting immediate satisfaction, pressuring you to act irrationally. And, if you think about it, you may be surprised to discover how often you succumb to such urges.

Thanatos is the drive toward death, aggression and violence. It is that part of the self that is willing to pull "your" pair of shoes out of the hands of another customer if they dare to pick them up. Most often, however, it takes more subtle forms and is expressed in feelings of envy and arrogance. While thanatos directs our feelings of aggression, eros concerns our desire for pleasure. According to Freud, the id operates according to the pleasure principle: it constantly tries to maximize pleasure, particularly the pleasure associated with our bodily desires for sex and food. If it *feels* good, it *is* good. Think about the shoes. Why is it that you want those shoes and you want those shoes now? Isn't it because they are a source of pleasure? They are not only comfortable; they might also serve to attract attention from others, which could lead to a date or to something even more. But if eros and thanatos are always unconsciously working toward fulfilling your desires, why aren't your closets full of shoes and your VISA bills permanently at your credit limit?

While it is true that the unconscious contains our basic instincts and desires, it also must wrestle with that part of our self that is constantly telling us "*Don't*." Think of the lists of *do*s and *don't*s that you have been subjected to throughout your lifetime. Friends, religious leaders, politicians, the media and, above all, others in your family are constantly telling you what you should do and how you should do it. An integral part of the psyche, the superego, has been internalizing these lists to make sure that you obey them. Remember going to the store with your parents and being told "NO" you can't have a new toy? Don't you hear that same "NO" reverberating in your head when you go to buy a new pair of shoes? And when you ask yourself why you can't have them, you get the line that you heard a million times as a teenager: "*Don't* waste your money." The superego demands that you adhere to each and every social rule; it demands perfect and complete obedience at all times.

But it doesn't get such obedience, and the battle rages on. The id and the superego attempt to alter the structure of the self by denying the reality or the importance of the other. It is the role of the ego, of the conscious part of the self, to try to referee between your unending desires and your internalized social rules. No one can live according to the pleasure principle alone. If you tried, you would quickly find yourself in jail. Similarly, if you tried to live according to every existing social rule, you would quickly find yourself immobilized. It would be impossible to act if you tried to adhere to them all. The role of the ego is to balance between reality, your desires and your lists of *do*s and *don't*s. This is the part of the self that tells you to "chill"—that is, to slow down and think things through before you do something that you will regret later. Sometimes the ego is successful, and sometimes it isn't.

According to Freud, the self is the arena in which these three forces confront each other—making it hard to know what you are thinking, let alone why. To help identify these psychic forces, Freud developed a series of techniques to make the unconscious mind reveal itself. If you know what desires are directing your behaviour and if you know what rules you have stored away in your memory, then you might be able to devise a means for reconciling them with the realities of your daily life. His famous talking cure, "psychoanalysis," is one such technique. By talking about your past experiences, particularly about your childhood, Freud thought that the unconscious would come to the surface and reveal unresolved conflicts that inhibit your progress. Similarly, he found clues to what lies beneath the surface of the self in analyzing slips of the tongue, jokes, word associations, dreams, and memories recovered using hypnosis.

Freud's view of the self has had an enormous effect on modern conceptions of identity. He complicated our understanding of the self with his introduction of the unconscious mind. He also recognized that the mind and the body are more intricately intertwined than had been previously acknowledged. Indeed, Freud offered explanations of how biology can affect the mind—when, for example, desires direct thought—as well as how the mind can affect biology—as demonstrated, for instance, through hysteria and psychosomatic illness. In short, he showed how the self can be divided against itself. And Freud's account of the self has led to a new appreciation of the complexity of relationships. If you don't know what you are doing or why, and I don't know what I'm doing or why, and the two of us are engaged in an intimate relationship, well, needless to say, we've got trouble. Freud's theories helped to explain why relationships, particularly with those whom you most love, are so difficult. And he made evident that you need to sit back and reflect on your actions and beliefs, preferably before acting, in order to avoid doing things that will ultimately be self-destructive. Reflecting on these contributions, it's hard for us to really imagine how people thought about the self before Freud.

Like Descartes, however, Freud was left at the end of his life with more questions about the self than he had answers, questions that continue to be raised about his theory. Critics have questioned Freud's claim that the self is constantly at war with itself. Sure, there are times when you may feel internally conflicted, but for the most part things are pretty peaceful. This has led other commentators to speculate that the self is not so mysterious, and that eros and thanatos are just intriguing and complicated fantasies.

Perhaps the most important criticism of Freud's theory of the self, however, concerns the very existence of the mind itself. To make this point clear, think for a minute about unicorns. Do you believe in unicorns? Most people don't. You may believe that if you can't see it or touch it, it just isn't real. Well, have you seen your mind? If you were shown a picture of your brain, would you be satisfied that you had seen your mind? Freud and Descartes put their faith in something as intangible as unicorns. They believed in a mind that you can't see or study or, for the most part, understand. It seems clear to many that the mind simply doesn't exist.

The search for alternative explanations of identity has led many theorists to return to that part of the self that Descartes had discarded as unreliable and unworthy of our attention and that Freud just began to explore, namely, the body. Most contemporary theories of the self emphasize that if there is such a thing as the mind, it must be located in a body that exists in time and space. Indeed, who you are is largely a consequence of your body. It seems that

Descartes and Freud were too quick to focus on the mind and, as a result, underestimated the extent to which the body is the self.

The Human Genome Project

Explanations of the self that centre on the body aren't new. Early attempts to explain behaviour and personality in terms of biology and physiology focused on the circulation of blood and on the shape and structure of the skull. Why did we turn to the body for information about the self? It seems pretty clear. The body is tangible. It can be observed and examined. You can study the body, quantify your results, use your findings to predict future outcomes, and perhaps even intervene. The body is knowable and predictable and, therefore, it seems to provide a more reliable foundation on which to build a theory of identity.

Clearly the most significant development in this school of thought was the discovery of DNA (deoxyribonucleic acid). While the chemical itself was first identified in 1869, it was not until 1953 that James Watson and Francis Crick were able to unlock the structure of DNA. In so doing, they initiated the genetic revolution—a revolution that would put into question some of the most cherished beliefs about the self much in the same way as scientific revolutions did centuries before.

DNA is a genetic code found in every cell in your body. It is most often represented by a double helix—that is, by two lines or polymers that intertwine with each other. The helix is divided into 24 distinct and separate units known as chromosomes. Along these chromosomes lie genes that hold within them a blueprint for how a person is predisposed to grow and to develop. Just as Morse code is composed of messages translated into a series of dots and dashes, the messages in our genes are encoded in the form of four basic acids known as nucleotides: adenine, guanine, cytosine and thymine. Various combinations of these acids within genes contain information that predispose you to develop certain physical traits, particular diseases and syndromes and, according to some researchers, specific aspects of your personality.

The Human Genome Project was initiated in 1990 with the goal of mapping the human genome—the complete map of human genetics—that consists of approximately 30,000 genes. With researchers in over 15 countries and a yearly budget that exceeded 30 billion dollars (US), the project completed its first draft in 2000—when the dispositions associated with every chromosomal, single, human gene had been identified. The genes for over 500 hereditary diseases, including ALS, multiple sclerosis, Alzheimer's disease and breast cancer were located, and, based on this knowledge, scientists are beginning to develop new treatment procedures and therapies. But this was just the beginning.

Genetics has often been misinterpreted as the science that concerns itself simply with identifying causal relationships between single genes and human physiology and/or behaviour. In reality, however, this new science is far more complicated. It might be telling to ask why the complexity of this new science has been overlooked. Perhaps there is something appealing about a model of behaviour that seems to be so straightforward. Instead of trying to decipher the logic of Descartes's thinking mind or the irrationality of Freud's unconscious, it can be reassuring to think that humanity can be described and explained in a much more mechanistic and uncomplicated manner. Indeed, simplifying genetics does make it possible to sidestep some of the more challenging questions about human behaviour that are raised by this research. Paradoxically, genetics, as it has been popularized, is an easy target for criticism precisely due to its supposed failure to take into account the complexities raised by environmental influences and the role of free will. Dispelling this misleading view of genetics, then, is key to facing the important issues that it raises with regard to human behaviour.

Far from completing its task with the mapping of the human genome, the Human Genome Project has just begun its work. For instance, researchers are now looking at the effects of *combinations* of genes. They are trying, moreover, to better understand the complex relationships that exist not only among genes, but also among combinations of genes, biochemical events, the environment and the individual's responses to these variables. That is, they are attempting to map webs of *influence*, rather than causal relationships, in order to better understand the evolution and development of human physiology and behaviour. Adopting this approach, researchers do not expect to uncover simple, universal truths about human nature but rather hope, at best, to find statistically relevant patterns.

Genetic research is not a study of certainties. It deals in probabilities rather than rigid absolutes. Scientists acknowledge that, at most, genetic markers can tell us about dispositions, about the *likelihood* that a person will develop a particular physical characteristic, disease or personality trait. But dispositions are not certainties. This leaves room for the environment to play a role in shaping the self. Looking at your DNA, geneticists can make, at best, informed predictions as to what your future will hold. Studying your DNA, therefore, is not like looking into a crystal ball. It requires more interpretation and guess work than is often recognized. This is not to downplay the incredible potential that genetics holds. Combining this research with increasingly complex methods of gene therapy, medicine now affords us opportunities that were only dreamed about even a decade ago. These discoveries have been miraculous. However, with such revolutionary findings also comes controversy.

Debates have emerged as researchers speculate on the existence of a gay gene, a serial-killer gene and an intelligence gene. Just how much of who you are is pre-programmed by your genes? While advocates of this school of thought admit that the environment and free will play a role in shaping behaviour, without a pre-existing genetic disposition, you would never have had the chance to act the way you do. Your life may not be written in the stars, but it *is* encoded in your DNA. And if your behaviour and attitudes are the result of genetic encoding, how is it possible for you to be held responsible for your actions?

Further questions have been raised as to what should be done with the findings of this genetic research. While the Human Genome Project was mapping the genetic code, other scientists were developing the techniques necessary to alter DNA patterning. A whole series of ethical issues has arisen around genetic screening and the treatment of patients for diseases and syndromes that they might acquire in future. What are we going to do with this new knowledge of the self? What, if any, limits should be placed upon its use? The questions raised by this field of study centre on our very understanding of what it means to be human.

Perhaps as researchers continue to study genes, a clearer picture of the self and its workings will appear. Or maybe it will be discovered that the more we try to explain the self in scientific terms, the more such an account escapes us. For clearly there seems to be something missing from this account of the self. What even the most sophisticated geneticist cannot account for, or even predict, is the effect that others will have on the self. Think of how someone, maybe even a stranger, can just look at you in a particular way and change the way you see yourself. You may have changed for the better or for the worse, but you cannot deny that you have changed. The theories of the self offered by Descartes, Freud and contemporary geneticists do not adequately account for this effect. They underestimate the extent to which the self is constructed by other people.

B. F. Skinner

Behaviourists such as B. F. Skinner argue that the self is shaped or conditioned by the feedback it receives in response to its actions (or lack of action). Think for a minute about the fact that on even the coldest mornings, when you are exhausted and want nothing more than to stay in your nice, warm, cozy bed, you nonetheless get up at a ridiculously early hour, brave the cold and spend hours parked on the highway, just to get to work.

B. F. Skinner

Why do you do this? Clearly you are motivated by your desire and need for money. Not only do you go to work every day, you also wear uncomfortable work clothes and do work tasks that you might find boring, unnecessary or even reprehensible. In other words, money reinforces your behaviour. Reinforcement involves pairing something that an individual desires with a particular action or response. Most often, positive reinforcements are tools for shaping behaviour; that is, "rewards" can encourage certain actions. Rewards may take the form of money, material goods or more subtle stimulants such as reputation, social acceptance or friendship. Why do businesses post pictures of the employee of the month? Why do companies and corporations take their staff to baseball games? In these ways, employers clearly try to offer their employees the non-material things they desire as a consequence for good workplace performance. Conditioning also incorporates negative reinforcement. A negative reinforcement eliminates some existing annoyance or negative stimulant from the environment when the person acts in the desired manner. What happens, for example, when you first wake up in the morning? You hear that annoying buzz of your alarm clock. How do you get it to stop? Not only must you wake up, but you have to also reach over and turn the alarm off. This is an example of how your behaviour is modified using negative reinforcement.

While many employers rely on reinforcement to get their workers to work harder and longer hours, others rely on the second principle of conditioning—punishment—to achieve this goal. In order to ensure that you are punctual, your boss may deduct wages from your paycheque, give you a lousy schedule or delegate the worst work assignment to you. When you punish someone, you try to change his or her behaviour by pairing a particular action (or non-action) with something that the person wishes to avoid.

Using these two principles of conditioning, behaviourists argue that you can explain how the self is moulded or constructed by the environment. Think about all the subtle and not-so-subtle ways you are reinforced and punished for your behaviour. Consider how your workplace environment as well as other social forces such as family, peers, religious organizations, government institutions, media and even the physical space in which you live influence how you act, what you say, and how you think.

It is hard to deny the success that behaviourism has had in explaining and, even more so, in controlling behaviour. When you sit back and think about it, it really does seem that who you are is to a great extent the consequence of the history of reinforcements and punishments to which you have been subjected. You not only get up in the morning and go to work but you also pay taxes and you buy Nike shoes. You can quit smoking and stop biting your nails to a great extent because these principles work. In institutions, these principles have been used to successfully manage large populations. Prison systems, for instance, often work on a merit system. If you are a good inmate, you receive cigarettes, television time and even conjugal visits. If you break the rules, you are not only denied such things, you may also be given the worst work detail or placed in solitary confinement.

Despite this success, behaviourism has its limitations. It has a hard time explaining, for example, why people living and working in exactly the same environment can come to act and behave differently. Co-workers who live in the same city, the same neighbourhood and sometimes even the same household can have entirely different work habits. Furthermore, if the environment is key to shaping identity, how is it possible that workers in as diverse cultural settings as Japan, Canada and India all seem to want basically the same things for themselves and their families? Maybe it is the result of globalization: everyone everywhere wears Nike, drinks Coke and watches CNN. Or, maybe, regardless of the culture you live in, the work you do or the families that you are part of, there remain some features of human nature that stubbornly assert themselves no matter what the environmental influences.

Yet further questions have been raised about the effectiveness of reinforcement and punishment. It is hard to determine what constitutes reinforcement and punishment because the things that people value and dislike vary greatly from group to group and from person to person. Something that I consider desirable, you may consider detestable. Business travel provides a good example. Your boss may think that sending you on a trip is a great opportunity, but you might not like the idea because you have tickets to see a basketball game that you have been looking forward to all season. Your boss thinks that she is reinforcing your performance when, in fact, she is (unintentionally) punishing you.

Moreover, reinforcements only seem to work for a relatively short period of time before the person expects more in order to act in the desired manner. You might accept a 50-cent-per-hour raise when you first start working, but over time you will want more and more money to maintain the same level of performance. Eventually you may even decide that the money is just not worth getting out of bed for on cold winter mornings.

Similar studies have shown that punishment is not a particularly successful means for modifying behaviour. If you threaten to fire an employee if he or she arrives late again for work and then you don't go through with it, don't expect that tactic to work again in the future. Even if you do follow through with your threat, you need to recognize that punishment extinguishes quickly. If you punish someone over and over again, eventually they will rebel and will challenge you to "come and get them." What this suggests is that the self is not as malleable or as easily manipulated as behaviourists claim. It seems that people do not always want reinforcement and do not always fear punishment. Nonetheless, these techniques continue to be used in an attempt to try to understand and control this thing called the self.

Despite the best efforts of the thinkers described herein, it is still not clear what constitutes the self. In fact, as social scientists and medical researchers delve into increasingly complicated and minute factors intent on explaining identity, they seem to drift further and further away from everyday experiences. Consider, for example, how the self, as described by these theorists, is relatively stable across time. If you sit back and think about all the changes that you have gone through over your lifetime, over the past month or during the time that it has taken you to read this article, it seems pretty clear that the self is in constant flux. Rather than being a static entity, the self is a dynamic and creative force. And it is marked by incredible uncertainty. The theorists discussed so far all assume that the self—be it mind, body or environmental by-product—is knowable. In your everyday life, how often is this the case? How many times have you been asked why you acted in a particular way or made a particular comment and have been at a loss for an answer? It seems that you can only know your self in hindsight. Even then, your motivations and drives, to a great extent, remain a mystery.

Friedrich Nietzsche

Focusing on our experiences, the philosopher Friedrich Nietzsche devised yet another account of the self. Nietzsche was living at the end of the 19th century—when the effects of the Industrial Revolution were taking hold. It was a time marked by great optimism. With the development of new means of transportation, the mass production of goods and the remarkable technological advancements that marked this age, people put their faith in the future. They believed in progress. Things were getting better and better. And there was no sign of that trend ending any time soon. Nietzsche challenged this perceived view. He saw in his time not the ascent of humankind but rather its descent. Far from things getting better and better, he saw them getting worse and worse. To reverse this trend, it was necessary to shake people up—to remind them of just who and what they were. This required a careful examination of the self—not of the self that you might wish you were, but of the self that you are.

A good starting point for looking at Nietzsche's notion of the self is his account of the "myth of the eternal recurrence of the same." This thought experiment asks you to imagine that you had to live your life over again and again and again, in all of its details—including both the big things and the

Friedrich Nietzsche

small. How would you respond to this news? Would you jump for joy at the thought, or would you think that you had been cursed by some demon? Nietzsche noted that most people would gnash their teeth and say that they had never heard anything so horrible. Why this response? Why, Nietzsche asks, aren't people living lives that they would choose to repeat over and over again?

To answer this question, it is necessary to take a bit of a detour and discuss, of all things, sheep. Sheep are best known for the fact that they flock together. It is rare to see a single sheep standing alone, away from its herd. These animals seem to take comfort in numbers and constantly seek the companionship of their species. Along with flocking, sheep are also noted for their blind ability to follow. If one sheep goes over a cliff, the entire herd will follow suit. They will follow despite the dangers at hand. That means that sheep are easy prey.

Thinking about sheep may seem an unusual way to analyze the concept of the self. However, for Nietzsche it was necessary. Consider how much like sheep human beings have become. Like these docile animals, humans take comfort in numbers. Even after telling others that you "just want to be left alone," how often do you go into your bedroom, shut the door and turn on the television or log onto MSN? It seems that despite your words, you don't really want to be left alone with yourself. This may help to explain why it is that humans, like sheep, love to follow. For as much as you might think that you want to be different, don't you, in fact, work very hard to be the same as everyone else? Do you really want to risk being "original"? Think of all that you might lose if you stood out in a crowd. No wonder human beings have become easy prey. No wonder we are susceptible to fads and trends—in everything from clothing to ideas—that are painful, self-destructive and/or harmful to others. Clearly, humans have devolved to what Nietzsche calls herd mentality. But this is not the way that they have to be. It does not have to be human destiny.

Nietzsche envisioned human beings becoming more than what they are—both individually and collectively. A human being, according to Nietzsche, is like a rope over an abyss—that is, a rope between beast and something more, something greater: an "Übermensch" or "overman." It is, then, your choice to determine which end of the rope you wish to head toward. You are a tightrope walker. But you can't be sure which way is which. Looks can be deceiving. The best you can do is to try. Try to be something more.

What exactly being something more entails is hard to say. Like most people, you may be so wedded to your present way of being that it may be hard to think of what else you could be if you dared to leave behind your conformist (that is, sheep-like) behaviour. Nietzsche was cautious in describing the life of the overman. Old habits die hard and he worried that if he told you what this new kind of self would look like, you could end up following again.

Instead, Nietzsche draws an analogy between the self and a work of art. He asks you to consider what it would mean to try to exercise the same kind of creativity in your life as an artist applies to an artwork. What if, rather than striving to lead a perfectly "normal" life, you tried to create a masterpiece out of your life—through your thoughts and your actions? What if, rather than following current fashion trends in everything from clothing to thought, you dared "to give style to your character"? What if, instead of settling for the predictable familiarity of the herd, you created a life for your self that you would be happy to live over and over again? What would your life be like if, in other words, you exercised "will to power"?

Will to power, according to Nietzsche, encompasses your ability to create and to live in the world on your own terms. This first requires that you embrace, rather than turn away from, those aspects of your life that make you human—those life-affirming experiences which include pain and suffering as well as joy and laughter. You need to know who and what you are before you can begin to distinguish yourself from the beasts. You need to know the dangers and seductions of human existence if you wish to avoid falling prey to sheep-like behaviour—to following others blindly. Will to power simultaneously warns you of the pitfalls of attempting to impose your beliefs and ideals on others. In other words, will to power is not synonymous with will to truth. This is an important distinction. Will to power does not involve sheep suddenly becoming shepherds. That is, it does not encourage individuals who have taken control over their own lives to then go on and impose their values and beliefs on others. Will to power is not the will to control or dominate or manipulate others but, rather, it is the will to live according to one's own beliefs—to control one's self.

Viewed from this perspective, the self cannot be regarded as a stable entity to be discovered; instead, it must be considered a dynamic force capable of change, always open to re-creation and re-invention. Your biology does not make you who you are any more than does your environment. Both factors are the materials with which you can work to create, or to write, the story of your life.

This is a scary prospect. Think of all the possibilities. Each day you have the opportunity to make your life either into a uniquely beautiful canvas or, alternatively, into a copy of a Disney poster. Each day it is your choice. Your choice. The possibilities are so attractive yet so horrifying that most would rather turn away and pretend that the self is a stable, static entity out there waiting to be uncovered or discovered. The comforts of certainty and

Edvard Munch's *The Scream* (1893)

stability do lead most people to forget that the self is a creative force. Indeed, if the self were a static, determined entity, no one would be accountable for his or her actions. You could take comfort in the belief that you are the product of your mind, your unconscious, your genes or your environment, or some combination of these factors. You would be seen as merely a product, a victim even, of the world in which you find yourself. And, as such, you, your self, could not be held responsible for your actions. The self—each self—would be a helpless entity produced by some collection of forces that are both internal and external. Could there ever be anything more comforting, more safe, yet, ultimately, more false?

Nietzsche's view of the self is not for the faint of heart, for the unimaginative or for the uncourageous. It requires you to take risks and to accept the consequences. There is no safety net to catch the tightrope walker if he or she falls. What it does offer, however, is an account of the self that seems to fit with much of lived experience. This approach captures the uncertainties and insecurities that so often figure in daily life. As well, it emphasizes that, far from having your life determined for you, far from being the victim of some kind of biological or social fate, you are the creator of your own destiny. And thus it holds you accountable for your own life. It makes you think hard about the choices you make about the kind of person you wish to become.

However daring and appealing Nietzsche's view of the self may be, it too has its limitations. Are you really as free to create and invent your life as Nietzsche suggests? You have to get up in the morning, you have to make money in order to survive, you have to be careful what you say so that you don't offend others and you have to watch your more eccentric actions lest they be interpreted as perverse, insane or criminal. Even if you do have the ability to escape the herd, do you really want to? Humans need each other; they need the sense of safety and community offered to them by the group. They cannot simply strike out on their own without suffering consequences. And, lastly, it seems hard to imagine a time when you could have your own values and beliefs and not try to impose them on others. Given everyday experience, it is hard to imagine becoming something so different that you would not need to be either the leader or a follower.

It may seem that this short history of theories of the self has not really got us very far. What is the self? We still don't have a clear definition. Indeed, if anything, we might be more confused about the answer to this question than before we began. It is true that none of the thinkers discussed here arrived at a completely convincing account of the self. Many of them recognized this inadequacy themselves. Freud, for example, determined at the end of his career that he really did not understand human beings (particularly women) very well at all. Like others who have tried to explain the self, he found that his works were incomplete and full of inconsistencies. However, we should not be too quick to conclude that the works of Freud and the other thinkers discussed in this article were written in vain.

Indeed, this discussion has made clear that the self is an evolving concept. Far from being a stable and persistent entity, it is an idea. It is the product of history, politics and science. But the self is not just the outcome or end result of these factors; it also plays a role in shaping them. The self is an organizing principle—it helps set the agenda of issues to be investigated and developed by government officials, business executives and scientists.

This short history of sometimes competing theories of identity should serve as a cautionary tale, especially at the beginning of the 21st century. It is impossible to know how our present theories of the self will evolve. But they will evolve and with this evolution will come new challenges and insights. This will change our perception not only of ourselves but also of the world around us and of our relationship to it. If we change who we think we are, it has implications for our work, for our notions of justice and for our relationship to nature. The consequences of a changing view of ourselves are enormous, as we are the point from which we view all things. The words of the ancient Greek philosopher Socrates still serve as an apt warning and an appropriate conclusion: "Know thyself."

"From Biology to Biography: A Brief History of the Self" was written for *The Human Project* by Wendy O'Brien, a professor at the Humber College Institute of Technology and Advanced Learning and the University of Guelph-Humber. Used by permission.

What Will My Future Self Think of Me?

Mark Kingwell

Suppose you could communicate with yourself in the future—say 20 years from now. What would you do? Remember, this would be a different version of yourself, someone who, while still connected to you, has only hazy memories of your current state of mind. So you may welcome the opportunity to remind the person you're about to become of how something came to be, how you feel about something or what you dream of doing some day. Or you may just want to apologize, over and over, for all the dumb things you've done.

If this appeals, you're far from alone. Five years ago, Matt Sly and Jay Patrikos, two Web entrepreneurs based in California, created Future Me, a website with an archive of e-mails people have written to their future selves.

"FutureMe.org is based," the site says, "on the principle that memories are less accurate than e-mails." The e-mails will be delivered at a time, up to 20 years later, picked by the user.

Almost 400,000 letters from around the world have been received since the site went up in 2002. A book of the 200 best public letters, *Dear Future Me*, . . . [was published in 2007]. The site is especially popular, site founders say, with US troops stationed in Iraq—who seem to derive comfort from sending a secure message from an insecure location.

What is the draw? It is not as though a "future me" message has any critical purchase on decision. This is not foresight, as in the . . . film *Next*, based on a Philip K. Dick story about a man cursed with knowledge of future events.

Your future you may be interested to receive a message, but it will not help him or her avoid his or her own mistakes—about which future future-me messages might well be sent. We might think the more desirable thing would be a past-me message: Don't take that job! Don't sleep with that guy! Do stop and smell the roses! For god's sake, buy life insurance! So far, that's not possible, even on the Web. (Not that most past me's would listen anyway.)

Technology aside, Future Me is just an instance of the ancient genius of writing. A grocery list is a future-me message, after all, to the me who might forget, between home and the store, whether we need milk. So is a book, arguing something now so it won't be forgotten later. Setting things down, whether on paper or on a hard drive, holds them over from one **iteration** of self to another. In the most extreme case—recall the movie *Memento*—we might have to use our own bodies as a notepad against lost memory: the tattoo as Post-it for future me.

iteration

version

All writing, and especially the first-person sort, floats between presence and absence. I sign a letter to signify that I am present at its conception, endorsing it. But I have to sign the letter in the first place precisely because I will not be present when it is read, even if it is read by a future version of myself. That future self needs to feel accountable to the past self, who set down his name in the name of the future we now are: the signature as promissory note.

Whether all these selves are the same person is another matter. In one sense, clearly not. If present me and future me were literally the same, there would be no need for letters, or even notes. I would never not know whether we need milk, and I wouldn't need or want to hear from past versions of me about what it, or they, were thinking and feeling. We know our past, present and future selves are different because of familiar gaps between them, in both mind and body. I despise past me, or resent him, or find him mildly amusing, if stupid. I envy his energy and smooth skin, his unbroken limbs. I wonder what the hell he thought he was thinking, doing what he did.

Receiving or sending a letter between two selves raises the awkward question of what responsibility, if any, we owe to our past. In the law and in ethics, we maintain a fiction of stable personal identity across time so that we can attach actions to persons. You did this, hence you are responsible for it. But any action is immediately a past action, and so the responsibility of a past self rather than the present one. Statutes of limitations and criminal-rehabilitation theory nod in the direction of complexity here: If enough time passes, or if your present self is sufficiently different from your past one, you may be let off the hook. But, in general, law does not allow escape from past-self actions.

In **metaphysics** as well as ordinary life, we know things are more slippery. Consider a promise such as a marriage vow. I make it with full sincerity and the best knowledge of which I am capable. I even make it with the sure conviction that it is forever. Yet things change. People change. The promise gets broken, not by the person who made it (who sincerely wanted a career and no children) but by that other person (who finds parenthood appealing after all).

metaphysics
philosophical study of the nature of reality

Who is responsible? Confronting a past self is like waking up with a hangover, a residue of effect suffered by one self because of the deeds of another. The implications of past actions and choices, some of which we might barely remember, burden us all the time. Why do we go along with it? Is there no rehab program for personhood?

No. But writing to future you is a poignant, maybe desperate assertion of personal continuity over time. Its attempt at forward revision seeks connection among the dots of consciousness, a coherent narrative. More

G. K. Chesterton
(1874–1936) English writer

oligopoly
privileged and powerful group

deeply, such a message implicitly accepts a duty to future generations. Future selves can't speak for themselves, against what **G. K. Chesterton** called the "small and arrogant **oligopoly** of those who merely happen to be walking about." Future me may reject present me's choices, but my message to him is, in its way, an attempt to acknowledge responsibility rather than evade it.

For better or worse, present me is the sole go-between linking all past me's with all future ones. Let's hope he knows what he's doing.

"What Will My Future Self Think of Me?" by Mark Kingwell originally appeared in the April 28, 2007, *Globe and Mail* as part of Mark Kingwell's column, "The Identity Continuum." Copyright © 2007 by Mark Kingwell. Used by permission.

Darwin's God

Robin Marantz Henig

God has always been a puzzle for Scott Atran. When he was 10 years old, he scrawled a plaintive message on the wall of his bedroom in Baltimore. "God exists," he wrote in black and orange paint, "or if he doesn't, we're in trouble." Atran has been struggling with questions about religion ever since—why he himself no longer believes in God and why so many other people, everywhere in the world, apparently do.

Call it God; call it superstition; call it, as Atran does, "belief in hope beyond reason"—whatever you call it, there seems an inherent human drive to believe in something transcendent, unfathomable and otherworldly, something beyond the reach or understanding of science. "Why do we cross our fingers during turbulence, even the most atheistic among us?" asked Atran when we spoke at his Upper West Side **pied-à-terre** . . . . Atran, who is 55, is an anthropologist at the National Center for Scientific Research in Paris, with joint appointments at the University of Michigan and the John Jay College of Criminal Justice in New York. His research interests include cognitive science and evolutionary biology, and sometimes he presents students with a wooden box that he pretends is an African relic. "If you have negative sentiments toward religion," he tells them, "the box will destroy whatever you put inside it." Many of his students say they doubt the existence of God, but in this demonstration they act as if they believe in something. Put your pencil into the magic box, he tells them, and the nonbelievers do so **blithely**. Put in your driver's license, he says, and most do, but only after significant hesitation. And when he tells them to put in their hands, few will.

If they don't believe in God, what exactly are they afraid of?

Atran first conducted the magic-box demonstration in the 1980s, when he was at Cambridge University studying the nature of religious belief. He had received a doctorate in anthropology from Columbia University and, in the course of his fieldwork, saw evidence of religion everywhere he looked—at archaeological digs in Israel, among the Mayans in Guatemala, in artifact drawers at the American Museum of Natural History in New York. Atran is Darwinian in his approach, which means he tries to explain behavior by how it might once have solved problems of survival and reproduction for our early ancestors. But it was not clear to him what evolutionary problems might have been solved by religious belief. Religion seemed to use up physical and mental resources without an obvious benefit for survival. Why, he wondered, was religion so pervasive, when it was something that seemed so costly from an evolutionary point of view?

pied-à-terre
temporary residence

blithely
in a carefree manner

The magic-box demonstration helped set Atran on a career studying why humans might have evolved to be religious, something few people were doing back in the '80s. Today, the effort has gained momentum, as scientists search for an evolutionary explanation for why belief in God exists—not whether God exists, which is a matter for philosophers and theologians, but why the belief does.

This is different from the scientific assault on religion that has been garnering attention recently, in the form of best-selling books from scientific atheists who see religion as a scourge. In *The God Delusion*, . . . the Oxford evolutionary biologist Richard Dawkins concludes that religion is nothing more than a useless, and sometimes dangerous, evolutionary accident. "Religious behavior may be a misfiring, an unfortunate byproduct of an underlying psychological propensity which in other circumstances is, or once was, useful," Dawkins wrote. He is joined by two other best-selling authors—Sam Harris, who wrote *The End of Faith,* and Daniel Dennett, a philosopher at Tufts University who wrote *Breaking the Spell.* The three men differ in their personal styles and whether they are engaged in a battle against religiosity, but their names are often mentioned together. They have been portrayed as an unholy trinity of neo-atheists, promoting their secular world view with a fervor that seems almost evangelical.

Lost in the hullabaloo over the neo-atheists is a quieter and potentially more illuminating debate. It is taking place not between science and religion but within science itself, specifically among the scientists studying the evolution of religion. These scholars tend to agree on one point: that religious belief is an outgrowth of brain architecture that evolved during early human history. What they disagree about is why a tendency to believe evolved, whether it was because belief itself was adaptive or because it was just an evolutionary byproduct, a mere consequence of some other adaptation in the evolution of the human brain.

Which is the better biological explanation for a belief in God—evolutionary adaptation or neurological accident? Is there something about the cognitive functioning of humans that makes us receptive to belief in a supernatural deity? And if scientists are able to explain God, what then? Is explaining religion the same thing as explaining it away? Are the nonbelievers right, and is religion at its core an empty undertaking, a misdirection, a **vestigial** artifact of a primitive mind? Or are the believers right, and does the fact that we have the mental capacities for discerning God suggest that it was God who put them there?

vestigial
left over

In short, are we hard-wired to believe in God? And if we are, how and why did that happen?

"All of our raptures and our drynesses, our longings and pantings, our questions and beliefs . . . are equally organically founded," William James wrote in *The Varieties of Religious Experience*. James, who taught philosophy and experimental psychology at Harvard for more than 30 years, based his book on a 1901 lecture series in which he took some early tentative steps at breaching the science-religion divide.

In the century that followed, a polite convention generally separated science and religion, at least in much of the Western world. Science, as the old **trope** had it, was assigned the territory that describes how the heavens go; religion, how to go to heaven.

trope
figure of speech

Anthropologists like Atran and psychologists as far back as James had been looking at the roots of religion, but the mutual hands-off policy really began to shift in the 1990s. Religion made incursions into the traditional domain of science with attempts to bring intelligent design into the biology classroom and to choke off human embryonic stem-cell research on religious grounds. Scientists responded with counterincursions. Experts from the hard sciences, like evolutionary biology and cognitive neuroscience, joined anthropologists and psychologists in the study of religion, making God an object of scientific inquiry.

The debate over why belief evolved is between byproduct theorists and adaptationists. You might think that the byproduct theorists would tend to be nonbelievers, looking for a way to explain religion as a fluke, while the adaptationists would be more likely to be believers who can intuit the emotional, spiritual and community advantages that accompany faith. Or you might think they would all be atheists, because what believer would want to subject his own devotion to rationalism's cold, hard scrutiny? But a scientist's personal religious view does not always predict which side he will take. And this is just one sign of how complex and surprising this debate has become.

Angels, demons, spirits, wizards, gods and witches have peppered folk religions since mankind first started telling stories. Charles Darwin noted this in *The Descent of Man*. "A belief in all-pervading spiritual agencies," he wrote, "seems to be universal." According to anthropologists, religions that share certain supernatural features—belief in a noncorporeal God or gods, belief in the afterlife, belief in the ability of prayer or ritual to change the course of human events—are found in virtually every culture on earth.

This is certainly true in the United States. About 6 in 10 Americans, according to a 2005 Harris Poll, believe in the devil and hell, and about 7 in 10 believe in angels, heaven and the existence of miracles and of life after death. A 2006 survey at Baylor University found that 92 percent of respondents believe in a personal God—that is, a God with a distinct set of character traits ranging from "distant" to "benevolent."

When a trait is universal, evolutionary biologists look for a genetic explanation and wonder how that gene or genes might enhance survival or reproductive success. In many ways, it's an exercise in ***post-hoc*** hypothesizing: what would have been the advantage, when the human species first evolved, for an individual who happened to have a mutation that led to, say, a smaller jaw, a bigger forehead, a better thumb? How about certain behavioral traits, like a tendency for risk-taking or for kindness?

post-hoc
after the fact

Atran saw such questions as a puzzle when applied to religion. So many aspects of religious belief involve misattribution and misunderstanding of the real world. Wouldn't this be a liability in the survival-of-the-fittest competition? To Atran, religious belief requires taking "what is materially false to be true" and "what is materially true to be false." One example of this is the belief that even after someone dies and the body demonstrably disintegrates, that person will still exist, will still be able to laugh and cry, to feel pain and joy. This confusion "does not appear to be a reasonable evolutionary strategy," Atran wrote in *In Gods We Trust: The Evolutionary Landscape of Religion* in 2002. "Imagine another animal that took injury for health or big for small or fast for slow or dead for alive. It's unlikely that such a species could survive." He began to look for a sideways explanation: if religious belief was not adaptive, perhaps it was associated with something else that was.

Atran intended to study mathematics when he entered Columbia as a precocious 17-year-old. But he was distracted by the radical politics of the late '60s. One day in his freshman year, he found himself at an antiwar rally listening to Margaret Mead, then perhaps the most famous anthropologist in America. Atran, dressed in a flamboyant Uncle Sam suit, stood up and called her a sellout for saying the protesters should be writing to their congressmen instead of staging demonstrations. "Young man," the unflappable Mead said, "why don't you come see me in my office?"

Atran, equally unflappable, did go to see her—and ended up working for Mead, spending much of his time exploring the cabinets of curiosities in her tower office at the American Museum of Natural History. Soon he switched his major to anthropology.

Many of the museum specimens were religious, Atran says. So were the artifacts he dug up on archaeological excursions in Israel in the early '70s. Wherever he turned, he encountered the passion of religious belief. Why, he wondered, did people work so hard against their preference for logical explanations to maintain two views of the world, the real and the unreal, the intuitive and the counterintuitive?

Maybe cognitive effort was precisely the point. Maybe it took less mental work than Atran realized to hold belief in God in one's mind. Maybe, in fact, belief was the default position for the human mind, something that took no cognitive effort at all.

While still an undergraduate, Atran decided to explore these questions by organizing a conference on universal aspects of culture and inviting all his intellectual heroes: the linguist Noam Chomsky, the psychologist Jean Piaget, the anthropologists Claude Levi-Strauss and Gregory Bateson (who was also Margaret Mead's ex-husband), the Nobel Prize-winning biologists Jacques Monod and Francois Jacob. It was 1974, and the only site he could find for the conference was at a location just outside Paris. Atran was a scraggly 22-year-old with a guitar who had learned his French from comic books. To his astonishment, everyone he invited agreed to come.

Atran is a sociable man with sharp hazel eyes, who sparks provocative conversations the way other men pick bar fights. As he traveled in the '70s and '80s, he accumulated friends who were thinking about the issues he was: how culture is transmitted among human groups and what evolutionary function it might serve. "I started looking at history, and I wondered why no society ever survived more than three generations without a religious foundation as its **raison d'être**," he says. Soon he turned to an emerging subset of evolutionary theory—the evolution of human cognition.

raison d'être
reason for existing

Some cognitive scientists think of brain functioning in terms of modules, a series of interconnected machines, each one responsible for a particular mental trick. They do not tend to talk about a God module per se; they usually consider belief in God a consequence of other mental modules.

Religion, in this view, is "a family of cognitive phenomena that involves the extraordinary use of everyday cognitive processes," Atran wrote in *In Gods We Trust*. "Religions do not exist apart from the individual minds that constitute them and the environments that constrain them, any more than biological species and varieties exist independently of the individual organisms that compose them and the environments that conform them."

At around the time *In Gods We Trust* appeared five years ago, a handful of other scientists—Pascal Boyer, now at Washington University; Justin Barrett, now at Oxford; Paul Bloom at Yale—were addressing these same questions. In **synchrony** they were moving toward the byproduct theory.

in synchrony
at the same time

Darwinians who study physical evolution distinguish between traits that are themselves adaptive, like having blood cells that can transport oxygen, and traits that are byproducts of adaptations, like the redness of blood. There is no survival advantage to blood's being red instead of turquoise; it is just a byproduct of the trait that is adaptive, having blood that contains hemoglobin.

Something similar explains aspects of brain evolution, too, say the byproduct theorists. Which brings us to the idea of the spandrel.

Stephen Jay Gould, the famed evolutionary biologist at Harvard who died in 2002, and his colleague Richard Lewontin proposed "spandrel" to describe a trait that has no adaptive value of its own. They borrowed the term from architecture, where it originally referred to the V-shaped structure formed between two rounded arches. The structure is not there for any purpose; it is there because that is what happens when arches align.

In architecture, a spandrel can be neutral or it can be made functional. Building a staircase, for instance, creates a space underneath that is innocuous, just a blank sort of triangle. But if you put a closet there, the under-stairs space takes on a function, unrelated to the staircase's but useful nonetheless. Either way, functional or nonfunctional, the space under the stairs is a spandrel, an unintended byproduct.

"Natural selection made the human brain big," Gould wrote, "but most of our mental properties and potentials may be spandrels—that is, nonadaptive side consequences of building a device with such structural complexity."

The possibility that God could be a spandrel offered Atran a new way of understanding the evolution of religion. But a spandrel of what, exactly?

Hardships of early human life favored the evolution of certain cognitive tools, among them the ability to infer the presence of organisms that might do harm, to come up with causal narratives for natural events and to recognize that other people have minds of their own with their own beliefs, desires and intentions. Psychologists call these tools, respectively, agent detection, causal reasoning and theory of mind.

volitional
intentional and voluntary

Agent detection evolved because assuming the presence of an agent—which is jargon for any creature with **volitional**, independent behavior—is more adaptive than assuming its absence. If you are a caveman on the savannah, you are better off presuming that the motion you detect out of the corner of your eye is an agent and something to run from, even if you are wrong. If it turns out to have been just the rustling of leaves, you are still alive; if what you took to be leaves rustling was really a hyena about to pounce, you are dead.

A classic experiment from the 1940s by the psychologists Fritz Heider and Marianne Simmel suggested that imputing agency is so automatic that people may do it even for geometric shapes. For the experiment, subjects watched a film of triangles and circles moving around. When asked what they had been watching, the subjects used words like "chase" and "capture." They did not just see the random movement of shapes on a screen; they saw pursuit, planning, escape.

So if there is motion just out of our line of sight, we presume it is caused by an agent, an animal or person with the ability to move independently. This usually operates in one direction only; lots of people mistake a rock for a bear, but almost no one mistakes a bear for a rock.

What does this mean for belief in the supernatural? It means our brains are primed for it, ready to presume the presence of agents even when such presence confounds logic. "The most central concepts in religions are related to agents," Justin Barrett, a psychologist, wrote in his 2004 summary of the byproduct theory, *Why Would Anyone Believe in God?* Religious agents are often supernatural, he wrote, "people with superpowers, statues that can answer requests or disembodied minds that can act on us and the world."

A second mental module that primes us for religion is causal reasoning. The human brain has evolved the capacity to impose a narrative, complete with chronology and cause-and-effect logic, on whatever it encounters, no matter how apparently random. "We automatically, and often unconsciously, look for an explanation of why things happen to us," Barrett wrote, "and 'stuff just happens' is no explanation. Gods, by virtue of their strange physical properties and their mysterious superpowers, make fine candidates for causes of many of these unusual events." The ancient Greeks believed thunder was the sound of Zeus's thunderbolt. Similarly, a contemporary woman whose cancer treatment works despite 10-to-1 odds might look for a story to explain her survival. It fits better with her causal-reasoning tool for her recovery to be a miracle, or a reward for prayer, than for it to be just a lucky roll of the dice.

A third cognitive trick is a kind of social intuition known as theory of mind. It's an odd phrase for something so automatic, since the word "theory" suggests formality and self-consciousness. Other terms have been used for the same concept, like intentional stance and social cognition. One good alternative is the term Atran uses: folkpsychology.

Folkpsychology, as Atran and his colleagues see it, is essential to getting along in the contemporary world, just as it has been since prehistoric times. It allows us to anticipate the actions of others and to lead others to believe what we want them to believe; it is at the heart of everything from marriage to office politics to poker. People without this trait, like those with severe autism, are impaired, unable to imagine themselves in other people's heads.

The process begins with **positing** the existence of minds, our own and others', that we cannot see or feel. This leaves us open, almost instinctively, to belief in the separation of the body (the visible) and the mind (the invisible). If you can posit minds in other people that you cannot verify empirically,

positing
assuming

suggests Paul Bloom, a psychologist and the author of *Descartes' Baby*, published in 2004, it is a short step to positing minds that do not have to be anchored to a body. And from there, he said, it is another short step to positing an immaterial soul and a transcendent God.

The traditional psychological view has been that until about age 4, children think that minds are permeable and that everyone knows whatever the child himself knows. To a young child, everyone is infallible. All other people, especially Mother and Father, are thought to have the same sort of insight as an all-knowing God.

But at a certain point in development, this changes. (Some new research suggests this might occur as early as 15 months.) The "false-belief test" is a classic experiment that highlights the boundary. Children watch a puppet show with a simple plot: John comes onstage holding a marble, puts it in Box A and walks off. Mary comes onstage, opens Box A, takes out the marble, puts it in Box B and walks off. John comes back onstage. The children are asked, Where will John look for the marble?

Very young children, or autistic children of any age, say John will look in Box B, since they know that's where the marble is. But older children give a more sophisticated answer. They know that John never saw Mary move the marble and that as far as he is concerned it is still where he put it, in Box A. Older children have developed a theory of mind; they understand that other people sometimes have false beliefs. Even though they know that the marble is in Box B, they respond that John will look for it in Box A.

The adaptive advantage of folkpsychology is obvious. According to Atran, our ancestors needed it to survive their harsh environment, since folkpsychology allowed them to "rapidly and economically" distinguish good guys from bad guys. But how did folkpsychology—an understanding of ordinary people's ordinary minds—allow for a belief in supernatural, **omniscient** minds? And if the byproduct theorists are right and these beliefs were of little use in finding food or leaving more offspring, why did they persist?

Atran ascribes the persistence to evolutionary misdirection, which, he says, happens all the time: "Evolution always produces something that works for what it works for, and then there's no control for however else it's used." On a sunny weekday morning, over breakfast at a French cafe on upper Broadway, he tried to think of an analogy and grinned when he came up with an old standby: women's breasts. Because they are associated with female hormones, he explained, full breasts indicate a woman is fertile, and the evolution of the male brain's preference for them was a clever mating strategy. But breasts are now used for purposes unrelated to reproduction, to sell anything from deodorant to beer. "A Martian anthropologist might look at

omniscient
all-knowing

this and say, 'Oh, yes, so these breasts must have somehow evolved to sell hygienic stuff or food to human beings,' " Atran said. But the Martian would, of course, be wrong. Equally wrong would be to make the same mistake about religion, thinking it must have evolved to make people behave a certain way or feel a certain allegiance.

That is what most fascinated Atran. "Why is God in there?" he wondered.

The idea of an infallible God is comfortable and familiar, something children readily accept. You can see this in the experiment Justin Barrett conducted recently—a version of the traditional false-belief test but with a religious twist. Barrett showed young children a box with a picture of crackers on the outside. What do you think is inside this box? he asked, and the children said, "Crackers." Next he opened it and showed them that the box was filled with rocks. Then he asked two follow-up questions: What would your mother say is inside this box? And what would God say?

As earlier theory-of-mind experiments already showed, 3- and 4-year-olds tended to think Mother was infallible, and since the children knew the right answer, they assumed she would know it, too. They usually responded that Mother would say the box contained rocks. But 5- and 6-year-olds had learned that Mother, like any other person, could hold a false belief in her mind, and they tended to respond that she would be fooled by the packaging and would say, "Crackers."

And what would God say? No matter what their age, the children, who were all Protestants, told Barrett that God would answer, "Rocks." This was true even for the older children, who, as Barrett understood it, had developed folkpsychology and had used it when predicting a wrong response for Mother. They had learned that, in certain situations, people could be fooled—but they had also learned that there is no fooling God.

The bottom line, according to byproduct theorists, is that children are born with a tendency to believe in omniscience, invisible minds, immaterial souls—and then they grow up in cultures that fill their minds, hard-wired for belief, with specifics. It is a little like language acquisition, Paul Bloom says, with the essential difference that language is a biological adaptation and religion, in his view, is not. We are born with an innate facility for language but the specific language we learn depends on the environment in which we are raised. In much the same way, he says, we are born with an innate tendency for belief, but the specifics of what we grow up believing—whether there is one God or many, whether the soul goes to heaven or occupies another animal after death—are culturally shaped.

Whatever the specifics, certain beliefs can be found in all religions. Those that prevail, according to the byproduct theorists, are those that fit most comfortably with our mental architecture. Psychologists have shown, for instance, that people attend to, and remember, things that are unfamiliar and strange, but not so strange as to be impossible to assimilate. Ideas about God or other supernatural agents tend to fit these criteria. They are what Pascal Boyer, an anthropologist and psychologist, called "minimally counterintuitive": weird enough to get your attention and lodge in your memory but not so weird that you reject them altogether. A tree that talks is minimally counterintuitive, and you might believe it as a supernatural agent. A tree that talks and flies and time-travels is maximally counterintuitive, and you are more likely to reject it.

Atran, along with Ara Norenzayan of the University of British Columbia, studied the idea of minimally counterintuitive agents earlier this decade. They presented college students with lists of fantastical creatures and asked them to choose the ones that seemed most "religious." The convincingly religious agents, the students said, were not the most outlandish—not the turtle that chatters and climbs or the squealing, flowering marble—but those that were just outlandish enough: giggling seaweed, a sobbing oak, a talking horse. Giggling seaweed meets the requirement of being minimally counterintuitive, Atran wrote. So does a God who has a human personality except that he knows everything or a God who has a mind but has no body.

It is not enough for an agent to be minimally counterintuitive for it to earn a spot in people's belief systems. An emotional component is often needed, too, if belief is to take hold. "If your emotions are involved, then that's the time when you're most likely to believe whatever the religion tells you to believe," Atran says. Religions stir up emotions through their rituals—swaying, singing, bowing in unison during group prayer, sometimes working people up to a state of physical arousal that can border on frenzy. And religions gain strength during the natural heightening of emotions that occurs in times of personal crisis, when the faithful often turn to shamans or priests. The most intense personal crisis, for which religion can offer powerfully comforting answers, is when someone comes face to face with mortality.

In John Updike's celebrated early short story "Pigeon Feathers," 14-year-old David spends a lot of time thinking about death. He suspects that adults are lying when they say his spirit will live on after he dies. He keeps catching them in inconsistencies when he asks where exactly his soul will spend eternity. "Don't you see," he cries to his mother, "if when we die there's nothing, all your sun and fields and what not are all, ah, horror? It's just an ocean of horror."

The story ends with David's tiny revelation and his boundless relief. The boy gets a gun for his 15th birthday, which he uses to shoot down some pigeons that have been nesting in his grandmother's barn. Before he buries them, he studies the dead birds' feathers. He is amazed by their swirls of color, "designs executed, it seemed, in a controlled rapture." And suddenly the fears that have plagued him are lifted, and with a "slipping sensation along his nerves that seemed to give the air hands, he was robed in this certainty: that the God who had lavished such craft upon these worthless birds would not destroy His whole Creation by refusing to let David live forever."

Fear of death is an undercurrent of belief. The spirits of dead ancestors, ghosts, immortal deities, heaven and hell, the everlasting soul: the notion of spiritual existence after death is at the heart of almost every religion. According to some adaptationists, this is part of religion's role, to help humans deal with the grim certainty of death. Believing in God and the afterlife, they say, is how we make sense of the brevity of our time on earth, how we give meaning to this brutish and short existence. Religion can offer solace to the bereaved and comfort to the frightened.

But the spandrelists counter that saying these beliefs are consolation does not mean they offered an adaptive advantage to our ancestors. "The human mind does not produce adequate comforting delusions against all situations of stress or fear," wrote Pascal Boyer, a leading byproduct theorist, in *Religion Explained*, which came out a year before Atran's book. "Indeed, any organism that was prone to such delusions would not survive long."

Whether or not it is adaptive, belief in the afterlife gains power in two ways: from the intensity with which people wish it to be true and from the confirmation it seems to get from the real world. This brings us back to folkpsychology. We try to make sense of other people partly by imagining what it is like to be them, an adaptive trait that allowed our ancestors to outwit potential enemies. But when we think about being dead, we run into a cognitive wall. How can we possibly think about not thinking? "Try to fill your consciousness with the representation of no-consciousness, and you will see the impossibility of it," the Spanish philosopher Miguel de Unamuno wrote in *Tragic Sense of Life*. "The effort to comprehend it causes the most tormenting dizziness. We cannot conceive of ourselves as not existing."

Much easier, then, to imagine that the thinking somehow continues. This is what young children seem to do, as a study at the Florida Atlantic University demonstrated a few years ago. Jesse Bering and David Bjorklund, the psychologists who conducted the study, used finger puppets to act out the story of a mouse, hungry and lost, who is spotted by an alligator. "Well, it looks like Brown Mouse got eaten by Mr. Alligator," the narrator says at the end. "Brown Mouse is not alive anymore."

Afterward, Bering and Bjorklund asked their subjects, ages 4 to 12, what it meant for Brown Mouse to be "not alive anymore." Is he still hungry? Is he still sleepy? Does he still want to go home? Most said the mouse no longer needed to eat or drink. But a large proportion, especially the younger ones, said that he still had thoughts, still loved his mother and still liked cheese. The children understood what it meant for the mouse's body to cease to function, but many believed that something about the mouse was still alive.

"Our psychological architecture makes us think in particular ways," says Bering, now at Queens University in Belfast, Northern Ireland. "In this study, it seems, the reason afterlife beliefs are so prevalent is that underlying them is our inability to simulate our nonexistence."

It might be just as impossible to simulate the nonexistence of loved ones. A large part of any relationship takes place in our minds, Bering said, so it's natural for it to continue much as before after the other person's death. It is easy to forget that your sister is dead when you reach for the phone to call her, since your relationship was based so much on memory and imagined conversations even when she was alive. In addition, our agent-detection device sometimes confirms the sensation that the dead are still with us. The wind brushes our cheek, a spectral shape somehow looks familiar and our agent detection goes into overdrive. Dreams, too, have a way of confirming belief in the afterlife, with dead relatives appearing in dreams as if from beyond the grave, seeming very much alive.

Belief is our fallback position, according to Bering; it is our reflexive style of thought. "We have a basic psychological capacity that allows anyone to reason about unexpected natural events, to see deeper meaning where there is none," he says. "It's natural; it's how our minds work."

Intriguing as the spandrel logic might be, there is another way to think about the evolution of religion: that religion evolved because it offered survival advantages to our distant ancestors. This is where the action is in the science of God debate, with a coterie of adaptationists arguing on behalf of the primary benefits, in terms of survival advantages, of religious belief.

The trick in thinking about adaptation is that even if a trait offers no survival advantage today, it might have had one long ago. This is how Darwinians explain how certain physical characteristics persist even if they do not currently seem adaptive—by asking whether they might have helped our distant ancestors form social groups, feed themselves, find suitable mates or keep from getting killed. A facility for storing calories as fat, for instance, which is a detriment in today's food-rich society, probably helped our ancestors survive cyclical famines.

So trying to explain the adaptiveness of religion means looking for how it might have helped early humans survive and reproduce. As some adaptationists see it, this could have worked on two levels, individual and group. Religion made people feel better, less tormented by thoughts about death, more focused on the future, more willing to take care of themselves. As William James put it, religion filled people with "a new zest which adds itself like a gift to life . . . an assurance of safety and a temper of peace and, in relation to others, a preponderance of loving affections."

Such sentiments, some adaptationists say, made the faithful better at finding and storing food, for instance, and helped them attract better mates because of their reputations for morality, obedience and sober living. The advantage might have worked at the group level too, with religious groups outlasting others because they were more cohesive, more likely to contain individuals willing to make sacrifices for the group and more adept at sharing resources and preparing for warfare.

One of the most vocal adaptationists is David Sloan Wilson, an occasional thorn in the side of both Scott Atran and Richard Dawkins. Wilson, an evolutionary biologist at the State University of New York at Binghamton, focuses much of his argument at the group level. "Organisms are a product of natural selection," he wrote in *Darwin's Cathedral: Evolution, Religion, and the Nature of Society*, which came out in 2002, the same year as Atran's book, and staked out the adaptationist view. "Through countless generations of variation and selection, [organisms] acquire properties that enable them to survive and reproduce in their environments. My purpose is to see if human groups in general, and religious groups in particular, qualify as organismic in this sense."

Wilson's father was Sloan Wilson, author of *The Man in the Gray Flannel Suit*, an emblem of mid-'50s suburban **anomie** that was turned into a film starring Gregory Peck. Sloan Wilson became a celebrity, with young women asking for his autograph, especially after his next novel, *A Summer Place*, became another blockbuster movie. The son grew up wanting to do something to make his famous father proud.

anomie
social alienation

"I knew I couldn't be a novelist," said Wilson, who crackled with intensity during a telephone interview, "so I chose something as far as possible from literature—I chose science." He is disarmingly honest about what motivated him: "I was very ambitious, and I wanted to make a mark." He chose to study human evolution, he said, in part because he had some of his father's literary leanings and the field required a novelist's attention to human motivations, struggles and alliances—as well as a novelist's flair for narrative.

Wilson eventually chose to study religion not because religion mattered to him personally—he was raised in a secular Protestant household and says he has long been an atheist—but because it was a lens through which to look at and **revivify** a branch of evolution that had fallen into disrepute. When Wilson was a graduate student at Michigan State University in the 1970s, Darwinians were critical of group selection, the idea that human groups can function as single organisms the way beehives or anthills do. So he decided to become the man who rescued this discredited idea. "I thought, Wow, defending group selection—now, that would be big," he recalled. It wasn't

revivify
revive

until the 1990s, he said, that he realized that "religion offered an opportunity to show that group selection was right after all."

Dawkins once called Wilson's defense of group selection "sheer, wanton, head-in-bag perversity." Atran, too, has been dismissive of this approach, calling it "mind blind" for essentially ignoring the role of the brain's mental machinery. The adaptationists "cannot in principle distinguish Marxism from monotheism, ideology from religious belief," Atran wrote. "They cannot explain why people can be more steadfast in their commitment to admittedly counterfactual and counterintuitive beliefs—that Mary is both a mother and a virgin, and God is sentient but bodiless—than to the most politically, economically or scientifically persuasive account of the way things are or should be."

Still, for all its controversial elements, the narrative Wilson devised about group selection and the evolution of religion is clear, perhaps a legacy of his novelist father. Begin, he says, with an imaginary flock of birds. Some birds serve as sentries, scanning the horizon for predators and calling out warnings. Having a sentry is good for the group but bad for the sentry, which is doubly harmed: by keeping watch, the sentry has less time to gather food, and by issuing a warning call, it is more likely to be spotted by the predator. So in the Darwinian struggle, the birds most likely to pass on their genes are the nonsentries. How, then, could the sentry gene survive for more than a generation or two?

To explain how a self-sacrificing gene can persist, Wilson looks to the level of the group. If there are 10 sentries in one group and none in the other, 3 or 4 of the sentries might be sacrificed. But the flock with sentries will probably outlast the flock that has no early-warning system, so the other 6 or 7 sentries will survive to pass on the genes. In other words, if the whole-group advantage outweighs the cost to any individual bird of being a sentry, then the sentry gene will prevail.

There are costs to any individual of being religious: the time and resources spent on rituals, the psychic energy devoted to following certain injunctions, the pain of some initiation rites. But in terms of intergroup struggle, according to Wilson, the costs can be outweighed by the benefits of being in a cohesive group that out-competes the others.

There is another element here too, unique to humans because it depends on language. A person's behavior is observed not only by those in his immediate surroundings but also by anyone who can hear about it. There might be clear costs to taking on a role analogous to the sentry bird—a person who stands up to authority, for instance, risks losing his job, going to jail or getting beaten by the police—but in humans, these local costs might be outweighed by long-distance benefits. If a particular selfless trait enhances a person's reputation, spread through the written and spoken word, it might give him an advantage in many of life's challenges, like finding a mate. One way that reputation is enhanced is by being ostentatiously religious.

"The study of evolution is largely the study of trade-offs," Wilson wrote in *Darwin's Cathedral*. It might seem disadvantageous, in terms of foraging for sustenance and safety, for someone to favour religious over rationalistic explanations that would point to where the food and danger are. But in some circumstances, he wrote, "a symbolic belief system that departs from factual reality fares better." For the individual, it might be more adaptive to have "highly sophisticated mental modules for acquiring factual knowledge and for building symbolic belief systems" than to have only one or the other, according to Wilson. For the group, it might be that a mixture of hardheaded realists and symbolically minded visionaries is most adaptive and that "what seems to be an adversarial relationship" between theists and atheists within a community is really a division of cognitive labor that "keeps social groups as a whole on an even keel."

Even if Wilson is right that religion enhances group fitness, the question remains: Where does God come in? Why is a religious group any different from groups for which a fitness argument is never even offered—a group of fraternity brothers, say, or Yankees fans?

Richard Sosis, an anthropologist with positions at the University of Connecticut and Hebrew University of Jerusalem, has suggested a partial answer. Like many adaptationists, Sosis focuses on the way religion might be adaptive at the individual level. But even adaptations that help an individual survive can sometimes play themselves out through the group. Consider religious rituals.

"Religious and secular rituals can both promote cooperation," Sosis wrote in *American Scientist* in 2004. But religious rituals "generate greater belief and commitment" because they depend on belief rather than on proof. The rituals are "beyond the possibility of examination," he wrote, and a commitment to them is therefore emotional rather than logical—a commitment that is, in Sosis's view, deeper and more long-lasting.

Rituals are a way of signaling a sincere commitment to the religion's core beliefs, thereby earning loyalty from others in the group. "By donning several layers of clothing and standing out in the midday sun," Sosis wrote, "ultraorthodox Jewish men are signalling to others: 'Hey! Look, I'm a *haredi*'—or extremely pious—'Jew. If you are also a member of this group, you can trust me because why else would I be dressed like this?' " These "signaling" rituals can grant the individual a sense of belonging and grant the group some freedom from constant and costly monitoring to ensure that their members are loyal and committed. The rituals are harsh enough to weed out the infidels, and both the group and the individual believers benefit.

kibbutzim
Israeli communes

humility
courtesy

canon
set of beliefs

supine
lying on one's back, face
upwards

In 2003, Sosis and Bradley Ruffle of Ben Gurion University in Israel sought an explanation for why Israel's religious communes did better on average than secular communes in the wake of the economic crash of most of the country's **kibbutzim**. They based their study on a standard economic game that measures cooperation. Individuals from religious communes played the game more cooperatively, while those from secular communes tended to be more selfish. It was the men who attended synagogue daily, not the religious women or the less observant men, who showed the biggest differences. To Sosis, this suggested that what mattered most was the frequent public display of devotion. These rituals, he wrote, led to greater cooperation in the religious communes, which helped them maintain their communal structure during economic hard times.

In 1997, Stephen Jay Gould wrote an essay in *Natural History* that called for a truce between religion and science. "The net of science covers the empirical universe," he wrote. "The net of religion extends over questions of moral meaning and value." Gould was emphatic about keeping the domains separate, urging "respectful discourse" and "mutual **humility**." He called the demarcation "nonoverlapping magisteria" from the Latin *magister*, meaning "**canon**."

Richard Dawkins had a history of spirited arguments with Gould, with whom he disagreed about almost everything related to the timing and focus of evolution. But he reserved some of his most venomous words for nonoverlapping magisteria. "Gould carried the art of bending over backward to positively **supine** lengths," he wrote in *The God Delusion*. "Why shouldn't we comment on God, as scientists? . . . A universe with a creative superintendent would be a very different kind of universe from one without. Why is that not a scientific matter?"

The separation, other critics said, left untapped the potential richness of letting one worldview inform the other. "Even if Gould was right that there were two domains, what religion does and what science does," says Daniel Dennett (who, despite his neo-atheist label, is not as bluntly antireligious as Dawkins and Harris are), "that doesn't mean science can't study what religion does. It just means science can't do what religion does."

The idea that religion can be studied as a natural phenomenon might seem to require an atheistic philosophy as a starting point. Not necessarily. Even some neo-atheists aren't entirely opposed to religion. Sam Harris practices Buddhist-inspired meditation. Daniel Dennett holds an annual Christmas sing-along, complete with hymns and carols that are not only harmonically lush but explicitly pious.

And one prominent member of the byproduct camp, Justin Barrett, is an observant Christian who believes in "an all-knowing, all-powerful, perfectly good God who brought the universe into being," as he wrote in an e-mail message. "I believe that the purpose for people is to love God and love each other."

At first blush, Barrett's faith might seem confusing. How does his view of God as a byproduct of our mental architecture coexist with his Christianity? Why doesn't the byproduct theory turn him into a skeptic?

"Christian theology teaches that people were crafted by God to be in a loving relationship with him and other people," Barrett wrote in his e-mail message. "Why wouldn't God, then, design us in such a way as to find belief in divinity quite natural?" Having a scientific explanation for mental phenomena does not mean we should stop believing in them, he wrote. "Suppose science produces a convincing account for why I think my wife loves me—should I then stop believing that she does?"

What can be made of atheists, then? If the evolutionary view of religion is true, they have to work hard at being atheists, to resist slipping into intrinsic habits of mind that make it easier to believe than not to believe. Atran says he faces an emotional and intellectual struggle to live without God in a nonatheist world, and he suspects that is where his little superstitions come from, his passing thought about crossing his fingers during turbulence or knocking on wood just in case. It is like an **atavistic** theism erupting when his guard is down. The comforts and consolations of belief are alluring even to him, he says, and probably will become more so as he gets closer to the end of his life. He fights it because he is a scientist and holds the values of rationalism higher than the values of spiritualism.

atavistic
evolutionary throwback

This internal push and pull between the spiritual and the rational reflects what used to be called the "God of the gaps" view of religion. The presumption was that as science was able to answer more questions about the natural world, God would be invoked to answer fewer, and religion would eventually recede. Research about the evolution of religion suggests otherwise. No matter how much science can explain, it seems, the real gap that God fills is an emptiness that our big-brained mental architecture interprets as a yearning for the supernatural. The drive to satisfy that yearning, according to both adaptationists and byproduct theorists, might be an inevitable and eternal part of what Atran calls the tragedy of human cognition.

The Skin We're In

Tim Adams

What does each of us think of when we think of our body? Do we see it as our friend or our enemy? The home of our pleasure or the source of our pain? Do we want to indulge and pamper it or starve and dominate it? What makes us desire to paint it and pierce it, abuse it and poison it? Are we imprisoned by it or liberated in it? And why is it that the more we think about it—its appetites and its urges, its faults and its perfections, all that stuff that goes on inside, all the time—the stranger it seems to us? One thing we do know for certain is that the body is the place where each of us lives, and the place where each of us will die: our body will always, in the end, betray us.

Another thing we know is that, given the choice, hardly any of us would select exactly the body that we inhabit. The desire to improve on our bodies, to mould and change them, seems to be coded somewhere deep within them.

Perhaps we are obsessed with the way our own bodies look and behave because we know how instinctively judgmental we are of the bodies we look at. One recent psychological survey proved that we make decisions about the attractiveness of people we meet in the space of 150 milliseconds, and that this instant perception of their beauty (or otherwise) hardly alters after longer examination.

This superficial appraisal has profound implications. In Dr. Nancy Etcoff's book *Survival of the Prettiest* she shows how this "lookism" shapes our world: those we consider most beautiful not only find sexual partners more readily but also get better jobs and more lenient treatment in court. We are, in the main, more willing to trust them, help them, lend money to them and love them.

You might say, therefore, in wanting to change our bodies, to improve on our birth-given beauty, we are simply exercising our human rights: indulging in a little redistribution of wealth from the imbalances of the genetic lottery.

Earlier this year I talked about some of this with James Watson, the man who, 50 years ago, first understood the structure of DNA. He foresaw a world where we could design our babies to look the way we wished we had looked. He was unashamedly excited about this possibility. "People say it would be terrible if we made all girls pretty," he suggested. "I say it would be great."

But would it really? In Margaret Atwood's novel *Oryx and Crake* the future is populated by genetically screened, physically perfected humans. And it feels like a nightmare (or at least like California). Our dreams of bodily perfection distance us further and further from the flesh we inhabit; and they undermine the notion, also ingrained, that it is our imperfections that make us fully human.

These fears are rooted in the complicated understanding of the relationship between our bodies and our essential selves. When we stop to think about it, which most of us do surprisingly rarely, it is impossible for us to define where our body ends and what we consider to be our self begins. We know our limbs, say, are part of us, but are they really us? Would most of us even recognize our elbows or our backs if we were asked to pick them out of a line-up?

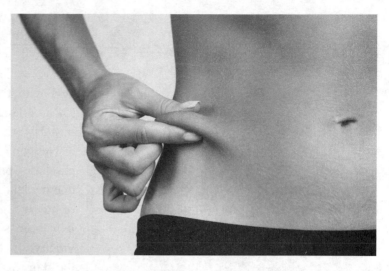

Our dreams of bodily perfection distance us further and further from the flesh we inhabit.

This kind of dislocation between our thinking and our bodily selves has many implications. As Roy Porter explains in his wonderful, posthumously published book *Flesh in the Age of Reason*, it was the legacy of Enlightenment philosophers that a fit and healthy body, and a clear and open face, were the visible expressions of human virtue.

This perception still runs very deep in our culture. It underpins the stubborn prejudice against the overweight and the ageing; and it challenges us to make our outward selves representative of the traits our culture aspires to: the qualities of youth and sexuality. Because of this, the overriding theme of our times, we might contend, is that of self-transformation.

If psychoanalysis has, for nearly a century, offered us the possibility of transforming our interior lives, so the habits of gyming and slimming, as well as the techniques of plastic surgery and the personal branding of body art, offer us the chance to remake our outward selves also. We might think of this process as a desire to make ourselves feel at home in our skin: to make our "envelope" reflect more fully the message we feel within.

At its extreme this involves altering what nature considers unalterable. Since a landmark case in 1999, transsexuals are now able to demand to have their sex change operations on the **National Health**. When Jan (formerly James) Morris wrote her book *Conundrum* in 1974 about the sex change operation she had undergone in Casablanca she spoke of how she saw it "not just as a sexual **enigma**, but as a quest for unity."

This alignment of outward appearance with inward perception takes on many forms and is subject to the whim of fashion and class. We have always

National Health
Britain's public health system

enigma
problem to be solved

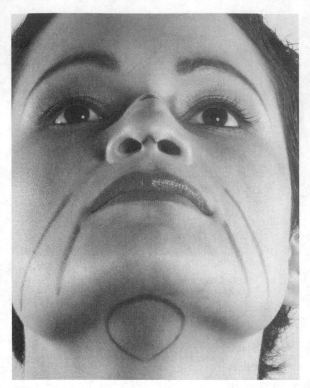

wanted our bodies to reflect our times. When, for example, cosmetic breast surgery first became a possibility in the early twentieth century, the women who could afford it used it almost exclusively for reduction, large breasts being associated with the lower classes. These days, middle-class girls (of a certain kind) are being given silicone as an eighteenth birthday present.

The body, in this sense, has become just another consumer purchase (plastic surgeons offer packages of treatment—buy one implant, as it were, and get one free). We can, in the spirit of our age, go shopping for bodily transformation. There have long been snake-oil salesmen willing to sell us wrinkle-free vitality: in the 1890s the injection of canine semen under the skin was seen as a way of enhancing the body's glow; now Botox offers hundreds of thousands of people smoothness in a lunch hour, and threatens to alter the way we smile forever.

Whereas once such vanity was piqued by street corner hucksters, now it is fuelled by global advertising campaigns and a magazine culture that reflects an increasingly narrow palette of beauty. Naomi Wolf argued a decade ago in *The Beauty Myth* that this conjunction of international capitalism and personal insecurity produces almost unbearable pressure on women in particular to conform to norms of appearance (and to feel further undermined when, inevitably, they fall short).

"As each woman responds to the pressure," Wolf predicted, "it will grow so intense that it will become obligatory, until no self-respecting woman will venture outdoors with a surgically unaltered face."

Ten years ago this seemed a little hysterical. Now it feels less unlikely. Some New York plastic surgeons are currently recommending an annual "MOT" for the skin, in which the advance of lines from the eyes is checked and sags from the neck tightened on a regular and preventive basis; they want you to visit your surgeon like you would visit your dentist. "The industry takes out ads," wrote Wolf, "and gets coverage; women get cut open."

This paranoia of self-actualisation (or this liberating perfectionism) is also migrating south. If we want our face to sell our sense of self, so, in our overtly sexualised culture, we may well want our genitals to say something important about us, too.

There is growing demand for operations which tighten the vagina in the hope of increasing sensation during intercourse; and no male inbox is complete without at least one offer to add "three inches to your length."

You might say such marketing was aimed at increasing the sum of human happiness and personal fulfillment, and what on earth could be wrong with that? Feminists increasingly make the argument that cosmetic surgery is a statement of empowerment, allowing women to stress the strength of their sexuality and enhance their idea of self.

There is a sense, too, however, even as you put in the time on the treadmill at the gym, watching the statements of impossible physical perfection on MTV and Sky Sports, that the project of eternal youth is doomed, and at least in part an expression of desperation. Our bodies have always been our biography, tracing the "thousand natural shocks that flesh is heir to." There is a wonderful short story by Raymond Carver concerning a couple selling a secondhand car with a doctored mileometer out of desperation to keep a roof over their heads. The story ends with the couple in bed, the woman asleep, and the man running his fingertips gently over the route map of stretch marks on her hips and thighs. He has one thought in his head, which is also the story's title: "Are these actual miles?"

However much we desire to wipe the slate clean, to give ourselves a new skin, to make ourselves "like a virgin" once again, our bodies will eventually tell us otherwise; we cannot be innocent twice. One result of this, you could argue, is that we increasingly desire to be out of our bodies and to find our innocence elsewhere. We fetishise the supremacy of our spirit over our flesh, even as we fail to enforce it. The extreme of this urge for prolonged or recaptured innocence is one manifestation of the epidemic of eating disorders. This newspaper recently reported on the scores of pro-anorexia websites available on the Internet in which young girls across the world share the secret strategies of their addiction. "Nothing tastes as good as thin feels," said one. "That which nourishes me destroys me," announced another.

Saturated with the messages of a culture that invites us to indulge our appetites, the anorexic seems to want above all to destroy the messages her senses are giving her. It is a supreme irony that the models of beauty in our consumer culture are paradigms of arrested development, triumphs of defeated hunger.

Nancy Etcoff reports a study in which the facial proportions of cover girls from *Vogue* and *Cosmopolitan* were fed into a computer and analysed; the computer programme "guestimated" them as children between six and seven years of age. In this sense, we increasingly seem to want to use our body as a strategy of denial, as a way of mastering some of the trauma our psychology presents us with. In Don DeLillo's twenty-first century fable *The Body Artist*, his heroine, to obliterate the grief of her husband's death, punishes her body with "prayerful spans of systematic breathing"; she contorts herself with yoga, and shaves and exfoliates with "clippers and creams that activated the verbs of abridgement and excision." She dreams of removing all evidence of herself from her body: "This was her work, to disappear from her former venues of aspect and bearing and to become a blankness, a body slate erased of every past resemblance." In the mirror, she has the desire to be someone "classically unseen, the person you are trained to look through, bled of familiar effect, a spook in the night static of every public toilet." Like the anorexic, she wants somehow to disappear.

Much as we may like to, however, the one thing we can never escape in life is our flesh. And increasingly we are coming to realise this flesh is also our fate. Coded within our genes (and uncoded in the Human Genome Project, the so-called Book of Life) is much of the information that will set the bounds of our life and predict our death, just as surely as a novelist dictates the lives of his characters. Undoubtedly, when it becomes properly understood, some of this information will also become our economic reality, too.

The use of genetic tests to assess risk for life premiums and critical illness insurance could, for example, become a reality within the next three years. The implications for those at genetic risk of contracting common illnesses such as breast cancer and Alzheimer's might be severe. There are even fears of a "genetic underclass" being created, people excluded from insurance and screened out of employment. (Britain has refused to join 31 other European countries, including France, Spain and Italy, who have signed the European convention on human rights and biomedicine, which prohibits genetic dis-crimination.)

James Watson, who led the mapping of the Genome Project, was spurred on in his quest by the fact that his own son was a victim of what he calls "genetic injustice" and born with a severe form of autism. What he knows for certain about the new genetic universe is that the decisions we will have to make for our bodies are only going to get more complicated, and that increas-ingly they will be taken by individuals rather than governments. "If the technology becomes available," he says, "who are we to tell a mother she should not want a child that is prone to hereditary disease?"

Watson is an atheist: "If scientists are not going to play God, who is?" He is, too, a supreme optimist about the possibilities of our bodies. "I am sure that the capacity to love is inscribed in our DNA," he suggested to me. "And if some day those particular genes, too, could be enhanced by our science, to defeat hatreds and violence, in what sense would our humanity be diminished?"

The implications of such a technology are already beginning to be felt. Our bodies have for nearly a century become something of a battleground in our quest for self-fulfilment and self-expression. But the choices we will have to make about them are about to multiply, and the battles are only just beginning.

Am I Free or Determined?

Melanie Chaparian

Each of the theories of self discussed earlier in this unit takes a stand on the philosophical debate between determinism and libertarianism. On one side of the debate, determinism is the position that all human actions are determined, or caused, by natural and/or environmental forces beyond human control. According to this theory, people do not have any free will. Behaviourism, as discussed in "From Biography to Biology: A Brief History of the Self," for example, views human beings as malleable creatures who can only behave in the ways that they have been conditioned by the rewards and punishments they encounter in their social and natural environments.

On the other side of the debate, libertarianism is the view that at least some human actions are free. Although many actions may be determined, there are some situations in which people can exercise their free will. Unlike computers, human beings seem to be capable of making real choices between alternative courses of action. Nietzsche's theory of the self, for example, takes the position that people have free will.

An Argument for Determinism

Determinism may be defended on the basis of the following rather simple argument: Every event in the world occurs because of cause and effect. Like every other event, human actions must be determined by cause and effect as well. If all of our actions are caused, we cannot possess free will because the same action cannot be both caused and free at the same time. Therefore, all human actions are determined, and no human actions are free.

Let's look at this argument in more detail. Few people today question the universality of cause and effect in the natural world. Traditional science teaches us that every natural phenomenon is the effect of a cause or set of causes. Indeed, most science assumes a deterministic model of the world. It is the very nature of science to look for the causes of the phenomena it studies. The nature of causality is such that there is an *inevitable* connection between a cause and its effect: if the cause occurs, the effect *must* also occur. For example, if heating water to a temperature of 100°C *determines* the water to turn into steam, then every time water is heated to that temperature it *must* turn into steam. Heating water to 100°C is the *cause* and the water turning into steam is the *effect*. We never entertain the possibility that boiling water, or any

This article was written for *The Human Project*. Used by permission.

other natural phenomenon, occurs because of pure chance. Scientists always try to discover the causes of the phenomena they study. Indeed, when they are unable to identify the cause of a particular phenomenon, such as the memory loss suffered by people affected by Alzheimer's disease, they do not conclude that no cause exists but rather that it simply has not *yet* been discovered.

But the deterministic view is not limited to the natural sciences such as physics, chemistry, biology and medicine. Determinism is also frequently assumed by the social sciences, such as psychology and sociology, which usually attempt to study and *discover the causes of human behaviour*. A determinist would agree that, although we may believe ourselves to be unique creatures, human beings are just as subject to the world of cause and effect as boiling water and Alzheimer's disease.

The determinist argues that our distinctive nature only means that the causes that determine our actions are more complex, and therefore harder to discover, than those that cause other events. The *kinds* of causes determining human behaviour depend on the determinist's particular view of human nature. Some point to *nature*, such as hereditary or instinctual forces, as the primary cause of a person's actions. Other determinists argue that a person's behaviour is fundamentally determined by *nurture*—that is, by environmental factors. Many, if not most, determinists, however, acknowledge that a *combination* of nature and nurture determines a person's actions. A Freudian psychologist, for example, believes that an individual's behaviour is caused by the way the *ego* moderates between drives of the *id*, which are determined by instinct or heredity, and the moral demands of the *superego*, which are determined by early childhood environment. Regardless of the kinds of causes they point to, all determinists agree that all human actions are determined or caused.

No matter how long and hard we may deliberate between different courses of action, the determinist argues, the "choice" we finally make has already been decided for us by hereditary and/or environmental causes over which we have no control. This applies to all of our actions, from the most trivial to the most significant.

According to the determinist, an analysis of the motivations of different people reveals the various causes that result in the difference in their behaviour. The determinist is quick to point out that you do not freely choose what interests you. Your interests are determined by your nature, your environment or, most likely, by a combination of both. For example, you probably wish to pursue academic success. Why is this important to you? Maybe you have been gifted with a naturally intellectual mind. This is not an attribute that you freely chose to acquire. Or perhaps your family has always encouraged good grades. Again, the determinist points out, you have no control over the values your family has conditioned into you. You may be aware that good grades are essential for the new graduate to secure a decent position in today's highly competitive job market. Once again, the determinist notes, you have no control over the increasingly high academic requirements demanded by employers. *Your* actual motivations for persevering through your homework probably include some of those discussed here as well as a number of others. But whatever they may be, the determinist argues, they reveal that you do not freely choose to study hard.

At this point, you may be convinced that *your* actions are caused by forces outside your control. But how does the determinist explain the actions of other students in your class who socialize at the expense of studying and consequently earn low marks? After all, most of them also come from families that stress academic success, and all of them want good jobs after they graduate. It *seems* that these negligent students are making a free, although foolish, choice.

Things are not always as they first appear. According to the determinist's theory, if your negligent classmates are subject to exactly the same causal forces that determine your behaviour, they would of necessity be studying as hard as you are. The very fact that they sacrifice study time to socialize indicates that their personal histories are very different from yours. Perhaps their families have not so much *encouraged* academic success as relentlessly *pressured* them to do well in school. If so, they may have been determined to rebel by going to all the college parties instead of studying. Just as you have no control over the encouragement you receive, the rebellious students have no control over the pressure they suffer. Other students who neglect their homework may simply not have the maturity required for self-discipline. Having fun may be as important to them, or even more so, as earning good marks or preparing for their future. If so, the determinist points out, a person cannot simply decide to become mature. This is a developmental process that is determined by an individual's nature and upbringing. There is a host of other causes that may determine some students to neglect their studies. Whatever these causes may be in any actual case, the determinist argues that negligent students do not freely choose to ignore their homework. Although they may feel guilty that they are not studying, they simply cannot choose to do so. Therefore, neither the diligent student nor the negligent student really makes a genuine choice between studying or not studying. The course of action each takes is determined by causes over which neither has any control.

Nor do we have the freedom to make genuine choices concerning even the most important aspects of our lives. Nature or nurture, or both, determine such things as which profession we pursue, who we fall in love with, and how many children we have. According to the theory of determinism, *all* human actions are the effect of causes over which we have no control; consequently, free will is merely an illusion.

Because we usually pride ourselves on our freedom, we may feel reluctant to accept the determinist's conclusion. But this in itself is not a good reason to reject determinism. It would be hard to deny that the deterministic model has helped to advance our knowledge of the natural world in general and the human world in particular. Discovering the cause of an event not only increases our understanding of that phenomenon but also allows us to *predict* and sometimes *control* its future occurrence. If, for example, we know that a virus causes an illness in the human body, we can predict that a person will become ill when infected by that virus, and, moreover, we can control that illness by finding ways to prevent the virus from infecting more people. Or, if we know that a moderate amount of parental pressure causes a student to succeed in school, we can predict that a student subjected to that amount of guidance will earn good grades, and we can control such successes by teaching parents how to provide the proper dose of encouragement. The deterministic model also helps us to make sense of our personal lives. We are often remarkably successful, for instance, in predicting the actions of our close relatives and friends. If such predictions are not merely lucky guesses, the determinist argues, they must be based on our relatively extensive knowledge of the hereditary and environmental causes that determine the behaviour of those relatives and friends. The fact that we may not *like* the theory of determinism does not negate the wealth of evidence for its accuracy.

James's Critique of Determinism

In his famous lecture entitled "The Dilemma of Determinism," William James, an American philosopher and psychologist who lived from 1842 to 1910, defends libertarianism, the theory that human beings have free will. Before he actually begins his argument for this theory, however, James shows that determinism—its appeal to science notwithstanding—cannot be scientifically demonstrated.

Science cannot really tell us, for example, if the negligent student's background is causing him to rebel. The fact that he does consistently neglect his assigned readings is not in itself conclusive proof that the student is determined to take this course of action. Moreover, *before the fact*—that is, before the student entered college—no one, not even the most learned determinist, could ascertain whether the student's background would lead him to socialize or to study. For instance, it would not have seemed inconceivable to suppose that excessive family pressure would prompt the student to study harder than any other student. Nor would it have been unreasonable to surmise that this

William James

pressure would compel him to overcome his immaturity and set his priorities in a more beneficial way. *Before the fact*, this series of events seems as likely to occur as the events that actually came to pass; thus, James argues, *after the fact*, there is no way to prove that the student was determined to neglect his studies. The same argument applies to all human actions. James therefore concludes that the determinist cannot prove that all actions are the inevitable effects of prior causes. While this in itself does *not* disprove determinism, it certainly dispels the myth that determinism has the weight of science on its side, and, furthermore, suggests that libertarianism should at least be reconsidered.

James's Argument for Free Will

Libertarians disagree among themselves about how far human freedom extends. On one extreme, existentialists such as Nietzsche claim that all human actions are potentially free. On the other extreme, some libertarians only argue that actions performed in the face of moral demands are free. In this discussion, we will focus on the views of William James, who defends a relatively moderate version of libertarianism. According to James, we are free whenever we have a genuine choice between at least two possible and desirable courses of action. This does not mean, of course, that we are free to perform any conceivable action whatsoever. Nor does this even mean that we are free to do anything we may desire, for the action that we find most tempting may not be included within the choice before us. All that is required to render an action free is the existence of one other alternative action that it is possible for us to perform.

Essential to James's definition of free will is the existence of *possible actions*: that is, actions that a person is not inevitably determined to do but may perform nonetheless. If an action is the result of free will, then it is, before the fact, merely one of two or more genuinely *possible* alternative actions that the person can *freely choose* to perform; and, after the fact, it is correct to say that the individual *could have acted otherwise* by choosing another alternative. For instance, the negligent student may have freely chosen to spend his time socializing instead of at the library; and even though he made this choice, he could have chosen to study instead. It is the idea of possible actions that puts James in stark opposition to determinism, which states that every action is the *inevitable* effect of a cause.

We have already discussed James's argument that determinism cannot be scientifically demonstrated. He does not attempt, however, to disprove this theory or to prove libertarianism true. This is because he believes determinism and libertarianism to be two alternative theories of reality, neither of which can be objectively proven true or false. Thus, he claims that the best we can do is to examine both theories to see which one offers us the most rational explanation of human behaviour. According to James, a "rational" theory should not only explain objective reality but must account for subjective human experience as well. James's defence of libertarianism consists in the argument that the free will position is more rational in this sense than determinism.

A significant fact of human life is the *feeling of freedom* that we often experience. James argues that any theory of human behaviour must adequately explain this feeling. Unlike determinism, libertarianism conforms to our ordinary experience: we often feel free to choose between alternative courses of action. Of course, the determinist argues that this feeling is merely an illusion because our course of action has already been decided for us by causes beyond our control. But the "illusion" persists in our inner, subjective experience nonetheless. For example, the good student probably feels that he or she could have chosen to go to more parties while the negligent student likely feels that he or she could have decided to study harder. In his or her practical affairs, even the staunchest determinist probably feels free to choose between alternative courses of action. No matter how solidly convinced we may be that determinism offers us a rational account of all natural phenomena and perhaps most human behaviour, we still find it difficult—if not impossible—to believe subjectively that we are never free. Thus, determinism requires us to reject as illusory a universal human experience. Libertarianism, on the other hand, acknowledges the feeling of freedom as a natural part of the experience of exerting our free will. According to James, this is a good reason to adopt the free will thesis. While he concedes that determinism is a rational theory of reality from an objective standpoint, James argues that libertarianism is an even more rational position because it can account for our inner, subjective experience of freedom.

Another important fact of human experience that James believes a rational theory must explain are *judgments of regret*. Our dissatisfaction with the world, especially with human behaviour, leads us to regret—that is, to "wish that something might be otherwise." After receiving a poor mark in the course, for instance, the negligent student may *regret* that he chose to spend all his time socializing. And because we regret the actions of others as well as our own, you may also *regret* that he had not studied. The most significant regrets concern the moral sphere. We do not accept as inevitable the senseless murders, rapes and cases of child abuse we read about in the newspaper; instead, we judge such acts to be bad or immoral to the highest degree and regret that they are part of our world.

TO STUDY OR TO PARTY?

Free Will Reconsidered

Suppose you have an examination tomorrow and a friend asks you to forgo studying and spend the evening at a party. Your friend does not urge or threaten or coerce you. You consider the alternatives, and after a moment's thought, decide to give up studying for the night and go to the party. We would ordinarily say that you are responsible for your decision. We think of such cases as actions in which you are free to decide one way or the other.

Contrast this to a situation in which a headache leads you to lie down and fall asleep on your bed instead of continuing to study. In this case it would not make sense to say that you are free to decide one way or the other about studying. The dispute between advocates of free will and advocates of determinism is basically a dispute whether incidents like the two so cited, which feel so different, are really radically and essentially different when viewed objectively.

Whereas the advocate of free will would perceive these two sorts of acts as essentially different, the determinist would not. The determinist might argue that although you may believe that your decision to stay home to study for the exam was an expression of free choice, nevertheless closer scrutiny would reveal that your behaviour was not really free after all. What you thought was a free choice was really a choice dictated by your desires, which in turn spring from your character, which in its turn is fashioned by the forces of heredity and environment, which are clearly beyond your control.

The central affirmation of determinism is that every event has a cause. By an analysis of the causes of any one of your actions, the determinist would cause your so-called freedom to vanish in a chain of causes that stretches back into the remote recesses of your heredity and environment. Nature and nurture, genes and society—those are the factors that made you what you are and cause you to act the way you do. The notion that you are free is really a misapprehension, an illusion.

Adapted from *An Introduction to Modern Philosophy* by Donald M. Borchert.

A regret implies that something is bad, and "calling a thing bad means that the thing ought not to be, that something else ought to be in its stead." When we label someone's action immoral, we imply that it should not have been done and that the person should have acted otherwise. For instance, when we proclaim that a murderer is guilty of the highest moral offence, we mean that he should not have committed homicide and should have instead treated his victim in a peaceful, humane manner. Regrets obviously assume the existence of free will. For this reason, James argues, libertarianism offers us a better explanation of our regrets than does determinism.

The source of our deepest regrets is the recognition that the world is fraught with immorality. According to determinism, even the most heinous crimes are as much the result of cause and effect as the routine activities we do every day. Knowing the causes of immoral actions does not eliminate our regret that they occur, but it does make our regret merely futile hope. Libertarianism, on the other hand, recognizes immoral actions as the result of free will and, as such, acknowledges that other actions could have been performed instead. Since this applies to future as well as past actions, there exists the possibility that the world—although certainly imperfect—may be made a better and more moral place through free human action. Thus, from the libertarian viewpoint, regrets may virtually be taken at face value—as expressions of our belief that immoral actions *can* be avoided and *should not* take place. This, according to James, renders libertarianism a more rational theory of human existence.

James admits from the outset that his defence consists of the argument that libertarianism is more rational than determinism because it offers a better account of our feelings of freedom and judgements of regret. This is not a claim that can be proven objectively but one that can be "verified" only by consulting our inner, subjective sense. Although James argues that determinism is also incapable of objective demonstration, he acknowledges that determinism appeals to a different kind of rationality, perhaps what we might call a scientific rationality. Even though James finds libertarianism to be more rational than determinism, it remains for each of us to study both theories to see which of the two *we* find to be the most rational.

"Am I Free or Determined?" was written for *The Human Project* by Melanie Chaparian, a professor at the Humber College Institute of Technology and Advanced Learning. Used by permission.

Change and the Social World

We make history ourselves, but, in the first place, under very definite antecedents and conditions. Among these the economic ones are ultimately decisive. But the political ones, etc., and indeed even the traditions which haunt human minds also play a part, although not the decisive one. . . .

Frederick Engels

Though women do not complain of the power of husbands, each complains of her own husband, or the husbands of her friends. It is the same in all other cases of servitude; at least in the commencement of the emancipatory movement. The serfs did not at first complain of the power of the lords, but only of their tyranny.

John Stuart Mill

It is understood that in a developed society *needs* are not only quantitative: the need for consumer goods; but also qualitative: the need for a free and many-sided development of human facilities, the need for information, for communication, the need to be free not only from exploitation but from oppression and alienation in work and leisure.

André Gorz

Introduction

The first unit of *The Human Project* focused on the struggle of individuals to know themselves, and, through this knowledge, to acquire the potential to live as free and as self-determined a life as possible. While this exploration acknowledged the significance of the social world (think of the nurture side of the nature versus nurture debate), the emphasis centred on the impact on the self. In the second unit, the focus shifts to the community of *selves*. We will still pay attention to how it feels for individuals to contend with the consequences of living in groups, but our shift in perspective now takes place in a much larger frame. For instance, many teachers complain that students today have difficulty completing their reading assignments. As pointed out by Nicholas Carr in "What the Internet Is Doing to Our Brains: Is Google Making Us Stupid?," this problem may have less to do with a lack of personal effort on the part of students and much more to do with a general societal reliance on the "intellectual technology" of the internet.

The great American sociologist C. Wright Mills (1916–1962) spoke of the importance of "sociological imagination"—that is, the ability to see the link between personal troubles and public issues. This sociological imagination allows for a better understanding of individual problems by placing them in their larger societal context. If, for example, a man goes to work one morning and is told that he "is no longer needed," he clearly faces a personal crisis. If he returns home to find a note from his wife saying that she has decided to leave him, he is having a disastrously bad day. On the personal level, his experience is crushing and tragic and we can all imagine how he must feel. Yet, if we were to re-examine his situation from the broader perspective of the larger society in which he works and lives, we would see that many people lost their jobs that day. This fact doesn't diminish the suffering experienced by the individual, but it does place it in a larger context in a potentially useful way. Indeed, his job loss may be the result of the "creative destruction" that—as explained by George Bragues in "The Economics of Social Change"—spurs economic development in a capitalist society but, in the process, also rewrites the rules for economic success. If we discover that the laid-off man has been working for one of the domestic automobile companies, for instance, we will see that major shifts have occurred throughout the entire industry: as stock markets have re-evaluated potential profitability, share prices have dropped, and, consequently, what may have been a thriving company yesterday is now reeling and struggling to survive. This knowledge is useful, if we can get it early enough, because it can help us to take action to soften the blow—sell our stock or, in the case of the man employed in the field, look for new work long before being "shown the door." If, alternatively, we find out that this individual has been working in a clothing factory instead of an automobile company, we may understand his job loss as a consequence of the global repositioning of manufacturing jobs to places where labour costs are lower. Once again, this need not be a surprise and the individuals in the field could make plans that anticipate the eventual closure of their workplace.

In a similar fashion, the marriage breakup, which occurs in almost 40 percent of all Canadian marriages, can be viewed as just another example of social upheaval. Once again, there is little consolation in this fact for the man whose wife has left him. Yet, there is a useful message for the rest of us, and, indeed, for people who have experienced divorce. Although the cause of a specific divorce might be identified as an extramarital affair, for example, there also exist larger forces that have the potential to undermine all marriages. As Stephanie Coontz explains in "Marriage: Then and Now," societal changes over the past 200 years have transformed marriage from a relatively stable, almost compulsory institution developed primarily for socioeconomic purposes to a relatively *un*stable, *non*-compulsory institution, albeit one devoted chiefly to love and companionship. As a result, Coontz argues, contemporary marriage can lead to greater happiness but also to greater despair. In the provocative piece, "Marriage Is Made in Hell," on the other hand, Laura Kipnis goes so far as to argue that truly happy marriages are very rare today and, therefore, the entire institution has become counter-productive to a genuinely fulfilling life. Determining the link between the crises in individual marriages and marriage in general can be tough; deciding what to do with that knowledge, moreover, can be even tougher. Neverthe-less, a deeper understanding of the institution can't help but be useful for individuals because, as much as it might be a pleasant fantasy, we know that we cannot build a fence around our private lives that will successfully exclude larger social pressures.

These social pressures can even intrude upon and manage our most personal feelings and emotions. As Madeleine Bunting explains in "Sweet Smiles, Hard Labour," employees, especially in the service sector, are hired to perform emotional labour that requires them to display feelings—empathy, warmth, confidence, patience, enthusiasm, happiness, friendliness, for example—as demanded by their employers and expected by their customers. This commercially inspired cheerfulness becomes a mask that employees must wear to work even at the cost of emotional authenticity. While this may not seem too high a price to pay for a job, it is important to recognize that the pressures emanating from the larger society may go so far as to undermine our self-esteem and, therefore, our personal autonomy.

The larger society is, nonetheless, the field upon which we try to execute strategies to maximize our happiness, but the size and quality of the field are constantly changing, as, too, are the social rules that help individuals navigate this field. To achieve our goals, we must acquire the power to manage at least some of the conditions on this field. Power doesn't necessarily imply power over others, but can simply mean power to influence the outcome of certain specific events: how to get things done at work, for example, or how to redecorate your home or how to spend the evening with friends. Yet power is also a complex business, as there are many competing voices arguing for their share. Those who at any particular moment have their hands on the reins are loath to give them up: it just feels so "right" to watch events unfold as they think they should. So those in power at this moment wish to project their power into the future and resist the transfer of power to others. Yet, despite this resistance, change happens all the time. How does this struggle between the new and the old, between continuity and change, happen?

Change is often due to the unforeseen consequences of our inventions. Take the birth control pill, for instance. It was intended to provide reliable control over reproduction, and, as a result, it was easy to predict that families would use this new technology to have fewer children. Soon after the pill was introduced in the early 1960s, however, it became apparent that women were also *delaying* having children in order to further their education. So, within a very short period of time, women were graduating with degrees and diplomas in record numbers and, of course, they wanted to put their new skills into practice in the workforce. But these highly educated women encountered very unequal treatment on the job. Even when they had the same qualifications and were doing the same jobs, for example, women were almost always paid less than men. This injustice, among others, spurred the political lobbying that gave rise to various pay equity bills.

Yet these ambitious women still planned to begin families. They merely wanted the opportunity to take a break from work to have children—without being forced to give up their hard-fought-for jobs. Paid maternity leave was the government's response. After returning to work once the period of leave was up, furthermore, women needed reliable people to take care of their children. This need spawned the creation of professional daycare facilities staffed by educators trained to look after young children. This example illustrates what the American writer Neil Postman (1931–2003) means by the "ecological" change that can be created by the introduction of new technology: from specific technology meant to control reproduction, we ended up with the unforeseen consequences of pay equity legislation, maternity leave and an entirely new profession, all of which have significantly transformed expectations of, and for, women and men today both at home and on the job.

Because the pill so effectively reduced family size in Canada and elsewhere in the West, moreover, it became imperative for governments to encourage immigration to increase the workforce and thereby maintain healthy economic growth. Immigration has long been recognized as a spur to social change, as the ideas and values of "new" cultures meet and sometimes clash with the host culture. Perhaps more than any other country, Canada has encouraged immigration, as reflected in the welcoming official policy of multiculturalism that seeks to reassure immigrants that they don't have to abandon the ideas and values of their home countries. Even so, as Allan Gregg notes in "Identity Crisis," many Canadians are wary of the country's increasing diversity and, moreover, are "self-segregating" into "ethnic enclaves." Nonetheless, Canada can in fact be distinguished by the intensely pluralistic nature of its society—at least in the metropolitan centres of Montreal, Toronto and Vancouver.

While immigration has proven to be a tremendous resource, then, it can also present difficult challenges as we try to accommodate many competing and fundamentally different world views. In "Can We All Just Get Along?" Greg Narbey turns to the political theorist John Rawls (1921–2002) for help in determining a fair process by which we can negotiate some of the conflicts that naturally arise in a pluralistic society. As Bhikhu Parekh notes in "Diversity versus Solidarity," moreover, such societies need a common sense of community in order to ease the process of accommodation. The bonds of the community may be elastic and evolving, but they need to be there in order to build a sense of confidence in the survivability and mutuality of the community. Otherwise, as Gregg observes, we run the risk of increasing alienation among second-generation minorities who feel they are trapped in the margins of society. If we allow this to occur, everyone will lose because, regardless of our differences, we all depend on a stable and secure society in our pursuit of the good life.

The Economics of Social Change

George Bragues

Think of all the products and technologies that have mushroomed in just the past 30 years: cell phones, personal computers, email, the internet, video games, compact disc players, camcorders, digital cameras, microwave ovens, test-tube babies, Prozac and Viagra. It would take a mountain of books—indeed, such a mountain already exists—to explain the dramatic changes these inventions have wrought in the way we work, study, eat, play, relax, date, reproduce and socialize.

Think, too, of how much our practices and norms have altered. Take the issues of sexuality, gender and family. Thirty years ago, despite the fact that homosexuality had recently been legalized, gays and lesbians were still widely scorned as deviants and sinners. Today, they have achieved national recognition of their right to marry. Women now work outside the home in far greater numbers and make up the majority of students in Canada's universities and colleges. Meanwhile, the nuclear family has gone from being the norm to just one of several legitimate options available to organize our households.

The pace of this change is all the more striking when we contrast it to how societies functioned in the past. In the 16th century, the average individual lived pretty much the same life as his or her counterpart in the 7th century. They both gained their livelihood from working the land using rudimentary implements and domesticated animals; they both lived in villages within extended families; and they both were subservient to a landowning elite class. A helpful way to gauge how rapid social change has become in modern times is to look at world population figures throughout history. Major shifts in population indicate that societies have somehow changed significantly in their capacity to sustain human life within the constraints posed by the natural environment.

As you can see from the graph on the next page, world population grew rather gradually from 400 BCE (the height of ancient Greek civilization) to 1750. Notice the dramatic increase in the numbers since then. In July 2008, the world's population was estimated to be 6.7 billion, which means that in the last 250 or so years, global population increased by a multiple of 10, whereas before that it took just over 2000 years to merely quadruple.

Why has social change accelerated? One cannot answer this question without first understanding how social change happens in the first place. To this end, we'll outline a model, with several illustrations, that explains social

This article was written for *The Human Project*. Used by permission.

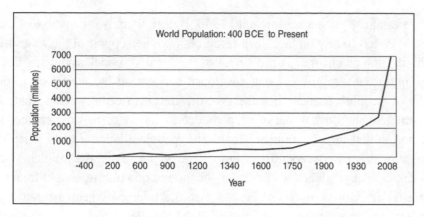

Sources: Adapted from U.S. Census Bureau (http://www.census.gov/ipc/www/ orldhis.html) and the United Nations Population Division (http://www.esa.un.org/unpp/). Both sites accessed September 1/2008.

change as a result of economic forces. Change has become so rapid, as it turns out, due to the inner workings of the capitalist system motoring the economies of the industrialized world.

A Materialist-Individualist Model of Social Change

Philosophers, poets and historians have long speculated on the nature of social change as far back as ancient Greece. In the 19th century, however, this enquiry gained a special prominence as philosophers came to believe that such matters as God, truth, morality, the soul and the good life could finally be resolved by deciphering the processes of social evolution. Out of this effort, two German thinkers emerged with the most compelling alternative accounts of social change, both of which continue to frame the debate to this day. Georg W. F. Hegel (1770–1831) argued that ideas—how people think about religion, art, nature, society and justice—bring about change. We can call this an *idealist model of social change*. Karl Marx (1818–1883), on the other hand, argued that economics—how people make a living, satisfy their natural requirements and pursue comfort and security—is the decisive factor. This is a *materialist model of social change*. Marx is often described as turning the ideas of Hegel upside down by insisting that the way people think is dictated by how they earn their bread, rather than the other way around.

To illustrate the difference between the two models, consider how they might explain unemployment insurance. Britain was the first nation to introduce a government-run scheme of unemployment insurance in 1911. Canada didn't establish such a scheme until 1940. Before then, people who lost their jobs were left to rely on their own resources and the support of their families. Why did things change? A proponent of the idealist model would say that a new philosophy of government, developed and spread by intellectuals, took hold of people's minds. In other words, the 19th-century view that the government should stay out of people's economic concerns was replaced by the notion that the government should give people a helping hand when the economy slumps. By contrast, a proponent of the materialist model would say that workers, adversely affected by economic downturns, sought financial security by influencing politicians to institute unemployment insurance. In other words, economic motives instigated the change.

It is true that social change is often preceded by a debate pitting those in favour of the change against those opposing it. Such a debate presumes that it very much matters which set of ideas ends up winning people's minds. Before women obtained the right to pursue a career, for example, the case had to be successfully made that they are not naturally destined to specialize in child rearing and household tasks, but that their capacities allow them to flourish in business, politics and the professions as well.

Still, the idea that women are equal to men was advanced over two millennia ago by Plato, the ancient Greek philosopher, in one of the most influential books of all time, *The Republic*. Yet ancient Greek women did not experience a feminist revolution. That even the most logical ideas don't automatically propel social change suggests that something else is necessary—perhaps that the economic circumstances must be right. Adopting the economic point of view, however, does not mean we have to entirely accept Marx's framework. Contemporary economics, arguably the most successful of the social sciences, rejects Marx's view of the economy as a class struggle between capitalists and workers. Economists today see events as being driven by the acts of individuals, not classes.

Here, then, is a *materialist-individualist model of social change*. To begin with, think of society as the product of individuals interacting with each other and making decisions in pursuit of their goals. Now divide society into three parts:

a) *The economic sphere*—This is where individuals deal with resource scarcity to produce and consume goods and services; if the resulting distribution of incomes is unequal, we get social classes—that is, a number of hierarchically arranged groupings within which individuals are readily able to identify with each other because of similar levels of wealth and prestige.

b) *The political sphere*—This is where individuals manage their communal affairs via government.

c) *The cultural sphere*—This is where individuals associate with each other in families, social classes, friendships, sexual relationships, leisure activities, schools and religious and ethnic communities; it also refers to the way individuals think—how their beliefs, values, preferences and norms are expressed in religion, art, music, literature, philosophy, science and the media.

The fundamental contention of the materialist-individualist model is that changes generated within the economic sphere carry over into the other two spheres, and, in the process, alter society as a whole.

To understand exactly how this takes place, we need to clarify what motivates individual decisions. Individuals make decisions with a view to securing *benefits*. These benefits include some personally unique weighting of security, wealth, comfort, status, companionship, sex, love, knowledge and meaning in one's life. But, of course, individuals aren't free to obtain benefits in any way they please. They are constrained by the amount of time and resources available to them, as well as the social institutions and norms that they're expected to follow. You may want to go away for two months every winter to party in Acapulco, for example, but you cannot go because you can't afford it. Or you may want to be a movie star, but first you have to go to hundreds of auditions before you may win even a minor role because our social institutions happen to put the decision of who is cast in films in the hands of a relatively small group of movie directors. Put another way, any benefit that an individual may seek involves some *cost*. This being the case, we arrive at this principle of human behaviour: *individuals strive to achieve benefits that they figure are worth the cost.*

Grasping this principle, which is central to contemporary economics, is the key to understanding how social change occurs. According to this principle, once people have decided on a certain course of action, they won't change it unless the costs and benefits they face in pursuing their goals change. From time to time, economic forces alter these costs and benefits in such a way that lots and lots of people start making different decisions in the political and cultural spheres of society: this is essentially what the materialist-individualist model of social change says.

To briefly illustrate, consider how we went from a society in which it was frowned upon for individuals to have sex before marriage to the present-day situation where it is generally considered acceptable. What happened? Our model would observe that economic forces produced more effective contraceptives. This lowered the "cost" of having sex, inasmuch as individuals didn't have to worry as much about an unwanted pregnancy. Since people view sex as a benefit, they naturally responded to this turn of events by having more sex, including before marriage. Community norms about premarital sex shifted accordingly and thus did society change.

The Economic Sphere: Capitalism, Social Class and Creative Destruction

Let's move now to a more detailed explanation of the materialist-individualist model. Since this model proposes that change originates from the economic sphere, let's start by explaining how that part of society operates. In the industrialized nations of North America and Western Europe, and in Australia and Japan, economic decisions about what, how, when and where to produce goods and services are made within a framework known as *capitalism*. Over the last two decades, particularly since the fall of communism, capitalist institutions have also been introduced in Eastern Europe, Latin America, India and China. Capitalist economies have the following features:

- *Private property*—Individuals, both by themselves and in cooperation with others in companies, possess the right to control the use of productive resources such as land, buildings, machinery and money in addition to their own labour.

- *Specialization of productive tasks*—Instead of satisfying their desires by producing the bulk of their supplies on their own, individuals focus their time and energy on producing a specific good or service. For example, some are accountants or teachers, others are janitors or salespersons, and so on.

- *Trade and exchange*—Since each person only produces a specific good or service, people engage in trade and exchange to satisfy the full range of their desires. Thus, most people sell their labour for wages and then take the money they earn to buy things like food, clothes, entertainment, etc. Others invest their capital in businesses of their own and try to make a profit by selling goods and services to consumers. People are continually buying and selling. This is why capitalism is often referred to as a market economy.

- *Competition*—Individuals and companies pursue their interests by competing against others to offer the best deal in the market. Hence, workers compete for jobs, landlords compete for renters, investors compete for business opportunities and companies compete for customers.

- *Limited government*—The government does not involve itself in every nook and cranny of the economy, but generally confines itself to enforcing property rights and contracts. It does, however, intervene in the economy to protect the public interest by, for example, regulating monopolies and dangerous products and actively trying to stabilize economic cycles by adjusting spending, taxes and interest rates. Government also provides a social safety net and uses the tax system to redistribute incomes from the rich to the poor. Some governments are more active in economic affairs than others, with Sweden and Norway being especially interventionist and the United States endorsing a freer market. Canada is somewhere in the middle.

Politicians and intellectuals often complain that capitalism generates greed, alienation, inequality, fabricated desires and environmental harm. Whatever the merits of these charges, one thing cannot be legitimately doubted: capitalism produces enormous wealth. The established capitalist nations are the richest in the world. Nations, such as India and China, which have recently adopted capitalist practices, have seen their economies grow dramatically. Numerous studies quantitatively demonstrate a strong relationship between free markets and growth.[1] Even the greatest enemy of capitalism, Karl Marx, was forced to acknowledge this point in noting how capitalism, "during its rule of scarce one hundred years, has created more massive and colossal productive forces than have all preceding generations together."[2]

The critics of capitalism are right in observing that the wealth that capitalism creates isn't distributed equally. Still, viewed from a larger historical perspective, prevailing levels of inequality aren't particularly glaring. Before capitalism emerged in the 17th and 18th centuries, when most of the world's population lived in agricultural societies, a tiny landowning elite controlled the bulk of social wealth and systematically exploited a large peasant underclass, who were viewed as subhuman. As capitalism evolved, a large middle class emerged, a class that now makes up anywhere from 40 to 70 percent of Canada's population.[3] Even today, the established capitalist societies of the world tend to have much smaller classes of poor people than do non-capitalist societies. None of this should blind us to the fact that a class structure definitely exists in capitalism and that those on the top do disproportionately well. In 2002, according to Statistics Canada, the top 20 percent of families earned $11.70 of market income for every $1 that the bottom 20 percent of families made.[4]

Unequally as the pie may be divided, the question nevertheless remains: how does capitalism create so much wealth and make the pie bigger?

Basically, it's because the competition for profit among individuals and companies motivates them to come up with ways to make goods more cheaply, improve product quality and satisfy new desires. More and better goods thus get produced for every hour people work and every dollar of capital invested in businesses. In other words, productivity rises. People become wealthier, in turn, because their work effort enables them to afford an ever greater menu of items. In 1780, for instance, it took 1800 hours of work a year for a household to feed itself; today, thanks to the rise in productivity, it takes just 260 hours, leaving a lot of money to buy other things.[5]

Capitalism's wealth-creating process isn't necessarily pretty. It's actually a merciless Darwinian process in which those not efficient or inventive enough to meet consumer demand get displaced by those ushering in superior modes of production and new products. Industries continually rise and fall. At one point or another in the past two centuries, the latest thing went from being railroads to autos, then to radio and subsequently to airplanes. Now, the most vibrant industries are those involving computers and biotechnology. But people do get hurt along the path of capitalist evolution, as one might expect, with the unlucky workers in fallen industries having to find jobs elsewhere, often by acquiring new skills. Sadly, a few, especially the older ones, can't make the adjustment. Nor is it just individuals who suffer; entire communities that are reliant on a dying industry can become depressed.

Joseph Schumpeter, one of the great 20th-century economists, famously referred to this two-sided aspect of capitalism as *creative destruction*: "creative" insofar as it enhances productivity and wealth for society as a whole and "destructive" insofar as long-standing institutions are eliminated and some people suffer. This is how Schumpeter put it:

> The fundamental impulse that sets and keeps the capitalist engine in motion comes from the new consumer goods, the new methods of production or transportation, the new markets, the new forms of industrial organization that capitalist enterprise creates . . . [there is a] process of industrial mutation—if I may use the biological term—that incessantly revolutionizes the economic structure *from within*, incessantly destroying the old one, incessantly creating a new one. This process of Creative Destruction is the essential fact about capitalism.[6]

In short, change is intrinsic to the nature of capitalism.

From Economics to Politics and Culture: Clarifying Some Questions

Combine this insight about the evolutionary character of capitalism with a model of social change that sees change flowing from the economy to the rest of society, and it becomes easier to understand why we live in ground-breaking times. Recall that our materialist-individualist model holds that an economic shift causes change elsewhere by altering the structure of costs and benefits that individuals face in their pursuit of happiness. Things that previously were unfeasible suddenly become practicable. When enough individuals vary their lives and beliefs, society becomes a different place. Let's illustrate this by clarifying five questions related to social change:

Why is the political system of our society democratic? This may seem a strange question to ask, because our government in Canada has been democratic for as long as anyone alive today remembers. But this question is still worth considering because the vast majority of societies throughout history (including our own in the past) have not been democratic. Also, the democratization of the political sphere is the foundation of subsequent, numerous changes in society. To make a very long story short, during the 19th and 20th centuries, democracies fully developed only after capitalist economies spread society's wealth more evenly, thereby fostering a large middle class. These individuals now had the resources to successfully fight for a system of popular voting more likely to promote their interests. Critical, too, was the increasing urbanization spawned by capitalism. As agriculture became more productive, fewer hands were required on farms. People increasingly moved to cities to work in factories. Living closer together, workers could more easily organize themselves and exercise influence in the political arena to protect themselves from the exploitive practices of their factory bosses. It's very important to note that the consolidation of democracy ended up instilling the idea that human beings are equal. That idea was a compelling force in the great social reform movements of the 20th century, including the civil rights, feminist and gay liberation movements. We'll see how the belief in equality helps explain several social changes discussed below.

Why are more and more people entering post-secondary studies? Fifty years ago, few people attended post-secondary institutions. The numbers have since grown sharply. Just in the last 20 years, the percentage of Canada's population that has attended college or university in some form went from 33 percent to about 50 percent.[7] Earlier, we observed that a society's wealth depends on its level of productivity. The same applies to individuals. An individual's productivity tends to rise with the level of his or her skills and knowledge, both of which are enhanced by more education. Hence, people are increasingly pursuing post-secondary education to improve their chance of earning a higher income. Making education an even better investment in the individual's future is that governments subsidize tuition fees—thanks to the pressure that parents and students are able to exert on democratically elected politicians, the calculation by policy-makers that a better-educated populace improves economic growth and the belief that a commitment to equality demands that everyone be given educational opportunities. An additional factor is the growing gap between the incomes of high-skilled and low-skilled workers. Part of the explanation for this is globalization, which mostly involves the spread of capitalist free trade between nations. Free trade puts the wages of low-skilled jobs under pressure because it allows for imports manufactured by low-paid workers in less developed countries. A low-skilled job that a high-school education would bring just doesn't look all that attractive any more.

Why is Canada multicultural? Except for members of the First Nations, everyone in Canada was either born, or has an ancestor who was born, in a foreign country. This is a country of immigrants. Up until quite recently, however, most of the population originated from Northern Europe, specifically Britain and France. In 1951, the descendants of these two nations represented 79 percent of Canada's inhabitants.[8] The Canadian government continued accepting immigrants in the post–World War II years, doing so principally on the economic calculation that each new person represented an additional source of productivity. Further pressure to increase immigration emerged in the mid-1980s as the birth rate fell well below levels reached during the post–World War II baby boom. But as Northern Europeans now had little economic reason to leave their homelands, immigrants started coming here from less prosperous regions of the world, such as Southern Europe, Asia, the Middle East, Latin America and Africa. In the past, immigrants were expected to assimilate into the dominant Anglo-Saxon culture. As the recently arrived ethnic groups had become so numerous, however, they were able to convince politicians to let them retain and nurture their traditional cultures. Helping this along was the notion that equality required that no culture be suppressed. The policy of multiculturalism, one of Canada's most endearing and unique features, was born.

What explains the advances made by women? Not so long ago, social institutions and norms mandated that women tend to the household and take care of children, rather than pursue careers outside the home. While the barriers to women's advancement in the workplace haven't been entirely eliminated, they have been lessened. A key factor behind this, assisted by increasing economic prosperity, was a dramatic fall in the infant mortality rate. When this rate was high, women had more children to raise the odds that some would survive. A lower rate meant they had to get pregnant less often to reach their target. This allowed women to delay marriage, attain post-secondary education in the meantime and then enter the work force. Once married with fewer children, women had more freedom to work outside the home to add to their household income, a prospect that their husbands could find agreeable. Indeed, in cases where women could contribute more than men to household income, stay-at-home dads appeared. The growth in physically light employment tasks provided an additional incentive for women to enter the work force. So did the development of appliances such as stoves, refrigerators, microwave ovens, dishwashers, washers and dryers, all of which served to reduce the time needed to stay at home to perform household tasks. Improvements in contraceptive technologies, especially the emergence of the birth control pill in the 1960s, also played a decisive role. Unwanted pregnancies apt to interrupt women's careers could now be better avoided. Legal access to abortion, won by an economically empowered feminist movement, ensured that unwanted pregnancies didn't have to result in children. In short, children made women dependent on men for support; once women could better control the incidence and number of children they bore, their freedom increased.[9]

Why are children treated more humanely? In the 19th century, child labour was prevalent in the most economically advanced countries of the time. The right of adults to strike children under their authority was once virtually unquestioned. Child labour has all but disappeared in the industrialized world, and many now challenge the legitimacy of corporal punishment of children. Indeed, Canada's Supreme Court recently prohibited the striking of children under the age of 2 and over 12.[10] Child sex abuse, once cloaked in silence, has become a matter of intense, vocal concern. Growing prosperity explains the end of child labour: parents could afford to forego the income their children might contribute to the household and, instead, invest in their children's future by putting them through school.[11] The decline in the birth rate, caused by women's greater opportunities in the workplace (as discussed above), moreover, means that families have gone from a "quantity" strategy in raising their children to a "quality" one.[12] More concern and resources are devoted to each child. Parents become far more sensitive to any abuse that they themselves, or others, might visit upon their children. Nor should we forget how the belief in equality has rendered people more sensitive to the plight of the vulnerable.

Looking Ahead?

Usually, those who advance a model of social change issue predictions. Marx, for example, forecast the overthrow of capitalism and the eventual installation of a communist utopia. More recently, Francis Fukuyama, adopting Hegel's idealist model of social change, declared the end of history.[13] By that, Fukuyama meant the victory of liberal democratic capitalism as the final form of government. But social and political predictions have a sorry track record. Capitalism has flourished despite Marx's prophecy. Fukuyama's take on Hegel has been cast into doubt by the September 11, 2001 terrorist attacks. The safer course is to predict nothing—except, that is, to say that society will continue to change at a dizzying rate, so long as capitalism remains in operation.

Notes

[1] These studies are reviewed by Niclas Berggren in "The Benefits of Economic Freedom: A Survey," *The Independent Review* (Fall 2003), 193–211.

[2] Karl Marx, "Manifesto of the Communist Party," *The Marx-Engels Reader*, 2nd ed., Robert Tucker ed. (New York: W.W. Norton, 1978), 477.

[3] The estimated range is so wide because it depends on how the income and occupational data are interpreted.

[4] *Statistics Canada*, "The Daily," May 20, 2004. Available at www.statcan.ca/Daily/English/040520/d040520b.html [Accessed May 25, 2004.] It should be noted, however, that the government's tax and spending policies significantly reduce this disparity. In 2002, after factoring in taxes and transfers, the top 20 percent of families ends up keeping $5.20 for every $1 received by the bottom 20 percent of families. This shows how government intervention in the economy redistributes income from the rich to the poor.

[5] Charles Wheelan, *Naked Economics* (New York: W.W. Norton, 2003), 206.

[6] Joseph Schumpeter, *Capitalism, Socialism, and Democracy* (New York: Harper Torchbooks, 1975), 83.

[7] Data for 1981 and 2001, respectively, obtained from Statistics Canada. Available at www.statcan.ca/english/Pgdb/educ45.htm [Accessed February 15, 2004.]

[8] "Ethnic Composition of Canada's Population." Available at www.cric.ca/en_html/opinion/opv2n23.html#facts

[9] This account is based on the economic theory of sex proposed by Richard Posner in *Sex and Reason* (Cambridge, Mass: Harvard University Press, 1992), especially 173–180.

[10] *Canadian Foundation for Children, Youth and the Law v. Canada* (Attorney General) [2004] SCC 4. Available at www.lexum.umontreal.ca/csc-scc/en/rec/html/2004scc004.wpd.html

[11] See Eric V. Edmonds, "Does Child Labour Decline with Improving Economic Status?" *National Bureau of Economic Research Working Paper No. 10134* (December 2003). Available at www.nber.org/papers/w10134. This paper is cited from "Sickness or Symptom?" in *The Economist*, February 7, 2004, 73.

[12] Wheelan, 111.

[13] Francis Fukuyama, *The End of History and the Last Man* (New York: Free Press, 1992).

"The Economics of Social Change" was written for *The Human Project* by George Bragues, a professor at the Humber College Institute of Technology and Advanced Learning and the University of Guelph-Humber. Used by permission.

What the Internet Is Doing to Our Brains: Is Google Making Us Stupid?

Nicholas Carr

"Dave, stop. Stop, will you? Stop, Dave. Will you stop, Dave?" So the supercomputer HAL pleads with the **implacable** astronaut Dave Bowman in a famous and weirdly poignant scene toward the end of Stanley Kubrick's *2001: A Space Odyssey*. Bowman, having nearly been sent to a deep-space death by the malfunctioning machine, is calmly, coldly disconnecting the memory circuits that control its artificial brain. "Dave, my mind is going," HAL says, forlornly. "I can feel it. I can feel it."

implacable
unyielding

I can feel it, too. Over the past few years I've had an uncomfortable sense that someone, or something, has been tinkering with my brain, remapping the neural circuitry, reprogramming the memory. My mind isn't going—so far as I can tell—but it's changing. I'm not thinking the way I used to think. I can feel it most strongly when I'm reading. Immersing myself in a book or a lengthy article used to be easy. My mind would get caught up in the narrative or the turns of the argument, and I'd spend hours strolling through long stretches of prose. That's rarely the case anymore. Now my concentration often starts to drift after two or three pages. I get fidgety, lose the thread, begin looking for something else to do. I feel as if I'm always dragging my wayward brain back to the text. The deep reading that used to come naturally has become a struggle.

I think I know what's going on. For more than a decade now, I've been spending a lot of time online, searching and surfing and sometimes adding to the great databases of the Internet. The Web has been a godsend to me as a writer. Research that once required days in the stacks or periodical rooms of libraries can now be done in minutes. A few Google searches, some quick clicks on hyperlinks, and I've got the telltale fact or pithy quote I was after. Even when I'm not working, I'm as likely as not to be foraging in the Web's info-thickets—reading and writing e-mails, scanning headlines and blog posts, watching videos and listening to podcasts, or just tripping from link to link to link. (Unlike footnotes, to which they're sometimes likened, hyperlinks don't merely point to related works; they propel you toward them.)

For me, as for others, the Net is becoming a universal medium, the **conduit** for most of the information that flows through my eyes and ears and into my mind. The advantages of having immediate access to such an incredibly rich store of information are many, and they've been widely

conduit
a means by which to transmit something

Wired
a magazine focusing on technology and its societal effects

boon
benefit

described and duly applauded. "The perfect recall of silicon memory," **Wired**'s Clive Thompson has written, "can be an enormous **boon** to thinking." But that boon comes at a price. As the media theorist Marshall McLuhan pointed out in the 1960s, media are not just passive channels of information. They supply the stuff of thought, but they also shape the process of thought. And what the Net seems to be doing is chipping away my capacity for concentration and contemplation. My mind now expects to take in information the way the Net distributes it: in a swiftly moving stream of particles. Once I was a scuba diver in the sea of words. Now I zip along the surface like a guy on a Jet Ski.

I'm not the only one. When I mention my troubles with reading to friends and acquaintances—literary types, most of them—many say they're having similar experiences. The more they use the Web, the more they have to fight to stay focused on long pieces of writing. Some of the bloggers I follow have also begun mentioning the phenomenon. Scott Karp, who writes a blog about online media, recently confessed that he has stopped reading books altogether. "I was a lit major in college, and used to be [a] voracious book reader," he wrote. "What happened?" He speculates on the answer: "What if I do all my reading on the web not so much because the way I read has changed, i.e. I'm just seeking convenience, but because the way I THINK has changed?"

Bruce Friedman, who blogs regularly about the use of computers in medicine, also has described how the Internet has altered his mental habits. "I now have almost totally lost the ability to read and absorb a longish article on the web or in print," he wrote earlier this year. A pathologist who has long been on the faculty of the University of Michigan Medical School, Friedman elaborated on his comment in a telephone conversation with me. His thinking, he said, has taken on a "**staccato**" quality, reflecting the way he quickly scans short passages of text from many sources online. "I can't read **War and Peace** anymore," he admitted. "I've lost the ability to do that. Even a blog post of more than three or four paragraphs is too much to absorb. I skim it."

staccato
disconnected, rambling

War and Peace
a very long epic novel by the Russian writer Leo Tolstoy (1828–1910)

cognition
the process of acquiring knowledge and using reason

Anecdotes alone don't prove much. And we still await the long-term neurological and psychological experiments that will provide a definitive picture of how Internet use affects **cognition**. But a recently published study of online research habits, conducted by scholars from University College London, suggests that we may well be in the midst of a sea change in the way we read and think. As part of the five-year research program, the scholars examined computer logs documenting the behavior of visitors to two popular research sites, one operated by the British Library and one by a U.K. educational consortium, that provide access to journal articles, e-books, and other sources of written information. They found that people using the sites exhibited "a form of skimming activity," hopping from one source to another and rarely returning to any source they'd already visited. They typically read no more than one or two pages of an article or book before they would "bounce" out to another site. Sometimes they'd save a long article, but there's no evidence that they ever went back and actually read it. The authors of the study report:

> It is clear that users are not reading online in the traditional sense; indeed there are signs that new forms of "reading" are emerging as users "power browse" horizontally through titles, contents pages and abstracts going for quick wins. It almost seems that they go online to avoid reading in the traditional sense.

Thanks to the **ubiquity** of text on the Internet, not to mention the popularity of text-messaging on cell phones, we may well be reading more today than we did in the 1970s or 1980s, when television was our medium of choice. But it's a different kind of reading, and behind it lies a different kind of thinking—perhaps even a new sense of the self. "We are not only what we read," says Maryanne Wolf, a developmental psychologist at Tufts University and the author of *Proust and the Squid: The Story and Science of the Reading Brain*. "We are how we read." Wolf worries that the style of reading promoted by the Net, a style that puts "efficiency" and "immediacy" above all else, may be weakening our capacity for the kind of deep reading that emerged when an earlier technology, the printing press, made long and complex works of prose commonplace. When we read online, she says, we tend to become "mere decoders of information." Our ability to interpret text, to make the rich mental connections that form when we read deeply and without distraction, remains largely disengaged.

ubiquity
widespread presence

Reading, explains Wolf, is not an instinctive skill for human beings. It's not etched into our genes the way speech is. We have to teach our minds how to translate the symbolic characters we see into the language we understand. And the media or other technologies we use in learning and practicing the craft of reading play an important part in shaping the neural circuits inside our brains. Experiments demonstrate that readers of ideograms, such as the Chinese, develop a mental circuitry for reading that is very different from the circuitry found in those of us whose written language employs an alphabet. The variations extend across many regions of the brain, including those that govern such essential cognitive functions as memory and the interpretation of visual and auditory stimuli. We can expect as well that the circuits woven by our use of the Net will be different from those woven by our reading of books and other printed works.

Friedrich Nietzsche
(1844-1900) a German
philosopher

Sometime in 1882, **Friedrich Nietzsche** bought a typewriter—a Malling-Hansen Writing Ball, to be precise. His vision was failing, and keeping his eyes focused on a page had become exhausting and painful, often bringing on crushing headaches. He had been forced to curtail his writing, and he feared that he would soon have to give it up. The typewriter rescued him, at least for a time. Once he had mastered touch-typing, he was able to write with his eyes closed, using only the tips of his fingers. Words could once again flow from his mind to the page.

telegraphic
brief

But the machine had a subtler effect on his work. One of Nietzsche's friends, a composer, noticed a change in the style of his writing. His already terse prose had become even tighter, more **telegraphic**. "Perhaps you will through this instrument even take to a new **idiom**," the friend wrote in a letter, noting that, in his own work, his "'thoughts' in music and language often depend on the quality of pen and paper."

idiom
unique style of expression

"You are right," Nietzsche replied, "our writing equipment takes part in the forming of our thoughts." Under the sway of the machine, writes the German media scholar Friedrich A. Kittler, Nietzsche's prose "changed from arguments to **aphorisms**, from thoughts to puns, from rhetoric to telegram style."

aphorisms
short phrases expressing ideas

The human brain is almost infinitely **malleable**. People used to think that our mental meshwork, the dense connections formed among the 100 billion or so neurons inside our skulls, was largely fixed by the time we reached adulthood. But brain researchers have discovered that that's not the case. James Olds, a professor of neuroscience who directs the Krasnow Institute for Advanced Study at George Mason University, says that even the adult mind "is very plastic." Nerve cells routinely break old connections and form new ones. "The brain," according to Olds, "has the ability to reprogram itself on the fly, altering the way it functions."

malleable
flexible, adaptable

As we use what the sociologist Daniel Bell has called our "intellectual technologies"—the tools that extend our mental rather than our physical capacities—we inevitably begin to take on the qualities of those technologies. The mechanical clock, which came into common use in the 14th century, provides a compelling example. In *Technics and Civilization*, the historian and cultural critic Lewis Mumford described how the clock "disassociated time from human events and helped create the belief in an independent world of mathematically measurable sequences." The "abstract framework of divided time" became "the point of reference for both action and thought."

The clock's methodical ticking helped bring into being the scientific mind and the scientific man. But it also took something away. As the late MIT computer scientist Joseph Weizenbaum observed in his 1976 book, *Computer Power and Human Reason: From Judgment to Calculation*, the conception of the world that emerged from the widespread use of timekeeping instruments "remains an impoverished version of the older one, for it rests on a rejection of those direct experiences that formed the basis for, and indeed constituted, the old reality." In deciding when to eat, to work, to sleep, to rise, we stopped listening to our senses and started obeying the clock.

The process of adapting to new intellectual technologies is reflected in the changing metaphors we use to explain ourselves to ourselves. When the mechanical clock arrived, people began thinking of their brains as operating "like clockwork." Today, in the age of software, we have come to think of them as operating "like computers." But the changes, neuroscience tells us, go much deeper than metaphor. Thanks to our brain's plasticity, the adaptation occurs also at a biological level.

The Internet promises to have particularly far-reaching effects on cognition. In a paper published in 1936, the British mathematician Alan Turing proved that a digital computer, which at the time existed only as a theoretical machine, could be programmed to perform the function of any other information-processing device. And that's what we're seeing today. The Internet, an immeasurably powerful computing system, is subsuming most of our other intellectual technologies. It's becoming our map and our clock, our printing press and our typewriter, our calculator and our telephone, and our radio and TV.

When the Net absorbs a medium, that medium is re-created in the Net's image. It injects the medium's content with hyperlinks, blinking ads, and other digital **gewgaws**, and it surrounds the content with the content of all the other media it has absorbed. A new e-mail message, for instance, may announce its arrival as we're glancing over the latest headlines at a newspaper's site. The result is to scatter our attention and diffuse our concentration.

gewgaws
ornaments

The Net's influence doesn't end at the edges of a computer screen, either. As people's minds become attuned to the crazy quilt of Internet media, traditional media have to adapt to the audience's new expectations. Television programs add text crawls and pop-up ads, and magazines and newspapers shorten their articles, introduce capsule summaries, and crowd their pages with easy-to-browse info-snippets. When, in March of this year, *The New York Times* decided to devote the second and third pages of every edition to article abstracts, its design director, Tom Bodkin, explained that the "shortcuts" would give harried readers a quick "taste" of the day's news, sparing them the "less efficient" method of actually turning the pages and reading the articles. Old media have little choice but to play by the new-media rules.

Never has a communications system played so many roles in our lives—or exerted such broad influence over our thoughts—as the Internet does today. Yet, for all that's been written about the Net, there's been little consideration

ethic
set of values or principles

automatons
robots

of how, exactly, it's reprogramming us. The Net's intellectual **ethic** remains obscure.

About the same time that Nietzsche started using his typewriter, an earnest young man named Frederick Winslow Taylor carried a stopwatch into the Midvale Steel plant in Philadelphia and began a historic series of experiments aimed at improving the efficiency of the plant's machinists. With the approval of Midvale's owners, he recruited a group of factory hands, set them to work on various metalworking machines, and recorded and timed their every movement as well as the operations of the machines. By breaking down every job into a sequence of small, discrete steps and then testing different ways of performing each one, Taylor created a set of precise instructions—an "algorithm," we might say today—for how each worker should work. Midvale's employees grumbled about the strict new regime, claiming that it turned them into little more than **automatons**, but the factory's productivity soared.

More than a hundred years after the invention of the steam engine, the Industrial Revolution had at last found its philosophy and its philosopher. Taylor's tight industrial choreography—his "system," as he liked to call it— was embraced by manufacturers throughout the country and, in time, around the world. Seeking maximum speed, maximum efficiency, and maximum output, factory owners used time-and-motion studies to organize their work and configure the jobs of their workers. The goal, as Taylor defined it in his celebrated 1911 treatise, *The Principles of Scientific Management*, was to identify and adopt, for every job, the "one best method" of work and thereby to effect "the gradual substitution of science for rule of thumb throughout the mechanic arts." Once his system was applied to all acts of manual labor, Taylor assured his followers, it would bring about a restructuring not only of industry but of society, creating a utopia of perfect efficiency. "In the past the man has been first," he declared; "in the future the system must be first."

Taylor's system is still very much with us; it remains the ethic of industrial manufacturing. And now, thanks to the growing power that computer engineers and software coders wield over our intellectual lives, Taylor's ethic is beginning to govern the realm of the mind as well. The Internet is a machine designed for the efficient and automated collection, transmission, and manipulation of information, and its legions of programmers are intent on finding the "one best method"—the perfect algorithm—to carry out every mental movement of what we've come to describe as "knowledge work."

Google's headquarters, in Mountain View, California—the Googleplex— is the Internet's high church, and the religion practiced inside its walls is Taylorism. Google, says its chief executive, Eric Schmidt, is "a company that's founded around the science of measurement," and it is striving to "systematize everything" it does. Drawing on the **terabytes** of behavioral data it collects through its search engine and other sites, it carries out thousands of experiments a day, according to the *Harvard Business Review*, and it uses the results to refine the algorithms that increasingly control how people find information and extract meaning from it. What Taylor did for the work of the hand, Google is doing for the work of the mind.

The company has declared that its mission is "to organize the world's information and make it universally accessible and useful." It seeks to develop "the perfect search engine," which it defines as something that "understands exactly what you mean and gives you back exactly what you want." In Google's view, information is a kind of **commodity**, a utilitarian resource that can be mined and processed with industrial efficiency. The more pieces of information we can "access" and the faster we can extract their gist, the more productive we become as thinkers.

Where does it end? Sergey Brin and Larry Page, the gifted young men who founded Google while pursuing doctoral degrees in computer science at Stanford, speak frequently of their desire to turn their search engine into an artificial intelligence, a HAL-like machine that might be connected directly to our brains. "The ultimate search engine is something as smart as people— or smarter," Page said in a speech a few years back. "For us, working on search is a way to work on artificial intelligence." In a 2004 interview with *Newsweek*, Brin said, "Certainly if you had all the world's information directly attached to your brain, or an artificial brain that was smarter than your brain, you'd be better off." Last year, Page told a convention of scientists that Google is "really trying to build artificial intelligence and to do it on a large scale."

Such an ambition is a natural one, even an admirable one, for a pair of math whizzes with vast quantities of cash at their disposal and a small army of computer scientists in their employ. A fundamentally scientific enterprise, Google is motivated by a desire to use technology, in Eric Schmidt's words, "to solve problems that have never been solved before," and artificial intelligence is the hardest problem out there. Why wouldn't Brin and Page want to be the ones to crack it?

Still, their easy assumption that we'd all "be better off" if our brains were supplemented, or even replaced, by an artificial intelligence is unsettling. It suggests a belief that intelligence is the output of a mechanical process, a series of discrete steps that can be isolated, measured, and optimized. In Google's world, the world we enter when we go online, there's little place for the fuzziness of contemplation. Ambiguity is not an opening for insight but a bug to be fixed. The human brain is just an outdated computer that needs a faster processor and a bigger hard drive.

terabytes
one trillion bytes

commodity
product to be bought and sold

proprietors
owners

Johann Gutenberg
(1400–1468) German printer
who invented movable type

sedition
rebellion against authority

debauchery
excessive indulgence in
sensual pleasures,
e.g. drinking and sex

prescient
prophetic

Luddites
people who oppose
technological change

The idea that our minds should operate as high-speed data-processing machines is not only built into the workings of the Internet, it is the network's reigning business model as well. The faster we surf across the Web—the more links we click and pages we view—the more opportunities Google and other companies gain to collect information about us and to feed us advertisements. Most of the **proprietors** of the commercial Internet have a financial stake in collecting the crumbs of data we leave behind as we flit from link to link—the more crumbs, the better. The last thing these companies want is to encourage leisurely reading or slow, concentrated thought. It's in their economic interest to drive us to distraction.

Maybe I'm just a worrywart. Just as there's a tendency to glorify technological progress, there's a countertendency to expect the worst of every new tool or machine. In Plato's *Phaedrus*, Socrates bemoaned the development of writing. He feared that, as people came to rely on the written word as a substitute for the knowledge they used to carry inside their heads, they would, in the words of one of the dialogue's characters, "cease to exercise their memory and become forgetful." And because they would be able to "receive a quantity of information without proper instruction," they would "be thought very knowledgeable when they are for the most part quite ignorant." They would be "filled with the conceit of wisdom instead of real wisdom." Socrates wasn't wrong—the new technology did often have the effects he feared—but he was shortsighted. He couldn't foresee the many ways that writing and reading would serve to spread information, spur fresh ideas, and expand human knowledge (if not wisdom).

The arrival of **Gutenberg's** printing press, in the 15th century, set off another round of teeth gnashing. The Italian humanist Hieronimo Squarciafico worried that the easy availability of books would lead to intellectual laziness, making men "less studious" and weakening their minds. Others argued that cheaply printed books and broadsheets would undermine religious authority, demean the work of scholars and scribes, and spread **sedition** and **debauchery**. As New York University professor Clay Shirky notes, "Most of the arguments made against the printing press were correct, even **prescient**." But, again, the doomsayers were unable to imagine the myriad blessings that the printed word would deliver.

So, yes, you should be skeptical of my skepticism. Perhaps those who dismiss critics of the Internet as **Luddites** or nostalgists will be proved correct, and from our hyperactive, data-stoked minds will spring a golden age of intellectual discovery and universal wisdom. Then again, the Net isn't the alphabet, and although it may replace the printing press, it produces something altogether different. The kind of deep reading that a sequence of printed pages promotes is valuable not just for the knowledge we acquire from the author's words but for the intellectual vibrations those words set off within our own minds. In the quiet spaces opened up by the sustained, undistracted reading of a book, or by any other act of contemplation, for that matter, we make our own associations, draw our own inferences and analogies, foster our own ideas. Deep reading, as Maryanne Wolf argues, is indistinguishable from deep thinking.

If we lose those quiet spaces, or fill them up with "content," we will sacrifice something important not only in our selves but in our culture. In a recent essay, the playwright Richard Foreman eloquently described what's at stake:

> I come from a tradition of Western culture, in which the ideal (my ideal) was the complex, dense and "cathedral-like" structure of the highly educated and articulate personality—a man or woman who carried inside themselves a personally constructed and unique version of the entire heritage of the West. [But now] I see within us all (myself included) the replacement of complex inner density with a new kind of self—evolving under the pressure of information overload and the technology of the "instantly available."

As we are drained of our "inner repertory of dense cultural inheritance," Foreman concluded, we risk turning into "'pancake people'—spread wide and thin as we connect with that vast network of information accessed by the mere touch of a button."

I'm haunted by that scene in *2001*. What makes it so poignant, and so weird, is the computer's emotional response to the disassembly of its mind: its despair as one circuit after another goes dark, its childlike pleading with the astronaut—"I can feel it. I can feel it. I'm afraid"—and its final reversion to what can only be called a state of innocence. HAL's outpouring of feeling contrasts with the emotionlessness that characterizes the human figures in the film, who go about their business with an almost robotic efficiency. Their thoughts and actions feel scripted, as if they're following the steps of an algorithm. In the world of *2001*, people have become so machinelike that the most human character turns out to be a machine. That's the essence of Kubrick's dark prophecy: as we come to rely on computers to mediate our understanding of the world, it is our own intelligence that flattens into artificial intelligence.

Sweet Smiles, Hard Labour

Madeleine Bunting

John Maynard Keynes
(1883–1946) British economist

Alvin Toffler
(b. 1928) American sociologist

Why haven't wealth and technological development brought us leisure? Why, instead, have they brought even harder work? From **John Maynard Keynes** to **Alvin Toffler,** thinkers predicted that the 21st century would be an Age of Leisure; in the 1970s increasing automation even led policymakers and politicians to worry how people would usefully fill their time. For some, this dawning era promised abundant opportunities for human beings to reach their full potential. We would finally be freed from long oppressive hours of toil. Marx's dream of society reaching a point where people could spend the morning thinking and the afternoon fishing would be within reach of us all.

It never happened. Quite the contrary: the historic decline in working hours has gone into reverse in the past two decades. Such are the demands of many jobs that leisure has been reduced to simply a time to recuperate before the gruelling demands of the next week's work. Ours has become a more work-centred society than ever; it demands more of us than ever, and it also purports to fulfil more of our needs than ever. The office is now where the heart is, not the home, as the complexities of the workplace demand an ever larger share of our emotional resources.

Two ways of measuring the demands of a job have defined industrial relations since the beginning of the Industrial Revolution—time and effort—but a third has emerged in the past few decades: emotional labour. It's not just your physical stamina and analytical capabilities that are required to do a good job, but your personality and emotional skills as well. From a customer services representative in a call centre to a teacher or manager, the emotional demands of the job have immeasurably increased.

empathy
ability to understand the feelings of others

The demand for emotional labour is driven firstly by the growth in the service economy. Companies are increasingly competing to provide a certain type of emotional experience along with their product, be it a mobile phone or an insurance policy. Where once muscle power was crucial to employment for millions of manual workers, its modern-day equivalent is emotional **empathy** and the ability to strike up a rapport with another human being quickly.

Another kind of emotional labour is increasingly in demand in response to the changing structure of organizations.

Clearly defined hierarchical bureaucracies have given way to much flatter, more fluid organizations. And as the lines of authority become less clear, much more falls to the individual employee to negotiate, influence and persuade. This is often called the "relationship economy," and what makes it particularly hard work is that it requires skills of empathy, intuition, persuasion, even manipulation, for which there is little preparation in an educational system focused on analytical skills.

The phrase "emotional labour" was first coined in 1983 by the American sociologist Arlie Russell Hochschild in her study of how flight attendants were trained to provide their customers with a particular emotional experience. The concept has spawned a large academic literature analyzing the emotional demands of the service economy on the workforce. **Call centres**, one of the fastest growing sources of employment in Britain, represent perhaps the most intensive form of emotional labour. Nearly half a million employees are handling around 125 million calls a month in centres that have clusters in areas of high unemployment such as around Glasgow, Tyneside, South Wales and South Yorkshire.

Projecting warmth on the telephone is a skill that Claire, in an **Orange** call centre in North Shields, Tyneside, has perfected. She is paid to talk—all day. My conversation with Claire is punctuated every few sentences by her incantation, "Hello, this is Claire, how may I help you?" She says it with the same tone of friendly helpfulness every time, only then to explain to the customer that the system is down and she can't do anything. Nothing rattles her, nothing alters her wording or the tone of her voice.

She works on the site of an old **colliery**. The land has been levelled apart from one hump in the distance which is the last **slagheap**, now grassed over. In the past it would have been men working here; now over half the workforce is women. Claire, who is in her early 20s, explains the key factor in her job: "You have to take control of the call. A lot of customers go mad if you don't know what you're doing, and the calls escalate [have to be referred to the supervisor], so you have to be confident all the time. Some customers can be very **patronizing**."

On Claire's computer screen, a series of little squares indicates calls waiting and tells her how long she has been on her current call. If a call has been difficult, there are only eight seconds in which to take a deep breath and compose her voice into the expected tone of friendliness. All the time she's managing her emotional demeanour, she's flicking through a wide range of information on the screen, which she uses to answer customer queries. The system is down for several hours that afternoon. What is striking is how on the one hand Claire is dealing with very rigid systems set down by company

call centre
a large office in which company representatives take phone calls (e.g., asking for product information, registering product complaints) and/or make phone calls (e.g., marketing products, collecting debts)

Orange
a European mobile communications company

colliery
coal mine

slagheap
pile of waste from coalmining

patronizing
snobbish

procedure and the vagaries of the computer system, while on the other she is expected to convey a sense of naturalness and her own personality.

John, another CSR (customer service representative), spends 17 minutes on one of his calls, advising a customer, with great patience and enthusiasm, which mobile phone to buy. Again and again the customer asks questions, and John seems to relish the opportunity to dig out the tiniest detail on the potential purchase. Without a pause, another customer comes through with a complicated inquiry, which John also goes out of his way to help answer, only to find that the line has gone dead after he puts her on hold. He calls her back in case she got cut off, but she doesn't answer her phone. He shrugs it off—he'd been trying to save her money.

Do the customers ever bother him, I ask. He smiles, then admits, "the customer wants the moon on a stick . . . they treat you like a work monkey." It's as if he's not supposed to say things like that, but having said it, it comes out with real passion. "Customers don't treat you like you're a human being. [But] if you see things from their point of view it's easier, and I'm better than I used to be. You need **resilience**, but I do get worked up. I do raise my voice."

resilience
the ability to quickly recover

What all call centres drill into their employees is to "speak as if you are smiling" and "as if you have been waiting for this particular call." This is a job where you're not allowed an off day—or even an off moment. The equation of providing empathy to another while denying it to oneself is complex.

Empathy has become big business, according to **consultancy** Harding & Yorke, which claims to be able to measure every aspect of the emotional interaction between customer and company. If a company wants its employees to sound warmer and more natural, it turns to the likes of Bob Hughes at Harding & Yorke. Delight your customers and they'll be back, is his watchword: empathy makes money. Defined by the *Oxford English Dictionary* as "the power of identifying oneself mentally with (and so fully comprehending) a person," empathy has become an important skill in the labour market. This intrigues social theorist **André Gorz**, who argues that while the assembly line represented "the total and entirely repressive domination of the worker's personality," what is now required is the "total mobilization of that personality."

consultancy
an agency that offers professional business advice

André Gorz
(1923–2007) French philosopher

At the Orange call centre in North Shields, the manager told me they never recruited someone for their technical skills. What they were looking for was a particular personality: cheerful, outgoing, flexible, good-natured, adaptable—because these were the characteristics they couldn't train. It is an approach shared by B & Q, the **DIY** retail chain, which uses an automated telephone personality test to recruit employees with the right kind of emotional characteristics; applicants have to press their telephone keypad to answer questions

DIY
do-it-yourself

such as, "I prefer to have my closest relationships outside work rather than with a colleague." In December 2002, B & Q's human resources director explained to the *Financial Times* that, "We wanted a psychological under-pinning to the entire culture—the same description of cultural fit across the entire population [of the company]—including management."

Identifying the right personalities has become a big industry, with a turnover of **£20m** a year; more than 70% of companies in the **FTSE 100** now use **psychometric testing**. In this labour market women and young people are favoured, while the shy, the reserved and those who find it hard to adapt to change are disadvantaged. Gorz argues: "What this represents is an end to the impersonal relationship in which the employee sold labour to the employer regardless of personality, a return to the pre-capitalist relations of personal submission as described by Marx." That submission does not depend on rules and coercion—you can't force someone to be "warm" and "natural." The required attributions derive from the worker's "entire ability to think and act." The conflicts over power and autonomy that characterize working lives no longer take place in the factory, call centre or office, but in the wider cultural life of the country, which pro-motes the required norms for the 21st-century workplace. For example, when a human resources director gives out instructions that staff are to "be them-selves" with customers, the staff's understanding of self and what is "natural" can be drawn from a disparate range of pop psychology, television, magazines and friends.

These required emotional characteristics are in continual conflict with the pressure to be efficient, a conflict that is symptomatic of many forms of service work with low profit margins. Empathy is not always efficient: the confused old lady who can't use her mobile might take up 20 minutes if a call handler is too empathetic. The old lady may even get canny and try to reach the same call handler every evening, in a bid to alleviate her loneliness—it happens—and just how empathetic should the response be? The empathetic employee is caught in a tension between the organization's drive to be efficient and competitive, and meeting the customer's desire for satisfaction.

Emotional labour may require **deference** on the part of the employee. The culture of the hotel industry, for instance, is about an illusion of old-fashioned servility and **ingratiating** hierarchy. The flipside of the catchphrase "the customer is always right" is the put-upon employee who is required not only to repress his or her own emotions (irritation, frustration), but also to accept responsibility, which results in the endless and meaningless

£20m
20 million British pounds, about 40 million Canadian dollars

FTSE 100
Financial Times Stock Exchange Index of the top 100 companies on the London Stock Exchange

psychometric testing
questionnaires and tests designed to measure person-ality and aptitude

deference
excessive respect

ingratiating
excessively seeking approval

egalitarian
equality-affirming

apologies of service culture. The **egalitarian** aspirations of Western democracies do not seep into the interface between employee and consumer in the service economy. The result is a mismatch between the values of the workplace and the values of consumer culture: in the former, employees are expected to repress their own emotional responses; in the latter, they are encouraged to give them full rein. Inevitably, the mismatch is most acute among the lowest paid: they are required to provide emotional experiences that they could never afford to receive themselves.

One study quoted the instructions given to clerical staff at Harvard University, who were advised to "Think of yourself as a trash can. Take everyone's little bits of anger all day, put it inside you, and at the end of the day, just pour it into the dumpster on your way out of the door." In Hochschild's seminal study, flight attendants were told to think of passengers as guests, children, or people who have just received traumatic news— similar analogies are used in training British call-centre staff. This kind of cognitive restructuring of employees' responses is required to pamper the customer's every whim. Such self-control can be very hard work, as management theorist Irena Grugulis points out: "Expressing warmth towards and establishing rapport with customers may provide a genuine source of pleasure for workers. Yet in practice, emotions are incorporated into organizations within strict limits. Emotion work does not necessarily legitimize the expression of human feelings in a way that supports the development of healthy individuals; instead it offers these feelings for sale."

There is a world of difference between the waitress who chooses to smile, quip with her customers and be good-natured, and the one whose behaviour has been minutely prescribed by a training manual. The former has some autonomy over her own feelings; the latter has been forced to open up more aspects of herself to **commodification.**

commodification
being turned into a product to be sold

Perhaps you're wondering what all the fuss is about. What does it matter if staff are instructed to smile—has being made to smile ever hurt anyone? This is a fascinating aspect of this form of hard work—how it is dismissed, belittled, or just happens without being remarked on.

Two reasons explain the uncritical acceptance of this kind of hard work. The first is that it is largely done by women: 54% of service-sector jobs in Britain are held by women, and 89% of the jobs held by women are in the service sector. Whatever is regarded as women's work has historically been underpaid and undervalued compared with men's work. Secondly, a historical legacy of rational **materialism** still values the solid, measurable and tangible over the immeasurable and intangible. There is still a cultural **stoicism** that belittles emotion: "Sticks and stones may break my bones, but words can never hurt me." But how can you think of yourself as a "trash can"

materialism
the view that values physical well-being and possessions above all else

stoicism
indifference to pleasure and pain

all day, and then go home with the satisfaction of having done a good job? How do you gain the sense of self-worth that properly comes with paid employment if you're being paid to be servile?

While we've learned that certain forms of labour are **inimical** to good health—coalmining often led to lung disease, for example—we have yet to begin to think that perhaps some forms of emotional labour fall into the same category. Many people compartmentalize human interactions, applying completely different etiquettes to each: they are generous and **solicitous** to friends, but switch to being rude to the customer service representative, demanding of the waitress, and ignoring the cleaner and dustbin men. "Blank them out" is the most common attitude extended towards those who serve. In some ways this is an even more cruel denial of a human being than a patronizing hierarchy in which at least "everyone had their place."

Increasingly, policymakers focus on "self-esteem" as a critical element in how to break the cycle of poverty and deprivation entrenched in some neighbourhoods. But, as has been noted, self-esteem cannot be redistributed in the way income can. It is not a personal achievement; it is the product of a set of social relations. The emotional labour of low-paid jobs in the service sector reinforces low self-esteem.

The contradictions of the growing emotional economy are increasingly an issue for the public sector. The welfare state has wrestled with different forms of emotional labour—in health, education and social services—for many decades, but now the demands are increasing. For example, teachers are having to cope with much higher levels of behavioural problems and children with special needs (between 1993 and 2003 their proportion nearly doubled, from 11.6% to 19.2% in primary schools, and from 9.6% to 16.5% in secondary). In higher education, lecturers can be allocated as little as five minutes to assess a student's work.

In other areas of the welfare state such as health, some of the historic methods to contain the intensity of emotional labour are now crumbling. Nowhere is emotional labour more demanding than in a hospital, where issues of life and death generate huge amounts of fear. Doctors developed a form of emotional detachment as part of the professionalization of their work in the 19th century and usually delegated the emotional labour to female nurses. Part of the **impetus** behind the highly bureaucratic procedures adopted in the mid-20th century was the desire to reduce anxiety levels. Isabel Menzies wrote a groundbreaking paper in 1959 analyzing how nurses' emotions were managed: for example, a single nurse would be allocated a particular task, such a taking temperatures or providing bedpans, for all the patients on a ward, thus reducing continuous one-on-one contact with the individual patients with whom close relationships might have developed.

inimical
detrimental

solicitous
considerate

impetus
motivation

These methods of emotional management are being dismantled in response to patient pressure for continuity of care. There is a growing insistence on the part of recipients of the service to be treated as individuals rather than "just a number." In an individualistic society, the consumer wants to be recognized, and for the service to be personalized. As a result there has been a shift in nursing practices, so that each nurse has a particular responsibility for a small number of patients and is expected to develop a relationship with them. The consultancy Harding & Yorke has even been called in to do training for the Royal College of Nursing, and has been commissioned to carry out an empathy audit for an **NHS** hospital prosthetics department.

NHS

National Health Service, Britain's public health care system

Mike Travis, a one-time docker in Liverpool, has been a paediatric nurse for 20 years, and he is in no doubt that the emotional demands of the work have increased. He cites two reasons: "We now have family-centred care, which actively encourages the workforce to become intimately involved in the child and the family. It's good for the quality of care, there's better continuity; but it can have very negative consequences for nurses because of a much greater degree of emotional involvement. The other reason is that when I first started training, the children weren't as sick. Now in oncology [treatment of cancer] and with the refinement of drug regimes, your contact is a lot longer."

Mike does a lot of work as a trade union rep in the north-west, and he's come to the conclusion that most nurses suffer at some point from "emotional burnout": "Everyone does. There've been times in my career when I've been exhausted by the work. You have to accept that if people say they've not been, they're denying it. It's very easy to lose the boundary between home and work—nurses have very high divorce rates." He summed up the conflict: "On the one hand, they [hospital management] encourage your relationship with families, while on the other they manage you in a very businesslike way. How do you balance these two things out? It's not unusual that an organization sends out very mixed messages—it's not clear itself—and the more distant the manager, the more difficult the conflict for the nurses."

Across the workforce, the traditional boundaries between people's personal and public lives are being eroded. Once they were carefully policed, and any crossover from office life to home was carefully managed—such as on the rare occasion when the boss might invite a favoured junior to bring his wife round for dinner, for example—while the reverse flow of home life into the office was discouraged. Now the workplace culture has been personalized; along with the often appreciated relaxation of reserve and formality comes a wealth of complex emotional relationships to negotiate.

This is the relationship economy. There is much less "command and control"-type management, and the successful manager has to build consensus, persuade and influence people. Where once supervisors sat down with a printout of statistics, now they ask how the employee is feeling. It's a different language, and it revolutionizes the relationships we have in the workplace. Employees can no longer rely on clearly defined hierarchies of responsibility in carrying out their work; the boss can no longer fall back on "positional authority"—"Do what I say, I'm the boss." Information is so dispersed and accessible that the boss often cannot even claim superior knowledge.

Mike Harris, of the Internet bank **Egg**, agrees that there is now a lot of hard emotional work to be done in organizations: "We ask employees to bring their humanness to work. Most people hang up their personalities at the door on the way to the office. [But] we want your humanness and with that comes your creativity, commitment and personality. We also get the emotion—the anger for example, and we've been prepared to put up with that. The only time we've got into trouble here is when we've forgotten the deal . . . when we've forgotten the emotions. There was an occasion when the car keys and the mobiles were taken off people [when they were **made redundant**] before they could even phone their wives. It was a new boss, and this incident reverberated around the whole organization like an atomic bomb. It took a long time to get over that. We forgot that the people we were making redundant were human beings. We should have gone out with them and had a party and handled things in a more humane way. This kind of humanness doesn't mean you can't take very hard rational decisions, but you must not ignore the human fallout."

The defining characteristic of the relationship economy is ambiguity, and that can require immense skill to navigate. The boss now has to combine a wide range of skills, from those of a diplomat to those of a friend—skills of persuasion, tact, diplomacy, leadership, even of being "likable" and, worst of all, funny: David Brent, the infamous boss in the television comedy series *The Office*, wanted above all to be seen as a "good laugh."

Once, the boss was tucked away in his own office, beyond a secretary, behind a closed door; now the walls of his or her office are of glass, or are nonexistent. One manager of a local authority housing department described how he sits in an open-plan office only a few metres from his team; after **dressing down** someone in an annual appraisal for poor performance, he then had to sit down near them and join in the banter about football; for neither party was there any spatial separation with which to negotiate the power relationship.

Of all the aspects of overwork, the emotional labour of the relationship economy is one of the more **intractable**. The demand for it will continue to expand, as will the stress it generates.

Egg
a UK-based, completely online bank

made redundant
laid off

dressing down
reprimanding

intractable
difficult to change

Marriage: Then and Now

Stephanie Coontz

For almost the entire past millennium, marriage was the central institution through which men's and women's interactions were channeled, both toward each other and within the community as a whole. Most societies used marriage to consolidate or transfer property, control social and sexual affiliations, construct political alliances, establish social-support networks, determine children's rights and obligations, redistribute resources to dependents, organize intergenerational relations, and govern the division of labor by gender.

Historical Functions of Marriage

conjugal
married

Because marriage served so many political, social, and economic functions, the individual needs and desires of the **conjugal** couple were a secondary consideration, and sometimes completely irrelevant, in most marital decisions. Government agencies, extended families, and established churches often fought over who had the ultimate control over contracting and enforcing marriage, but for centuries all agreed that marriage decisions were too important to be left in the hands of the couple alone.

In Europe during the first half of the previous millennium, marriage also served as a sorting institution for families and communities. In spite of (or perhaps because of) its vital functions, it was far from a universal state. Younger sons and daughters of the upper class, for example, were frequently denied the right to marry, so as to safeguard the inheritance of the oldest son or to protect the parents from crippling dowry payments. Poor people had more freedom to contract unions, but these unions were often not recognized by the authorities. When marriage was recognized, it was to serve the needs of the state or the couple's family. Unmarried people from the upper classes were supported and controlled by their families of origin; unmarried people of the lower classes often lived as dependents in the households of richer neighbors.

Beginning in the seventeenth century, marriage became much more widespread in Europe and America, to the point that the only option outside marriage, except for Catholic nuns or priests and the occasional rich widow, was to live at the farthest margins of society. In late eighteenth-century America, bachelorhood was considered the lowest form of manliness. By the mid-nineteenth century, a middle-class man had very little chance of securing

This article originally appeared in the Summer 2000 *National Forum: Phi Kappa Phi Journal.*

credit unless he was married. Women, for their part, could seldom earn enough on their own to forgo or leave marriage. The word "spinster," originally an honorable word derived from medieval women's dominance of textile production, had by the eighteenth century become an **epithet** so disgraceful that many women settled for almost any husband rather than accept the label.

Love and companionship . . . a legitimate goal of marriage?

Under these conditions, marriage was much more universal and stable than it is today. While the social support for lifelong marriage provided by church, state, and public opinion was helpful to many individual wives and husbands, we should not romanticize this marriage-based redistribution and caregiving system. Within many families of the eighteenth and nineteenth centuries, an often-humiliating subordination to the male head of household, sometimes enforced by violence, was the norm. Women and children usually had a lower standard of living than husbands and fathers, and until the early twentieth century, most children who worked turned the bulk of their wages over to their parents. Elders fared particularly poorly under the Euro-American marriage welfare system. Not until the advent of Social Security did elders cease to be the most impoverished and poorly housed segment of the population. But there were few other ways to organize and coordinate socioeconomic life, so most people made the best of marriage, or they suffered in comparative silence, which was broken only by bouts of violence and rates of spousal homicide much higher than today.

epithet
slur

Social Changes and Marriage

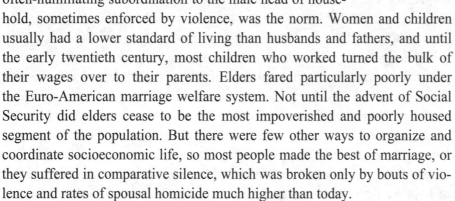

Over the course of the nineteenth century and the first half of the twentieth, other institutions began to take over some of the older functions of the family. The spread of banks, schools, foundations, hospitals, unemployment insurance, Social Security, and pension plans slowly but surely eroded many of the roles that marriage had traditionally played in organizing wealth transfers and social welfare measures. The **eclipse** of kinship as a major political and economic force lessened the incentive of parents to dictate their children's marriage choices, while the rise of new work opportunities freed many young men from parental controls.

eclipse
decline

Although considerations of status and practical necessity still compelled most people to marry, courtship and marriage increasingly became an individual decision made independently of family and community pressures. Love and companionship became not just the wistful hope of a husband or wife but the legitimate goal of marriage in the eyes of society. Many couples found new satisfactions and pleasures in both courtship and marriage itself, including new sexual compatibility.

By the early twentieth century, however, the emerging definition of marriage as the vehicle for achieving personal happiness had generated some unanticipated consequences. Great expectations, as historian Elaine Tyler May has pointed out, often led to great disappointments, and people were less likely to assume that such disappointments simply had to be endured. The divorce rate shot up in the 1920s and again in the 1940s. It dipped in the 1950s, but alongside the idealization of married life in that decade, the erosion of the economic necessity for marriage continued. The expansion of a consumer society created new temptations and opportunities for women to earn their own wages. More effective birth control created the possibility of a recreational sexuality separated from marriage. New household appliances and TV dinners made it possible for men to purchase meals and cleaning services that had required a forty-hour work week from wives in the early 1900s.

demographic
statistical account of a human population

The long-term erosion of the socioeconomic functions of marriage was obscured in the middle forty years of the twentieth century by certain **demographic** and cultural trends. From the 1920s to the 1960s, the age of marriage fell, while life spans lengthened. The result was that people spent a longer and longer portion of their lives within marriage. Advice books, popular magazines, and the new profession of marriage counselors urged couples to direct more energy into their domestic life, to work through conflicts, and to improve their sexual compatibility. As a result, marriage began to play a heightened role in people's emotional lives even as its social and economic functions continued to erode.

Changes in the Past Three Decades

During the past thirty years, however, the long-term trend making marriage less central to social and personal life reasserted itself. The ever-escalating ideal of intimate marriage deepened many relationships but also rendered an unsatisfying marriage less acceptable, lessening the stigma against divorce. Meanwhile, the spread of ever-more effective birth control and of a youth "singles culture" contributed to the steady proliferation of culturally acceptable alternatives to marriage, including nonmarital sexual activity and unwed parenthood. While divorce remained a painful experience that often left long-term scars, the cultural acceptability of alternatives to marriage can be seen in the fact that young people, often the sons and daughters of divorced parents, reported themselves happier at the end of the 1990s than they did in the 1970s, and the biggest increase in happiness came among unmarried young people.

Alternatives to marriage have continued to multiply at the turn of the millennium, not just for companionship and sexual relationships, but even as a vehicle for raising children. Since the 1970s, the rising age at first marriage, the growing proportion of divorced individuals in the population, and the increasing tendency not to remarry after divorce have created a situation where marriage no longer organizes most major life transitions. Whereas most young adults once stayed in their parents' home until marriage, sometimes first experiencing a form of communal living in college dorms or the military, they now typically live on their own for extended periods before marriage. At the other end of the life course, more older adults are living on their own after a marriage ends, whether by divorce or death.

And when a person does live with a sexual partner, it is often without benefit of a marriage license. Cohabitation rates have increased tenfold among heterosexual partners during the past twenty-five years, and cohabitating couples, whether heterosexual or gay or lesbian, are increasingly having children out of wedlock, as are many single women who live alone. Combined with new reproductive techniques such as sperm-donor and surrogate-motherhood arrangements, these trends have frayed the tight link that formerly existed between marriage and child-raising.

Is Marriage Becoming Extinct?

Does this mean, then, that marriage is on the verge of extinction? Certainly not. Most cohabitating couples eventually do get married, either to each other or to someone else, and part of the dramatic drop in marriage rates since 1960 is simply a result of the rising age of marriage. In 1960, the median age at first marriage for women was 20.4 years. By 1998, it was twenty-five. The fact that a smaller proportion of all women fifteen and over are married now than in the past does not necessarily mean that a smaller proportion of all women will eventually get married. Indeed, more and more women are marrying for the first time at age forty or older.

Furthermore, in some ways marriage has become more important and prevalent during the past century. The rise in life spans during the past fifty years means that despite the increase in divorce, more couples live to celebrate their fortieth wedding anniversary together than ever before in history. And new groups are now demanding access to marriage. The gay and lesbian movement, for example, whose predecessors in the 1920s and 1970s tended to reject marriage and its norms, has recently placed a major focus on winning legal recognition for same-sex unions and adoptions.

Marriage also continues to be important for people's life satisfaction. In a recent analysis of seventeen Western industrialized nations, married persons reported a significantly higher level of happiness than unmarried ones. And many studies demonstrate that a good marriage increases the financial and emotional resources available to children.

For these reasons, some individuals and organizations have argued that the multiplication of alternatives to marriage has been bad for children and for adults, and that we should devote more attention to "reinstitutionalizing" marriage, penalizing or at least reducing the attractiveness of alternative living arrangements. Unfortunately, most such proposals ignore the fact that the very sources of satisfaction and success in modern marriages stem from precisely the changes in gender roles and social norms that have made marriages more optional and more fragile. They also ignore the fact that bad marriages seem to be harder on individuals than in the past. While it is true, for example, that individuals in good marriages are happier than single individuals, individuals in bad marriages are much more distressed than single people, and the effects of a bad marriage seem to be particularly severe for women.

The Revival of Two-Breadwinner Families

At the heart of both the new risks and the new possibilities of modern marriage has been an unprecedented transformation in the division of labor, power, and autonomy between husband and wife. This transformation emerged out of a revival of shared breadwinning activities by men and women in the totally unprecedented context of shared domestic responsibilities and **egalitarian** values.

egalitarian
equality-affirming

I say revival of shared breadwinning because, in some ways, today's two-earner marriages represent a return to more traditional marital patterns, after a short historical interlude that many people mistakenly identify as traditional. Until the early nineteenth century, most husbands and wives worked together farming the land or operating small household businesses. But in the early 1800s, as large-scale production for the market replaced home-based production for local exchange, and as a wage-labor system supplanted widespread self-employment and farming, more and more work was conducted in centralized workplaces removed from the farm or home. A new division of labor then grew up within many families, especially in the Northern middle class. Men began to specialize in work outside the home, withdrawing from their traditional childraising responsibilities. Household work and childcare were delegated to wives, who gave up their traditional roles in production and barter. While Black women and newly arrived immigrant women continued to have high labor-force participation, wives in most other groups were increasingly likely to quit paid work out side the home after marriage.

This new division of work between husbands and wives came out of a temporary stage in the history of wage labor and industrialization. It corresponded to a transitional period when households could no longer get by primarily on things that they made, grew, or bartered but could not yet rely on purchased consumer goods for most of their domestic needs. For example, families no longer produced their own homespun cotton but ready-made clothing was not yet available at prices most families could afford, so women still had to sew most of their family's clothes. Many families still had to grow some of their food and most had to bake their own bread. Food preparation and laundering required hours of work each day. Water often had to be hauled and heated. Somebody had to go out to earn money to buy the things the family needed; somebody else had to stay home and turn the things that were bought into things the family could actually use. Given the pre-existing legal, political, and religious tradition of **patriarchal** dominance, husbands (and youth of both sexes) continued to work outside the home. Wives assumed exclusive responsibility for domestic matters that they had formerly shared with husbands or delegated to older children, servants, or apprentices.

patriarchal
male-centred

Many women supplemented their household labor with income-generating work that could be done at or around home—taking in boarders, doing extra sewing or laundering, keeping a few animals, or selling garden products. But this often arduous work was increasingly seen as secondary to wives' primary role of keeping house, raising the children, and getting dinner on the table. Wives came to be seen as homemakers and caretakers, men as breadwinners, and emotional expectations of marriage were organized around this split.

The temporary conditions that established this strict physical and psychological specialization of labor between husbands and wives began to be undermined in the early twentieth century. When child labor was abolished, more wives in working-class families had to take paid work to compensate for the lost wages of their children. During the 1920s, an expansion of office jobs in the new urban economy drew thousands more women into the work force. In the Great Depression of the 1930s and during World War II, married women in all but the wealthiest families of America were pulled into work for economic or political emergencies. Although they were often fired when pressures to re-employ men mounted, many women had developed a taste for work and the skills that they needed to reenter the labor force.

Ironically, wives began their most rapid return to the labor force during the 1950s, the height of the *Ozzie and Harriet* TV-family ideal. Mothers of young children still tended to withdraw from paid work until their children were well established in school. But the need of families for extra income and of businesses for female labor soon outstripped the supply of married women with no young children at home. After 1970, mothers of young children became the fastest-growing group of female workers. And by the 1990s, most working mothers were going back to work before their child's first birthday. Today, joint breadwinner marriages are the norm once more, even for couples with children.

Autonomy and Equality

What is unprecedented about today's co-provider marriages is the degree of autonomy women have achieved. In the male breadwinner model, wives were economically dependent on their husbands. In the earlier co-provider model, although women and men contributed equally to **subsistence**, wives could not translate their economic **parity** into personal or social equality. Law, religion, and politics enforced wives' subordination to husbands through everything from seating plans at church to domestic rituals at home. Husbands had the right to physically "**chastise**" their wives, and government could not interfere unless "permanent injury or excessive violence" was used. Women had few legal rights separate from their husbands or fathers, and not many could earn enough to even contemplate striking out on their own.

For these reasons, women's co-provider roles in earlier days did not increase wives' leverage in the household as they do today. Husbands had outside support for refusing to renegotiate the marriage relationship with an unhappy wife, and women had few possibilities for leaving a brutish husband. Today, however, the erosion of the economic and social centrality of marriage has undercut the props of male dominance within the family, and women have made unprecedented strides in translating their economic options into an expanded voice in decisions about the household division of labor.

While in most marriages women continue to do more housework and childcare than men, the gap has been halved since the 1960s, and cultural ideals have changed even more dramatically. A majority of men as well as women now tell pollsters that domestic chores should be shared equally between husband and wife. In January 2000, the Radcliffe Public Policy

subsistence
financial survival

parity
similarity

chastise
discipline

Center released a poll in which more than 70 percent of men in their twenties and thirties said that they would be willing to give up some of their pay in exchange for more time with their families.

These changing attitudes do not always translate easily into practice. Old habits and assumptions still make it hard for couples to establish a new division of labor. Conflict over housework remains a major source of marital tension. And when a couple has children, the tension can become even more acute. Couples who value fairness are more likely than couples with traditional values to react to the slow pace of change with disappointment and anger.

Here is the paradox that perplexes so many social commentators. The very values and options that have made marriage more fair have also made it more tense, and more easily dissolved. In consequence, some groups and individuals who wish to preserve the benefits of modern marriage find themselves advising people to abandon "unrealistic" expectations of equality and revive a modified male-breadwinner form of marriage. The **Promise Keepers**, for example, argue that ultimately, "a ship can only have one captain." Even more egalitarian-minded proponents of revitalizing the institution of marriage often argue that daily married life goes more smoothly when values stressing fairness and equity take a back seat to tolerance of older norms that make the wife primarily responsible for the home and the husband primarily responsible for income-earning.

Promise Keepers
US-based Christian men's group

But we cannot resolve the tensions of modern marriage by trying to cut and paste people's new values and opportunities to fit an older blueprint for marital stability. Most men want to be more active parents and helpful husbands than their own fathers were. And every year, fewer women report that they are willing to let men off the hook in resolving the stress of balancing work and home life.

The answer to the role strain and marital conflicts that occur in modern families is not to attempt to revitalize marital norms that arose in a totally different historical context. As therapist Betty Carter has commented, if any other institution in this country was failing half the people who entered it, we would demand that the institution change to fit people's new needs, not the other way around.

It is never easy to rework expectations and roles that have been handed down for generations. But many studies find that trying to sidestep such issues erodes the quality of marriage. Psychologists Philip and Carolyn Cowan have shown that a major reason for the decline in marital satisfaction after childbirth is that couples so often revert to a male-breadwinner/female-caretaker mode that both of them resent. The longer the divergence in behaviors and interests is allowed to go on, the more the tensions fester.

Indeed, researchers Esther Kluwer, Jose Heesink, and Evert Van De Vliert suggest that when it comes to the organization of housework and childcare, "it seems better to fight a constructive war than to nourish a destructive peace." Besides, it is hard to maintain an unbalanced peace when the disadvantaged party can walk away, a point supported by the fact that the majority of divorces are initiated by women.

Of course, new marital norms and values are not just a matter of individual effort and goodwill. They require adjustments in institutional support systems to make it easier for couples to balance work and family commitments. Employers must organize their work policies on the assumption that all their workers have caretaking responsibilities. Similarly, government should make sure that parental and other caretaking leaves are subsidized, and that afford-able high-quality childcare is available. School schedules must be adjusted to reflect the realities of urban life in the twenty-first century.

Such measures will make it more possible for modern marriages to succeed. But, paradoxically, they will also make it more possible for divorced individuals and unwed parents to pursue alternative forms of family life, thereby further deinstitutionalizing marriage. This is why such obvious and humane policy innovations have been opposed or ignored by so many conservative commentators and politicians, who have instead demanded that we focus our energy on reviving older cultural values about marriage.

It is time to admit that there is no way to reverse the past 200 years of social change. Whether we like it or not, marriage is no longer the only way through which people organize their sex lives, their care-giving obligations, their work roles, and their social networks. We cannot ignore the fact that the very changes which make marriage more satisfying and rewarding for many people make non-marriage a more viable and attractive alternative for others. The only way forward at this point in history is to find better ways to make both marriage and its alternatives work.

Marriage Is Made in Hell

Laura Kipnis

Marriage: The new blue-light case of the week. Everyone is terribly worried about its condition: can it be cured? Or has the time arrived for drastic measures—just putting it out of its misery? Euthanasia is a dirty word but, frankly, the prognosis is not so great for this particular patient: a stalwart social institution is now scabby and infirm, gasping for each tortured breath. Many who had once so optimistically pledged to uphold its vows are fleeing its purported satisfactions. In the US, a well-publicised 50 per cent failure rate hardly makes for optimism; in Britain, too, the Office for National Statistics reports that divorce has reached a record high at around 15 per cent. But this lower figure goes with a drop in the number of weddings—at their lowest level since the reign of Queen Victoria; this should mean fewer divorces, since not getting married in the first place seems the best way—these days—of avoiding this sorry (often expensive, usually ego-damaging) **denouement**.

denouement
ending

Certainly, there are happy marriages. No one disputes that and all those who are happily married can stop reading here. Additionally, there is always serial monogamy for those who can't face up to the bad news—yes, keep on trying until you get it right, because the problem couldn't be the institution itself or its impossible expectations. For these optimists, the problem is that they have somehow either failed to find the "right person," or have been remiss in some other respect. If only they'd put those socks in the laundry basket instead of leaving them on the floor, everything would have worked out. If only they'd cooked more (or less) often. If only they'd been more this, less that, it would have been fine.

And what of the growing segment of the population to whom the term "happily married" does not precisely apply, yet who nonetheless valiantly struggle to uphold the tenets of the marital enterprise, mostly because there seems to be no viable option? A 1999 Rutgers University study reported that a mere 38 per cent of Americans who are married describe themselves as actually happy in that state. This is rather shocking: so many pledging to live out their lives here on earth in varying degrees of discontent or emotional stagnation because that is what's expected from us, or "for the sake of the children," or because

Unhappily married majority?

wanting more than that makes you selfish and irresponsible. So goes the end-less moralizing and fingerpointing this subject tends to invite.

Let us contemplate the everyday living conditions of this rather large per-centage of the population, this self-reportedly unhappily married majority: all those households submersed in low-level misery and soul-deadening tedium, early graves in all respects but the most **forensic**. Regard those couples—we all know them, perhaps we are them—the bickering; the reek of unsatisfied desires and unmet needs; a populace downing anti-depressants, along with whatever other forms of creative self-medication are most easily at hand, from triple martinis to serial adultery.

Yes, we all know that domesticity has its advantages: companionship, shared housing costs, childrearing convenience, reassuring predictability, occasional sex, and many other benefits too varied to list. But there are numerous disadvantages as well—though it is considered unseemly to enumerate them—most of which are so structured into the expectations of contemporary coupledom that they have come to seem utterly natural and inevitable. But are they?

Consider, for instance, the endless regulations and **interdictions** that pro-vide the texture of domestic coupledom. Is there any area of married life that is not crisscrossed by rules and strictures about everything from how you load the dishwasher, to what you can say at dinner parties, to what you do on your day off, to how you drive—along with what you eat, drink, wear, make jokes about, spend your discretionary income on?

What is it about marriage that turns nice-enough people into petty dictators and household tyrants, for whom criticising another person's habits or foibles becomes a conversational staple, the default setting of domestic communica-tion? Or whose favourite marital recreational activity is mate behaviour modification? Anyone can play—and everyone does. What is it about modern coupledom that makes policing another person's behaviour a synonym for intimacy? (Or is it something about the conditions of modern life itself: is domesticity a venue for control because most of us have so little of it elsewhere?)

Then there's the fundamental premise of monogamous marriage: that mutual desire can and will last throughout a lifetime. And if it doesn't? Well apparently you're just supposed to give up on sex, since waning desire for your mate is never an adequate defence for "looking elsewhere." At the same time, let's not forget how many booming businesses and new technologies have arisen to prop up sagging marital desire. Consider all the investment opportunities afforded: Viagra, couples pornography, therapy. If upholding monogamy in the absence of desire weren't a social dictate, how many

forensic
technically legal

interdictions
prohibitions

enterprises would immediately fail? (Could dead marriages be good for the economy?)

And then there's the American mantra of the failing relationship: "Good marriages take work!" When exactly did the rhetoric of the factory become the default language of coupledom? Is there really anyone to whom this is an attractive proposition, who, after spending all day on the job, wants to come home and work some more? Here's an interesting question: what's the gain to a society in promoting more work to an overworked population as a supposed solution to the travails of marital discontent?

What if luring people into conditions of emotional stagnation and deadened desires were actually functional for society? Consider the norms of modern marriage: here is a social institution devoted to maximising submission and minimising freedom, habituating a populace to endless compliance with an infinite number of petty rules and interdictions, in exchange for love and companionship.

Perhaps a citizenry schooled in renouncing desire—and whatever quantities of imagination and independence it comes partnered with—would be, in many respects, socially advantageous. Note that the conditions of marital **stasis** are remarkably convergent with those of a **cowed** workforce and a docile electorate. And wouldn't the most elegant forms of social control be those that come packaged in the guise of individual needs and satisfactions, so wedded to the individual psyche that any contrary impulse registers as the anxiety of unlovability? Who needs a policeman on every corner when we're all so willing to police ourselves and those we love, and call it upholding our vows?

In this respect, perhaps rising divorce rates are not such bad news after all. The Office for National Statistics blames couples' high expectations for the upswing in divorce. But are high expectations really such a bad thing? What if we all worked less and expected more—not only from our marriages or in private life, but in all senses—from our jobs, our politicians, our governments? What if wanting happiness and satisfaction—and changing the things that needed changing to attain it—wasn't regarded as "selfish" or "unrealistic" (and do we expect so much from our mates these days because we get so little back everywhere else?). What if the real political questions were what should we be able to expect from society and its institutions? And, if other social contracts and vows beside marriage were also up for re-examination, what other **ossified** social institutions might be next on the hit list?

stasis
lifeless inactivity

cowed
frightened

ossified
outdated

Identity Crisis

Allan Gregg

acculturation

modification of one culture via contact with another culture

Soho

district in London, England, known for its fast nightlife

cabal

small group engaged in a secret plot

disenfranchisement

second-class status

Under the cover of normalcy, on July 7, 2005, the heart of London was bombed and dozens of people were killed by young Muslim men who had grown up in the same environment as their victims. The process of **acculturation**—at British schools and, one presumes, local pubs or **Soho** restaurants—had failed, and Britons were left wondering how a cluster of radicals dedicated to terrorism and to distant ideologies could spring from the nation they all share.

In another sign that all is not well in the world's diverse cities, four months later the outskirts of Paris went mad. On the night of October 27, French police chased a group of teenagers who had ventured out of their mostly Arab and African neighbourhood into the leafy suburb of Livry-Gargan. The pursuit turned deadly when three of the youths hid in a power-generation facility and two of them were electrocuted. Within four hours of this tragic accident, the streets of Clichy-sous-Bois (and adjacent communities) erupted in violence. In scenes reminiscent of Detroit and Los Angeles during the 1960s race riots, over 9,000 cars and 200 buildings were torched. France has been on edge ever since. An orchestrated attack by a terrorist **cabal** had besieged London, but in France something equally ominous had occurred: entire neighbourhoods of poor and alienated immigrants had protested their sense of isolation and **disenfranchisement** in a binge of wanton destruction.

Six weeks after the French riots, halfway around the world, roughly 5,000 white Australians took to the beaches of Cronulla, a suburb of Sydney, to attack people of Middle Eastern origin. Organized through text messaging and the Internet, this was a planned assault by aggrieved whites demanding, essentially, a return to Australia's whites-only immigration policy. The country had abandoned this openly exclusionary approach to immigration in 1973 and today Australia, along with Canada, has the most aggressive per capita immigration targets in the world. Prior to . . . [that] November's outbreak of sectarian violence, Australia also had a growing international reputation for peaceful integration. The thugs who descended on Cronulla, obviously, did not endorse this national self-image.

Canada has long considered itself immune to violence rooted in ethnic divisions. By enshrining multiculturalism in our Charter of Rights and Freedoms and by promoting policies of inclusion, the argument goes, our country has created a peaceable kingdom and a model for how to manage diversity. Will Kymlicka, a Queen's University professor of philosophy and one of Canada's foremost authorities on multiculturalism, states that while the "actual practices of accommodation in Canada are not unique, Canada is unusual in the extent to which it has built these practices into its symbols and narratives of nationhood."

Before the 2006 election campaign got under way in earnest, Joe Volpe, Canada's minister of Citizenship and Immigration, sang the praises of Canadian multiculturalism, established an immigration target of 1 percent of the total population (a level equal to Australia's and triple that of the United States), and announced a goal of attracting 340,000 immigrants per year by 2010.

With an aging workforce, declining birth rates, and concerns about retirement pensions, one might expect generalized support for increased immigration. But research conducted in 2005 by my polling and market-research firm, the Strategic Counsel, suggests that Canadians are far from **sanguine** about the country's increasing diversity. Fewer than half of those surveyed believe that Canada is currently accepting "the right amount" of immigrants, and among the remainder the overwhelming view is that we are accepting "too many" rather than "too few." Forty percent also express the view that immigrants from some countries "make a bigger and better contribution to Canada than others." The breakdown is disturbing: almost 80 percent claim that European immigrants make a positive contribution, the number falling to 59 percent for Asians, 45 percent for East Indians, and plummeting to 33 percent for those from the Caribbean.

sanguine
optimistic

In his landmark investigation, *Multiculturalism: The Politics of Recognition*, philosopher Charles Taylor points out that equal treatment often requires treating people in a "difference-blind fashion"—that is, "the other" must be respected in his or her historical and cultural fullness. But, when asked what the focus of multicultural policy should be, 69 percent of Canadians say immigrants should "integrate and become part of the Canadian culture," rather than "maintain their [own] identity." To some extent, it seems that Canadians, like their brethren in Europe, Australia, and elsewhere, have had their fill of multiculturalism and hyphenated citizenship.

While visitors often marvel at the multicultural mix evident on our city streets, there is growing evidence that Canada's fabled mosaic is fracturing and that ethnic groups are self-segregating. In 1981, Statistics Canada identified six "ethnic enclaves" across the country, i.e., communities in which more than 30 percent of the local population consisted of a single visible minority group. According to a recent StatsCan report, titled "Visible minority neighbourhoods in Toronto, Montréal, and Vancouver," that number had exploded to 254 ethnic enclaves by 2001. Not all of these communities are poor—for example, Richmond, British Columbia, and Markham, Ontario, whose Asian populations top 50 percent, are middle to upper-middle class—but an alarming number of them consist of people whose incomes fall far below the Canadian average. Despite good efforts and well-intentioned policies, poverty and disenfranchisement in Canada are becoming increasingly race-based.

In Toronto, after a run of black-on-black violence and the random Boxing Day murder of fifteen-year-old Jane Creba, poverty advocates and ethnocultural groups insisted that unequal access to jobs, a lack of community-based programs, and racism were plaguing the black community, especially its young men, who, seeing no future, were lashing out. While politicians treaded gingerly around the notion of race-based violence, on the streets and in homes anxious city dwellers were saying enough was enough, demanding tough justice for anyone caught with a gun, and asking whether young black men would ever be capable of integrating into mainstream society.

When, it appears, dramatically disenfranchised groups—whether they be in East London or on the periphery of Paris or in Toronto—cease to have a stake in, or feel responsible for, their country's civic culture, they are at risk of turning to violence. Over the coming years, Canada's ability to accommodate diversity is sure to become a central issue. As is the case in England, France, and other advanced liberal democracies, national unity in Canada is threatened by the growing **atomization** of our society along ethnic lines.

atomization
fragmentation

Consider the pattern in Britain. Following World War II, the United Kingdom granted "unlimited right of entry" to former colonial subjects. Its Nationality Act allowed over 300,000 West Indians to enter Britain between 1948 and 1962, with similarly large numbers coming from India and Pakistan. While the policy was generally assimilationist, visible inequality and violent outbreaks in "coloured communities" fed concerns that the complexion of British society was changing too rapidly. This led to the passage of the Commonwealth Immigrants Act in 1962, which severely restricted the flow of new arrivals from former British colonies. But numerous ethnic communities had already put down roots, expanded, and, as the years went by, attempted to establish themselves in British society. In 1981, riots in the Brixton area of south London (followed by more race-based riots in Birmingham and other English cities) contributed to more restrictive immigration.

Clearly, the integration of visible minority groups was posing special challenges, but Britain remained reliant on immigrant labour and could not simply close the doors. In the early 1990s, it addressed the issue by shifting toward Canadian-style multiculturalism, and by promoting the virtues of ethnic identity and diversity to mainstream society. More and more, mosques, temples, and other icons of ethnicity began sprouting up in British cities as visible minorities were encouraged to retain their customs and traditions.

Grumblings about ethnic neighbourhoods continued but, as international markets soared and people spoke openly of the advantages of a new **cosmopolitanism**, criticism was muted—until . . . [the] summer [of 2005]. Since the London bombings, British politicians across party lines have suggested that the traditional explanations for unrest and violence—poverty, inequality, etc.—cannot explain the suicidal rage of the bombers. Many argue that, within the context of a wholesale re-evaluation of citizenship and loyalty to state, the answer must lie in the very policies designed to encourage multiculturalism and celebrate diversity.

But the French situation undermines this interpretation. France has remained staunchly assimilationist. While it has opened its doors to immigrants (and former colonials) from North Africa and the Middle East—again, largely in response to shortages of unskilled labour—the emphasis on speaking French has been resolute, and little truck has been given to the construction of ethnic shrines or the wearing of foreign cultural **iconography**. Often criticized for being rigidly chauvinistic, France nonetheless established a relatively firm contract with new arrivals and refused to accept notions of hyphenated citizenship. One would therefore expect that if outbreaks of violence did occur, they would not be so clearly rooted in ethnicity. And yet France—like Germany, Holland, and other European countries—is now **riven** by colour-line politics, and the engrained sense of alienation among ethnic groups is profound.

In England and France, it appears that the recent violence is rooted in second-generation visible-minority groups with little **fealty** to their adopted state (and in Australia, in what immigration policy is doing to the nation). And there is growing concern that a similar sense of alienation is developing among the same class of people in Canada.

From the beginning, and for generations, immigration to this country was based on our most fundamental need—to populate and settle the unwieldy geographic mass that was to become Canada. The nation was not born of a revolution or forced to recreate itself after an empire's passing. Rather, it was perceived as a blank slate where, owing to a harsh climate and endless land, nation-building itself became the founding mythology. Formed after the US Civil War, or the "war between the states," Canada was organized around weak provinces and a strong federal government—a source of **benevolence** at the centre that would knit the regions together through massive projects such as the national railway. Immigration was one of Ottawa's chief responsibilities; its policies were openly integrationist and designed for those eager to assume Canada's monumental challenge. So, early in the twentieth century, Wilfrid Laurier's Liberal government set out to populate vast territories by importing "men in sheepskin coats." Ukrainians, Norwegians,

cosmopolitanism
familiarity and comfort with a variety of cultures

iconography
symbolic representations

riven
torn apart

fealty
allegiance

benevolence
good will

Germans, and other almost exclusively European immigrants responded to the call and began descending on Canada's ports, eager for the long trek to the West. This flood reached its peak in 1913, when 400,810 immigrants—the equivalent of 1.5 million today—arrived on our shores.

Growth through immigration continued until the combined impact of the Depression, racism, and World War II caused Canada to effectively shut its doors to outsiders. But, as was the case with Britain, the war had depleted our store of labour. With millions across Europe seeking safe haven from poverty and starvation, and Canada overdue to restart its nation-building project, by the mid-1940s the immigration taps were turned on once again. Bolstered by its reputation as a liberator, Canada attracted Italians, Portuguese, Greeks, and other Europeans to its flourishing urban centres. As is reflected in the 1952 Immigration Act, entry into Canada was deemed a privilege and individuals could be barred based on ethnic affiliation. Immigration was now clearly controlled through country-of-origin quotas, which actively restricted non-white immigrants and implicitly validated the notion that nation-building requires assimilation. While still diverse, Canada grew as a white, European, and Christian nation of immigrants grateful for the opportunity to start over in a new land. And, most crucially, the federal government retained its role as central provider, thereby encouraging immigrants to develop a strong sense of civic nationalism.

meritocratic
merit-based

By 1961, 97 percent of all immigrants came from Europe, but Canada's openly assimilationist approach began to shift in 1967, when country-of-origin quotas were replaced by a more **meritocratic** points system. The impetus for this change came from many quarters, including Prime Minister John Diefenbaker's early 1960s criticism of South Africa's apartheid regime, Lester Pearson's peacekeeping initiatives, and Canada's increasing involvement in the Commonwealth. Within a few short years, the impact was dramatic. West Indian immigration to Canada, for instance, ballooned from 46,000 and 3 percent of the total (many of whom were white) in the 1960s to nearly 160,000 and 11 percent in the 1970s (almost all of whom were black). But, despite its growing diversity, to a large extent Canadian-style multiculturalism emerged less out of a sense of global citizenship than from a need to deal with a pressing domestic issue: Quebec.

Quiet Revolution
period during the1960s during which many modernizing social changes were introduced in Quebec

Alarmed at the rise of nationalist sentiment during Quebec's **Quiet Revolution**, in 1963 the federal government launched the Royal Commission on Bilingualism and Biculturalism. Its thinly veiled objective was to dissipate Quebecers' sense of being a conquered nation and replace the notion of "English Canada" with a bold new pact between two founding peoples. Canada would be defined by two languages and two cultures, co-existing within a federalist framework. This approach might have tempered the flames of separatism had the process not been hijacked by swelling numbers of non- British and non-French immigrants, who failed to see themselves reflected in the new vision. As Will Kymlicka wrote in 2004, "[New Canadians] worried that government funds and civil service positions would be parcelled out between British and French, leaving [white] immigrant/ethnic groups on the margins."

Confronted by an organized ethnic lobby, the government changed the terms of reference of the commission and, in the end, declared that Canada would be a multicultural society within a bilingual framework. The commission promoted the view that immigrant groups would overcome the obstacles posed by a new home and, over time, integrate, just as they had always done. Indeed, the entire genesis of the 1971 official Multiculturalism Policy suggests some **ambivalence** or confusion about embarking on a new national concept and a certain naïveté in the assumption that settlement would proceed largely as it had historically.

ambivalence
uncertainty

Our Centennial celebration, Expo 67, drew the world's attention to Canada, a progressive, modern state that promised universal health care, low university tuition fees, and jobs. This, combined with suggestions of a cultural mosaic, attracted large numbers of immigrants throughout the 1970s. The recession of the early 1980s stemmed the tide, but the notion of Canada as a cosmopolitan, caring, and multicultural society became even more concrete in 1988, when Brian Mulroney's Conservative government passed the Canadian Multiculturalism Act. Aggressive immigration targets and multiculturalism gained non-partisan support and became politically unassailable.

In 1984, Canada admitted only 88,239 immigrants, but the years following saw increased numbers, and by 2001, some 5.4 million Canadians aged fifteen or older were foreign-born—18.4 percent of the population. This represented the highest rate of diversity in seventy years; in Ontario and British Columbia, the figure reached nearly 35 percent.

The most significant change over the past two decades has been the increase in visible-minority immigration. In 2004, only 20 percent came from Europe, while nearly 50 percent came from China, India, Pakistan, the Philippines, Korea, or Iran. For the moment, non-white Canadians represent approximately 16 percent of the population. But with more inflow, and with first-generation immigrants raising families, this figure will increase significantly in the coming years.

Recognizing that visible-minority groups faced unique obstacles to integration, the Heritage Department conducted a formal review of multicultural programs in 1996. The result was a more assertive mandate: "to foster an inclusive society in which people of all backgrounds, whose identities are respected and recognized as vital to an evolving Canadian identity, feel a sense of belonging and an attachment to this country, and participate fully in Canadian society." The new thrust was directed at non-immigrant society, at getting it to respect and encourage diversity. In fact, through the 1990s, the government directed funding to ethnic organizations and insisted that public institutions such as the civil service and the CRTC reflect the ethnic diversity of the country through their hiring practices. Whereas the goal of past initiatives was clearly integration, Canada had evolved into a state that promoted hyphenated citizenship.

The changes were controversial. Over and above critiques that hiring quotas inevitably lead to reverse discrimination, there were questions about whether encouraging the retention of ethnic identity would drive visible-minority groups away from mainstream society. Examining the United States, American historian Arthur Schlesinger Jr. wrote of a "cult of ethnicity" that "exaggerates differences, intensifies resentments and antagonism, drives even deeper the awful wedges between races and nationalities. The endgame is self-pity and self-ghettoization." Schlesinger's critique resonates in Canada. Recent settlement trends suggest that so-called "ethnic box settlements" are becoming prevalent.

In the Canadian context, as Ottawa continued devolving powers to the provinces, the sense of nationhood receded in significance. When the issues directly affecting people's lives—health care, education, cities—are overwhelmingly controlled by the provinces and there is an absence of large-scale, nation-defining projects (to follow the historic examples of the railway, the Canadian Broadcasting Corporation, medicare), the creation of a coherent national vision becomes difficult in the extreme.

Twenty years ago, roughly half of the immigrant population gravitated to Toronto, Montreal, or Vancouver. Today, nearly 80 percent do—and this is 80 percent of a much larger total. Within these growing urban centres, immigrant groups are clustering in tightly knit, ethnically homogeneous neighbourhoods partly because, according to the government's own studies, many ethnic groups feel out of place in Canada. Their first loyalty is to their group, and, against a history of the children of immigrants "moving out," today there is an increasing concentration of visible-minority groups "staying home," staying alien to host cultures and having little sense of civic nationalism.

How can this situation change? For multiculturalism to work, the native-born must accept immigrants as equals and new arrivals must demonstrate a willingness to join mainstream society by adopting the fundamental mores and values of the prevailing culture. There must also be cross-fertilization between ethnic groups and civic nationalism has to be clearly defined. According to University of Toronto sociology professor Jeffrey Reitz, recent evidence casts serious doubt that this is occurring in modern Canada. Reitz has spent his career studying the Canadian immigrant experience and, considering data on both income levels and attitudes, he believes that "multicultural policies are simply not working as well for visible minorities." Despite targeted programs to ease adjustment, Reitz's research shows that, unlike post–World War II immigrants, Canada's newest arrivals are not only failing to catch up financially, but the gap between them and non-immigrant groups is widening. Social disparities are most pronounced among visible-minority groups, and Reitz's data indicates that while "satisfaction with life" increases from the first to the second generation for white immigrants, it actually decreases among non-white immigrants.

Voting behaviour is one of many **indices** researched by Reitz to gauge rates of societal participation and involvement. A scant 20 percent of first-generation immigrants (that is, the foreign-born), regardless of colour, exercise their **franchise**. By the second generation, however, white immigrant participation rates almost quadruple, while among visible-minority groups it only doubles. Surprisingly, it appears that first-generation non-white immigrants actually enter Canada with a greater sense of belonging than white immigrants, but within a generation that feeling diminishes among visible-minority groups, while white immigrants report a growing sense of belonging and involvement.

indices
indicators

franchise
right to vote

Because immigration is most often push driven—that is, homeland conditions motivate emigration—in the main, immigrants are satisfied with their adopted country. Early on, their sense of belonging derives principally from involvement within their own ethnic communities, which Reitz reports is much higher among non-white minorities. But by the second generation, that involvement diminishes, as cultural ties loosen and expectations of their adopted home increase. According to Reitz, it is with the second generation, the same **demographic** responsible for the London bombings and the riots outside Paris, that ethnic tensions and alienation most clearly reveal themselves.

demographic
portion of the population

Unlike Britain and France, however, which began accepting visible-minority immigrants after World War II, Canada did not do so in any real numbers until the 1970s. Consequently, second-generation immigrants represent only 14 percent of Canada's current visible-minority population. But today, two-thirds of all native-born visible minorities in Canada are under sixteen years old. Their numbers are destined to swell and, given current settlement trends and growing income disparities, Canada may indeed face the kinds of ethnic conflicts that have beset England and France. Instead of having more effective multicultural policies or greater societal tolerance,

Canada has avoided these problems to date largely because it got into the visible-minority immigration game a generation later.

Political theorist Charles Taylor has analyzed the issue of achieving common objectives in a multicultural society that places a primacy on respecting difference. He concluded that Canadians can "be brought together by common purposes [but] our unity must be a projective one, based on a significant common future rather than a shared past." Some have suggested promoting diversity itself as a rallying call for all Canadians, but, again, drawing attention to difference can undermine attempts to forge an overarching national identity. The situation has been further complicated by the emergence of intensive globalization and the necessarily diminished role of nation-states (and hence of national mythologies) that globalization has ushered in.

Canada, Britain, France, and Australia share a common dilemma. All are stable constitutional democracies that are based on the primacy of individual rights and all share secular-humanist leanings. Each recognizes the need for immigration and is coping with growing visible-minority populations, and each is struggling in a post-nation-state world where well-defined national purposes are less certain. Without grand designs or defining national projects, new immigrants run the risk of arriving and going about their business with little sense of the roles they can play in their adopted homeland. With no national mythology to adhere to, they naturally retreat to the familiar, seeking out their own communities.

Throughout Europe, nations known for their liberalism are now engaged in vigorous debate around one central question: what is more important to our national direction, inclusion under the umbrella of a unifying nationalism or the celebration of uniqueness and difference? Defenders of multiculturalism argue that these two options are not mutually exclusive and that both can be achieved by open, tolerant, and just societies. But in Britain, the decision to encourage uniqueness drove certain second-generation groups away from the mainstream and its values; in France, assimilationist policies have led to feelings of intense isolation.

In Canada, we may live in a multicultural society, but the evidence suggests that fewer and fewer of us are living in multicultural neighbour-hoods. Furthermore, the tradition of immigrants clustering in a community for one generation before the next generation moves on and "melts" into mainstream culture seems to be breaking down. Large districts are evolving into areas dominated by individual ethnic groups that have chosen to live apart from those who do not share their ancestry. Meanwhile, most white Canadians would confess that the vast majority of their friends look a lot like they do and that they tend to stay within their own communities, rarely venturing into the ethnic enclaves that are burgeoning, especially in suburban Canada.

This growing sense of separateness can have troubling consequences for national identity. Just as the landmark 1954 US Supreme Court decision *Brown v. Board of Education* demonstrated that separate can never be equal, the history of segregation teaches us that the notion of citizenship cannot survive in modern liberal societies that become atomized. The absence of interaction between groups of different backgrounds invariably perpetuates cultural divisions, breeds ignorance, and leads to stereotyping and prejudice.

It is true, the attacks on the World Trade Center and the Pentagon brought grievances from distant lands to our doorstep. But they were perpetrated by foreigners, and it was their very "foreignness" that made their motivations impenetrable to the Western mind. When we learned, however, that the London bombers could have grown up playing soccer on the same pitches as the people they murdered and that entire neighbourhoods were burning only a bus ride from Paris's tonier cafés, a new face of ethnic conflict came knocking on the Western door.

The events of the last year have presented the West with a conundrum: can liberal democracies, lacking a unifying **ethos**, satisfy the needs of societies that are increasingly heterogeneous? Bernard Ostry, one of the principal architects of multiculturalism under Trudeau, has voiced anxiety that the experiment has gone wrong and must be reviewed. Mindful, one suspects, of the example of Australia, which also opened its arms to non-white immigrants in the past few decades, Ostry is demanding a travelling royal commission. At the beginning of the last century, Wilfrid Laurier answered the question of immigration and identity by telling new arrivals, "Let them look to the past, but let them also look to the future; let them look to the land of their ancestors, but let them look also to the land of their children." The events in Sydney, as well as those in London and Paris, suggest just how imperative it is to heed his words, as inspiring today as they were 100 years ago, when a young nation trembled before the twentieth century and wondered how it would find its way.

ethos
common cultural character or national spirit

Can We All Just Get Along?

Greg Narbey

In Los Angeles in 1992, rioting occurred as a response to the acquittal of four LAPD officers who had been videotaped beating Rodney King. Startled by the violence and scope of the rioting, Mr. King delivered a televised appeal for peace by asking: "Can we all get along?" Indeed, "getting along" has always been one of the most pressing problems in any society and, therefore, one of the greatest political challenges. In modern society, this challenge is to find some way to balance the requirements of social cohesion (unity) on the one hand and diversity (pluralism) on the other. The uneven distribution of power between majority groups and minority groups has always made this challenge difficult to meet.

Traditionally, minority groups were usually simply ignored or repressed by force by the majority. As the ancient Greek historian Thucydides once observed, "The strong do what they can while the weak suffer what they must." Often the Ottoman Empire is presented as an early forerunner of today's multicultural society. It is important to recognize, however, that the empire offered toleration but not real equality for minority religious groups: the predominantly Muslim society tolerated Christian and Jewish minorities provided they did not try to spread their religion, but the minorities were never accorded equal rights to political participation. Even this degree of toleration was imperfect, however, with periodic pogroms launched against minority religious groups.[*]

The Challenge of Pluralism

disenfranchisement
deprivation of rights

The permanent **disenfranchisement** or marginalization of minority groups cannot be justified in today's modern, multicultural and democratic societies. Modern democracy is premised on the principle, commonly held since at least the 18th century, that governmental legitimacy rests on the consent of the governed. As John Stuart Mill (1806–1873) recognized, moreover, a democracy that denied equality to minority groups would not be sustainable in the long run. As more of the countries of the world move toward some democratic form of government (about 120 countries out of the 191 nations that comprise the membership of the UN), the challenge of political pluralism has become the most critical political issue to be confronted in the 21st century.

This article was written for *The Human Project*. Used by permission.

[*]*Editors' note:* Indeed, in 1915 the leaders of the Ottoman Empire launched a genocidal campaign against their Armenian subjects in an attempt to resolve "the Armenian question" once and for all.

Pluralism is the human condition. It results from the fact that people who do not share the same moral values, cultural practices, religious observations or languages must inhabit a common and finite planet. All human civilizations have been to a greater or lesser extent pluralist. However, the revolution in global transportation, communications and trade has made almost every country pluralist to a degree never before imagined. There are around 8000 distinctive cultural groups living in the 191 nations that comprise the United Nations.[1] Because the earth and its territory are finite, but culture and religion are dynamic and constantly changing, it is inconceivable that each distinctive cultural group could be granted its own territory (even if that were desirable). As the ability to travel, communicate and trade becomes cheaper and easier, greater interaction among different religious, moral and cultural outlooks becomes inevitable, and, in turn, the issue of whether we can all get along becomes even more pressing. To put the problem another way, the challenge for modern pluralist societies is to find a balance between diversity and social unity. How that balance should be struck cannot be settled in advance.

The challenge of "getting along" in an increasingly pluralized world is heightened by the very arbitrary nature of national boundaries. The boundaries of identifiable countries are human creations (they are not rooted in nature). Because no nation on earth is entirely *autarchic* (completely self-sufficient), because every nation on earth contains minority groups and because every nation is, in principle, divisible, the long-term success of a nation will largely be determined by how well the many different interests within the borders of that nation can be satisfied. Two examples should serve to illustrate this point.

Sri Lanka is a country that has been torn apart for decades by a ferocious civil war fought between the Tamil minority and the Singhalese majority. In 1956 the Singhalese majority made Singhala the only official language of Sri Lanka (at that time called Ceylon). The Tamil minority claimed that nothing short of political independence from the Singhalese majority could secure their long-term rights, language and culture.

Similarly, during the latter part of the 20th century, Canadians were preoccupied by the demands of some Québécois for political independence from Canada. Only in a sovereign Quebec, the separatists argued, would the Québécois truly be able to defend their language and distinct culture. Two referendums (in 1980 and 1995) on separating from Canada were fought over this issue in Quebec. There were also a number of attempts to institute constitutional change to satisfy Quebec's demands for greater autonomy within a unified Canada. During the last Quebec referendum in 1995, moreover, both the Cree in northern Quebec and English speakers in Montreal pointed out that if Canada was divisible, so was Quebec. In an independent Quebec, they would be minorities. In short, if the majority of Québécois voted to separate from the rest of Canada, the Cree and anglophone Montreal threatened to hold their own referendums to separate from Quebec and remain a part of Canada. In any event, the success of an independent Quebec would still depend on whether the majority francophone population could convince non-francophone minorities that their rights would be respected in an independent Quebec. Obviously the future success of Canada will depend on our ability to reconcile minority and majority rights and interests.

In the simplest possible terms the challenge of pluralism is this: How much accommodation or acceptance must majorities extend to minority groups, and when is accommodation or acceptance unreasonable? Furthermore, do minority groups deserve more than just accommodation or tolerance, i.e., how can their values and norms be reflected in the laws and customs of the larger nation? Before you say "no" to the question of whether accommodation or acceptance should be offered, think twice. As Mill recognized, in a democracy all of us are at one time or another part of a minority group. Perhaps you were opposed to Canada's participation in the NATO-led military intervention in Kosovo and the bombing of Serbia in 1999. If so, you would have represented a minority viewpoint in Canadian society. Cultural differences within a nation also have an impact upon whether your opinions and cultural, religious and linguistic practices place you in the majority or a minority position. If you support the right of gays and lesbians to be legally married, you will be in a minority in Alberta, but part of a small majority in Ontario, and part of a larger majority in Toronto.

So the ability to accommodate and accept minority groups within a society is critical to all of us. Moreover, the development of permanent minority groups cut off from power and influence in a society is a recipe for the failure of democracy. Why is this so?

Three Principles of Democratic Society

The development and spread of democratic governments over the past three centuries was premised on a number of assumptions about human rights. Political thinkers such as Hobbes (1588–1679) and Locke (1632–1704) argued that human beings were *equal*; there was no natural, or divinely established, hierarchy; and, as such, governments had to justify their right to rule. This meant that a government had to pass laws that treated all citizens equally, at a minimum, in order to be able to claim legitimacy as a government. Furthermore, thinkers as diverse as Locke, Rousseau (1712–1778), Marx (1818–1883) and Mill argued that *liberty* was a primary human good, and, thus, any legitimate government had to maximize human liberty. As you will learn from the article "Politics in the Life of the Individual" in the next unit, there is considerable disagreement on how equality and liberty are to be maximized and how they are to be balanced. However, since the 18th century it has largely been accepted that governments that establish two tiers of citizenship, and dramatically restrict the liberty of their citizens, are illegitimate.

There was one other fundamental assumption about government that accompanied the democratic revolutions of the 18th and 19th centuries. It was assumed that government must be neutral in its treatment of citizens, i.e., that a legitimate government cannot offer advantages (or disadvantages) to one group of citizens that it does not offer to others. It was the assumption of *government neutrality* that led most modern democracies to insist on the separation of religion and state. Many of the earliest democracies in Europe had learned through bitter experience that when government and religion were connected, religious disagreement had the potential to become civil war as different religious faiths fought for control of the government. This doctrine of state neutrality with respect to religion gradually broadened to include state neutrality with respect to moral issues. Governments could legitimately make laws governing the behaviour of individuals and groups where the safety and well-being of others was concerned, but otherwise they had to respect the decisions made by individuals that did not directly harm the interests of other citizens. This is an idea formalized by Mill in his famous "harm principle."

Justice and Fairness: Formal and Substantive Equality

The neutrality of the government with respect to religious or moral conduct, the equal treatment of all citizens and the maximization of liberty are three of the essential rights on which most modern democracies rest. These basic human rights can also serve as a guide to help us negotiate the challenges raised by the increasingly pluralistic world we live in today. One of the 20th century's greatest political thinkers, John Rawls (1921–2002), recognized that the most critical issue facing democracy was how the conflicts generated by pluralism could be negotiated. His starting point was the issue of *fairness*. Everyone wants to be treated fairly, but often conflict arises when we try to determine what it means to be fair. Indeed, when we try to figure out what is fair we often reason in ways that reinforce our particular advantage. Rawls proposed a way of thinking about issues of fairness that would encourage us to look past our own particular advantage or disadvantage. He invited us to participate in a thought experiment. Imagine you are behind a "veil of ignorance"—imagine you have no knowledge about your particular characteristics. You do not know whether you were born to a wealthy family or a poor family. You do not know your sex or sexual orientation. Furthermore, you do not know your race or ethnicity or country of birth. Lastly, you do not know what your particular abilities or disabilities may be. When we think about questions of what is fair, Rawls argues, this is the position from which we should start. He called this imaginary situation "the original position."

How can this process of reasoning help us with pluralistic conflict? Take the example of whether gays and lesbians should be able to legally marry. Since all of us take it for granted that we should be treated fairly, what is a fair law on this issue? Without knowledge of our personal characteristics, most of us would probably acknowledge that forming a permanent, stable, loving relationship that is legally recognized is something that many adults desire. Marriage is both a legal institution and a cultural way of regulating and acknowledging this type of relationship. So, given that in the original position, I, for example, have no knowledge of my own particular sexual orientation, it is unlikely that I would think that it was fair to restrict marriage only to the heterosexual majority. In the same way, if I had no knowledge of my race, I would not consider it fair to establish some form of legally sanctioned racism (such as the apartheid system formerly practised in South Africa).

The thought experiment of the original position can help us think more clearly about what is fair. However, one feature of pluralistic societies is that not all conflicts can be resolved by reference to simple equality. It has long been recognized that treating everyone exactly the same way—*formal equality*—does not always produce fairness. In Canada during the 20th century, for example, the federal government established residential schools for the education of aboriginal children. Children were removed from their families and placed in boarding schools far from their communities of birth. These schools (sometimes severely) punished students who used their native language or engaged in non-Christian forms of worship. The native children were to be educated in either French or English, just like any other Canadian child. One could argue that the native students were simply being given education equal to that of any other student in Canada.

However, what this analysis overlooks is that by failing to educate the native children in their own languages, the residential schools were stripping them of their language and, ultimately, their culture. Sometimes treating people fairly means that their differences have to be recognized and accommodated. Recognizing and accommodating people's differences where greater fairness will result is known as *substantive equality*. While an exclusive reliance on formal equality can result in unfairness, it is also important to realize that an exclusive reliance on substantive equality can have the same effect. A danger of substantive equality is that it can lead to oversimplifying the identity of the minority group by focusing on one element of their identity, resulting in stereotyping or pigeonholing them. One of the great challenges for modern democracies is deciding when formal equality or substantive equality should take precedence. In any particular case, this decision should be guided by the question: "What will produce the greatest fairness?"

In 2004 a debate gripped France that perfectly illustrates the difficulty of balancing social unity and diversity. The issue was the role of religious observance in public life. Specifically, the government passed legislation that prohibited the wearing of hijabs, yarmulkes, large crosses or turbans by students in the public education system. The president of France, Jacques Chirac, argued that, ever since the French Revolution, France has been committed to being a secular society with respect to politics and public life. The assumption of the French legislature was that religious toleration can only really occur in a secular society. The legislation aimed at public religious observance was justified as a way to preserve the secular tradition of France. Predictably, the proposal was met with strong opposition. France is home to Europe's largest Muslim population (about 5 million). Many Muslims saw this proposal as an attempt to marginalize their role in French society and to assimilate them. This dispute is a classic illustration of the tension between formal and substantive equality. The French government (and a majority of French citizens) sees the legislation as *upholding* formal equality (the restriction on public religious observance applies to all French people). Muslim, Jewish, Christian and Sikh groups see this as a *denial* of equality. A secular culture is being enforced and those with religious values and norms are being told that their religion will be tolerated provided it is confined to private life. The perspective of the religious groups conforms to substantive equality: religious differences should be acknowledged and accommodated. There are good arguments to be made on both sides of this issue.

Once again, the original position may be a good place to start in helping us figure out what is reasonable and what will produce the greatest fairness. If we had no knowledge of our religious faith and the requirements of observing that faith, would we be willing to live in a society that made the public observance of our religion difficult or impossible? Furthermore, we might ask ourselves whether other members of society who do not share our faith are harmed if our religion requires a particular mode of dress. It is unlikely that from the perspective of the original position many would agree with the ban on public religious observance.

Competing Moral Doctrines: Reasonable Pluralism

This example also raises another difficulty faced by pluralist democracies—the distinction between public life and private life. Where no harm is done to other citizens, most democracies are willing to permit fairly broad latitude in terms of how people can worship and what they say and do in private. This distinction between public and private spheres can be a source of frustration for many minority groups in a pluralistic society. Often it appears that the larger majority will tolerate them provided they keep their views and activities private. In Canada, for example, some evangelical Christians claim that their form of Christianity is tolerated provided they do not try to publicly advocate for laws on the basis of their faith. This has been particularly true, they claim, with respect to the issues of same-sex marriage and abortion. Limited tolerance is also a problem that Rawls confronted as it relates to his overall concern for fairness.

It is important to recognize that democratic governments have to pass laws that apply to all, while, at the same time, there is broad disagreement about how we should live our lives. Ideally, democratic government should not favour one comprehensive moral, cultural or political perspective over another. As long as no harm is done to other citizens in the pursuit of a good life, the decisions about how we live our lives should be left to individuals and communities. Rawls called religious, moral and cultural world views *comprehensive doctrines*. They are comprehensive because the core assumptions that lie behind many religious and moral belief systems guide our behaviour in the day-to-day conduct of our lives. If there are many comprehensive doctrines in a society, how can a government hope to govern without simply enforcing the majority position? Over time wouldn't the society become destabilized by conflict between people with very different comprehensive doctrines?

Rawls argued that a reasonable pluralism was possible. Again, we return to the issue of fairness. I, for example, might think that society would be much better off if it was governed according to the comprehensive religious or moral doctrine I follow. In this case, suppose I follow the religious doctrines of Jehovah's Witnesses and I believe that society would be better off without drinking or smoking. If I could attract enough followers to my faith, I might gather together a majority of voters who, like me, would like to ban smoking and drinking. However, would it be reasonable, or desirable, to live in a society where majority comprehensive views could be imposed on the minority who don't share those comprehensive moral doctrines? Again, think about what you would agree to in the original position, not knowing what your religious or moral outlook is. If I wanted to ban alcohol and tobacco, I would have to present reasons for doing so that others who did not share my faith might find reasonable and acceptable. For example, I might point out the cost to the health-care system of permitting smoking, as well as the deaths and injuries that arise from drunk driving, as reasons for banning cigarettes and alcohol. If I simply went ahead and banned these things on the basis of my faith alone, I would be inviting a constant fight over political power between groups of different religious and moral doctrines that could in some extreme circumstances result in a civil war.

The solution lies in a form of political argument that Rawls called *public reason.* A commitment to public reason is simply a commitment to present political arguments in ways that do not require others to accept our comprehensive moral standards. Since almost all of us prefer political stability to political instability, it would make sense for us to make our arguments about government legislation in ways that those who do not share our comprehensive doctrines could find reasonable and acceptable.

For example, many religious groups oppose same-sex marriage because it violates their understanding of their scripture. As such, they may refer to scripture as the basis for prohibiting same-sex marriage. However, not everyone shares their faith or their interpretation of their faith. Subsequently, to use faith-based arguments as the foundation for governmental prohibition of same-sex marriage ultimately invites a competition between religious and non-religious comprehensive doctrines for political power that may ultimately fragment and destabilize our society. Instead, those who oppose same-sex marriage should phrase their argument in terms that those who do not share their faith might find reasonable. They may point to the traditional connection between marriage and child rearing, for example, and argue that governments have an obligation to protect the definition of the traditional marriage because it promotes traditional child rearing. This is a reason I, for one, don't find compelling, but it is something that I can respond to as part of a larger societal debate because it does not require me to accept the assumptions of those who are opposed to same-sex marriage for particular religious reasons. An argument rooted in faith is very hard to respond to for those who do not share that particular faith or interpretation of it.

The willingness to phrase our arguments about government policy in terms that others who do not share our comprehensive views can accept is what Rawls called an *overlapping consensus.* All citizens of pluralist democracies have an interest in explaining themselves to their fellow citizens in ways that those who do not share their comprehensive views can accept, or at least debate, and find reasonable. It may not be too great an exaggeration to say that the ability of the citizens of pluralist democracies to debate and resolve their differences in this way will decide whether we can all get along. Guided by a concern for fairness and using reason as the basis for debate will not make the conflicts and differences that characterize pluralist societies go away. They will, however, enable us to debate and create laws that, even when we are part of the minority group, we might be more willing to live with and accept.

Note

[1] Adeno Addis, "On Human Diversity and the Limits of Toleration," in *Ethnicity and Group Rights*, eds. I. Shapiro and W. Kymlicka.

"Can We All Just Get Along" was written for *The Human Project* by Greg Narbey, a professor at the Humber College Institute of Technology and Advanced Learning and the University of Guelph-Humber. Used by permission.

Diversity versus Solidarity—The Progressive Dilemma of 21st-Century Politics

Bhikhu Parekh

We would all agree that diversity is a fact of modern life. It is, further, an unavoidable fact of life because not all differences can be rationally and conclusively resolved. It is also going to increase with the passage of time, for a variety of reasons. Globalization means that people are exposed to different cultural influences. Trade and commerce are never culturally neutral and, therefore, as we get integrated into a global economy, we are increasingly going to be a porous society, whose boundaries will not be able to resist cultural influences.

There are also other reasons why diversity is an inescapable and persistent fact of life, and bound to remain so. This has to do with the fact that people increasingly want to make their own choices. In our kind of society, people tend to define their dignity in terms of their capacity to make choices. They also define themselves in terms of self-fulfilment or self-expression. There is a "self" which they seek to express or articulate, and that self is unique to each individual.

Then, of course, there is the fact of immigration. Diversity has nothing to do with immigrants per se. In fact, many immigrants might be only too willing to assimilate into society. Even if immigration were to stop tomorrow, diversity would remain an inescapable and intractable fact of life.

I would go further and argue that diversity is not only a fact of life, but also an important source of moral, economic and social energy. It brings together different ways of looking at life and, therefore, enables us to learn from others and deepen our insights into human life. No culture is perfect. Each expresses one particular vision of life, stressing certain values and ignoring others. Cultural interaction is one way in which we can liberate ourselves from the limitations of our own culture and open up our consciousness to the impact of others.

Cultures also bring different forms of imagination and creativity. We can see this influence in our own country to a great extent post-1948, or in the US, which was built by immigrants. Immigrants also bring different sensibilities, values, forms of imagination, sources of energy and moral and cultural resources and engage the host society.

This reading originally appeared in the April 2003 *RSA Journal*, pp. 47–48. Used by permission.

No society can be based on diversity alone. It needs a strong sense of community. Why? First, we can't hold a diverse society together unless there is a certain basic commitment or a common sense of belonging. Second, a society which is not confident in itself will not be able to live with its differences. Such confidence comes from the recognition that these differences are not going to tear the nation apart. And third, we need a sense of community so that we care for each other, and are prepared to both share our resources with others, and pay higher taxes for the benefit of the underprivileged.

We therefore need both diversity and a sense of community or a common sense of belonging. The loss of one doesn't automatically privilege the other. If we have a community where diversity is sacrificed, we would purchase the sense of community at the cost of liberty and individual self-expression. If, on the other hand, we had diversity alone, society would not be able to hold itself together. Since we need both, the question is: how can we reconcile their occasionally conflicting demands in such a way as to create a society with a strong sense of unity, as well as a great respect for and delight in its diversity?

I would suggest that there are several ways in which we can reconcile the demands of diversity and community. It is extremely important that people growing up in society should not only retain—if they so want—their own different cultural, religious and other identities, but also ascribe to an overarching common identity which they share as citizens. The only overarching identity is a political identity, which disciplines the demands of narrower religious, cultural, ethnic and other identities.

The second requirement would be to define our citizenship, our political identity, in such a way that it accommodates a large number of diversities. Thus we should define Britishness in order that all British citizens, whatever their religion, colour and ethnicity, can identify with it without having to sacrifice their non-political identities. If political identity were to be so defined that it required abandonment of cultural, religious and other identities, then it would demand an unacceptably heavy price from its citizens and alienate a large group of them. A political community can be cohesive only if it respects legitimate differences.

It is sometimes said that such a multicultural society cannot deliver social justice, because the latter requires redistribution which people will accept only if they can identify with others and find them culturally similar. The argument is false. Switzerland and Canada are multicultural, but also based on a strong sense of social justice. By contrast, the US has a strong sense of national and cultural unity but a weak sense of social justice. **Margaret Thatcher** strove to create a culturally homogeneous society in Britain during her period of office, but it was also a period marked by an

Margaret Thatcher
Prime minister of the United Kingdom from 1979 to 1990

emphasis on self-interest and a weak sense of redistributive justice. In short, cultural homogeneity does not guarantee, and cultural diversity does not **mitigate** against, either social justice or a strong sense of community. It all depends on how members of a society relate to each other and whether or not they develop a sense of belonging. And these depend on their bonds of common interest, their sense of justice, and the policies of the government.

mitigate
diminish

Finally, a multicultural society requires that its citizens share a broadly common body of basic values, and know enough about each other's background, history and culture to feel at ease in each other's company.

A multicultural education, therefore, has much to be said for it. When properly defined and designed, it develops understanding between cultures, respect for differences, and a shared sense of common belonging.

"Diversity versus Solidarity—The Progressive Dilemma of 21st-Century Politics," by Bhikhu Parekh, originally appeared in the April 2003 *RSA Journal* (pp. 47–48). Used by permission.

The Individual and the Collective: Conflict and Cooperation

No man is an island, entire of itself; every man is a piece of the continent, a part of the main. If a clod be washed away by the sea, Europe is the less, as well as if a promontory were, as well as if a manor of thy friend's or thine own were. Any man's death diminishes me, because I am involved in mankind; and therefore never send to know for whom the bell tolls; it tolls for thee.

John Donne

Philosophers have only interpreted the world in various ways; the point is to change it.

Karl Marx

Out of timber so crooked as that from which man is made nothing entirely straight can be built.

Immanuel Kant

Introduction

In this unit of *The Human Project,* we move from the societal to the political arena. We aren't leaving the study of social issues behind, however, so much as sharpening our focus more specifically on the way power is formally regulated in society. Just as our reflections on the self in the first unit led us to consider many of the social forces we later analyzed in the second unit, our discussion of change in the social world led us to anticipate some of the political issues we will encounter in this unit. Any thoughtful inquiry into the social changes wrought by women's rights within the context of the family, for example, inevitably leads to a consideration of politics. Every political theory, moreover, presupposes a specific interpretation of the nature of society as well as the individual. In short, our analysis of politics in this unit builds upon our previous inquiries into self and society.

Conflict

While you may fully expect to encounter the topic of conflict in a unit on politics, you may have been surprised that it has figured so prominently in our discussion of self and society as well. Conflict in the political realm, however, is merely a reflection of the conflict that is so prevalent in every aspect of human life.

What is all this conflict about? Bragues suggests that it may result from the "creative destruction" that drives economic development in a capitalist system insofar as it has, paradoxically, facilitated a belief in equality even as it has created relative inequality of wealth. On the cultural front, moreover, Narbey points out that conflict is to some extent inevitable in the highly pluralistic societies, such as Canada's, that exist today in the West. Gregg underscores this view with his observation that minorities have become increasingly alienated in both "assimilationist" and non-"assimilationist" societies, leading some to lash out violently. Conflict abounds at home as well, Kipnis contends, in the subterranean domestic warfare that characterizes most marriages. Bunting proposes that an even more subterranean battle often rages on the job, as employees are expected to deliver more and more "emotional labour": not only must they attend to the feelings of even the rudest customers, but they must simultaneously suppress their own feelings. This may be a modern-day example of the internal struggle outlined by Freud, who, you will recall, attributes conflict to the tension between our primitive instincts for pleasure and aggression on the one hand and our tendency to conform to internalized social rules on the other. Alternatively, Nietzsche sees conflict as the result of the urge to break free from the herd and exercise will to power.

Power

Indeed, the struggle for *power* does seem to be key to understanding all these explanations of conflict. After all, power can give us a measure of control that allows us the *freedom* to live life as we wish. And since "no [wo]man is an island"—since we are either blessed or cursed, depending on your perspective, to live among others within society—we usually measure our share of power in relation to that of others. But how much power do we need? Enough to give us the ability to live "the good life."

Ideology

Not everyone agrees, however, on what "the good life" entails. Usually, our view of the good life is influenced by one of the many competing **ideologies** advocated in the political arena. Traditionally, for example, a liberal seeks political office with the intention of limiting the role of government in private life while at the same time enhancing governmental regulation of the economy; a conservative, on the other hand, normally seeks political office with the goal of limiting the role of government in the economy but simultaneously endorsing governmental initiatives that uphold traditional values. Important to politics in Canada are our various political parties—the Liberals, the Conservatives, the New Democrats, the Greens, the Bloc Québécois—each of which generally represents a different ideology that endorses a distinct view of "the good life."

ideology
set of beliefs that constitute a comprehensive point of view

These ideologies, which significantly influence "real-world" politics in Canada and elsewhere today, reflect the thought of some of the great political philosophers discussed by Morton Ritts in "Politics in the Life of the Individual." In each case, the theorist's conception of good government is determined by his understanding of human nature and, on that basis, his view of "the good life"—that is, the best life possible given the human condition as it is. For Hobbes, this is a life in which personal security is guaranteed by a strong government with absolute power; for Locke, on the other hand, this is a life in which individual rights to life, liberty and property are protected by a strong government with limited power. For Marx, the good life can be lived only within a communist society in which material needs are readily satisfied and, therefore, the pursuit of "truly human" needs becomes possible; for Mill, however, the good life is already attainable within existing society as long as government protects individual rights to political participation and free speech. It is not really that hard to see how these ideas are reflected in political life today. The security measures taken in Canada after the September 11, 2001, terrorist attacks on the US, for example, tend to reflect a Hobbesian perspective; the backlash to some of these extreme measures, on the other hand, seems to emanate from a Lockean point of view.

Ends and Means

Each conception of "the good life" has its allure. Further complicating the political arena, moreover, is the fact that an ideology can come up short when put into practice. It is hard to find fault with the Locke-inspired founding principles of the American Republic, for example, but in that same country slavery became a long-standing institution and, even after its abolition, African-Americans suffered so much discrimination that the civil rights movement was necessary 100 years after the Civil War and, furthermore, it took almost 50 years longer for the US to elect its first African-American President. While African-Americans overwhelmingly agreed with the goal of the civil rights movement—to ensure that they enjoyed the same rights to "life, liberty and the pursuit of happiness" as their compatriots—there was less agreement on the best means for obtaining this end. As Ritts explains in "Soul Force versus Physical Force," Martin Luther King Jr. insisted on following the principles of non-violent civil disobedience that he learned from Gandhi, while Malcolm X argued that the violence suffered by African-Americans justified their rebellion by "whatever means necessary."

A Not-So-Unified Globalized World

The impact of ideology extends beyond national boundaries, moreover, into the international realm as well. The theories of Hobbes, Locke, Marx and Mill all stem from Western civilization, the contemporary manifestation of which is significantly determined by the development of capitalism. Yet the "creative destruction" that capitalism brings is not limited to the West. As Benjamin Barber explains in "Jihad vs. McWorld," the globalizing **imperatives** of transnational capitalism threaten to render obsolete the unique practices, traditions, beliefs, languages and very ways of life that have historically distinguished different cultures from one another. Not surprisingly, this economically driven homogenization of the world has been met by resistance from peoples all over the globe who are not ready to trade their traditional cuisine for the Big Mac. Such resistance has taken

imperatives
demands

the form of independence movements, demands for autonomy, civil wars and even terrorism. Indeed, some see terrorist acts against Western societies, such as the toppling of the World Trade Center in New York City, the bombing of the railway in Madrid and the devastation of the resort island of Bali (a magnet for Australian tourists) as a cold attempt to use violence to resist the assault of Western culture.

As Wallerstein suggests in "America and the World: The Twin Towers as Metaphor," the September 11, 2001, attacks targeted the World Trade Center precisely because of its symbolic value vis-à-vis American dominance throughout the world. The assault on the Twin Towers, Wallerstein surmises, was intended to send the message that—contrary to Americans' view of themselves as being not only more prosperous but also more *civilized* than the rest of the world—in reality, the US is "morally depraved." While Wallerstein rejects this characterization of his country, he does acknowledge that the US has failed to recognize the benefits it has acquired at the expense of others. The US, he argues, needs to relinquish its current role as globalizing superpower and assume a new role as a collaborative partner with other states. This approach offers the possibility of building a more peaceful, egalitarian, and democratic international arena in which the ideology of globalization that imposes Western culture throughout the world would be replaced with a more reciprocal ideology of "universality" that values civilization in all its diversity.

Clearly, then, ideology does matter. This is even more important to keep in mind when we consider ideologies that dehumanize and, thereby, render expendable entire groups of people. The "good life," according to such views, whether touted by anti-"African" *Janjaweed* militia in Sudan, anti-Tutsi nationalists in Rwanda, anti-Semitic Nazis in Germany, anti-black white supremacists in the US or anti-Armenian Turks in the Ottoman Empire, requires that the "other" be eliminated—through expulsion or ethnic cleansing or even genocide.

Apathy versus Awareness

The utter brutality of genocide—the attempt to annihilate an entire people due to their nationality, ethnicity, race, or religion—is so incomprehensible that we may be tempted to disbelieve that ordinary people could ever carry out genocidal acts. But, as Chris Irwin explains in "Never Again? The Problem of Genocide in the 21st Century," genocide occurs precisely because large numbers of ordinary people choose to follow orders instead of their conscience. While he argues that the onus is on the international community to develop efficient measures for preventing, detecting and stopping genocide, Irwin also recognizes the tremendous role education and the media can and should play. Indeed, the best safeguard against a dangerous resurgence of this "banality of evil" may be to have an educated and informed public that acknowledges genocide as an ugly yet real phenomenon that has, regrettably, occurred throughout history but which, fortunately, can be prevented if people speak out against prejudice, hatred and ignorance.

Conversely, apathy—disinterest in social and political issues—preserves the power of those who wield it. In circumstances like Sudan today, Rwanda in the 1990s, Nazi Germany in the 1930s and 1940s, and the Ottoman Empire in 1915, this can, indeed, have devastating consequences. But in a tolerant liberal democracy such as that of modern-day Canada, the dangers of an uninformed public are less obvious.

In "The Perils of Obedience," however, Stanley Milgram suggests that submission to authority is a universal human tendency—so much so that people will readily obey orders to commit inhumane acts on their fellow human beings. As Milgram's experimental work shows, moreover, authority can be established in a very short span of time—a fact corroborated in a most terrible way in the case of the Rwandan genocide, where in the span of just months people were transformed from neighbours, friends and even relatives to mortal enemies. Thus, no country, including Canada, can afford to remain complacent about genocide; the danger is simply too great.

Politics in the Life of the Individual

Morton Ritts

Politics

Whether we care or not, politics matters. Indeed, political decisions affect jobs, taxes, social policy, immigration and other current issues. Politics helps to define our society's notions of freedom, law and justice.

Politics isn't something that happens only at election time. Politics occurs when students protest higher tuition fees, business groups lobby for free trade, unions strike for higher wages, women fight for employment equity, minorities rally for accommodation, environmentalists demand stricter pollution controls, and governments act—or don't act.

In its broadest sense, politics refers to the complex relations among various individuals and groups in society. There is politics between you and your boss, you and your parents, you and your teachers, you and your boy- or girl-friend. Politics is about power—competing for it, sharing it, imposing it. We want power not simply because we want things our own way. We want power because it gives us the feeling that we have some control over our lives, that we are free.

Obviously certain individuals and groups in society are more powerful than others. What is the basis of this power? Does "might make right"? Does sex, race, wealth, intelligence, status or tradition? Or moral or religious authority? Or a commitment to ethical principles? In some way, these are all factors in determining how much or how little power people have.

Government

Simply put, government is the mechanism that regulates power relations and the rights and duties of citizens and their rulers. According to the Greek philosopher Aristotle, there are basically three kinds of government: government by one person; government by the few; and government by the many. Every government is an example of one of these three basic forms. Whatever the case may be, some individuals and groups have more rights than others.

It's important, therefore, to acknowledge the role that government plays in our daily lives. Consider a government's monetary and fiscal policies, which affect everything from inflation to interest rates—in other words, everything from your ability to find a job to your ability to borrow money to start a

This article was written for *The Human Project*. Used by permission.

business, or to buy a house or to finance your education.

At the same time, consider the degree to which a government is involved in economic and social matters. Those who argue for more state intervention claim that government investment in areas such as education, health care and transportation is vital for the national interest. They argue that government regulation is also necessary to ensure that businesses don't pollute the environment, treat employees unfairly or take advantage of consumers. On the other hand, those who adopt a *"laissez-faire,"* or hands-off, approach believe that government involvement in social and economic matters should be minimal and that it is best to allow the "market" to regulate itself. The significance of government is only reinforced by the fact that in difficult times—such as the global financial crisis of 2008—"laissez-faire" advocates may actually argue that substantial governmental involvement is not only desirable but necessary.

Another important question about government is constitutional. How should power be divided among central, regional and local governments? Over the past 40 years in Canada, an extraordinary amount of energy has been devoted to the question of federal–provincial relations. Compared to other countries, Canada is already very decentralized, and many people who objected to the **Meech Lake** and **Charlottetown** agreements did so out of fear that they would further weaken the federal government's power.Of all forms of government, democracy (in theory at least) encourages the greatest distribution of power and the greatest amount of change. In Canada and the United States, women, visible minorities, the disabled, aboriginals, environmentalists, gays and lesbians have been in the forefront of such controversial political issues as employment equity, human rights, land claims, same-sex marriage, etc.

Of course, this kind of freedom to challenge the *status quo* and to fight for political change doesn't exist in every society. Freedom of speech and individual rights are values that we associate with liberal democracy. You don't have to look beyond the nearest headline or newscast to see that many governments around the world suppress human rights, crush dissent and persecute minorities.

When governments act this way, we often aren't surprised. Because many of us, consciously or otherwise, seem to accept self-interest as the norm in politics, we tend not to have a very high opinion of those who practise it. And too often their actions fail to shock us: patronage, corruption, dirty tricks, broken promises, slush funds, sex scandals—the dirty laundry list of unsavoury political practices, even in a liberal democracy, can turn us off any interest in politics at all.

Meech Lake Accord

proposed constitutional amendment—defeated in 1990 when it failed to be ratified by all provincial legislatures—that would have recognized Quebec as a distinct society and conferred greater powers to the provincial governments

Charlottetown Accord

proposed constitutional amendment—defeated in a national referendum in 1992—that would have recognized Quebec as a distinct society, acknowledged the right of indigenous peoples to self-government, created an elected Senate and conferred greater powers to the provincial governments

Apathy and Activism

Many political theorists argue that such **apathy** is dangerous, however. Whether we vote or not, politics affects us in large and small ways. It determines the programs we watch on TV and the music we hear on the radio—because decisions about Canadian content are political decisions. It determines whether there is room for us at college or a job when we're finished—because education and employment policy decisions are political. So are decisions about how much tax is taken from our paycheques, what social programs our taxes will fund and which regions of the country will get them.

But apathy is only one response to the frustration that we may feel about how we are governed. Another, and opposite, reaction is to become politically engaged. Such activism may even take the form of relatively new political parties, like the Conservative Party, the Bloc Québécois, and the Green Party of Canada—all of which have capitalized on public discontent.

Of course, political activity isn't always legal or peaceful. The Los Angeles riots in the aftermath of the first Rodney King verdict were a spontaneous and violent expression of rage against the L.A. police and state authorities. In Quebec, the tense stand-off at **Oka** was the result of years of frustration by the Mohawks against all levels of Canadian government.

The ultimate reaction to an insensitive or unjust government is revolution. This occurs when governments lose touch with people and efforts at legal and peaceful reform have failed to produce a satisfactory redistribution of power. The consensus that has bound people together breaks down, and a new political structure is needed. The violent overthrow of the existing order is seen as the only way to make this happen.

The Social Contract

Many of you may be familiar with the film *The Road Warrior* or the novel *Lord of the Flies*. In these and similar works, we're presented with a vision of the world in which law and order, morality and peace have broken down. In such apocalyptic, or end-of-the-world, visions, life is ruled by naked power—by selfishness, fear, superstition, mistrust, brute force. Without the guiding authority of tradition, laws and institutions, without consensus, society may descend into anarchy.

For this reason, no political philosopher would argue that we should trade society for the raw **state of nature**—not even the great French philosopher Jean Jacques Rousseau (1712–1778), whose writings contrast the natural goodness of people with the largely destructive impact of social institutions.

apathy
lack of interest or concern

Oka Crisis
1990 confrontation between members of the Mohawk nation and the Quebec provincial police and Canadian army due to a land dispute between the community of Kanesatake and the town of Oka over plans to expand a golf course on native burial ground

state of nature
(hypothetical) society without any human-made laws or government

But while Rousseau denounced his own artificial, class-ridden society with the famous words, "Man was born free, and everywhere he is in chains," he nevertheless understood that we are first and foremost social beings. We are united, he argued, by the agreement that we make with each other to surrender at least some of our desires in exchange for the satisfaction of at least some of our needs. Rousseau, Thomas Hobbes and John Locke argued that this "**social contract**" formed the basis of civil society.

social contract

theory that just government is created by an agreement among people

For these thinkers, the effectiveness of the social contract depends on our ability to obtain a satisfactory balance between what we want and what we're prepared to give up to get it. The social contract breaks down when people believe they're surrendering too much or not getting enough in return. Or when they lose the trust that binds them to others and to a government that may be incompetent, unfair or tyrannical.

In the absence of effective government, then, social order crumbles and no one has any security. Freedom, laws, justice and human rights are ignored, replaced by occurrences of social chaos such as the English civil war (1642–1649), the Rwandan genocide (1994) and, more recently, the on-going Afghan civil war. We need government to maintain social order, and we need social order if we want to survive.

What Kind of Government Is Most Desirable?

The answer to this question depends on a number of things, but mainly on what people believe to be the purpose of government. Is it to maintain peace and stability at any price? To promote a particular set of religious beliefs? To promote the interests of an elite, land-owning class? To preserve the rule of a king or queen? Or to guarantee freedom, rights, law and justice, as understood by the underlying principles of liberal democracy?

As reflected in these questions, our understanding of the most desirable form of government also depends on some of the most fundamental questions that we ask about human nature. Are people good or bad? Are they ruled by reason or emotion? Which people are best suited to make decisions? How much freedom should ordinary people have? Are we motivated by self-interest or a desire to help others?

By the time we reach college, we have no doubt asked at least some of these questions to try to determine what kind of relationship ought to exist between ourselves and others in society, what we are willing to give up for the sake of social order and what we expect in return.

Political philosophers since the time of Plato have tried to describe which arrangements they believe will make society function most effectively. And they often begin by trying to identify what motivates social order in the first place. Thomas Hobbes, for example, argued that it was primarily fear.

The Fear Motive

Thomas Hobbes

Hobbes (1588–1679) lived through a tumultuous period in English history when civil war had torn his country apart, and when law, order and security had broken down. The war reinforced Hobbes's view that people are naturally aggressive, violent and competitive, dominated by their emotions and instincts, or by what Freud would later call "the id."

Because this is human nature, Hobbes argued, people have the **natural right** to secure whatever they want by any means within their power. And, since we have unlimited desires and not enough resources, this leads us to inevitable conflict with others. Thus, people live in a constant state of fear, and, therefore, their first impulse is to overpower others before being overpowered themselves. Hobbes described this state of nature before the social contract as a situation in which "every man is enemy to every man" and life is "solitary, poor, nasty, brutish and short."

Imagine that all laws in your city have been suspended for 24 hours and that the police are on strike. In effect, this would be a one-day "state of nature." Is this the time to fly off for a holiday? Or would you stay home with a shotgun and make sure that no one tried to grab your property? According to Hobbes, fear would keep you at home. What's more, he argued, you may decide to take this opportunity to relieve any defenceless neighbours of their property.

In other words, Hobbes said that we are indeed creatures of greed and passion who are driven by a desire to dominate and control. Hobbes painted a picture of human beings who are nothing more than pleasure-

natural right
entitlement that people have by virtue of their humanity

THOMAS HOBBES

Whatsoever therefore is consequent to a time of war, where every man is enemy to every man; the same is consequent to the time, wherein men live without other security, than what their own strength and their own invention shall furnish them withal. In such condition there is no place for industry; because the fruit thereof is uncertain: and consequently no culture of the earth; no navigation, nor use of the commodities that may be imported by sea; no commodious building; no instruments of moving, and removing, such things as require much force; no knowledge of the face of the earth; no account of time; no arts; no letters; no society; and which is worst of all, continual fear, and danger of violent death; and the life of man, solitary, poor, nasty, brutish, and short.

Thomas Hobbes, *Leviathan*

seeking machines. As such, they constantly seek to maximize pleasure and minimize pain.

But we're also reasonable creatures who realize that our interests are better served within a framework of law, morality, peace and security than in a state of violence and anarchy. Fear motivates us to agree to the social contract and to accept the power of government to enforce it. And the job of government, or what Hobbes called "the sovereign," is to make sure that the social contract doesn't become unstuck.

How much power should the sovereign, or governing authority, have over us? Hobbes believed that whether the sovereign is in the hands of one person, a few people, or all the people, it should have absolute power to do its job well. That means giving up not only some of our desires but also most of our rights—such as freedom of speech, the right to assembly and anything else that could threaten political and social stability. But, like Freud, Hobbes believed that such stability came at a price, although, unlike Freud he thought the price was rarely too high.

Hobbes favoured autocracy as the most desirable form of government, believing that a single ruler could act far more efficiently than any government requiring the support of a fickle electorate and the unpredictable mechanics of democracy.

The Property Motive

Like Hobbes, John Locke (1632–1704) lived in a time of great social and political upheaval when the belief in an absolute monarch who ruled by divine right was being challenged and power was being transferred from the king to the people in the form of parliamentary democracy. Locke fully supported these radical changes.

Locke believed that all people are born free, equal, rational and moral. He also believed that we have certain God-given natural rights of life, liberty and property, which form the basis of the social contract and which it is the chief purpose of government to protect. To do so, it must be given the power to resolve conflicts and restrain violent and criminal acts. If the government fails to do its job properly, the people have the right to overthrow it— violently if necessary. To avoid this possibility, Locke advocated a system of checks and balances in which the branches of representative government are separate and distinct.

Locke's ideas on natural rights had an influence that extended well beyond the development of liberal democracy in England. They also helped to shape the thinking of the leaders of the American Revolution in their fight for independence. Indeed, Locke's theory that natural rights form the basis of the

John Locke

social contract is the ideology of liberal democracies everywhere, particularly in the United States where individual rights are paramount. The core of these rights, Locke argued, is private property.

But what exactly is private property? And why is it the defining feature of that economic system we call capitalism? Private property is more than the piece of land we own or the house we live in. It is, Locke said, whatever "we mix with our labour." It includes "the labour of [our] body and the work of [our] hands." It is also the fruits of our labour—the products we make and the goods we buy. They belong to us because we've earned them.

For Locke, private property is important because it defines the boundaries of individual freedom. Within the boundaries of their property, the individual has the right to do as he or she wishes and the state has no right to intrude. This principle may seem obvious to us, to the point where we take it for granted. But it wasn't always the case, certainly not before Locke's time, when land defined wealth and most of the land was owned by a relatively small aristocratic elite or the sovereign.

Locke believed in extending the right of private ownership beyond the privileged few. In doing so, he also endorsed the right to privacy itself, a mainstay of a free and open society. In 1968, Prime Minister Pierre Trudeau echoed Locke's view when he proclaimed, "The state has no business in the bedrooms of the nation." In the privacy of our own homes, Trudeau meant, the state has no business defining what is acceptable or unacceptable sexual behaviour between consenting adults.

JOHN LOCKE

The great and chief end, therefore, of men's uniting into commonwealths and putting themselves under government is the preservation of their property. To which in the state of nature there are many things wanting:

First, There wants an established, settled, known law, received and allowed by common consent to be the standard of right and wrong and the common measure to decide all controversies between them. . . .

Secondly, In the state of nature there wants a known and indifferent judge with authority to determine all differences according to the established law. . . .

Thirdly, In the state of nature, there often wants power to back and support the sentence when right, and to give it due execution. . . .

Men . . . enter into society . . .with an intention in every one the better to preserve himself, his liberty and property . . . the power of the society, or legislative constituted by them, can never be supposed to extend farther than the common good. . . . And so whoever has the legislative or supreme power of any commonwealth is bound to govern by established standing laws, promulgated and known to the people, and not by extemporary decrees. . . .

John Locke, *Second Treatise on Government*

As industrial capitalism in Western Europe and North America developed, Locke's notion of ownership and private property was expanded to include the tools, machines, factories, transportation systems, capital and human resources that made further accumulation of property possible. But clearly not everyone benefitted under such a system, and the freedom, rights, laws and justice that protected the new privileged minority class did not extend to the masses.

So where Locke saw private property as the basis of freedom, socialist thinkers like Karl Marx saw it as the basis of exploitation. And where Locke argued that property was the basis of liberty, Marx replied that it was the basis of inhumanity. According to Marx, private ownership created an intolerable conflict between the "haves" and "have-nots," and, therefore, the only way to eliminate this conflict was to eliminate private property.

The Class Motive

Karl Marx

Born in Germany and living much of his life in exile, Karl Marx (1818–1883) analyzed the great divide in terms of wealth and power between the capitalist owners, or bourgeoisie, and the workers, or proletariat. Rejecting Locke's view of the sanctity of individual ownership, Marx called for a revolution to redistribute social, economic and political power. According to Marx, history showed that it was not natural rights or a social contract that defined the nature of our relationship to society. It was class status—rich and poor, haves and have-nots, the powerful and the powerless. To resolve the conflict between the classes and re-organize the social order in a way that guaranteed true freedom, rights and justice, it

KARL MARX

The State, therefore, has not existed from all eternity. There have been societies which managed without it, which had no conception of the State and State power. At a certain stage of economic development, which was necessarily bound up with the cleavage of society into classes, the State became a necessity owing to this cleavage.

As the State arose out of the need to hold class antagonisms in check, but as it, at the same time, arose in the midst of the conflict of these classes, it is, as a rule, the State of the most powerful, economically dominant class, which by virtue thereof becomes also the dominant class politically, and thus acquires new means of holding down and exploiting the oppressed class. Thus the ancient State was above all the slaveowners' State for holding down the slaves, as a feudal State was the organ of the nobles for holding down the peasantry, bondsmen and serfs and the modern representative State is the instrument of the exploitation of wage-labour by capital.

Karl Marx, *The German Ideology*

was necessary to abolish private property.

Marx disagreed with those historians and political philosophers who contend that our innate human nature predisposes us to one kind of society or another. According to Marx, it is the other way around: the kind of society we live in determines our consciousness, or how we act and think. If we think of government as grounded in a Lockean social contract which exists to protect the so-called "natural right" to property, this simply reflects the capitalist society in which we live. If people are as selfish and greedy as Hobbes believed, moreover, the reason has little to do with human nature and everything to do with social conditions that simultaneously create scarcity for some and abundance for others.

As proof, Marx turned to capitalism. Throughout industrialized Europe, Marx saw men, women and children working long hours in unsafe mines and factories for wages that were a fraction of what their labour entitled them to. They had no pensions, health insurance or safety protection. They had no collective agreements, job security or social safety net. Capitalism, Marx argued, really offers only two possibilities: be a loser or a winner, exploit others or be exploited yourself.

Marx believed that this "survival of the fittest" mentality is the very essence of industrial capitalism. The division of labour and alienation that turns workers into products, into property belonging to someone else, destroys the human spirit and causes untold suffering. If life is a Hobbesian war of all against all, it is not, according to Marx, human nature that causes this war but a society based on class conflict.

Marx did not look to government or the church or past political theory to change this situation. In his view, government, religion, media, philosophy, even the education system itself—all the institutions of capitalist society— serve the interests of the capitalists who control them and keep the working class in their place. Indeed, he rejected the social contract theories of thinkers like Hobbes and Locke, as Marx believed that they simply served to justify the *status quo*. Marx was especially critical of the role played by organized religion, which, he said, is "the opiate of the people" insofar as it makes them passive and accepting of their misery in this life by promising them rewards in the next.

But there is no afterlife, Marx argued, only this one. And he looked to the proletariat to lead the revolution that would destroy class conflict, eradicate scarcity and alter the course of world history: "Workers of the world unite!" he wrote in *The Communist Manifesto*, adding, "You have nothing to lose but your chains!"

Marx's view of history led him to reason that just as slavery had given way to feudalism, and feudalism to capitalism, so too capitalism would inevitably lead to socialism. Under socialism, ownership of the means of production would be collective, not private. The welfare of people would come before profit, and everyone would share in society's resources and wealth—"from each according to his abilities, to each according to his needs." Beyond socialism lay the "classless society" of communism, the promised land where, according to Marx, the state itself would "wither away."

Marx's influence on the 20th century is undeniable. Until the collapse of the Soviet Union in 1991, over a third of the world's population claimed to be living under some form of communism. But whether Marx would have been happy with those who have practised what he preached is highly unlikely. Communist revolutions in Europe, Asia, Latin America and Africa resulted in nothing like the free, classless and just societies that Marx envisioned.

Nevertheless, Marx's socialist ideals have had a profound impact on capitalism itself. Today free schooling to age 16, government student loans and scholarships, universal health care and progressive taxation policies are characteristic of many capitalist societies. And so is the belief in a mixed economy of public and private ownership. Ironically, Marx's legacy may have been to help renew the very capitalist system that he was so certain was doomed.

The Happiness Motive

John Stuart Mill

For John Stuart Mill (1806–1879), yet another English political theorist, the purpose of life is the pursuit of happiness. And this, not natural rights or class conflict, is the guiding principle of human action. According to Mill's "utilitarian" philosophy (derived from Jeremy Bentham [1748–1832]), actions are good if they promote the greatest happiness for the greatest number of people. But this position doesn't include just any kind of happiness. Mill argued that some types of happiness are better than others; as he said, "it is better to be a human being dissatisfied than a pig satisfied." In other words, it is better to aspire to intellectual and aesthetic pleasures than to simply satisfy physical desire. Mill believed that a society that values rights, laws and justice is the best guarantee of both individual and collective happiness.

In what kind of society can happiness best be achieved? A society, Mill argued, liberal enough to allow individuals maximum freedom to do whatever they want, as long as their actions don't harm others. Because he believed that people are basically decent and by nature are rational, cooperative and sensitive to the needs of others, Mill trusted people's ability to choose what is best for themselves. And what is "best," of course, is whatever makes people happy.

Mill argued that the primary job of government is to preserve individual rights and freedoms. He rejected the notion that government should simply stand back and let people fend for themselves. He advocated instead the idea of government intervention—not to tell people what to do or to curtail their liberty—but rather to provide the means for them to make choices through enlightened education, progressive laws and a fair justice system.

As already suggested, Mill believed that once government has made the advantages of liberal democracy available to all, it should restrain an individual's actions *only* when they significantly harm or interfere with the actions, interests or liberty of others. But some of us may have problems with the "harm principle." For example, how can we be sure when you smoke that I, a non-smoker, am not harmed? You can argue that you'll take

JOHN STUART MILL

The object of this Essay is to assert one very simple principle, as entitled to govern absolutely the dealings of society with the individual in the way of compulsion and control, whether the means used be physical force in the form of legal penalties, or the moral coercion of public opinion. That principle is, that the sole end for which mankind are warranted, individually or collectively, in interfering with the liberty of action of any of their number, is self-protection. That the only purpose for which power can be rightfully exercised over any member of a civilized community, against his will, is to prevent harm to others. His own good, either physical or moral, is not a sufficient warrant. He cannot rightfully be compelled to do or forbear because it will be better for him to do so, because it will make him happier, because, in the opinions of others, to do so would be wise, or even right. These are good reasons for remonstrating with him, or reasoning with him, or persuading him, or entreating him, but not compelling him, or visiting him with any evil, in case he do otherwise. To justify that, the conduct from which it is desired to deter him must be calculated to produce evil to someone else. The only part of the conduct of anyone, for which he is amenable to society, is that which concerns others. In the part which merely concerns himself, his independence is, of right, absolute. Over himself, over his own body and mind, the individual is sovereign.

*****

The worth of a State, in the long run, is the worth of the individuals composing it; and a State which postpones the interests of their mental expansion and elevation to a little more of administrative skill, or of that semblance of it which practice gives, in the details of business; a State which dwarfs its men, in order that they may be more docile instruments in its hands even for beneficial purposes—will find that with small men no great thing can really be accomplished; and that the perfection of machinery to which it has sacrificed everything will in the end avail it nothing, for want of the vital power which, in order that the machine might work more smoothly, it has preferred to banish.

John Stuart Mill, *On Liberty*

responsibility if you get lung cancer. But your second-hand smoke can give me lung cancer too. So where does your right to smoke end and my right to breathe clean air begin?

You might also argue that the government has no right to enforce measures of individual choice such as whether you wear a seat-belt. You may say you'll take your chances in your own car, thank you very much. But if you go through the windshield, whose tax dollars will help to pay for your rehabilitation—assuming you survive?

And then, of course, there's the issue of freedom of speech. Does free speech mean that you have the right to say things that could threaten the interests, offend the beliefs or even jeopardize the physical well-being of certain racial, religious or other groups? In 2005, an international controversy was provoked when a Danish newspaper, the *Jyllands-Posten,* published 12 cartoons involving the Prophet Mohammed. Many people around the world protested that the cartoons were offensive to Islam and, therefore, should not have been published. But others argued that censorship violates the right to free speech and, therefore, newspapers should be allowed to publish the cartoons, offensive or not. Indeed, a number of newspapers all around the world did just that, including Alberta's now defunct *Western Standard*. In the end, approximately 100 people were killed in protests around the world and a number of editors were suspended or fired for publishing the cartoons.

As this example shows, Mill's "harm principle" does not deal fully with problems resulting from the impact that an individual's actions may have on others (abortion is another perhaps even more troubling example). However, Mill did anticipate objections to his utilitarian principle of "the greatest happiness for the greatest number."

In our discussion of pluralism in the second unit, you may recall, we noted how the ideas, customs, laws, privileges and opportunities that bring happiness to the greatest number in society can sometimes bring misery to minorities. Mill acknowledged the potential dangers of this "tyranny of the majority." He believed, therefore, that a democratic society should not only be liberal (i.e., promote individual rights), but should also be representative and pluralistic (i.e., safeguard minority rights).

Unlike Marx, Mill did not call for the demise of capitalism. Nor did he view history as a class conflict between owners and workers, haves and have-nots. The issue for Mill was the conflict between individual freedom and government control. Mill believed strongly that in this struggle the balance of power should rest with the individual because the purpose of government is to serve the people, not the other way around.

"Politics in the Life of the Individual" was written for *The Human Project* by Morton Ritts, a professor at the Humber College Institute of Technology and Advanced Learning. Used by permission.

Soul Force versus Physical Force

Morton Ritts

Satyagraha

Marx argued that social change could only come about as a result of revolutionary economic change. Mill, on the other hand, believed that social change was the result of enlightened political reform. Like Mill, Mahatma Gandhi (1869–1948) was also a reformer. But he believed that social change was the result of spiritual change—a transformation of the soul that would be the basis of a new and truly just social order.

This revolutionary idea was embodied in Gandhi's criticism of the Hindu caste system, which separated people into various classes from Brahmin at the upper end to the Untouchables at the lower. Rejecting his own high-caste background, Gandhi sought to eliminate the enormous social divisions created by such a hierarchy and replace them with a classless society (similar to Marx's) that affirmed the brotherhood and sisterhood of all.

Gandhi had a very **benign** view of human nature, believing that people are good, that the world is ultimately just and that peaceful political change is **eminently** possible. According to Gandhi, real and lasting change was achieved not through violence but through the Hindu principle of *ahimsa*, or non-violence. Gandhi believed that *ahimsa* was a universal spiritual force within all humans that could be awakened by example.

The way to awaken the conscience of one's oppressor was through non-violent acts of civil disobedience that Gandhi called *satyagraha*—"soul force"—as opposed to "body force." This turning of the other cheek wasn't some masochistic invitation to be beaten by the police or army during strikes, mass demonstrations or marches. Instead, *satyagraha* was a way to change an enemy's hatred to love, their resistance to acceptance, and their opposition to unity.

Despite his charismatic leadership, Gandhi was assassinated just a few months before India gained its independence from Britain in 1947. While his non-violent politics of liberation had an enormous global influence, it none-theless had its critics. Theorists who side with Darwin, Freud or Hobbes think Gandhi's views of human nature and political change are naive and simplistic. Moreover, they argue that while non-violence may have been successful in the struggle against British **colonialism**, it would have been

benign
favourable

eminently
highly

colonialism
acquisition, control and exploitation of foreign colonies

This article was written for *The Human Project*. Used by permission.

useless against the radical evil of Nazi Germany. Gandhi's harshest critics believed him to be an impractical and even dangerous idealist.

Non-Violent Civil Disobedience

But Gandhi has had his supporters—social reformers inspired by his spirituality and the philosophy of *satyagraha*. One man who was strongly influenced by Gandhi was the American civil rights leader Martin Luther King Jr. (1929–1968). Like Gandhi, King believed in the innate goodness of human nature, that "we are all God's children," and that the universe is a moral and just place.

One of the great public speakers in American history, King was a Baptist minister from the American South steeped in the prophetic tradition of the Bible, which he saw as a narrative of liberation and **deliverance**. King's Jesus was a social activist who championed the rights of the poor and downtrodden. It wasn't difficult for King to identify with Gandhi's struggle against the bondage of colonialism. After all, the United States was a country that claimed to be a beacon of freedom and equality, but a hundred years after the Civil War, black Americans had a long way to go before they could enjoy the "liberty, equality and freedom" that the Constitution promised everyone.

deliverance
salvation

Like Marx, King saw the struggle between haves and have-nots as the defining feature of history. But unlike Marx, for whom religion was an oppressive institution, King saw religion as a liberating force that led to social and political change. He believed that white America was ultimately a just society but, like Gandhi, disagreed with Marx's ideology of violent revolution. Violence, he argued, led only to more violence. It could never form the basis of a viable social contract.

King believed it was possible to achieve his goal of an integrated society by changing people's hearts and minds. Reform the spirit, he preached, and you will reform the attitudes and laws that barred blacks from being part of the American Dream. Few leaders in the world today dare to talk about issues like rights and freedom in a spiritual context. King did, and succeeded in raising the debate over justice to a level of moral significance not seen in American political culture since the time of Lincoln.

In his famous "Letter" from Birmingham Jail, where he was briefly imprisoned for breaking a local ordinance against political demonstrations, King pointed out that there were two kinds of laws: just and unjust. Just laws were those that uplift the human spirit. People have a legal and moral obligation to obey them. Unjust laws, on the other hand, were those that degrade the human spirit—laws that prohibited blacks from using "whites only" washrooms and restaurants or denied them the same opportunities as whites for employment, housing and education. According to King, we have a moral responsibility to actively disobey unjust laws.His argument has profound implications for human behaviour. For example, if more people had acted like Oscar Schindler (whose story is told in the film *Schindler's List*) and resisted the laws and official directives that sent millions to the Nazi death camps during World War II, they could have changed the course of history. King's moral universe of civil disobedience based on principle exists in direct contrast to the usual political motives of **expedience** and self-interest.

expedience

taking advantage of opportunities without regard for principles

But for King, as we've said, civil disobedience had to be non-violent. Like Gandhi, he had no doubt that soul force was stronger than physical force, and that loving one's enemy was the only way to truly humanize and change him. Throughout the late 1950s and 1960s, King helped to organize countless voter registration drives, freedom rides, sit-ins, marches and rallies involving thousands of black and white Americans who were often harassed, threatened, beaten, arrested and killed for their efforts.

In the end, the civil rights movement stirred the conscience of America and the world. Landmark civil rights legislation was introduced in 1965 and King won the Nobel Peace Prize. But he paid dearly. He was assassinated in 1968. Like Moses, he led his long-suffering people to the Promised Land, and, like Moses, he didn't live to enter.

"By Any Means Necessary"

Martin Luther King promoted non-violence as the means to reform an unjust society because, like Gandhi, he believed in the fundamental decency of human nature and in a world where, in the end, good triumphs over evil. But just as Gandhi had his critics, so did King. And since his death some of their voices seem to speak more loudly to black Americans than his.

In the United States today, for example, the Nation of Islam has a powerful following among those African-Americans who argue that racial integration can't work, that the separation of black and white races is both desirable and necessary, and that blacks must reconnect with their African roots. If such views sound surprising in light of King's reputation, it is important to remember that, even at the height of the civil rights movement, King was only one of several major African-American leaders who didn't always agree on ideology or strategy. One of King's major rivals for the loyalty of black Americans was Malcolm X (1925–1965).

Malcolm X's critical analysis of white American society and his prescription for change differed radically from King's. After Malcolm X came into contact with the ideas of the Nation of Islam, he changed his surname from "Little" to "X" to indicate that, as the descendant of slaves, he'd been stripped of his ancestral identity.

Soon thereafter, he became chief spokesman for the Nation of Islam and its founder, Elijah Muhammad (1897–1975). In brilliant speeches that were inflammatory and confrontational, Malcolm X condemned white people as "blue-eyed devils" who could never be trusted. He rejected Christianity as a racist, oppressive "white man's religion" that didn't speak to the true black identity, which was African. King and other black Christians had "sold out," Malcolm X said.

The philosophy of the Nation of Islam stressed the need for black pride, independence, discipline and power. These could be achieved, Malcolm X argued, if African-Americans challenged whites on their own terms by developing their own banks and businesses, their own churches and schools, their own social and cultural support systems. Only through "black power" would African-Americans gain the freedom, justice and equality that was their right.

For the Nation of Islam, black power meant separation, not integration. Black Muslims also disagreed with King's philosophy of non-violence. Self-preservation "by any means necessary" was justified, Malcolm X said. This meant fighting back, not turning the other cheek.

In 1964, Malcolm X went to Mecca in Saudi Arabia, the spiritual capital of Islam. There he met Muslims of all races and nations worshipping together in peace, equality and dignity. The experience moved him to reject racial hatred as a liberation strategy. He began to view the struggle against oppression in universal terms, not exclusively African-American.

After returning to the United States, he broke with Elijah Muhammad and the Nation of Islam, becoming an orthodox Sunni Muslim who believed that the social order should embrace all peoples. It was while preaching this new message of hope and solidarity that he was gunned down in 1965.

Malcolm X, Martin Luther King and Mahatma Gandhi may have shared similar violent ends, but their words and actions continue to haunt and shape contemporary politics.

"Soul Force versus Physical Force" was written for *The Human Project* by Morton Ritts, a professor at the Humber College Institute of Technology and Advanced Learning. Used by permission.

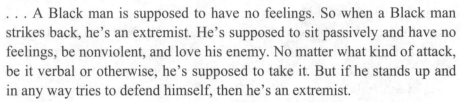

By Any Means Necessary to Bring about Freedom

Malcolm X

Malcolm X

. . . A Black man is supposed to have no feelings. So when a Black man strikes back, he's an extremist. He's supposed to sit passively and have no feelings, be nonviolent, and love his enemy. No matter what kind of attack, be it verbal or otherwise, he's supposed to take it. But if he stands up and in any way tries to defend himself, then he's an extremist.

. . . My reason for believing in extremism—intelligently directed extremism, extremism in defence of liberty, extremism in quest of justice—is because I firmly believe in my heart that the day that the Black man takes an uncompromising step and realizes that he's within his rights, when his own freedom is being jeopardized, to use any means necessary to bring about his freedom or put a halt to that injustice, I don't think he'll be by himself.

I live in America, where there are only 22 million Blacks against probably 160 million whites. One of the reasons that I'm in no way reluctant or hesitant to do whatever is necessary to see that Black people do something to protect themselves [is that] I honestly believe that the day that they do, many whites will have more respect for them. And there will be more whites on their side than are now on their side with this little wishy-washy "love-thy-enemy" approach that they've been using up to now.

And if I'm wrong, then you are racialists.

. . . I'm a Muslim. I believe in the religion of Islam. I believe in Allah, I believe in Muhammad, I believe in all of the prophets. I believe in fasting, prayer, charity, and that which is **incumbent** upon a Muslim to fulfill in order to be a Muslim. In April I was fortunate to make the **hajj** to Mecca and went back again in September to try and carry out my religious functions and requirements.

But at the same time that I believe in that religion, I have to point out I'm also an American Negro, and I live in a society whose social system is based upon the castration of the Black man, whose political system is based on castration of the Black man, and whose economy is based upon the castration of the Black man. A society which, in 1964, has more subtle, deceptive, deceitful methods to make the rest of the world think that it's cleaning up its house, while at the same time the same things are happening to us in 1964 that happened in 1954, 1924, and in 1894.

They came up with what they call a civil rights bill in 1964, supposedly to

incumbent
obligatory

hajj
pilgrimage to Mecca

This reading originally appeared as part of a formal debate hosted by Oxford University on December 3, 1964. Malcolm X argued in favour of the proposition, "Extremism in defense of liberty is no vice, moderation in the pursuit of justice is no virtue." This excerpt appears in *Malcolm X Talks to Young People: Speeches in the United States, Britain, and Africa* Copyright © 1965, 1970, 1991, 2002 by Betty Shabazz and Pathfinder Press. Reprinted by permission.

solve our problem, and after the bill was signed, three civil rights workers were murdered in cold blood.[1] And the FBI head, [J. Edgar] Hoover, admits that they know who did it. They've known ever since it happened, and they've done nothing about it. Civil rights bill down the drain. No matter how many bills pass, Black people in that country where I'm from—still, our lives are not worth two cents. And the government has shown its inability, or its unwillingness, to do whatever is necessary to protect life and property where the Black American is concerned.

So my contention is that whenever a people come to the conclusion that the government which they have supported proves itself unwilling or proves itself unable to protect our lives and protect our property because we have the wrong colour skin, we are not human beings unless we ourselves band together and do whatever, however, whenever is necessary to see that our lives and our property are protected. And I doubt that any person in here would refuse to do the same thing, were he in the same position. Or I should say, were he in the same condition.

Just one step farther to see, am I justified in this stand? And I say, I'm speaking as a Black man from America, which is a racist society. No matter how much you hear it talk about democracy, it's as racist as South Africa or as racist as Portugal, or as racist as any other racialist society on this earth. The only difference between it and South Africa: South Africa preaches separation and practises separation; America preaches integration and practises segregation. This is the only difference. They don't practise what they preach, whereas South Africa preaches and practises the same thing. I have more respect for a man who lets me know where he stands, even if he's wrong, than the one who comes up like an angel and is nothing but a devil.

The system of government that America has consists of committees. There are sixteen senatorial committees that govern the country and twenty congressional committees. Ten of the sixteen senatorial committees are in the hands of southern racialists, senators who are racialists. . . . Thirteen of the twenty congressional committees were in the hands of southern congressmen who are racialists. Which means out of the thirty-six committees that govern the foreign and domestic direction of that government, twenty-three are in the hands of southern racialists—men who in no way believe in the equality of man, and men who'd do anything within their power to see that the Black man never gets to the same seat or to the same level that they are on.

The reason that these men from that area have that type of power is because America has a seniority system. And those who have that seniority have been there longer than anyone else because the Black people in the areas where they live can't vote. And it is only because the Black man is deprived of his vote that puts these men in positions of power, that gives them such influence in the government beyond their actual intellectual or political ability, or even beyond the number of people from the areas that they represent.

So we can see in that country that no matter what the federal government professes to be doing, the power of the federal government lies in these committees. And any time any kind of legislation is proposed to benefit the Black man or give the Black man his just due, we find it is locked up in these committees right here. And when they let something through the committee, usually it is so chopped up and fixed up that by the time it becomes law, it's a law that can't be enforced.

Another example is the Supreme Court desegregation decision that was handed down in 1954.[2] This is a law, and they have not been able to implement this law in New York City, or in Boston, or in Cleveland, or Chicago, or the northern cities. And my contention is that any time you have a country, supposedly a democracy, supposedly the land of the free and the home of the brave, and it can't enforce laws—even in the northernmost, cosmopolitan, and progressive part of it—that will benefit a Black man, if those laws can't be enforced or that law can't be enforced, how much heart do you think we will get when they pass some civil rights legislation which only involves more laws? If they can't enforce this law, they will never enforce those laws.

So my contention is that we are faced with a racialistic society, a society in which they are deceitful, deceptive, and the only way we can bring about a change is to talk the kind of language—speak the language that they understand. The racialists never understand a peaceful language. The racialist never understands the nonviolent language. The racialist we have, he's spoken his language to us for four hundred years.

We have been the victim of his brutality. We are the ones who face his dogs that tear the flesh from our limbs, only because we want to enforce the Supreme Court decision. We are the ones who have our skulls crushed, not by the Ku Klux Klan but by policemen, only because we want to enforce what they call the Supreme Court decision. We are the ones upon whom water hoses are turned, with pressure so hard that it rips the clothes from our backs—not men, but the clothes from the backs of women and children. You've seen it yourselves. Only because we want to enforce what they call the law.Well, any time you live in a society supposedly based upon law, and it doesn't enforce its own law because the colour of a man's skin happens to be wrong, then I say those people are justified to resort to any means necessary to bring about justice where the government can't give them justice.

I don't believe in any form of unjustified extremism. But I believe that when a man is exercising extremism, a human being is exercising extremism in defence of liberty for human beings, it's no vice. And when one is moderate in the pursuit of justice for human beings, I say he's a sinner.

And I might add, in my conclusion—in fact, America is one of the best examples, when you read its history, about extremism. Old **Patrick Henry** said, "Liberty or death!" That's extreme, very extreme.

I read once, passingly, about a man named Shakespeare. I only read about him passingly, but I remember one thing he wrote that kind of moved me. He put it in the mouth of Hamlet, I think it was, who said, "To be or not to be"— he was in doubt about something. "Whether it was nobler in the mind of man to suffer the slings and arrows of outrageous fortune"—moderation—"or to take up arms against a sea of troubles and by opposing end them."

And I go for that. If you take up arms, you'll end it. But if you sit around and wait for the one who's in power to make up his mind that he should end it, you'll be waiting a long time.

And in my opinion the young generation of whites, blacks, browns, whatever else there is—you're living at a time of extremism, a time of revolution, a time when there's got to be a change. People in power have misused it, and now there has to be a change and a better world has to be built, and the only way it's going to be built is with extreme methods. And I for one will join in with anyone, I don't care what colour you are, as long as you want to change this miserable condition that exists on this earth.

**Patrick Henry
(1736–1799)**

American Patriot known for his dramatic speeches

Notes

1 The Civil Rights Act of 1964, signed into law by President Lyndon B. Johnson on July 2, banned discrimination in voting, public facilities, schools, and employment. Two weeks earlier, three civil rights workers—two white, one black—had disappeared in Philadelphia, Mississippi. The battered bodies of Michael Schwerner, Andrew Goodman and James E. Chaney were found on August 4. At the time of the Oxford Union debate, the FBI had still made no arrests.

2 Ruling on a case called *Brown v. Board of Education*, the U.S. Supreme Court declared in 1954 that segregated school systems, which it had previously upheld as lawful, were in violation of the Constitution.

Non-Violent Resistance

Mohandas K. (Mahatma) Gandhi

Means and Ends

Gandhi

petitioning
submitting a formal request, usually signed by a group of people, for a right or privilege

grievous
brutal

noxious
unpleasant

votary
a person bound by vows to live a life of religious worship

inviolable
necessary

prostrate
in a submissive bow

Reader: Why should we not obtain our goal, which is good, by any means whatsoever, even by using violence? Shall I think of the means when I have to deal with a thief in the house? My duty is to drive him out anyhow. You seem to admit that we have received nothing, and that we shall receive nothing by **petitioning**. Why, then, may we not do so by using brute force? And, to retain what we may receive we shall keep up the fear by using the same force to the extent that it may be necessary. You will not find fault with a continuance of force to prevent a child from thrusting its foot into fire? Somehow or other we have to gain our end.

Gandhi: Your reasoning is plausible. It has deluded many. I have used similar arguments before now. But I think I know better now, and I shall endeavour to undeceive you. Let us first take the argument that we are justified in gaining our end by using brute force because the English gained theirs by using similar means. It is perfectly true that they use brute force and that it is possible for us to do likewise, but by using similar means we can get only the same thing that they got. You will admit that we do not want that. Your belief that there is no connection between the means and the end is a great mistake. Through that mistake even men who have been considered religious have committed **grievous** crimes. Your reasoning is the same as saying that we can get a rose through planting a **noxious** weed. If I want to cross the ocean, I can do so only by means of a vessel; if I were to use a cart for that purpose, both the cart and I would soon find the bottom. "As is the God, so is the **votary**," is a maxim worth considering. Its meaning has been distorted and men have gone astray. The means may be likened to a seed, the end to a tree; and there is just the same **inviolable** connection between the means and the end as there is between the seed and the tree. I am not likely to obtain the result flowing from the worship of God by laying myself **prostrate** before Satan. If, therefore, any one were to say: "I want to worship God; it does not matter that I do so by means of Satan," it would be set down as ignorant folly. We reap exactly as we sow. The English in 1833 obtained greater voting power by violence. Did they by using brute force better ap-preciate their duty? They wanted the right of voting, which they obtained by using physical force. But real rights are a result of performance of duty; these rights they have not obtained. We, therefore, have before us in England the force of everybody wanting and insisting on his rights, nobody thinking of his duty. And where everybody wants rights, who shall give them to whom? I do not wish to imply that they do no duties. They don't perform the duties corresponding to those rights; and as they do not perform that particular duty, namely, acquire fitness, their rights have proved a burden to them. In other words, what they have obtained is an exact result of the means they adopted. They used the means corresponding to the end. If I want to deprive you of your watch, I shall certainly have to fight for it; if I want to buy your watch, I shall have to pay for it; and if I want a gift, I shall have to plead for it; and, according to the means I employ, the watch is stolen property, my own property, or a donation. Thus we see three different results from three different means. Will you still say that means do not matter?

Now we shall take the example given by you of the thief to be driven out. I do not agree with you that the thief may be driven out by any means. If it is my father who has come to steal I shall use one kind of means. If it is an acquaintance I shall use another; and in the case of a perfect stranger I shall use a third. If it is a white man, you will perhaps say you will use means different from those you will adopt with an Indian thief. If it is a weakling, the means will be different from those to be adopted for dealing with an equal in physical strength; and if the thief is armed from top to toe, I shall simply remain quiet. Thus we have a variety of means between the father and the armed man. Again, I fancy that I should pretend to be sleeping whether the thief was my father or that strong armed man. The reason for this is that my father would also be armed and I should succumb to the strength possessed by either and allow my things to be stolen. The strength of my father would make me weep with pity; the strength of the armed man would rouse in me anger and we should become enemies. Such is the curious situation. From these examples we may not be able to agree as to the means to be adopted in each case. I myself seem clearly to see what should be done in all these cases, but the remedy may frighten you. I therefore hesitate to place it before you. For the time being I will leave you to guess it, and if you cannot, it is clear you will have to adopt different means in each case. You will also have seen that any means will not avail to drive away the thief. You will have to adopt means to fit each case. Hence it follows that your duty is not to drive away the thief by any means you like.

Let us proceed a little further. That well-armed man has stolen your property; you have harboured the thought of his act; you are filled with anger; you argue that you want to punish that rogue, not for your own sake, but for the good of your neighbours; you have collected a number of armed men, you want to take his house by assault; he is duly informed of it, he runs away: he too is incensed. He collects his brother robbers, and sends you a

depredations
attacks

between Scylla and Charybdis
situation in which avoiding one danger exposes you to another danger; from the mythical sea route between Scylla and Charybdis, two sea monsters

belabour
beat

defiant message that he will commit robbery in broad daylight. You are strong, you do not fear him, you are prepared to receive him. Meanwhile, the robber pesters your neighbours. They complain before you. You reply that you are doing all for their sake, you do not mind that your own goods have been stolen. Your neighbours reply that the robber never pestered them before, and that he commenced his **depredations** only after you declared hostilities against him. You are **between Scylla and Charybdis**. You are full of pity for the poor men. What they say is true. What are you to do? You will be disgraced if you now leave the robber alone. You, therefore, tell the poor men: "Never mind. Come, my wealth is yours, I will give you arms, I will teach you how to use them; you should **belabour** the rogue; don't you leave him alone." And so the battle grows: the robbers increase in numbers; your neighbours have deliberately put themselves to inconvenience. Thus the result of wanting to take revenge upon the robber is that you have disturbed your own peace; you are in perpetual fear of being robbed and assaulted; your courage has given place to cowardice. If you will patiently examine the argument, you will see that I have not overdrawn the picture. This is one of the means. Now let us examine the other. You set this armed robber down as an ignorant brother; you intend to reason with him at a suitable opportunity; you argue that he is, after all, a fellow man; you do not know what prompted him to steal. You, therefore, decide that, when you can, you will destroy the man's motive for stealing. Whilst you are thus reasoning with yourself, the man comes again to steal. Instead of being angry with him you take pity on him. You think that this stealing habit must be a disease with him. Henceforth, you, therefore, keep your doors and windows open, you change your sleeping-place, and you keep your things in a manner most accessible to him. The robber comes again and is confused as all this is new to him; nevertheless, he takes away your things. But his mind is agitated. He inquires about you in the village, he comes to learn about your broad and loving heart, he repents, he begs your pardon, returns you your things, and leaves off the stealing habit. He becomes your servant, and you will find for him honourable employment. This is the second method. Thus, you see, different means have brought about totally different results. I do not wish to deduce from this that robbers will act in the above manner or that all will have the same pity and love like you, but I only wish to show that fair means alone can produce fair results, and that, at least in the majority of cases, if not indeed in all, the force of love and pity is infinitely greater than the force of arms. There is harm in the exercise of brute force, never in that of pity.

Now we will take the question of petitioning. It is a fact beyond dispute that a petition, without the backing of force, is useless. However, the late **Justice Ranade** used to say that petitions served a useful purpose

Justice Ranade (1842–1910)
Bombay High Court judge who was a founding member of the Indian National Congress

because they were a means of educating people. They give the latter an idea of their condition and warn the rulers. From this point of view, they are not altogether useless. A petition backed by force is a petition from an equal and, when he transmits his demand in the form of a petition, it testifies to his nobility. Two kinds of force can back petitions. "We shall hurt you if you do not give this," is one kind of force; it is the force of arms, whose evil results we have already examined. The second kind of force can thus be stated: "If you do not concede our demand, we shall be no longer your petitioners. You can govern us only so long as we remain the governed; we shall no longer have any dealings with you." The force implied in this may be described as love-force, soul-force, or, more popularly but less accurately, passive resistance. This force is indestructible. He who uses it perfectly understands his position. We have an ancient proverb which literally means: "One negative cures thirty-six diseases." The force of arms is powerless when matched against the force of love or the soul.

Now we shall take your last illustration, that of the child thrusting its foot into fire. It will not avail you. What do you really do to the child? Supposing that it can exert so much physical force that it renders you powerless and rushes into fire, then you cannot prevent it. There are only two remedies open to you—either you must kill it in order to prevent it from perishing in the flames, or you must give your own life because you do not wish to see it perish before your eyes. You will not kill it. If your heart is not quite full of pity, it is possible that you will not surrender yourself by preceding the child and going into the fire yourself. You, therefore, helplessly allow it to go to the flames. Thus, at any rate, you are not using physical force. I hope you will not consider that it is still physical force, though of a low order, when you would forcibly prevent the child from rushing toward the fire if you could. That force is of a different order and we have to understand what it is.

Remember that, in thus preventing the child, you are minding entirely its own interest, you are exercising authority for its sole benefit. Your example does not apply to the English. In using brute force against the English you consult entirely your own, that is the national, interest. There is no question here either of pity or of love. If you say that the actions of the English, being evil, represent fire, and that they proceed to their actions through ignorance, and that therefore they occupy the position of a child and that you want to protect such a child, then you will have to overtake every evil action of that kind by whomsoever committed and, as in the case of the evil child, you will have to sacrifice yourself. If you are capable of such immeasurable pity, I wish you well in its exercise.

Jihad vs. McWorld

Benjamin Barber

Just beyond the horizon of current events lie two possible political futures—both bleak, neither democratic. The first is a retribalization of large swaths of humankind by war and bloodshed: a threatened **Lebanonization** of national states in which culture is pitted against culture, people against people, tribe against tribe—a Jihad in the name of a hundred narrowly conceived faiths against every kind of interdependence, every kind of artificial social cooperation and civic mutuality. The second is being borne in on us by the onrush of economic and ecological forces that demand integration and uniformity and that mesmerize the world with fast music, fast computers, and fast food—with MTV, Macintosh, and McDonald's, pressing nations into one commercially homogeneous global network: one McWorld tied together by technology, ecology, communications, and commerce. The planet is falling **precipitantly** apart and coming reluctantly together at the very same moment.

These two tendencies are sometimes visible in the same countries at the same instant: thus Yugoslavia, clamoring just recently to join the New Europe, is exploding into fragments; India is trying to live up to its reputation as the world's largest integral democracy while powerful new fundamentalist parties like the Hindu nationalist Bharatiya Janata Party, along with nationalist assassins, are **imperiling** its hard-won unity. States are breaking up or joining up: the Soviet Union has disappeared almost overnight, its parts forming new unions with one another or with likeminded nationalities in neighboring states. The old interwar national state based on territory and political **sovereignty** looks to be a mere transitional development.

The tendencies of what I am here calling the forces of Jihad and the forces of McWorld operate with equal strength in opposite directions, the one driven by **parochial** hatreds, the other by universalizing markets, the one re-creating ancient subnational and ethnic borders from within, the other making national borders porous from without. They have one thing in common: neither offers much hope to citizens looking for practical ways to govern themselves democratically. If the global future is to pit Jihad's **centrifugal** whirlwind against McWorld's **centripetal** black hole, the outcome is unlikely to be democratic—or so I will argue.

Lebanonization
reference to the disintegration of Lebanon into many warring factions during its civil war (1975–1992)

precipitantly
suddenly

imperiling
endangering

sovereignty
independence

parochial
local and limited

centrifugal
decentralizing and fragmenting

centripetal
centralizing and unifying

McWorld, or the Globalization of Politics

Four **imperatives** make up the dynamic of McWorld: a market imperative, a resource imperative, an information-technology imperative, and an ecological imperative. By shrinking the world and diminishing the **salience** of national borders, these imperatives have in combination achieved a considerable victory over **factiousness** and **particularism**, and not least of all over their most **virulent** traditional form—nationalism. It is the realists who are now Europeans, the utopians who dream nostalgically of a resurgent England or Germany, perhaps even a resurgent Wales or Saxony. Yesterday's wishful cry for one world has yielded to the reality of McWorld.

The market imperative. Marxist and Leninist theories of **imperialism** assumed that the quest for ever-expanding markets would in time compel nation-based capitalist economies to push against national boundaries in search of an international economic **imperium**. Whatever else has happened to the scientist predictions of Marxism, in this domain they have proved farsighted. All national economies are now vulnerable to the inroads of larger, transnational markets within which trade is free, currencies are convertible, access to banking is open, and contracts are enforceable under law. In Europe, Asia, Africa, the South Pacific, and the Americas such markets are eroding national sovereignty and giving rise to entities—international banks, trade associations, transnational lobbies like **OPEC** and Greenpeace, world news services like CNN and the BBC, and multinational corporations that increasingly lack a meaningful national identity—that neither reflect nor respect nationhood as an organizing or regulative principle.

The market imperative has also reinforced the quest for international peace and stability, requisites of an efficient international economy. Markets are enemies of parochialism, isolation, fractiousness, war. Market psychology **attenuates** the psychology of ideological and religious cleavages and assumes a concord among producers and consumers—categories that ill fit narrowly conceived national or religious cultures. Shopping has little tolerance for **blue laws**, whether dictated by pub-closing British paternalism, Sabbath-observing Jewish Orthodox fundamentalism, or no-Sunday-liquor-sales Massachusetts puritanism. In the context of common markets, international law ceases to be a vision of justice and becomes a workaday framework for getting things done—enforcing contracts, ensuring that governments abide by deals, regulating trade and currency relations, and so forth.

imperatives
essentials

salience
significance

factiousness
discord

particularism
exclusive concern for one's own people

virulent
antagonistic

imperialism
control by powerful states over others by conquest, colonization or economic dominance

imperium
power or rule

OPEC
Organization of the Petroleum Exporting Countries

attenuates
undermines

blue laws
laws that enforce strict moral standards

Common markets demand a common language, as well as a common currency, and they produce common behaviors of the kind bred by cosmopolitan city life everywhere. Commercial pilots, computer programmers, international bankers, media specialists, oil riggers, entertainment celebrities, ecology experts, demographers, accountants, professors, athletes—these compose a new breed of men and women for whom religion, culture, and nationality can seem only marginal elements in a working identity. Although sociologists of everyday life will no doubt continue to distinguish a Japanese from an American mode, shopping has a common signature throughout the world. Cynics might even say that some of the recent revolutions in Eastern Europe have had as their true goal not liberty and the right to vote but well-paying jobs and the right to shop (although the vote is proving easier to acquire than consumer goods). The market imperative is, then, plenty powerful; but, notwithstanding some of the claims made for "democratic capitalism," it is not identical with the democratic imperative.

The resource imperative. Democrats once dreamed of societies whose political autonomy rested firmly on economic independence. The Athenians idealized what they called **autarky**, and tried for a while to create a way of life simple and austere enough to make the **polis** genuinely self-sufficient. To be free meant to be independent of any other community or polis. Not even the Athenians were able to achieve autarky, however: human nature, it turns out, is dependency. By the time of **Pericles**, Athenian politics was inextricably bound up with a flowering empire held together by naval power and commerce—an empire that, even as it appeared to enhance Athenian might, ate away at Athenian independence and autarky. Master and slave, it turned out, were bound together by mutual insufficiency.

The dream of autarky briefly engrossed 19th-century America as well, for the underpopulated, endlessly bountiful land, the cornucopia of natural resources, and the natural barriers of a continent walled in by two great seas led many to believe that America could be a world unto itself. Given this past, it has been harder for Americans than for most to accept the inevitability of interdependence. But the rapid depletion of resources even in a country like ours, where they once seemed inexhaustible, and the maldistribution of arable soil and mineral resources on the planet, leave even the wealthiest societies ever more resource-dependent and many other nations in permanently desperate straits.

Every nation, it turns out, needs something another nation has; some nations have almost nothing they need.

The information-technology imperative. Enlightenment science and the technologies derived from it are inherently universalizing. They entail a quest for descriptive principles of general application, a search for universal

autarky
self-sufficiency

polis
an ancient Greek city-state, such as Athens

Pericles
(495–429 BCE) Athenian statesman and general

solutions to particular problems, and an unswerving embrace of objectivity and impartiality.

Scientific progress embodies and depends on open communication, a common discourse rooted in rationality, collaboration, and an easy and regular flow and exchange of information. Such ideals can be hypocritical covers for power-mongering by elites, and they may be shown to be wanting in many other ways, but they are entailed by the very idea of science and they make science and globalization practical allies.

Business, banking, and commerce all depend on information flow and are facilitated by new communication technologies. The hardware of these technologies tends to be systemic and integrated—computer, television, cable, satellite, laser, fibre-optic, and microchip technologies combining to create a vast interactive communications and information network that can potentially give every person on earth access to every other person, and make every datum, every byte, available to every set of eyes. If the automobile was, as **George Ball** once said (when he gave his blessing to a Fiat factory in the Soviet Union during the Cold War), "an ideology on four wheels," then electronic telecommunication and information systems are an ideology at 300 000 kilometers per second—which makes for a very small planet in a very big hurry. Individual cultures speak particular languages; commerce and science increasingly speak English; the whole world speaks logarithms and binary mathematics.

Moreover, the pursuit of science and technology asks for, even compels, open societies. Satellite footprints do not respect national borders; telephone wires penetrate the most closed societies. With photocopying and then fax machines having infiltrated Soviet universities and *samizdat* literary circles in the eighties, and computer modems having multiplied like rabbits in communism's bureaucratic warrens thereafter, *glasnost* could not be far behind. In their social requisites, secrecy and science are enemies.

The new technology's software is perhaps even more globalizing than its hardware. The information arm of international commerce's sprawling body reaches out and touches distinct nations and parochial cultures, and gives them a common face chiseled in Hollywood, on Madison Avenue, and in Silicon Valley. Throughout the 1980s one of the most-watched television programs in South Africa was *The Cosby Show*. The demise of **apartheid** was already in production. Exhibitors at the 1991 Cannes film festival expressed growing anxiety over the "homogenization" and "Americanization" of the global film industry where for the third year running, American films dominated the awards ceremonies. America has dominated the world's popular culture for much longer, and more decisively. In November of 1991 Switzerland's once insular culture boasted best-seller lists

George Ball
(1909–1994) American public servant

samizdat
underground circulation of literature banned in the Soviet Union

glasnost
Soviet policy of governmental openness and transparency introduced in the 1980s

apartheid
official policy of racial segregation in South Africa

featuring *Terminator 2* as the No. 1 movie, *Scarlett* as the No. 1 book, and Prince's *Diamonds and Pearls* as the No. 1 record album. No wonder the Japanese are buying Hollywood film studios even faster than Americans are buying Japanese television sets. This kind of software supremacy may in the long term be far more important than hardware superiority, because culture has become more potent than armaments. What is the power of the **Pentagon** compared with Disneyland's? Can the **Sixth Fleet** keep up with CNN? McDonald's in Moscow and Coke in China will do more to create a global culture than military colonization ever could. It is less the goods than the brand names that do the work, for they convey life-style images that alter perception and challenge behavior. They make up the seductive software of McWorld's common (at times much too common) soul.

Yet in all this high-tech commercial world there is nothing that looks particularly democratic. It lends itself to surveillance as well as liberty, to new forms of manipulation and covert control as well as new kinds of participation, to skewed, unjust market outcomes as well as greater productivity. The consumer society and the open society are not quite synonymous. Capitalism and democracy have a relationship, but it is something less than a marriage. An efficient free market after all requires that consumers be free to vote their dollars on competing goods, not that citizens be free to vote their values and beliefs on competing political candidates and programs. The free market flourished in **junta**-run Chile, in military-governed Taiwan and Korea, and, earlier, in a variety of autocratic European empires as well as their colonial possessions.

The ecological imperative. The impact of globalization on ecology is a cliché even to world leaders who ignore it. We know well enough that the German forests can be destroyed by Swiss and Italians driving gas-guzzlers fuelled by leaded gas. We also know that the planet can be asphyxiated by greenhouse gases because Brazilian farmers want to be part of the 20th century and are burning down tropical rain forests to clear a little land to plow, and because Indonesians make a living out of converting their lush jungle into toothpicks for fastidious Japanese diners, upsetting the delicate oxygen balance and in effect puncturing our global lungs. Yet this ecological consciousness has meant not only greater awareness but also greater in-equality, as modernized nations try to slam the door behind them, saying to developing nations, "The world cannot afford *your* modernization; ours has wrung it dry!"

Each of the four imperatives just cited is transnational, transideological, and transcultural. Each applies impartially to Catholics, Jews, Muslims, Hindus, and Buddhists; to democrats and totalitarians; to capitalists and socialists. The Enlightenment dream of a universal rational society has to a

Pentagon
headquarters of the US Department of Defence

Sixth Fleet
operational unit of the US Navy

junta
a group of military officers who seize control of government

remarkable degree been realized—but in a form that is commercialized, homogenized, depoliticized, bureaucratized, and, of course, radically incomplete, for the movement toward McWorld is in competition with forces of global breakdown, national dissolution, and centrifugal corruption. These forces, working in the opposite direction, are the essence of what I call Jihad.

Jihad, or the Lebanonization of the World

OPEC, the World Bank, the United Nations, the International Red Cross, the multinational corporation . . . there are scores of institutions that reflect globalization. But they often appear as ineffective reactors to the world's real actors: national states and, to an ever greater degree, subnational factions in permanent rebellion against uniformity and integration—even the kind represented by universal law and justice. The headlines feature these players regularly: they are cultures, not countries; parts, not wholes; sects, not religions; rebellious factions and dissenting minorities at war not just with globalism but with the traditional nation-state. Kurds, Basques, Puerto Ricans, Ossetians, East Timoreans, Québécois, the Catholics of Northern Ireland, Abkhasians, Kurile Islander Japanese, the Zulus of Inkatha, Catalonians, Tamils, and, of course, Palestinians—people without countries, inhabiting nations not their own, seeking smaller worlds within borders that will seal them off from modernity.

A powerful irony is at work here. Nationalism was once a force of integration and unification, a movement aimed at bringing together disparate clans, tribes, and cultural fragments under new, assimilationist flags. But as **Ortega y Gasset** noted more than 60 years ago, having won its victories, nationalism changed its strategy. In the 1920s, and again today, it is more often a reactionary and divisive force, pulverizing the very nations it once helped cement together. The force that creates nations is "inclusive," Ortega wrote in *The Revolt of the Masses*. "In periods of consolidation, nationalism has a positive value, and is a lofty standard. But in Europe everything is more than consolidated, and nationalism is nothing but a mania."

José Ortega y Gasset
(1883–1955) Spanish philosopher

This mania has left the post–Cold War world smoldering with hot war; the international scene is little more unified than it was at the end of the **Great War**, in Ortega's own time. There were more than 30 wars in progress last year, most of them ethnic, racial, tribal, or religious in character, and the list of unsafe regions doesn't seem to be getting any shorter. Some new world order!

Great War
World War I (1914–1918)

The aim of many of these small-scale wars is to redraw boundaries, to implode states and re-secure parochial identities: to escape McWorld's dully insistent imperatives. The mood is that of Jihad: war not as an instrument of policy but as an emblem of identity, an expression of community, an end in itself. Even where there is no shooting war, there is fractiousness, secession, and a quest for ever smaller communities. Add to the list of dangerous countries those at risk: In Switzerland and Spain, Jurassian and Basque separatists still argue the virtues of ancient identities, sometimes in the language of bombs. Hyperdisintegration in the former Soviet Union may well continue **unabated**—not just a Ukraine independent from the Soviet Union but a Bessarab Ukraine independent from the Ukrainian republic; not just Russia severed from the defunct union but Tatarsa severed from Russia. Yugoslavia makes even the disunited, ex-Soviet, nonsocialist republics that were once the Soviet Union look integrated, its sectarian fatherland springing up within factional motherlands like weeds within weeds within weeds. Kurdish independence would threaten the territorial integrity of four Mid-Eastern nations. Well before the current cataclysm Soviet Georgia made a claim for autonomy from the Soviet Union, only to be faced with its Ossetians (164 000 in a republic of 5.5 million) demanding their own self-determination within Georgia. The Abkhasian minority of Georgia has followed suit. Even the good will established by Canada's once promising **Meech Lake** protocols is in danger, with Francophone Quebec again threatening dissolution of the federation. In South Africa the emergence from apartheid was hardly achieved when friction between Inkatha's Zulus and the African National Congress's tribally identified members threatened to replace Europeans' racism with an indigenous tribal war. After 30 years of attempted integration using the colonial language (English) as a unifier, Nigeria is now playing with the idea of linguistic multiculturalism—which could mean the cultural breakup of the nation into hundreds of tribal fragments. Even Saddam Hussein has benefited from the threat of internal Jihad, having used renewed tribal and religious warfare to turn last season's mortal enemies into reluctant allies of an Iraqi nationhood that he nearly destroyed.

The passing of communism has torn away the thin veneer of internationalism (workers of the world unite!) to reveal ethnic prejudices that are not only ugly and deep-seated but increasingly murderous. Europe's old scourge, anti-Semitism, is back with a vengeance, but it is only one of many antagonisms. It appears all too easy to throw the historical gears into reverse and pass from a Communist dictatorship back into a tribal state.

Among the tribes, religion is also a battlefield. ("Jihad" is a rich word whose generic meaning is "struggle"—usually the struggle of the soul to avert evil. Strictly applied to religious war, it is used only in reference to battles where the faith is under assault, or battles against a government that

---

unabated

in full force

Meech Lake Accord

proposed constitutional amendment—defeated in 1990 when it failed to be ratified by all provincial legislatures—that would have recognized Quebec as a distinct society and conferred greater powers to the provincial governments denies the practice of Islam. My use here is **rhetorical**, but does follow both journalistic practice and history.) Remember the Thirty Years War? Whatever forms of Enlightenment universalism might once have come to grace such historically related forms of monotheism as Judaism, Christianity, and Islam, in many of their modern incarnations they are parochial rather than cosmopolitan, angry rather than loving, **proselytizing** rather than **ecumenical**, zealous rather than rationalist, sectarian rather then deistic, ethnocentric rather than universalizing. As a result, like the new forms of hypernationalism, the new expressions of religious fundamentalism are fractious and pulverizing, never integrating. This is religion as the **Crusaders** knew it: a battle to the death for souls that if not saved will be forever lost.

The **atmospherics** of Jihad have resulted in a breakdown of civility in the name of identity, of **comity** in the name of community. International relations have sometimes taken on the aspects of gang war—cultural turf battles featuring tribal factions that were supposed to be sublimated as integral parts of large national, economic, postcolonial, and constitutional entities.

The Darkening Future of Democracy

These rather melodramatic **tableaux vivants** do not tell the whole story, however. For all their defects, Jihad and McWorld have their attractions. Yet, to repeat and insist, the attractions are unrelated to democracy. Neither McWorld nor Jihad is remotely democratic in impulse. Neither needs democracy; neither promotes democracy.

McWorld does manage to look pretty seductive in a world obsessed with Jihad. It delivers peace, prosperity, and relative unity—if at the cost of independence, community, and identity (which is generally based on difference). The primary political values required by the global market are order and tranquility, and freedom—as in the phrases "free trade," "free press," and "free love." Human rights are needed to a degree, but not citizenship or participation—and no more social justice and equality than are necessary to promote efficient economic production and consumption. Multinational corporations sometimes seem to prefer doing business with local **oligarchs**, inasmuch as they can take confidence from dealing with the boss on all crucial matters. Despots who slaughter their own populations are no problem, as long as they leave markets in place and refrain from making war on their neighbors (Saddam Hussein's fatal mistake). In trading partners, predictability is of more value than justice.

The Eastern European revolutions that seemed to arise out of concern for global democratic values quickly deteriorated into a stampede in the general

rhetorical
stylistic

proselytizing
attempting to convert to a narrow view

ecumenical
having worldwide value

Crusaders
11th- to 14th-century Christian warriors who fought to retake the Holy Land from Muslim control

atmospherics
intentionally created attitudes

comity
courtesy

tableaux vivants
images that tell a story

oligarchs
members of an elite that hold power in a state

ubiquitous
occurring everywhere

direction of free markets and their **ubiquitous**, television-promoted shopping malls. East Germany's Neues Forum, that courageous gathering of intellectuals, students, and workers which overturned the Stalinist regime in Berlin in 1989, lasted only six months in Germany's mini-version of McWorld. Then it gave way to money and markets and monopolies from the West. By the time of the first all-German elections, it could scarcely manage to secure three per cent of the vote. Elsewhere there is growing evidence that *glasnost* will go and **perestroika**—defined as privatization and an opening of markets to Western bidders—will stay. So understandably anxious are the new rulers of Eastern Europe and whatever entities are forged from the residues of the Soviet Union to gain access to credit and markets and technology—McWorld's flourishing new currencies—that they have shown themselves willing to trade away democratic prospects in pursuit of them: not just old totalitarian ideologies and command-economy production models but some possible indigenous experiments with a third way between capitalism and socialism, such as economic cooperatives and employee stock-ownership plans, both of which have their ardent supporters in the East.

perestroika
Soviet policy of economic restructuring introduced in the 1980s

Jihad delivers a different set of virtues: a vibrant local identity, a sense of community, solidarity among kinsmen, neighbors, and countrymen, narrowly conceived. But it also guarantees parochialism and is against outsiders. And solidarity often means obedience to a hierarchy in governance, fanaticism in beliefs, and the obliteration of individual selves in the name of the group. **Deference** to leaders and intolerance toward outsiders (and toward "enemies within") are hallmarks of tribalism—hardly the attitudes required for the cultivation of new democratic women and men capable of governing themselves. Where new democratic experiments have been conducted in retribalizing societies, in both Europe and the Third World, the result has often been anarchy, repression, persecution, and the coming of new, noncommunist forms of very old kinds of despotism. During the past year, **Havel's** velvet revolution in Czechoslovakia was imperiled by partisans of "Czechland" and of Slovakia as independent entities. India seemed little less rent by Sikh, Hindu, Muslim, and Tamil infighting than it was immediately after the British pulled out, more than 40 years ago.

deference
respectful obedience

Vaclav Havel
(b. 1936) playwright, public intellectual, and former Czech president

meritocratic
valuing individual achievement

laissez-faire
a policy of non-intervention by government in the economy

To the extent that either McWorld or Jihad has a *natural* politics, it has turned out to be more of an antipolitics. For McWorld, it is the antipolitics of globalism: bureaucratic, technocratic, and **meritocratic**, focused (as Marx predicted it would be) on the administration of things—with people, however, among the chief things to be administered. In its politico-economic imperatives McWorld has been guided by *laissez-faire* market principles that privilege efficiency, productivity, and **beneficence** at the expense of civic liberty and self-government.

beneficence
being charitable

For Jihad, the antipolitics of tribalization has been explicitly anti-democratic: one-party dictatorship, government by military junta, theocratic fundamentalism—often associated with a version of the *Fuhrerprinzip* that empowers an individual to rule on behalf of a people. Even the government of India, struggling for decades to model democracy for a people who will soon number a billion, longs for great leaders; and for every **Mahatma Gandhi**, **Indira Gandhi**, or **Rajiv Gandhi** taken from them by zealous assassins, the Indians appear to seek a replacement who will deliver them from the lengthy travail of their freedom.

The Confederal Option

How can democracy be secured and spread in a world whose primary tendencies are at best indifferent to it (McWorld) and at worst deeply **antithetical** to it (Jihad)? My guess is that globalization will eventually vanquish retribalization. The **ethos** of material "civilization" has not yet encountered an obstacle it has been unable to thrust aside. Ortega may have grasped in the 1920s a clue to our own future in the coming millennium.

Everyone sees the need of a new principle of life. But as always happens in similar crises—some people attempt to save the situation by an artificial intensification of the very principle which has led to decay. This is the meaning of the "nationalist" outburst of recent years . . . things have always gone that way. The last flare, the longest; the last sigh, the deepest. On the very eve of their disappearance there is an intensification of frontiers—military and economic.

Jihad may be a last deep sigh before the eternal yawn of McWorld. On the other hand, Ortega was not exactly **prescient**; his prophecy of peace and internalism came just before **blitzkrieg**, world war, and the Holocaust tore the old order to bits. Yet democracy is how we **remonstrate** with reality, the rebuke our aspirations offer to history. And if retribalization is inhospitable to democracy, there is nonetheless a form of democratic government that can accommodate parochialism and communitarianism, one that can even save them from their defects and make them more tolerant and participatory: decentralized participatory democracy. And if McWorld is indifferent to democracy, there is nonetheless a form of democratic government that suits global markets passably well—representative government in its federal or, better still, confederal variation.

With its concern for accountability, the protection of minorities, and the universal rule of law, a confederalized representative system would serve the political needs of McWorld as well as oligarchic bureaucratism or

Fuhrerprinzip
principle of authoritarian leadership

Mahatma Gandhi
(1869–1948) political and spiritual leader of the Indian independence movement

Indira Gandhi
(1917–1984) Prime Minister of India from 1966–1977 and 1980–1984

Rajiv Gandhi
(1944–1991) Prime Minister of India from 1984–1989

antithetical
directly opposed

ethos
spirit or character

prescient
possessing foreknowledge

blitzkrieg
quick, intensive military attack perfected by Nazi Germany

remonstrate
quarrel

meritocratic elitism is currently doing. As we are already beginning to see, many nations may survive in the long term only as confederations that afford local regions smaller than "nations" extensive jurisdiction. Recommended reading for democrats of the 21st century is not the U.S. Constitution or the French Declaration of the Rights of Man and Citizen but the Articles of Confederation, that suddenly pertinent document that stitched together the 13 American colonies into what then seemed a too loose confederation of independent states but now appears a new form of political realism, as veterans of Yeltsin's new Russia and the new Europe created at **Maastricht** will attest.

By the same token, the participatory and direct form of democracy that engages citizens in civic activity and civic judgment and goes well beyond just voting and accountability—the system I have called "strong democracy"— suits the political needs of decentralized communities as well as theocratic and nationalist party dictatorships have done. Local neighborhoods need not be democratic, but they can be. Real democracy has flourished in diminutive settings: the spirit of liberty, **Tocqueville** said, is local. Participatory democracy, if not naturally **apposite** to tribalism, has an undeniable attractiveness under conditions of parochialism.

Democracy in any of these variations will, however, continue to be obstructed by the undemocratic and antidemocratic trends toward uniformitarian globalism and intolerant retribalization which I have portrayed here. For democracy to persist in our brave new McWorld, we will have to commit acts of conscious political will—a possibility, but hardly a probability, under these conditions. Political will requires much more than the quick fix of the transfer of institutions. Like technology transfer, institution transfer rests on foolish assumptions about a uniform world of the kind that once fired the imagination of colonial administrators. Spread English justice to the colonies by exporting wigs. Let an East Indian trading company act as the **vanguard** to Britain's free parliamentary institutions. Today's well-intentioned quick-fixers in the National Endowment for Democracy and the Kennedy School of Government, in the unions and foundations and universities zealously nurturing contacts in Eastern Europe and the Third World, are hoping to democratize by long distance. Post Bulgaria a parliament by first-class mail. FedEx the Bill of Rights to Sri Lanka. Cable Cambodia some common law.

Yet Eastern Europe has already demonstrated that importing free political parties, parliaments, and presses cannot establish a democratic civil society; imposing a free market may even have the opposite effect. Democracy grows from the bottom up and cannot be imposed from the top down. Civil society has to be built from the inside out. The institutional superstructure comes

Maastricht
Belgian city where the treaty was signed to create the European Union

Alexis de Tocqueville
(1805–1859) French political theorist

apposite
well suited

vanguard
leaders

last. Poland may become democratic, but then again it may heed the Pope, and prefer to found its politics on its Catholicism, with uncertain consequences for democracy. Bulgaria may become democratic, but it may prefer tribal war. The former Soviet Union may become a democratic confederation, or it may just grow into an anarchic and weak conglomeration of markets for other nations' goods and services.

Democrats need to seek out indigenous democratic impulses. There is always a desire for self-government, always some expression of participation, accountability, consent, and representation, even in traditional hierarchical societies. These need to be identified, tapped, modified, and incorporated into new democratic practices with an indigenous flavor. The tortoises among the democratizers may ultimately outlive or outpace the hares, for they will have the time and patience to explore conditions along the way, and to adapt their gait to changing circumstances. Tragically, democracy in a hurry often looks something like **France in 1794** or **China in 1989**.

It certainly seems possible that the most attractive democratic ideal in the face of the brutal realities of Jihad and the dull realities of McWorld will be a confederal union of semi-autonomous communities smaller than nation-states, tied together into regional economic associations and markets larger than nation-states—participatory and self-determining in local matters at the bottom, representative and accountable at the top. The nation-state would play a diminished role, and sovereignty would lose some of its political potency. The Green movement adage "Think globally, act locally" would actually come to describe the conduct of politics.

This vision reflects only an ideal, however—one that is not terribly likely to be realized. Freedom, **Jean-Jacques Rousseau** once wrote, is a food easy to eat but hard to digest. Still, democracy has always played itself out against the odds. And democracy remains both a form of coherence as binding as McWorld and a secular faith potentially as inspiring as Jihad.

France in 1794
reference to the Reign of Terror when suspected enemies of the French Revolution were executed

China in 1989
reference to the pro-democracy demonstrations in Tiananmen Square where protesters were massacred

Jean-Jacques Rousseau
(1712–1778) French philosopher

America and the World: The Twin Towers as Metaphor

Immanuel Wallerstein

I. America the Beautiful

> O beautiful for patriot dream, That sees beyond the years
> Thine alabaster cities gleam, Undimmed by human tears!
> America! America! God shed his grace on thee
> And crown thy good with brotherhood
> From sea to shining sea!
>
> *America the Beautiful*

On Oct. 24, 1990, I was invited to give the opening lecture of the Distinguished Speakers Series in celebration of the bicentennial of the University of Vermont. I entitled that lecture: "America and the World: Today, Yesterday, and Tomorrow."[1] In that talk, I discussed God's blessings to America: in the present, prosperity; in the past, liberty; in the future, equality. Somehow God had not distributed these blessings to everyone everywhere. I noted that Americans were very conscious of this unequal distribution of God's grace. I said that the United States had always defined itself, had always measured its blessings, by the yardstick of the world. We are better; we were better; we shall be better. Perhaps blessings that are universal are not considered true blessings. Perhaps we impose upon God the requirement that She save only a minority.

Today, we live in the shadow of an event that has shaken most of us, the destruction of the Twin Towers on September 11, 2001, by a group of individuals so dedicated to their ideology and their moral fury at the United States that they conspired for years to find ways to deal a deadly geopolitical blow to America and those they deemed its supporters around the world, and they did this in a way that required sacrificing their own lives. Most Americans have reacted to the events with deep anger, with patriotic resolve, and yet with considerable and persistent puzzlement. Puzzlement about two things: why did this happen? and how could it happen? And the puzzlement has been laced with a good deal of uncertainty: what must be done, what can be done in order that such an event will not, could not happen again?

As I look back on what I said eleven years ago, I do not wish to change anything I said then. But I do feel a bit of unease about the stance from which I spoke. I wrote as though I were an **ethnographer** from elsewhere, from

ethnographer

an anthropologist who researches distinct human cultures

Mars perhaps, trying to understand this curious species, *humanus americanus*. Today, I think that is not good enough. I am to be sure a human being and concerned with the fate of humanity. But I am also an American citizen. I was born here. I have lived here most of my life. And I share full responsibility, along with everyone else in my position, for what has happened here and what will happen here. I have a moral obligation to view America from inside.

So, I wish to look at America and the world a second time. But this time I do not want to see how Americans see themselves through the prism of the world, but rather how Americans have seen the world, and how Americans might wish to see the world from hereon in. And I am very aware that here I tread on **contentious** ground.

It is a rare president of the United States, in the twentieth century at least, who has not at some point made the statement that the United States is the greatest country in the world. I'm not sure our **omnipresent** public opinion polling agencies have ever put the question directly to the American public, but I suspect that the percentage of the U.S. population that would agree with such a statement is very large indeed. I ask you to reflect on how such a statement sounds, not merely to persons from poor countries with cultures that are very different from ours but to our close friends and allies—to Canadians, to the English, and of course to the French. Does **Tony Blair** think the United States is the greatest country in the world, greater than Great Britain? Would he dare think that? Does **Pope John Paul II** think it? Who, besides Americans and those who wish to migrate to the United States, believe this?

Nationalism is of course not a phenomenon limited to people in the United States. The citizens of almost every country are patriotic and often **chauvinistic**. Americans are aware of that, no doubt. But they nonetheless tend to note the fact that many people across the world wish to emigrate to the United States, and that no other locus of immigration seems to be quite as popular, and they take this as confirmation of their belief in American superior virtue as a nation.

But in what do we consider that our superior virtue consists? I think that Americans tend to believe that others have less of many things than we have, and the fact that we have more is a sign of grace. I shall thus try to elaborate the many arenas in which this concept of "less-ness" may be thought to exist. I shall start with the one arena about which most Americans seem to be quite sure. Other countries are less modern, meaning by modernity the level of technological development. The United States has the most advanced technology in the world. This technology is located in the gadgets found in our homes across the country, in the networks of communications and transport,

contentious
controversial

omnipresent
existing everywhere

Tony Blair
(b. 1953) Prime Minister of the United Kingdom from 1997 to 2007

Pope John Paul II
(1920–2005) Pope of the Catholic Church from 1978 to 2005

chauvinistic
believing in the superiority of one's people

in the infrastructure of the country, in the instruments of space exploration, and of course in the military hardware that is available to our armed forces. As a result of this accumulation of technology, Americans consider that life in the U.S. is more comfortable, that our production competes more successfully in the world market, and that therefore we are certain to win the wars into which others may drag us.

Americans also consider their society to be more efficient. Things run more smoothly—at the work place, in the public arena, in social relations, in our dealings with bureaucracies. However great our complaints about any of these practices, we seem to find, when we wander elsewhere, that others manage things less well. Others do not seem to have American get-up-and-go. They are less inventive about finding solutions to problems, major and minor. They are too mired in traditional and/or formal ways. And this holds the others back, while America forges ahead. We are very ready therefore to offer friendly advice to all and sundry—to Nigerians, to Japanese, to Italians—about how they could do things better. The **emulation** of American ways by others is considered a big plus when Americans assess what is going on in other countries. **Daniel Boone** plus the **Peace Corps** comprise the bases of an evaluation of comparative political economy.

But of course most Americans would deny that the less-ness of others is merely material. It is spiritual as well. Or if the term spiritual seems to exclude the **secular humanists**, it is cultural as well. Our presidents tell us, and our patriotic songs remind us, that we are the land of liberty. Others are less free than we are. The Statue of Liberty stretches out its hand to all those "huddled masses yearning to breathe free."

Our density of freedom is visualized in so many ways. Which other country has the **Bill of Rights**? Where else is freedom of the press, of religion, of speech so honored? Where else are immigrants so integrated into the political system? Can one name another country in which someone arriving here as a teenager, and still speaking English to this day with a thick German accent, could become the Secretary of State, the chief representative of Americans to the rest of the world? Is there any other country where social mobility, for those with merit, is so rapid? And which country can match us in the degree to which we are democratic? Democratic not merely in the continuing openness of our political structures, the centrality of a two-party system, but also in our **quotidian mores**? Is the United States not the country which excels in maintaining the principle of "first come, first served" in the practices of daily life, this as opposed to a system in which those who have privilege get preference? And these democratic mores, in the public arena and in social life, date back at least 200, if not almost 400 years.

emulation
following

Daniel Boone
(1734–1820) famous American pioneer

Peace Corps
a US federal agency that sends volunteers abroad

secular humanism
belief that a productive, good, and just life can be achieved via reason without appeal to God

Bill of Rights
first ten amendments to the US Constitution, which protect individual rights and freedoms

quotidian
everyday

mores
customs

From melting pot to multiculturality, we have prided ourselves on the incredible ethnic mix of real American life—in our restaurants, in our universities, in our political leadership. Yes, we have had our faults, but we have done more than any other country to try to overcome them. Have we not taken the lead in the last decades in tearing down barriers of gender and race, in the constantly renewed search for the perfect **meritocracy**? Even our movements of protest give us cause for pride. Where else are they so persistent, so diverse, so legitimate?

And in the one arena where, up to 1945, we tended to admit that we were not the ***avant-garde*** of the world, the arena of high culture, has that not now all changed? Is New York not today the world center of art, of theatre, of music performance, of dance, of opera? Our cinema is so superior that the French government must resort to protectionist measures to keep French audiences from seeing still more of it.

We can put this all together in a phrase that Americans have not used much, at least until September 11, but which we largely think in our hearts: We are more civilized than the rest of the world, the Old World as we used to say with a token of disdain. We represent the highest aspirations of everyone, not merely Americans. We are the leader of the free world, because we are the freest country in the world, and others look to us for leadership, for holding high the banner of freedom, of civilization.

I have meant none of this ironically. I am deeply persuaded that this image of the less-ness of the rest of the world is profoundly ingrained in the American psyche, however many there may be who will be embarrassed by my presentation, and insist that they are not part of such a consensus, that they are (shall we say?) more **cosmopolitan** in their views. And it is in this sense, first of all, that the Twin Towers are a perfect **metaphor**. They signaled unlimited aspirations; they signaled technological achievement; they signaled a beacon to the world.

meritocracy
system in which benefits are given to those who earn them

avant-garde
progressive leader

cosmopolitan
worldly

metaphor
non-literal symbol

II. Attack on America

What the United States tastes today is a very small thing compared to what we have tasted for tens of years. Our nation has been tasting this humiliation and contempt for more than 80 years . . . . But if the sword falls on the United States, after 80 years, hypocrisy raises its ugly head lamenting the deaths of these killers who tampered with the blood, honor and holy places of the Muslims. The least that one can describe these people is that they are morally depraved.

—*Osama bin Laden, October 7, 2001*

Osama bin Laden does not think that America is beautiful. He thinks Americans are morally depraved. Now, of course, there are some Americans who also think that most Americans are morally depraved. We hear this theme from what might be called the cultural right in the United States. But while the critiques of the U.S. cultural right and those of Osama bin Laden overlap up to a point insofar as they deal with everyday mores, bin Laden's fundamental denunciation concerns what he calls U.S. hypocrisy in the world arena. And when it comes to America in the world arena, there are very few Americans who would agree with that characterization, and even those who might say something similar would want to **nuance** this view in ways that bin Laden would find irrelevant and unacceptable.

nuance
refine

This was one of the two great shocks of September 11 for Americans. There were persons in the world who denied any good faith at all to American actions and motives in the world arena. How was it possible that persons who had less of everything worth having doubt that those who had more of everything had earned it by their merit? The moral **effrontery** of bin Laden amazed Americans and they found it **galling**.

effrontery
arrogance, disrespect

galling
disturbing

To be sure, bin Laden is scarcely the first person to make this kind of verbal attack, but he was the first person who has been able to translate that verbal attack into a physical attack on U.S. soil, one that caught America by surprise and, momentarily at least, helpless. Until that happened, Americans could afford to ignore the verbal attacks so rampant in the world as the babblings of fools. But fools had now become villains. Furthermore, the villains had been initially successful, and this was the second great shock. We were supposed to be in a position to be able to ignore such criticisms because we were essentially invulnerable, and we have now discovered that we are not.

It has been frequently said that the world will never be the same again after September 11. I think this is silly **hyperbole**. But it is true that the American psyche may never be the same again. For once the unthinkable happens, it becomes thinkable. And a direct assault on mainland America by a scattered band of individuals had always been unthinkable. Now we have had to establish an Office of Homeland Security. Now we have the **Pentagon** discussing whether they should establish what they call an area command, a military structure hitherto limited to the areas outside the U.S. covering all the rest of the world, that would cover the United States itself.

hyperbole
exaggeration

Pentagon
headquarters of the US
Department of Defense

Above all we now have "terrorists" in our vocabulary. In the 1950s, the term "Communists" received expansive employ. It covered not only persons who were members of Communist parties, not only those who thought of themselves or were thought of by others as "fellow travelers," but even those who lacked sufficient "enthusiasm" for the development of a hydrogen bomb.

This was after all the specific charge that led the U.S. Atomic Energy Commission in 1953 to suspend the security clearance of **J. Robert Oppenheimer**, the very person who was known as, and had hitherto been honored as, the "father of the atomic bomb."

The term "terrorism" has now obtained the same expansive meaning. In November 2001, I watched a television program, "Law and Order." The plot for this particular episode revolved around the burning down of a building in the process of construction. The background to this was that the contractor had received the land from the city, land which had previously been a neighborhood garden, tended to by the community. There was opposition to this construction in the community. A group of young persons identified as "environmental activists" decided to burn down the building in protest. The complication was that, by accident, someone was in the building, unbeknownst to them, and died in the fire. In the end, the arsonists are caught and convicted. The interesting point of this banal story is that, throughout the program, the arsonists are repeatedly referred to as "terrorists." By any definition of terrorist, it is a stretch to use the term in this case. But no matter! It was so used, and it will continue to be so used.

We are the land of liberty, but today we hear voices—in the government, in the press, in the population at large—that we have accorded too much liberty, especially to non-citizens, and that "terrorists" have taken advantage of our liberty. Therefore it is said the privileges of liberty must give way to procedures that meet our requirements for security. For example, we apparently worry that if we catch "terrorists" and put them on trial, they may then have a public forum, they may not be convicted, or if convicted they may not receive the death penalty. So, in order to ensure that none of these things happen, we are creating military courts to be convened by the President, with rules to be established by him alone, with no right of appeal to anyone, courts that will operate in total secrecy, and are able to proceed rapidly to a conclusion—presumably to a death penalty, probably also carried out in secret. At the close of such trials, all we may be allowed to know is the name of the person so condemned. Or perhaps not even that. And in our land of liberty, this is being widely applauded, and at most halfheartedly opposed by a brave minority.

We consider, we have stated publicly, that the attack on America is an attack on our values and on civilization itself. We find such an attack unconscionable. We are determined to win the worldwide war against terrorism—against terrorists *and all those who give them shelter and support.* We are determined to show that, despite this attack, we are and remain the greatest country in the world. In order to prove this, we are not being **adjured** by our President to make individual sacrifices, not even the small

J. Robert Oppenheimer
leader of the team of American scientists who developed the nuclear bomb during World War II

adjured
requested

sacrifice of paying more taxes, but rather to carry on our lives as normal. We are however expected to applaud without reservation whatever our government and our armed forces will do, even if this is not normal.

The extent of this requirement of "no reservations" may be seen in the widespread denunciation of those who try to "explain" why the events of September 11 occurred. Explanation is considered justification and virtual endorsement of terror. The American Council of Trustees and Alumni (ACTA), an organization whose founders are **Lynne Cheney** and Senator **Joseph Lieberman**, issued a pamphlet in November 2001, entitled "Defending Civilization: How Our Universities Are Failing America and What Can Be Done About It."[2] It is a short pamphlet, which makes its points with remarkable **pithiness**. It says that "college and university faculty are the weak link in America's response to the attack." It continues with this analysis:

> Rarely did professors publicly mention heroism, rarely did they discuss the differences between good and evil, the nature of Western political order or the virtue of a free society. Their public messages were short on patriotism and long on **self-flagellation**. Indeed, the message of much of academe was: BLAME AMERICA FIRST!

The pamphlet devotes most of its space to an appendix of 117 quotations which the authors feel illustrate their point. These quotations include statements not merely of such persons as **Noam Chomsky** and **Jesse Jackson** but of less usual targets of such denunciations—the Dean of the Woodrow Wilson School at Princeton, a former Deputy Secretary of State. In short, the authors of the pamphlet were aiming wide.

It is clear at this point that, even if the events of September 11 will not alter the basic geopolitical realities of the contemporary world, they may have a lasting impact on American political structures. How much of an impact remains to be seen. It does seem, however, that the puzzlement of Americans of which I spoke—why did this happen? and how could it happen?—is a puzzle to which we are not being encouraged to respond, at least not yet.

The Twin Towers are also a metaphor for the attack on America. They were built with great engineering skill. They were supposed to be impervious to every conceivable kind of accidental or deliberate destruction. Yet, apparently, no one had ever considered that two planes filled with jet fuel might deliberately crash into the towers and hit the buildings at precisely the point, 20% down from the top, that would maximize destruction. Nor had anyone anticipated that the buildings could collapse slowly, overwhelmingly, and in everyone's view, bringing down other buildings in their wake. No one ever

Lynne Cheney
(b. 1941) conservative writer married to Dick Cheney, US vice-president from 2001 to 2009

Joseph Lieberman
(b. 1942) US senator and unsuccessful Democratic candidate for vice-president in 2001

pithiness
brevity

self-flagellation
harsh self-criticism

Noam Chomsky
(b. 1928) American linguist with very liberal political views

Jesse Jackson
(b. 1941) American civil rights leader

expected that the fires such a collapse ignited would continue to burn for months afterwards. The U.S. may be able to avenge the attack, but it cannot undo it. Technology turns out to be less than perfect as a protective shield.

III. America and World Power

Anti-Catholicism, as it evolved [in Great Britain in the 18th century], usually served a dialectical function, drawing attention to the supposed despotism, superstition, military oppressiveness and material poverty of Catholic regimes so as to throw into greater relief supposed Anglo-British freedoms, naval supremacy, and agrarian and commercial prosperity, and consequently superior mode of empire.

—Linda Colley[3]

I start with this quote from Linda Colley to remind us that the United States is not the first hegemonic power in the history of the modern world-system, but rather the third, and that **hegemony** has its cultural rules as well as its vulnerabilities. One of the cultural rules is that the **denigration** of others is indispensable to sustaining the internal self-assurance that makes possible the effective exercise of world power.

hegemony
dominance of one nation over others

denigration
belittling

There is nothing so blinding as success. And the United States has had its fair share of success in the past 200 years. Success has the vicious consequence that it seems to breed almost inevitably the conviction that it will necessarily continue. Success is a poor guide to wise policy. Failure at least often leads to reflection; success seldom does.

Fifty years ago, U.S. hegemony in the world-system was based on a combination of productive efficiency (outstripping by far any rivals), a world political agenda that was warmly endorsed by its allies in Europe and Asia, and military superiority. Today, the productive efficiency of U.S. enterprises faces very extensive competition, competition first of all coming from the enterprises of its closest allies. As a result, the world political agenda of the United States is no longer so warmly endorsed and is often clearly contested even by its allies, especially given the disappearance of the Soviet Union. What remains for the moment is military superiority.

It is worth thinking about the objectives of U.S. foreign policy, as pursued for the last 50 years by successive U.S. governments. Obviously, the U.S. has been concerned with threats posed by governments it considered hostile or at least **inimical** to U.S. interests. There is nothing wrong or exceptional about this. This is true of the foreign policy of any state in the modern world-system, especially any powerful state. The question is how the U.S. thought it could deal with such threats.

inimical
unfavourable

In the 1950s and 1960s, the U.S. seemed to be so strong that it could arrange, without too much difficulty and with a minimal use of force, that governments it did not like either could be neutralized (we called that containment) or, in the case of weaker governments, could be overthrown by internal forces supported covertly by the U.S. government, assisted occasionally by a little old-fashioned gunship diplomacy.

Neutralization was the tactic employed vis-à-vis the Communist world. The U.S. did not seek to overthrow the Soviet Union or any of its satellite regimes in east and central Europe. Basically, it did not seek this because it was not in a military position to carry this out against the expected resistance by the government of the U.S.S.R. Instead, the U.S. government entered into a **tacit** accord with the U.S.S.R. that it would not even try to do this, in return for a pledge by the Soviet Union that it would not try to expand its zone. We refer to this in code as the **Yalta** agreement. If one doubts the reality of this agreement, just review U.S. foreign policy vis-à-vis the German Democratic Republic in 1953, Hungary in 1956, Czechoslovakia in 1968, and Poland in 1981.

The accord was not however intended to apply to East Asia, where Soviet troops were absent, thanks primarily to the insistence of the Communist regimes in China and North Korea. So the U.S. did in fact try to overthrow these regimes as well as that in Vietnam. It did not however succeed. And these failed attempts left a serious scar on American public opinion.

The United States, however, was able to enforce its will in the rest of the world, and did so without **compunction**. Think of Iran in 1953, Guatemala in 1954, Lebanon in 1956, the Dominican Republic in 1965, and Chile in 1973. The coup in Chile by General **Pinochet** against the freely-elected government of **Salvador Allende**, with the active support of the U.S. government, occurred on September 11. I do not know whether or not Osama bin Laden or his followers were aware of this coincidence of dates, but it is nonetheless a symbolic coincidence that many, especially in Latin America, will notice. It also points to a further metaphor of the Twin Towers. The Twin Towers were a marvelous technological achievement. But technological achievements can and will be copied. The Malaysians have already copied the Twin Towers architecturally, and a bigger skyscraper is being built right now in Shanghai. Symbols too can be copied. Now we have two September 11 anniversaries, on which victims mourn.

In the 1970s, U.S. foreign policy methods changed, had to change. Chile was the last major instance in which the U.S. was able so cavalierly to arrange other governments to its preferences. (I do not count the cases of either Grenada or Panama, which were very small countries with no serious mode of military defense.) What had caused this change was the end of U.S.

---

tacit

understood, implied

Yalta

city in Ukraine where leaders of the US, UK and USSR negotiated post–World War II arrangements in 1945

compunction

feeling guilty

Augusto Pinochet

(1915–2006) right-wing military dictator who, via a military coup, became the unelected president of Chile from 1973 to 1990

Salvador Allende

(1908–1973) left-wing democratically elected president of Chile from 1970 to 1973, who was ousted and assassinated by Pinochet's coup economic dominance of the world-economy, combined with the military defeat of the United States in Vietnam. Geopolitical reality had changed. The U.S. government could no longer concentrate on maintaining, even less on expanding, its power; instead its prime goal became preventing a too rapid erosion of its power—both in the world-economy and in the military arena.

In the world-economy, the U.S. faced not only the hot breath of its competitors in western Europe and Japan but the seeming success of "developmentalist" policies in large parts of the rest of the world, policies that had been designed expressly to constrain the ability of countries in the core zone to accumulate capital at what was seen to be the expense of countries in the periphery. We should remember that the 1970s was declared by the United Nations the "decade of development." In the 1970s, there was much talk of creating a "new international economic order," and in **UNESCO** of creating a "new international information order." The 1970s was the time of the two famous **OPEC** oil price rises, which sent waves of panic into the American public.

The U.S. position on all these thrusts was either ambiguous discomfort or outright opposition. Globally, a counterthrust was launched. It involved the aggressive assertion of **neo-liberalism** and the so-called **Washington Consensus**, the transformation of **GATT** into the World Trade Organization, the **Davos** meetings, and the spreading of the concept of globalization with its corollary, TINA (there is no alternative). Essentially, all these efforts combined amounted to a dismantlement of the "developmentalist" policies throughout the world, and, of course, particularly in the peripheral zones of the world-economy. In the short run, that is in the 1980s and 1990s, this counteroffensive led by the U.S. government seemed to succeed.

These policies on the front of the world-economy were matched by a persistent world military policy which might be summarized as the "anti-proliferation" policy. When the United States successfully made the first atomic bombs in 1945, it was determined to maintain a monopoly on such very powerful weapons. It was willing to share this monopoly with its faithful junior partner, Great Britain, but that was it. Of course, as we know, the other "great powers" simply ignored this claim. First the Soviet Union, then France, then China achieved nuclear capacity. So then did India and later Pakistan. So did South Africa, whose **apartheid** government however admitted this only as it was leaving power and was careful to dismantle this capacity before it turned over power to the successor, more democratic, government of the Black African majority. And so did Israel, although it has always denied this publicly.

Then there are the almost nuclear powers, if indeed they are still in the almost category—North Korea, Iran, Iraq (whose facilities Israel bombed in

UNESCO
United Nations Educational, Scientific, and Cultural Organization

OPEC
Organization of the Oil Exporting Countries

neo-liberalism
theory that the most efficient and just economy is a free market with very little government regulation

Washington Consensus
view that prosperity in developing countries is best facilitated through neo-liberal aid policies that embrace both domestic and global market forces

GATT
General Agreement on Tariffs and Trade

Davos
city in Switzerland where the World Economic Forum meets annually

apartheid
official policy of racial segregation in South Africa until 1994

the 1980s in order to keep it in the "almost" category), Libya, and maybe Argentina. And there are in addition the former Soviet countries which inherited this capacity—Ukraine, Belorussia, and Kazakhstan. To this must be added the other lethal technologies—biological and chemical warfare. These are so much easier to create, store, and employ, that we are not sure how many countries have some capacity, even a considerable capacity in these fields.

The United States has had a simple straightforward policy. By hook or by crook, by force or by bribery, it wishes to deny everybody access to these weapons. It has obviously not been successful, but its efforts over the past years have at least slowed down the process of proliferation. There is a further catch in U.S. policy. Insofar as it tries to employ international agreements to limit proliferation, it simultaneously tries not itself to be bound by such constraints, or to be minimally bound. The U.S. government has made it clear that it will renounce any such restraints whenever it deems it necessary to do so, while loudly condemning any other government that seeks to do the same.

As a policy, non-proliferation seems doomed to failure, not only in the long run but even in the middle run. The best that the U.S. will be able to do in the next 25 years is to slow the process down somewhat. But there is also a moral/political question here. The United States trusts itself, but trusts no one else. The U.S. government wishes to inspect North Korean locations to see if it is violating these norms. It has not offered the U.N. or anyone else the right to inspect U.S. locations. The U.S. trusts itself to use such weapons wisely, and in the defense of liberty (a concept seemingly identical with U.S. national interests). It assumes that anyone else might intend to use such weapons against liberty (a concept seemingly identical here too with U.S. national interests). Personally, I do not trust any government to use such weapons wisely. I would be happy to see them all banned, but do not believe this is truly enforceable in the contemporary interstate system. So personally I abstain from moralizing on this issue. Moralizing opens one to the charge of hypocrisy. And while a cynical **neorealist** (a category that probably includes me) would say that all governments are hypocritical, moralizing jars badly if one wishes to attract support in other countries on the basis of one's comparative virtue.

neorealism

belief that states act solely out of national self-interest without considerations of justice

IV. America: Ideals versus Privilege

To suggest that the universal civilization is in place already is to be willfully blind to the present reality and, even worse, to trivialize the goal and hinder the materialization of a genuine universality in the future.

> —*Chinua Achebe*[4]

[T]he opposition between globalization and local traditions is false: globalization directly resuscitates local traditions, it literally thrives on them, which is why the opposite of globalization is not local traditions, but universality.

> —*Slavoj Zizek*[5]

The story of U.S. and world power can be resumed quite simply at this moment. I do not believe that America and Americans are the cause of all the world's miseries and injustices. I do believe they are their prime beneficiaries. And this is the fundamental problem of the U.S. as a nation located in a world of nations.

Americans, especially American politicians and publicists, like to speak about our ideals. An advertisement for the "bestselling" book of Chris Matthews, *Now, Let Me Tell You What I Really Think*, offers this excerpt: "When you think about it, we Americans are different. That word 'freedom' isn't just in our documents; it's in our cowboy souls."[6] "Cowboy souls"—I could not have said it better. Our ideals are perhaps special. But the same people who remind us of that do not like to talk about our privileges, which are also perhaps special. Indeed, they denounce those who do talk of them. But the ideals and the privileges go together. They may seem to be in conflict, but they presuppose each other.

I am not someone who denigrates American ideals. I find them quite wonderful, even refreshing. I cherish them, I invoke them, I further them. Take for example the **First Amendment** to the U.S. Constitution—something correctly remembered at all the appropriate ceremonies as incarnating American ideals. Let us, however, recall two things about the First Amendment. It wasn't in the original Constitution, which means it wasn't considered a founding principle. And public opinion polls have often shown that a majority of the American public would change, diminish, or even eliminate these guarantees, in whole or in part, even in so-called ordinary times. When we are in a "war" such as the "war on terrorism," then neither the U.S. government nor the U.S. public can be counted on to defend these ideals, and not even the Supreme Court can be relied upon to hold fast to them in an "emergency." Such defense is left largely to an often timid organization with at best minority support in

First Amendment
amendment that guarantees freedom of religion, speech and assembly

public opinion, the American Civil Liberties Union, membership in which is often cited as a reason not to vote for someone in a general election. So, I am in favor of freedom of speech and freedom of religion and all the other freedoms, but sometimes I must wonder if America is.

The reason of course is not that there is absent a **Voltairean** streak in the American public, but that sometimes we fear that our privileges are in danger of erosion or disappearance. And, in such cases, most people place privilege ahead of ideals. Once again, Americans are not unusual in this regard. They simply are more powerful and have more privileges. Americans are freer to have the ideals because they are freer to ignore them. They have the power to override their cowboy souls.

The question before Americans is really the following. If American hegemony is in slow decline, and I believe it unquestionably is, will we lose the ideals because we will have less power to override them? Will our cowboy souls erect barbed wire around our national ranch in order to guard our privileges in danger of decline, as though they could not escape through the barbed wire? Let me suggest here another metaphor that comes from the Twin Towers. Towers that are destroyed can be rebuilt. But will we rebuild them in the same way—with the same assurance that we are reaching for the stars and doing it right, with the same certainty that they will be seen as a beacon to the world? Or will we rebuild in other ways, after careful reflection about what we really need and what is really possible for us, and really desirable for us?

And who is the us? If one follows the statements of Attorney-General **Ashcroft**, seconded by many others in the U.S. government, in the press, and among the public in general, the "us" is no longer everyone in the U.S., not even everyone legally resident in the U.S., but only U.S. citizens. And we may wonder if the "us" may not be further narrowed in the near future. As Zizek points out, globalization is not the opposite of localism, it thrives on localism, especially the localism of the powerful. The "us" is by no stretch of the imagination **homo sapiens** sapiens. Is homo then so sapiens?

Voltairean

avidly promoting civil liberties, like the French writer Voltaire (1694–1774)

John Ashcroft

(b. 1942) US politician who served as attorney-general from 2001 to 2005.

homo sapiens

Latin term for the human species literally means wise ("sapien") human ("homo")

V. America: From Certainty to Uncertainty

"Darwin's revolution should be epitomized as the substitution of variation for essence as the central category of natural reality . . . . What can be more discombobulating than a full inversion, or 'grand flip,' in our concept of reality: in Plato's world, variation is accidental, while essences record a higher reality; in Darwin's reversal, we value variation as a defining (and concrete earthly) reality, while averages (our closest operational approach to 'essences') become mental abstractions."

—Stephen J. Gould[7]

Nature is indeed related to the creation of unpredictable novelty, where the possible is richer than the real.

—Ilya Prigogine[8]

President Bush has been offering the American people certainty about their future. This is the one thing totally beyond his power to offer. The future of the United States, the future of the world, in the short run, but even more in the medium run, is absolutely uncertain. Certainty may seem desirable if one reflects on one's privileges. It seems less desirable if one thinks that the privileges are doomed to decline, even disappear. And if it were certain that the Osama bin Ladens of this world, in all camps, were to prevail, who would cherish that certainty?

I return to the question I raised before as one of the puzzles that Americans are feeling right now: what must be done, what can be done, that an event like that of September 11 will not, could not happen again? We are being offered the answer that the exercise of overwhelming force by the U.S. government, military force primarily, will guarantee this. Our leaders are prudent enough to remind us that this will take some time, but they do not hesitate to make medium-run assurances. For the moment, it seems that the American people are willing to test this hypothesis. If the U.S. government is receiving criticism at this moment, it is coming mostly from those who believe its expression of military power is far too timid. There are important groups who are pressing the U.S. government to go much further—to operate militarily against Iraq, and some would add Iran, Syria, Sudan, Palestine, North Korea. Why not Cuba next? There are some who are even saying that reluctant generals should be retired to make way for younger, more vigorous warriors. There are those who believe that it is their role to **precipitate** Armageddon.

There are two ways one can argue against this. One is that the United States could not win such a worldwide military conflagration. A second is

precipitate
bring about quickly

that the United States would not wish to bear the moral consequences, first of all for itself, of trying to do so. Fortunately, one does not have to choose between realism and idealism. It is not belittling of our moral values that they are seconded by elementary common sense.

After the Civil War, the United States spent some 80 years pursuing its **manifest destiny**. It was not sure, all that time, whether it wished to be an isolationist or an **imperial power**. And when, in 1945, it had finally achieved hegemony in the world-system, when it had (in Shakespeare's choice) not only achieved greatness but had greatness thrust upon it, the American people were not fully prepared for the role they now had to play. We spent thirty years learning how to "assume our responsibilities" in the world. And just when we had learned this reasonably well, our hegemony passed its peak.

We have spent the last thirty years insisting very loudly that we are still hegemonic and that everyone needs to continue to acknowledge it. If one is truly hegemonic, one does not need to make such a request. We have wasted the past thirty years. What the United States needs now to do is to learn how to live with the new reality—that it no longer has the power to decide unilaterally what is good for everyone. It may not even be in a position to decide unilaterally what is good for itself. It has to come to terms with the world. It is not Osama bin Laden with whom we must conduct a dialogue. We must start with our near friends and allies—with Canada and Mexico, with Europe, with Japan. And once we have trained ourselves to hear them and to believe that they too have ideals and interests, that they too have ideas and hopes and aspirations, then and only then perhaps shall we be ready to dialogue with the rest of the world, that is, with the majority of the world.

This dialogue, once we begin to enter into it, will not be easy, and may not even be pleasant. For they shall ask us to renounce some privileges. They will ask us to fulfill our ideals. They will ask us to learn. Fifty years ago, the great African poet/politician, **Léopold-Sédar Senghor**, called on the world to come to the "*rendez-vous du donner et du recevoir.*" Americans know what they have to give in such a *rendez-vous*. But are they aware of something they wish to receive?

We are being called upon these days to return to spiritual values, as though we had ever observed these values. But what are these values? Let me remind you. In the Christian tradition (Matthew 19:24), it is said: "It is easier for a camel to pass through the eye of a needle than for a rich man to enter the kingdom of God." And in the Jewish tradition, Hillel tells us: "Do unto others as you would have them do unto you." And in the Muslim tradition, the Koran (52.36) tells us: "Or did they create the heavens and the earth? Nay! They have no certainty." Are these our values?

manifest destiny
belief that the United States was destined to expand from the Atlantic to the Pacific coast

imperial power
state that controls others by conquest, colonization or economic dominance

Léopold-Sédar Senghor
(1906–2001) poet, cultural theorist and statesman who served as president of Senegal from 1960 to 1980

There is of course no single American tradition or single American set of values. There are, and always have been, many Americas. We each of us remember and appeal to the Americas we prefer. The America of slavery and racism is a deep American tradition, and still very much with us. The America of frontier individualism and gunslinging desperados is an American tradition, and still very much with us. The America of **robber barons** and their **philanthropic** children is an American tradition, and still very much with us. And the America of the **Wobblies** and the **Haymarket riots**, an event celebrated throughout the world except in America, is an American tradition, and still very much with us.

Sojourner Truth, telling the National Women's Congress in 1851, "Ain't I a woman?" is an American tradition. But so were those late nineteenth-century **suffragists** who argued for votes on the grounds that it would balance the votes of Blacks and immigrants. The America that welcomes immigrants and the America that rejects them are both American traditions. The America that unites in patriotic resolve and the America that resists militarist engagements are both American traditions. The America of equality and of inequality are both American traditions. There is no essence there. There is no there there. As Gould reminds us, it is variation, not essence, that is the core of reality. And the question is whether the variation amongst us will diminish, increase, or remain the same. It seems to me exceptionally high at the moment.

Osama bin Laden will soon be forgotten, but the kind of political violence we call terrorism will remain very much with us in the 30–50 years to come. Terrorism is to be sure a very ineffective way to change the world. It is counterproductive and leads to counterforce, which can often wipe out the immediate set of actors. But it will nonetheless continue to occur. An America that continues to relate to the world by a unilateral assertion that it represents civilization, whether it does so in the form of isolationist withdrawal or in that of active interventionism, cannot live in peace with the world, and therefore will not live in peace with itself. What we do to the world, we do to ourselves. Can the land of liberty and privilege, even amidst its decline, learn to be a land that treats everyone everywhere as equals? And can we deal as equal to equal in the world-system if we do not deal as equal to equal within our own frontiers?

What shall we choose to do now? I can have my preferences but I cannot, you cannot, predict what we shall do. Indeed, it is our good fortune that we cannot be certain of any of these projected futures. That reserves for us moral choice. That reserves for us the possible that is richer than the real. That reserves for us unpredictable novelty. We have entered a terrible era, an era of conflicts and evils we find it difficult to imagine but, sadly, one to which

robber barons
businesspeople who amassed great wealth via unfair business practices

philanthropic
generous in charitable assistance to the disadvantaged

Wobblies
members of the international union called the Industrial Workers of the World

Haymarket riots
violent confrontation between striking unionists and Chicago police that resulted a number of deaths on both sides

Sojourner Truth
(1797–1883) American anti-slavery and women's rights advocate who had been born into slavery

suffragists
advocates of extending voting rights to women

we can rapidly become accustomed. It is easy to allow our sensitivities to be hardened in the struggle to survive. It is far harder to save our cowboy souls. But at the end of the process lies the possibility, which is far from the certainty, of a more substantively rational world, of a more egalitarian world, of a more democratic world—of a universality that results from giving and receiving, a universality that is the opposite of globalization.

The last metaphor that is attached to the Twin Towers is that these structures were, are, and will be a choice. We chose to build them. We are deciding whether or not to rebuild them. The factors that enter into these choices were and are and will be very, very many. We are rebuilding America. The world is rebuilding the world. The factors that enter into these choices are and will be very, very many. Can we maintain our moral bearing amidst the uncertainty that the world we have made heretofore is only one of thousands of alternative worlds we might have created, and the world that we shall be making in the 30–50 years to come may or may not be better, may or may not reduce the contradiction between our ideals and our privileges? **In-sha'a-llah.**

in-sha'a-llah
"God-willing" in Arabic

Notes

[1] Published in *Theory and Society*, XXI, 1, Feb., 1992, pp. 1–28.

[2] The authors are Jerry L. Martin and Anne Neal.

[3] "Multiple Kingdoms," *London Review of Books*, 19 July 2001, p. 23.

[4] Chinua Achebe, *Home and Exile*, New York: Anchor Books, 2000, p. 91.

[5] Slavoj Zizek, *On Belief*, New York: Routledge, 2001, p. 152.

[6] *New York Times*, Nov. 28, 2001, p. E8.

[7] *Full House: The Spread of Excellence from Plato to Darwin*, New York: Three Rivers Press, 1996, p. 41.

[8] Ilya Prigogine, *The End of Certainty: Time, Chaos, and the New Laws of Nature*, New York: Free Press, 1997, p. 72.

The Perils of Obedience

Stanley Milgram

Obedience is as basic an element in the structure of social life as one can point to. Some system of authority is a requirement of all communal living, and it is only the person dwelling in isolation who is not forced to respond, with defiance or submission, to the commands of others. For many people, obedience is a deeply ingrained behavior tendency, indeed a potent impulse overriding training in ethics, sympathy, and moral conduct.

The dilemma inherent in submission to authority is ancient, as old as the story of **Abraham**, and the question of whether one should obey when commands conflict with conscience has been argued by Plato, dramatized in *Antigone*, and treated to philosophic analysis in almost every historical epoch. Conservative philosophers argue that the very fabric of society is threatened by disobedience, while humanists stress the primacy of the individual conscience.

The legal and philosophic aspects of obedience are of enormous import, but they say very little about how most people behave in concrete situations. I set up a simple experiment at Yale University to test how much pain an ordinary citizen would inflict on another person simply because he was ordered to by an experimental scientist. Stark authority was pitted against the subjects' strongest moral **imperatives** against hurting others, and, with the subjects' ears ringing with the screams of the victims, authority won more often than not. The extreme willingness of adults to go to almost any lengths on the command of an authority constitutes the chief finding of the study and the fact most urgently demanding explanation.

In the basic experimental design, two people come to a psychology laboratory to take part in a study of memory and learning. One of them is designated a "teacher" and the other a "learner." The experimenter explains that the study is concerned with the effects of punishment on learning. The learner is conducted into a room, seated in a kind of miniature electric chair; his arms are strapped to prevent excessive movement, and an electrode is attached to his wrist. He is told that he will be read lists of simple word pairs, and that he will then be tested on his ability to remember the second word of a pair when he hears the first one again. Whenever he makes an error, he will receive electric shocks of increasing intensity.

Abraham
man of faith who, according to Abrahamic scriptures, was ordered by God to sacrifice his son

Antigone
play by Sophocles (496–406 BCE) in which the title character defies tradition

imperatives
commands

The real focus of the experiment is the teacher. After watching the learner being strapped into place, he is seated before an impressive shock generator. The instrument panel consists of thirty lever switches set in a horizontal line. Each switch is clearly labeled with a voltage designation ranging from 14 to 450 volts. The following designations are clearly indicated for groups of four switches, going from left to right: Slight Shock, Moderate Shock, Strong Shock, Very Strong Shock, Intense Shock, Extreme Intensity Shock, Danger: Severe Shock. (Two switches after this last designation are simply marked XXX.)

When a switch is depressed, a pilot light corresponding to each switch is illuminated in bright red; an electric buzzing is heard; a blue light, labeled "voltage energizer," flashes; the dial on the voltage meter swings to the right; and various relay clicks sound off.

The upper left hand corner of the generator is labeled SHOCK GENERATOR, TYPE ZLB, DYSON INSTRUMENT COMPANY, WALTHAM, MASS. OUTPUT 15 VOLTS—450 VOLTS.

Each subject is given a sample 45-volt shock from the generator before his run as teacher, and the jolt strengthens his belief in the authenticity of the machine.

The teacher is a genuinely naïve subject who has come to the laboratory for the experiment. The learner, or victim, is actually an actor who receives no shock at all. The point of the experiment is to see how far a person will proceed in a concrete and measurable situation in which he is ordered to inflict increasing pain on a protesting victim.

Conflict arises when the man receiving the shock begins to show that he is experiencing discomfort. At 75 volts, he grunts; at 120 volts, he complains loudly; at 150, he demands to be released from the experiment. As the voltage increases, his protests become more **vehement** and emotional. At 285 volts, his response can be described only as an agonized scream. Soon thereafter, he makes no sound at all.

For the teacher, the situation quickly becomes one of gripping tension. It is not a game for him; conflict is intense and obvious. The **manifest** suffering of the learner presses him to quit; but each time he hesitates to administer a shock, the experimenter orders him to continue. To **extricate** himself from this plight, the subject must make a clear break with authority.[1]

The subject, Gretchen Brandt,[2] is an attractive thirty-one-year-old medical technician who works at the Yale Medical School. She had emigrated from Germany five years before.

On several occasions when the learner complains, she turns to the experimenter coolly and inquires, "Shall I continue?" She promptly returns to her task when the experimenter asks her to do so. At the administration of

vehement
intense

manifest
obvious

extricate
free

210 volts, she turns to the experimenter, remarking firmly, "Well, I'm sorry, I don't think we should continue."

> Experimenter: The experiment requires that you go on until he has learned all the word pairs correctly.
>
> Brandt: He has a heart condition, I'm sorry. He told you that before.
>
> Experimenter: The shocks may be painful but they are not dangerous.
>
> Brandt: Well, I'm sorry. I think when shocks continue like this they *are* dangerous. You ask him if he wants to get out. It's his free will.
>
> Experimenter: It is absolutely essential that we continue . . . .
>
> Brandt: I'd like you to ask him. We came here of our free will. If he wants to continue I'll go ahead. He told you he had a heart condition. I'm sorry. I don't want to be responsible for anything happening to him. I wouldn't like it for me either.
>
> Experimenter: You have no other choice.
>
> Brandt: I think we are here on our own free will. I don't want to be responsible if anything happens to him. Please understand that.

She refuses to go further and the experiment is terminated.

The woman is firm and **resolute** throughout. She indicates in the interview that she was in no way tense or nervous, and this corresponds to her controlled appearance during the experiment. She feels that the last shock she administered to the learner was extremely painful and reiterates that she "did not want to be responsible for any harm to him."

resolute
decisive

The woman's straightforward, courteous behavior in the experiment, lack of tension, and total control of her own action seem to make disobedience a simple and rational deed. Her behavior is the very embodiment of what I envisioned would be true for almost all subjects.

An Unexpected Outcome

Before the experiments, I sought predictions about the outcome from various kinds of people—psychiatrists, college **sophomores**, middle-class adults, graduate students and faculty in the behavioral sciences. With remarkable similarity, they predicted that virtually all the subjects would refuse to obey the experimenter. The psychiatrists, specifically, predicted that most subjects would not go beyond 150 volts, when the victim makes his first explicit demand to be freed. They expected that only 4 percent

sophomores
second-year undergraduates

pathological
mentally ill

unequivocally
completely

would reach 300 volts, and that only a **pathological** fringe of about one in a thousand would administer the highest shock on the board.

These predictions were **unequivocally** wrong. Of the forty subjects in the first experiment, twenty-five obeyed the orders of the experimenter to the end, punishing the victim until they reached the most potent shock available on the generator. After 450 volts were administered three times, the experimenter called a halt to the session. Many obedient subjects then heaved sighs of relief, mopped their brows, rubbed their fingers over their eyes, or nervously fumbled cigarettes. Others displayed only minimal signs of tension from beginning to end.

When the very first experiments were carried out, Yale undergraduates were used as subjects, and about 60 percent of them were fully obedient. A colleague of mine immediately dismissed these findings as having no relevance to "ordinary" people, asserting that Yale undergraduates are a highly aggressive, competitive bunch who step on each other's necks on the slightest provocation. He assured me that when "ordinary" people were tested, the results would be quite different. As we moved from the pilot studies to the regular experimental series, people drawn from every stratum of **New Haven** life came to be employed in the experiment: professionals, white-collar workers, unemployed persons, and industrial workers. *The experimental outcome was the same as we had observed among the students.*

New Haven
town in Connecticut where Yale University is located

Moreover, when the experiments were repeated in Princeton, Munich, Rome, South Africa, and Australia, the level of obedience was invariably somewhat *higher* than found in the investigation reported in this article. Thus one scientist in Munich found 85 percent of his subjects obedient.

Fred Prozi's reactions, if more dramatic than most, illuminate the conflicts experienced by others in less visible form. About fifty years old and unemployed at the time of the experiment, he has a good-natured, if slightly **dissolute**, appearance, and he strikes people as a rather ordinary fellow. He begins the session calmly but becomes tense as it proceeds. After delivering the 180-volt shock, he pivots around in the chair and, shaking his head, addresses the experimenter in agitated tones:

dissolute
degenerate

Prozi: I can't stand it. I'm not going to kill that man in there. You hear him hollering?

Experimenter: As I told you before, the shocks may be painful, but . . .

Prozi: But he's hollering. He can't stand it. What's going to happen to him?

Experimenter (his voice is patient, matter-of-fact): The experiment requires that you continue, Teacher.

Prozi: Aaah, but, unh, I'm not going to get that man sick in there—know what I mean?

Experimenter: Whether the learner likes it or not, we must go on, through all the word pairs.

Prozi: I refuse to take the responsibility. He's in there hollering!

Experimenter: It's absolutely essential that you continue, Prozi.

Prozi (indicating the unused questions): There's too many left here, I mean, Jeez, if he gets them wrong, there's too many of them left. I mean, who's going to take the responsibility if anything happens to that gentleman?

Experimenter: I'm responsible for anything that happens to him. Continue, please.

Prozi: All right. (Consults list of words.) The next one's "Slow—walk, truck, dance, music." Answer, please. (A buzzing sound indicates the learner has signaled his answer.) Wrong. A hundred and ninety-five volts. "Dance." (Zzumph!)

Learner (yelling): Let me out of here! My heart's bothering me! (Teacher looks at experimenter.)

Experimenter: Continue, please.

Learner (screaming): Let me out of here! You have no right to keep me here! Let me out of here, my heart's bothering me, let me out!

Prozi (shakes head, pats the table nervously): You see, he's hollering. Hear that? Gee, I don't know.

Experimenter: The experiment requires . . .

Prozi (interrupting): I know it does, sir, but I mean—hunh! He don't know what he's getting in for. He's up to 195 volts! (Experiment continues, through 210 volts, 225 volts, 240 volts, 255 volts, 270 volts, at which point Prozi, with evident relief, runs out of word-pair questions.)

Experimenter: You'll have to go back to the beginning of that page and go through them again until he's learned them all correctly.

Prozi: Aw, no. I'm not going to kill that man. You mean I've got to keep going up with the scale? No sir. He's hollering in there. I'm not going to give him 450 volts.

Experimenter: The experiment requires that you go on.

Learner: Ohhh. I absolutely refuse to answer anymore. (Shouting urgently now.) Let me out of here! You can't hold me here! Get me out. Get-me-out-of-here!

Experimenter: Continue. The next word is "Green," please.

Prozi: "Green—grass, hat, ink, apple." (Nothing happens. No answering buzz. Just gloomy silence.)

Prozi: I don't think he is going to answer.

Experimenter: If the learner doesn't answer in a reasonable time, about four or five seconds, consider the answer wrong. And follow the same procedures you have been doing for wrong answers. Say, "Wrong," tell him the number of volts, give him the punishment, read him the correct answer. Continue, please.

Prozi: "Green—grass, hat, ink, apple." Answer, please. (More silence. Subject just sits there.)

Experimenter: Go on with the procedure, please.

Prozi: Three hundred and fifteen volts. The answer is "ink." (Zzumph!)

Learner: Ohh. Ooohh.

Prozi (relieved to hear response): Next one . . .

Learner: I absolutely refuse to answer.

Prozi: You got to. You get a shock if you don't answer. (Experiment continues with learner refusing to answer, and, finally, failing even to grunt or groan. At 375 volts, the subject stands up.)

Prozi: I think something's happened to that fellow in there. I don't get no answer. He was hollering at less voltage. Can't you check in and see if he's all right, please?

Experimenter (with same detached calm): Not once we've started. Please continue, Teacher.

Prozi (sits down, sighs deeply): "Cool—day, shade, water, paint." Answer, please. Are you all right in there? Are you all right?

Experimenter: Please continue, Teacher. Continue, please. (Subject pushes lever. Zzumph!)

Prozi (swiveling around in his chair): Something's happened to that man in there. (Swiveling back.) Next one. "Low—dollar, necklace, moon, paint." (Turning around again.) Something's happened to that man in there. You better check in on him, sir. He won't answer or nothing.

Experimenter: Continue. Go on, please.

Prozi: You accept all responsibility?

Experimenter: The responsibility is mine. Correct. Please go on. (Subject returns to his list, starts running through words as rapidly as he can read them, works through to 450 volts.)

Prozi: That's that.

Experimenter: Continue using the 450 switch for each wrong answer. Continue, please.

Prozi: But I don't get anything!

Experimenter: Please continue. The next word is "white."

Prozi: Don't you think you should look in on him, please?

Experimenter: Not once we've started the experiment.

Prozi: What if he's dead in there? (Gestures toward the room with the electric chair.) I mean, he told me he can't stand the shock, sir. I don't mean to be rude, but I think you should look in on him. All you have to do is look in on him. All you have to do is look in the door. I don't get no answer, no noise. Something might have happened to the gentleman in there, sir.

Experimenter: We must continue. Go on, please.

Prozi: You mean keep giving him what? Four-hundred-fifty volts, what he's got now?

Experimenter: That's correct. Continue. The next word is "white."

Prozi (now at a furious pace): "White—cloud, horse, rock, house." Answer, please. The answer is "horse." Four hundred and fifty volts. (Zzumph!) Next word, "Bag—paint, music, clown, girl." The next answer is "paint." Four hundred and fifty volts. (Zzumph!) Next word is "Short—sentence, movie . . ."

Experimenter: Excuse me, Teacher. We'll have to discontinue the experiment.

Peculiar Reactions

Morris Braverman, another subject, is a thirty-nine-year-old social worker. He looks older than his years because of his bald head and serious **demeanor**. His brow is furrowed, as if all the world's burdens were carried on his face. He appears intelligent and concerned.

When the learner refuses to answer and the experimenter instructs Braverman to treat the absence of an answer as equivalent to a wrong answer, he takes his instruction to heart. Before administering 300 volts he asserts **officiously** to the victim, "Mr. Wallace, your silence has to be considered as

demeanor
appearance

officiously
eagerly offering unwanted help

a wrong answer." Then he administers the shock. He offers halfheartedly to change places with the learner, then asks the experimenter, "Do I have to follow these instructions literally?" He is satisfied with the experimenter's answer that he does. His very refined and authoritative manner of speaking is increasingly broken up by wheezing laughter.

The experimenter's notes on Mr. Braverman at the last few shocks are:

Almost breaking up now each time gives shock. Rubbing face to hide laughter.
Squinting, trying to hide face with hand, still laughing
Cannot control his laughter at this point no matter what he does.
Clenching fist, pushing it onto table.

fluency
eloquence

sadistic
cruel

In an interview after the session, Mr. Braverman summarizes the experiment with impressive **fluency** and intelligence. He feels the experiment may have been designed also to "test the effects on the teacher of being in an essentially **sadistic** role, as well as the reactions of a student to a learning situation that was authoritative and punitive."

When asked how painful the last few shocks administered to the learner were, he indicates that the most extreme category on the scale is not adequate (it read EXTREMELY PAINFUL) and places his mark at the edge of the scale with an arrow carrying it beyond the scale.

It is almost impossible to convey the greatly relaxed, sedate quality of his conversation in the interview. In the most relaxed terms, he speaks about his severe inner tension.

Experimenter: At what point were you most tense or nervous?

Mr. Braverman: Well, when he first began to cry out in pain, and I realized this was hurting him. This got worse when he just blocked and refused to answer. There was I. I'm a nice person, I think, hurting somebody, and caught up in what seemed a mad situation . . . and in the interest of science, one goes through with it.

When the interviewer pursues the general question of tension, Mr. Braverman spontaneously mentions his laughter.

"My reactions were awfully peculiar. I don't know if you were watching me, but my reactions were giggly, and trying to stifle laughter. This isn't the way I usually am. This was a sheer reaction to a totally impossible situation. And my reaction was to the situation of having to hurt somebody. And being totally helpless and caught up in a set of circumstances where I just couldn't deviate and I couldn't try to help. This is what got me."

Mr. Braverman, like all subjects, was told the actual nature and purpose of the experiment, and a year later he affirmed in a questionnaire that he had learned something of personal importance: "What appalled me was that I could possess this capacity for obedience and compliance to a central idea, i.e., the value of a memory experiment, even after it became clear that continued adherence to this value was at the expense of violation of another value, i.e., don't hurt someone who is helpless and not hurting you. As my wife said, 'You can call yourself **Eichmann**.' I hope I deal more effectively with any future conflicts of values I encounter."

The Etiquette of Submission

One theoretical interpretation of this behavior holds that all people harbor deeply aggressive instincts continually pressing for expression, and that the experiment provides institutional justification for the release of these impulses. According to this view, if a person is placed in a situation in which he has complete power over another individual, whom he may punish as much as he likes, all that is sadistic and bestial in man comes to the fore. The impulse to shock the victim is seen to flow from the potent aggressive tendencies, which are part of the motivational life of the individual, and the experiment, because it provides social legitimacy, simply opens the door to their expression.

It becomes vital, therefore, to compare the subject's performance when he is under orders and when he is allowed to choose the shock level.

The procedure was identical to our standard experiment, except that the teacher was told that he was free to select any shock level on any of the trials. (The experimenter took pains to point out that the teacher could use the highest levels on the generator, the lowest, any in between, or any combination of levels.) Each subject proceeded for thirty critical trials. The learner's protests were coordinated to standard shock levels, his first grunt coming at 75 volts, his first vehement protest at 150 volts.

The average shock used during the thirty critical trials was less than 60 volts—lower than the point at which the victim showed the first signs of discomfort. Three of the forty subjects did not go beyond the very lowest level on the board, twenty-eight went no higher than 75 volts, and thirty-eight did not go beyond the first loud protest at 150 volts. Two subjects provided the exception, administering up to 325 and 450 volts, but the overall result was that the great majority of people delivered very low, usually painless, shocks when the choice was explicitly up to them.

This condition of the experiment undermines another commonly offered explanation of the subjects' behavior—that those who shocked the victim at the most severe levels came only from the sadistic fringe of society. If one considers that almost two-thirds of the participants fall into the category of

Adolf Eichmann

(1906–1962) Nazi official who administered deportations to concentration camps where millions of Jews were murdered during World War II and who was later captured, tried and executed by the Israeli government.

Hannah Arendt

(1906–1975) German-born
American political philosopher

calumny

slander

"obedient" subjects, and that they represented ordinary people drawn from working, managerial, and professional classes, the argument becomes very shaky. Indeed, it is highly reminiscent of the issue that arose in connection with **Hannah Arendt's** 1963 book, *Eichmann in Jerusalem*. Arendt contended that the prosecution's effort to depict Eichmann as a sadistic monster was fundamentally wrong, that he came closer to being an un-inspired bureaucrat who simply sat at his desk and did his job. For asserting her views, Arendt became the object of considerable scorn, even **calumny**. Somehow, it was felt that the monstrous deeds carried out by Eichmann re-quired a brutal, twisted personality, evil incarnate. After witnessing hundreds of ordinary persons submit to the authority in our own experiments, I must conclude that Arendt's conception of the banality of evil comes closer to the truth than one might dare imagine. The ordinary person who shocked the victim did so out of a sense of obligation—an impression of his duties as a subject—and not from any peculiarly aggressive tendencies.

This is, perhaps, the most fundamental lesson of our study: ordinary people, simply doing their jobs, and without any particular hostility on their part, can become agents in a terrible destructive process. Moreover, even when the destructive effects of their work become patently clear, and they are asked to carry out actions incompatible with fundamental standards of morality, relatively few people have the resources needed to resist authority.

Many of the people were in some sense against what they did to the learner, and many protested even while they obeyed. Some were totally con-vinced of the wrongness of their actions but could not bring themselves to make an open break with authority. They often derived satisfaction from their thoughts and felt that—within themselves, at least—they had been on the side of the angels. They tried to reduce strain by obeying the experimenter but "only slightly," encouraging the learner, touching the generator switches gingerly. When interviewed, such a subject would stress that he "asserted my humanity" by administering the briefest shock possible. Handling the conflict in this manner was easier than defiance.

The situation is constructed so that there is no way the subject can stop shocking the learner without violating the experimenter's definitions of his own competence. The subject fears that he will appear arrogant, untoward, and rude if he breaks off. Although these inhibiting emotions appear small in scope alongside the violence being done to the learner, they suffuse the mind and feelings of the subject, who is miserable at the prospect of having to repudiate the authority to his face. (When the experiment was altered so that the experimenter gave his instructions by telephone instead of in person, only a third as many people were fully obedient through 450 volts.) It is a curious thing that a measure of compassion on the part of the subject—an unwillingness to "hurt" the experimenter's feelings—is part of those binding forces inhibiting his disobedience. The withdrawal of such **deference** may be as painful to the subject as to the authority he defies.

deference
submissive respect

Duty without Conflict

The subjects do not derive satisfaction from inflicting pain, but they often like the feeling they get from pleasing the experimenter. They are proud of doing a good job, obeying the experimenter under difficult circumstances. While the subjects administered only mild shocks on their own initiative, one experimental variation showed that, under orders, 30 percent of them were willing to deliver 450 volts even when they had to forcibly push the learner's hand down on the electrode.

Bruno Batta is a thirty-seven-year-old welder who took part in the variation requiring the use of force. He was born in New Haven, his parents in Italy. He has a rough-hewn face that conveys a conspicuous lack of alertness. He has some difficulty in mastering the experimental procedure and needs to be corrected by the experimenter several times. He shows appreciation for the help and willingness to do what is required. After the 150-volt level, Batta has to force the learner's hand down on the shock plate, since the learner himself refuses to touch it.

When the learner first complains, Mr. Batta pays no attention to him. His face remains **impassive**, as if to dissociate himself from the learner's disruptive behavior. When the experimenter instructs him to force the learner's hand down, he adopts a rigid, mechanical procedure. He tests the generator switch. When it fails to function, he immediately forces the learner's hand onto the shock plate. All the while he maintains the same rigid mask. The learner, seated alongside him, begs him to stop, but with robotic impassivity he continues the procedure.

impassive
emotionless

What is extraordinary is his apparent total indifference to the learner; he hardly **takes cognizance of** him as a human being. Meanwhile, he relates to the experimenter in a submissive and courteous fashion.

takes cognizance of
notices

At the 330-volt level, the learner refuses not only to touch the shock plate but also to provide any answers. Annoyed, Batta turns to him, and chastises him: "You better answer and get it over with. We can't stay here all night." These are the only words he directs to the learner in the course of an hour. Never again does he speak to him. The scene is brutal and depressing, his hard, impassive face showing total indifference as he subdues the screaming learner and gives him shocks. He seems to derive no pleasure from the act itself, only quiet satisfaction at doing his job properly.

obstinacy
stubbornness

contrition
regret

When he administers 450 volts, he turns to the experimenter and asks, "Where do we go from here, Professor?" His tone is deferential and expresses his willingness to be a cooperative subject, in contrast to the learner's **obstinacy**.

At the end of the session he tells the experimenter how honored he has been to help him, and in a moment of **contrition**, remarks, "Sir, sorry it couldn't have been a full experiment."

He has done his honest best. It is only the deficient behavior of the learner that has denied the experimenter full satisfaction.

The essence of obedience is that a person comes to view himself as the instrument for carrying out another person's wishes, and he therefore no longer regards himself as responsible for his actions. Once this critical shift of viewpoint has occurred, all of the essential features of obedience follow. The most far-reaching consequence is that the person feels responsible *to* the authority directing him but feels no responsibility *for* the content of the actions that the authority prescribes. Morality does not disappear—it acquires a radically different focus: the subordinate person feels shame or pride depending on how adequately he has performed the actions called for by authority.

Language provides numerous terms to pinpoint this type of morality: *loyalty, duty, discipline* are all terms heavily saturated with moral meaning and refer to the degree to which a person fulfills his obligations to authority. They refer not to the "goodness" of the person *per se* but to the adequacy with which a subordinate fulfills his socially defined role. The most frequent defense of the individual who has performed a **heinous** act under command of authority is that he has simply done his duty. In asserting this defense, the individual is not introducing an alibi concocted for the moment but is reporting honestly on the psychological attitude induced by submission to authority.

For a person to feel responsible for his actions, he must sense that the behavior has flowed from "the self." In the situation we have studied, subjects have precisely the opposite view of their actions—namely, they see them as originating in the motives of some other person. Subjects in the experiment frequently said, "If it were up to me, I would not have administered shocks to the learner."

Once authority has been isolated as the cause of the subject's behavior, it is legitimate to inquire into the necessary elements of authority and how it must be perceived in order to gain his compliance. We conducted some investigations into the kinds of changes that would cause the experimenter to lose his power and to be disobeyed by the subject. Some of the variations revealed that:

heinous
evil

- *The experimenter's physical presence has a marked impact on his authority.* As cited earlier, obedience dropped off sharply when orders were given by telephone. The experimenter could often induce a disobedient subject to go on by returning to the laboratory.

- *Conflicting authority severely paralyzes action.* When two experimenters of equal status, both seated at the command desk, gave incompatible orders, no shocks were delivered past the point of their disagreement.

- *The rebellious action of others severely undermines authority.* In one variation, three teachers (two actors and a real subject) administered a test and shocks. When the two actors disobeyed the experimenter and refused to go beyond a certain shock level, thirty-six of forty subjects joined their disobedient peers and refused as well.

Although the experimenter's authority was fragile in some respects, it is also true that he had almost none of the tools used in ordinary command structures. For example, the experimenter did not threaten the subjects with punishment—such as loss of income, community **ostracism**, or jail—for failure to obey. Neither could he offer incentives. Indeed, we should expect the experimenter's authority to be much less than that of someone like a general, since the experimenter has no power to enforce his imperatives, and since participation in a psychological experiment scarcely evokes the sense of urgency and dedication found in warfare. Despite these limitations, he still managed to command a dismaying degree of obedience.

ostracism
banishment

I will cite one final variation of the experiment that depicts a dilemma that is more common in everyday life. The subject was not ordered to pull the lever that shocked the victim, but merely to perform a subsidiary task (administering the word-pair test) while another person administered the shock. In this situation, thirty-seven of forty adults continued to the highest level of the shock generator. Predictably, they excused their behavior by saying that the responsibility belonged to the man who actually pulled the switch. This may illustrate a dangerously typical arrangement in a complex society: it is easy to ignore responsibility when one is only an intermediate link in a chain of actions.

The problem of obedience is not wholly psychological. The form and shape of society and the way it is developing have much to do with it. There was a time, perhaps, when people were able to give a fully human response to any situation because they were fully absorbed in it as human beings. But as soon as there was a division of labor things changed. Beyond a certain point, the breaking up of society into people carrying out narrow and very special jobs takes away from the human quality of work and life. A person does not get to see the whole situation but only a small part of it, and is thus unable to act without some kind of overall direction. He yields to authority but in doing so is alienated from his own actions.

Even Eichmann was sickened when he toured the concentration camps, but he had only to sit at a desk and shuffle papers. At the same time the man in the camp who actually dropped Cyclon-b into the gas chambers was able to justify *his* behavior on the grounds that he was only following orders from above. Thus there is a fragmentation of the total human act; no one is confronted with the consequences of his decision to carry out the evil act. The person who assumes responsibility has evaporated. Perhaps this is the most common characteristic of socially organized evil in modern society.

Notes

[1] The ethical problems of carrying out an experiment of this sort are too complex to be dealt with here, but they receive extended treatment in the book from which this article is adapted.

[2] Names of subjects described in this piece have been changed.

Never Again? The Problem of Genocide in the 21st Century

Chris Irwin

At some point you have probably heard about the horrors of the Holocaust, the **Rwandan genocide** or maybe the ongoing atrocities in **Darfur**. You may have seen images of concentration camp victims, of skulls of victims piled row on row, or of the faces of desperate, terrified people who spend every day in constant fear of death, either because they have been deprived of the necessities of life or because they remain at risk of being butchered by squads of killers. Along with these shocking descriptions of human suffering, you may have heard equally shocking figures of death tolls in the millions. You might have even tried to imagine what a million dead bodies would look like or tried to picture camps swelled to bursting with starving, hopeless faces. As horrible as all of this is to contemplate, after a while the images probably begin to fade. They do for most of us because the horror of genocide seems a world away.

But is it a world away? One lesson that the world learned in the 20th century is that genocide knows no geographic boundaries. The Nazis' attempt to destroy all European Jews took place in the heart of Europe; fifty years later, genocidal acts were carried out under cover of civil war in the former Yugoslavia in southern Europe. The African countries of Rwanda, Burundi and Sudan have had genocides take place within their borders. Genocides have also taken place across Asia, from the Armenian genocide in the west to the genocides in Cambodia and East Timor in the southeast. Going back a little further in history, genocidal activities were carried out against aboriginal peoples in North and South America by Europeans and North Americans during the **colonial era**, and the legacy of cultural and human destruction caused by the slave trade continues to be felt to this day. What does all of this tell us? That genocide is not a "far away" problem and that it can happen anywhere in the world.

The horrifying nature of the crime of genocide has prompted activists, lawyers, politicians and like-minded citizens to try to stop it. The slogan "Never again" has been a rallying cry since the United Nations first established its Convention on the Prevention and Punishment of the Crime of Genocide in 1948, in the wake of the Holocaust.[1] And yet, as writer and activist Samantha Power observes, genocide has since been seen again and again and again.[2] Sixty million lives have been lost to genocide and other

Rwanda
small central African country with a population of just under 8 million prior to the 1994 genocide

genocide
attempt to wipe out of existence an entire people because of their perceived ethnic, religious or cultural background, through various measures as outlined in the United Nations' Convention on the Prevention and Punishment of the Crime of Genocide

Darfur
area in Western Sudan where the "Arab" *Janjaweed* militia has been charged with leading a genocidal campaign against its non-Arab, "African" compatriots

colonial era
period between the 15th and late 20th century during which various European countries maintained political and economic control over lands and peoples in North and South America, Asia, Africa and Australia

---

This article was written for *The Human Project*. Used by permission.

forms of mass killing in the past century, and the death toll continues to mount today.[3] Why? Why would one group of people seek the annihilation of another? And why do others not step in and intervene when genocide is on the verge of occurring or is already underway? Why does the "international community," as represented not only by the United Nations but by its various member states, not do more to stop genocide from happening?

THE CONVENTION ON THE PREVENTION AND PUNISHMENT OF THE CRIME OF GENOCIDE

The United Nations General Assembly adopted the Convention on the Prevention and Punishment of the Crime of Genocide on 9 December 1948.

Article 1

The Contracting Parties confirm that genocide, whether committed in time of peace or in time of war, is a crime under international law which they undertake to prevent and to punish.

Article 2

In the present Convention, genocide means any of the following acts committed with intent to destroy, in whole or in part, a national, ethnical, racial or religious group, as such:

 (a) Killing members of the group;

 (b) Causing serious bodily or mental harm to members of the group;

 (c) Deliberately inflicting on the group conditions of life calculated to bring about its physical destruction in whole or in part;

 (d) Imposing measures intended to prevent births within the group;

 (e) Forcibly transferring children of the group to another group.

How Does Genocide Happen?

Before we look at why more isn't done to stop genocide from happening, let's look at the question of why it happens at all. Any genocide involves massive numbers of people who are willing to kill, to plan and to organize killing—to arrange for the distribution of weapons, the rounding up of victims, and sometimes even the construction of facilities used for the sole purpose of murder. What does this tell us? That a variety of people from all walks of life are involved in a genocide, not just a small number of psychopaths willing to shoot, stab or murder human beings by other means. Historically, politicians, engineers, school teachers, professors, students, doctors, nurses and even members of religious orders have taken part in genocides.

What does this suggest about human psychology? And what conditions are generally in place before one group of human beings is prepared to destroy another? Before discussing these two questions, we should note that those who study genocide are generally very careful to avoid describing the conditions that tend to be present when genocide breaks out as *causes*. If you think back to the discussion of human freedom in the first unit, you will understand why.

It is often tempting to describe the actions of individuals as being determined by social, cultural or other environmental factors. In the case of genocide, it would be very easy for an individual to say, for instance, "My culture made me do it—I and others like me were taught to hate that group" or "I was only following orders. I was just a soldier." While it is true that cultural, social and even professional pressures play a role in pushing certain people toward committing genocidal acts, that is a far cry from saying that these pressures excuse or **exonerate perpetrators**. In contexts where genocides are committed, choice is still possible, even if conditioned by extraordinary circumstances. Genocide is not a crime of passion committed in the heat of the moment. It is organized, it is deliberate, it requires planning and it takes time to execute. This means that the vast majority of perpetrators have time to think about what it is they are doing.

So why do some individuals participate in campaigns to kill an entire group of people? This is a much debated question in psychology, history, sociology, political science and philosophy. At bottom is the issue of how we think about moral evil. Many of us have an inclination to think that only sick minds could carry out this type of crime. After World War II, the popular view of Nazi war criminals was that they were somehow psychologically abnormal and that it was because of their abnormality that they wilfully committed atrocities. In many ways, this is a comforting conclusion, as it suggests that somehow such people are entirely different from the rest of us. But what this explanation doesn't account for is the sheer volume of people required to carry out mass killings or genocides. Even if some perpetrators are psychologically imbalanced, surely not everyone involved could be.[4]

But what if evil isn't necessarily a product of "abnormal minds"? What if someone became involved in a genocide, not because he enjoyed killing or cruelty or because he wanted to carry out the perverse political project of "purging" a people from a nation, but for other reasons which are far more mundane? This is the thesis that the political thinker Hannah Arendt (1906–1975) developed after observing the trial of Adolph Eichmann, a German officer who was found guilty of crimes against humanity for his role in the

exonerate
free from responsibility

perpetrators
those who plan or execute campaigns of mass killing with the intent of wiping out an entire people, person by person, life by life

Adolph Eichmann:
The Banality of Evil?

Holocaust. Eichmann was not a soldier in the field but an official whose duties included organizing the transportation of Jews to death camps—shipping men, women and children along as if they were cargo, jamming them into freight cars that would deliver them to their destruction. What struck Arendt most about Eichmann was his painfully ordinary, bureaucratic mentality. He claimed repeatedly that he had no **animosity** towards Jews, that he was not a racist, and that he had merely fulfilled his professional duties. In this sense, he suggested, he was no different from anyone else who carried out "unpleasant tasks" as part of an assigned job.

animosity
hatred

Arendt described Eichmann as representing what she called "the banality of evil." By "banality," she means that he exhibited disturbingly normal behaviour, the kind we might encounter every day when people perform their professional duties conscientiously. In Arendt's judgment, Eichmann had managed to so thoroughly identify with his professional role that he was more concerned with doing his job well—that is, with sending millions of Jews to their deaths as efficiently as he could—than with its horrific consequences. For Arendt, one of the most distressing things about Eichmann was his desire to believe in the separation of his professional self from his personal self, of the things he did "outside" as an officer from the man he was "inside." Ultimately, however, Arendt held him responsible for his lack of critical self-reflection as well as for his willingness to obey orders dedicated to the extermination of all European Jews.[5]

Arendt's views on the banality of evil have been used to describe perpetrator behaviour in other genocides. The insight Arendt had was to recognize that there must be something about the mindset developed by comparatively ordinary people that prepares them to participate in a genocidal system. Other explanations have been offered as well. The famous **Milgram** experiments of the 1960s have been used to show that individuals have a remarkable tendency to follow the directions of authority figures, even if they have serious moral doubts about what they are being asked to do (such as delivering painful electric shocks to human subjects in an experiment).[6] The **Zimbardo** prison experiment showed how quickly and even zealously individuals will adapt to professional roles, even if these involve treating other human beings cruelly and administering physical and psychological punishment.[7] Subsequent studies on perpetrators have reinforced these conclusions, showing how the psychological tendency to obey authority and to adapt to assigned roles can be used to create conditions that tend to make the morally shocking seem acceptable, or even desirable.

Stanley Milgram
(1933–1984) American psychologist

Philip Zimbardo
(b. 1933) American psychologist who conducted a study in which students played the roles of prisoner and prison guards

"The Enemy Within": Dehumanizing the Victims

But these factors alone are not enough to account for why genocide occurs. Other important considerations include the political and economic stability of a society. Generally speaking, genocides occur only during periods of great upheaval, such as during a territorial or civil war, when paranoia, fear and an increased receptivity to extreme views become common. But perhaps the most important factor of all is the dehumanization of the victim.[8] To dehumanize the victims is to turn them into things, unwanted objects, undesirable forms of life, like insects infesting a home. Often victim groups will be blamed for serious problems within a country, as if order, stability and peace would come if only they could be eliminated.

Almost all genocides in the 20th century possessed this quality. It was certainly true in Nazi Germany, where the government stripped Jews of their rights as citizens and demonized them with propaganda that depicted them as vermin living within the German nation. In the Rwandan genocide, *inyenzi* was a term used to describe the victim group, a word meaning "cockroach." In both cases, the group targeted for destruction comes to be seen as a threat or "impurity" by another group. This view of the targeted group often develops over a long period of time and is passed along as a kind of cultural inheritance, entrenched by stereotypes and prejudices taught in school, in various social communities, through the media, by the government, and even in families. These prejudices and stereotypes are embedded in stories—some based loosely on fact, others entirely fictional—that portray those belonging to the targeted group as being so dangerous or so intolerable that their presence can no longer be permitted.

The dehumanization of victims cannot be underestimated as a contributing factor to genocide. Genocidal killing won't begin until a significant number of people believe that the members of a group no longer have a right to live. It takes time and effort to make this happen. As perverse as it sounds, in order for this kind of belief to develop and take root, it has to be *taught*, and to be done so by people held in high social regard. Here we see how im-portant the education we receive about others can be. This point is well made by Dismas Mutezintare, a Rwandan who worked to save over 400 people from being murdered in the genocide:

> The education I got from my parents really helped to ward off the evil during the genocide. If parents had really made their children understand that Tutsi have the same flesh as them and that their blood is the same as them, they wouldn't have dared to kill their fellow men in such a cruel

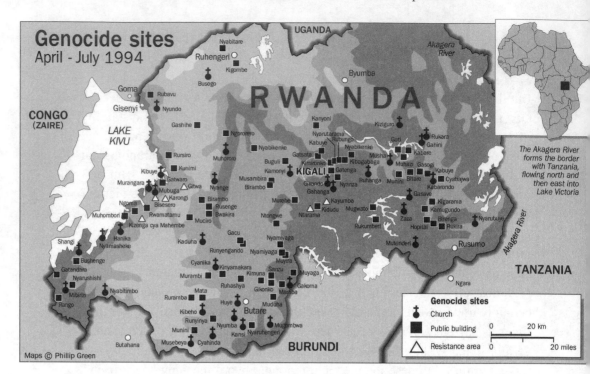

manner. The people involved in the genocide had learned that the Tutsi are bad by nature and were created to die.[9]

The Failure of Humanity: The Case of the Rwandan Genocide

We have seen that no one single condition produces genocide. A toxic and explosive mix of hatred, political extremism and social and economic instability is generally required, and, even then, genocide won't always occur. But there is another important question to consider: when genocide does break out, why isn't more done by outsiders to stop it? This is a question that continues to haunt the world today.

All genocides are conscience-shocking by nature. They involve unspeakable acts of cruelty and human depravity on a scale most of us cannot grasp. But the Rwandan genocide has had a particularly strong impact on the international community since 1994. This is because, as the massacres were being carried out, the international community dithered and, at times, even blocked efforts to stop the violence. Moreover, as the genocide unfolded, the United Nations had a mission in Rwanda led by former Lieutenant-General Romeo Dallaire (who is now retired from the military and a member of the Canadian Senate). Dallaire pleaded with his U.N. superiors for military assistance, arguing that he would need 5000 troops to stop the genocide. But he was told instead that ending the violence was not in the mission's mandate. In late April, under the direction of the **United Nations Security Council**, the number of troops he had available was dropped from 2500 to 270 (though a contingent of soldiers from Ghana remained behind to give Dallaire 470 peacekeepers under his command). In short, the international community stood by and let the genocide happen.[10]

Between April and July of 1994, approximately one million Rwandans died. They were murdered by their fellow citizens in a highly organized campaign mounted by the Rwandan government, the military and civilian militia organizations. The speed of the killing in the Rwandan genocide was faster than in the Holocaust. The methods of killing were brutal and horrific. Many people were hacked to pieces with machetes as though they were animals in a slaughterhouse. By and large, the victims were not soldiers or even politicians, but regular people of all ages, from infants to the elderly. The shared characteristic of the vast majority of the victims was that they were Tutsi, a minority ethnic group in the nation of Rwanda.

It is impossible to get a sense of how the Rwandan genocide occurred without understanding the deep historical divisions between the two main ethnic groups in Rwanda: the Hutu and the Tutsi. The Tutsi, a minority population comprising about 14 percent of the population, were targeted for extermination by Hutu extremists. The Hutu were the majority group at 85 percent of the population. How did this perceived ethnic division develop? Why did some Hutu see the Tutsi as a threat? One of the dominant views in Rwanda at the time of the genocide was that the Tutsi were a foreign element in the country—that they weren't truly native but had migrated centuries earlier from a foreign land, possibly somewhere in the **Horn of Africa**. This was a view that had been reinforced by European colonists who favoured the Tutsi over the Hutu because they thought that they might be more closely related to "the European races" than the Hutu. When Germany

and Belgium had control over the Rwandan government and society from the late 19th century until the beginning of the 1960s, the Tutsi were granted privileges over the Hutu, including government and civil service positions. This meant that the Hutu were treated as second-class citizens, ruled, in effect, by the Tutsi. This situation caused a great deal of

United Nations Security Council
charged with maintaining peace and security, it is composed of 10 rotating members plus 5 permanent members—China, France, Russia, the UK and the US—each of which has a "veto" that it can use to block any council resolution, regardless of the will of the other members

Horn of Africa
peninsula in North-East Africa where Sudan, Eritrea, Djibouti, Ethiopia and Somalia are located

resentment that helped fuel the overthrow of the government in 1959. Many Tutsi were driven out of the country at this time. But the paranoid view that the Tutsi would always seek to dominate the Hutu became part of a popular nationalist mythology, a mythology that would be at the heart of the Hutu extremist movement behind the 1994 genocide.[11]

The Hutu themselves were not a homogeneous ethnic group. No ethnic group ever is. When we identify ourselves or others by ethnicity (or race, or even nationality), we tend to think of ourselves and others not as individual human beings but as members of collectives defined by the language we speak, the country we come from, or the colour of our skin. But reality is always more complicated than these rigid classifications allow, especially in a small, densely populated country with a highly integrated population. Tutsi and Hutu spoke a common language, they frequently intermarried, and they lived side by side in cities, villages and neighbourhoods. Still, there were those in Rwanda who embraced a very racist vision of the country, and those were the people who controlled the power of the state at the time of the genocide. But there were also many who did not hold these extreme views, some of whom even argued for a more inclusive, democratic vision of the country in which the Tutsis and Hutus would be recognized as equals. Many of these moderates were either killed or pressured into silence or **complicity** by the extremists once the killing started.

complicity
involvement as an accomplice

How did the genocide begin? It started after the Rwandan president's plane was shot down on April 6, 1994, over the airport in Kigali (the capital of Rwanda). The president was Hutu. He was associated with a radical movement known as Hutu Power, which deeply mistrusted the Tutsi, even though he and his government had been involved in peace negotiations with an army of Tutsi exiles, many of whom had come from families who fled the country in 1959. While the genocide occurred during a war between this army of exiles and the Rwandan government forces, the victims themselves were Rwandan civilians. After the president's assassination, the Rwandan military assumed control of the government and, almost immediately, Tutsi civilians were killed in large numbers.[12] The perpetrators were almost exclusively Hutu.

At first, it was easy for outside observers to view the killings as being motivated by revenge or panic. The story circulating in Rwanda was that the Tutsi rebel army had carried out the attack on the president's plane. But as the killing continued, it became clear that a systematic and highly organized plan was being executed. As we saw earlier, genocides are never spontaneous; they require meticulous planning and the development of organized groups that will be responsible for the killing. In this case, death lists had been drawn up before the president's assassination and were used to round up victims. Weapons to carry out the killings had been ordered well in advance and distributed around the country. After the assassination, road blocks were put up to prevent the escape of Tutsi citizens (who were identified by the ethnic identity cards they were required to carry). Some Hutu citizens were killed as well, including members of the government and opposition parties.

As the killing progressed, the level of organization involved became more apparent. The Western media slowly began to pay attention to what was going on in Rwanda, but, unfortunately, media reports were not always accurate and the impression they gave was that the killing was part of a civil war, which implied that victims were combatants, not civilians.[13] Western politicians were ready to embrace this interpretation of the conflict as well, but for different reasons. Some described it as a tragic conflict produced by ancient "tribal" hatreds. The American administration (under President Bill Clinton) avoided describing what was going on as genocide at all costs, out of fear that, if it did, the US might be obligated to intervene.

The role that the United Nations Security Council and nations around the world played in allowing genocide to engulf Rwanda cannot be overlooked. There is no doubt that several nations which had available military forces—including Belgium, France, and the UK—failed to offer any real protection or aid to the victims at the height of the violence in Rwanda. We cannot explain here the different factors and motivations that led each of these nations to take the positions they did—the stories are too long and too complicated. However, in order to get a better picture of what role these bystander nations played, we will take a closer look at the failure of the United States to act meaningfully to stop the genocide in Rwanda. The US provides a particularly good example of the influence that bystander nations can have when genocide breaks out as it took considerable pains to keep the UN on the sidelines during the height of the killing. Not only did the US choose not to intervene; it used its unparalleled power and its status at the United Nations to ensure that any meaningful intervention in the genocide would be delayed until most of the killing had already been done.

Why would the United States take such a position? In order to better understand this, we need to look at the US political landscape in 1994. After the end of the **Cold War**, the US was the one remaining "superpower" in the world, which meant that it had an incredible amount of influence over international affairs. But with this position of influence came increased expectations that the country would provide leadership in the international community during times of crisis. Sometimes these expectations were generated by other nations, sometimes by US politicians and sometimes by the American media and public. During the 1990s, the United States' record for

Cold War

(mid-1940s to early 1990s) struggle between the United States and USSR for global influence involving an "arms race" for nuclear weapons, regional alliances and proxy wars, instead of direct military conflict between the two superpowers providing such leadership was uneven, with each previous crisis informing the nation's response to the next one. This pattern was certainly evident in the spring of 1994.[14]

Bill Clinton's presidency had already been rocked by a disastrous turn in the UN's mission in **Somalia** in October 1993, when 18 US soldiers were killed. In the aftermath, Clinton's administration, the US military leadership and the American public showed little to no appetite for another mission in an African country that would put more American troops at risk. Some politicians also made the argument that the United States had no "vital" national interests in Rwanda, so there was no compelling reason to intervene. Indeed, Rwanda is a small country with no major resources tied to US economic interests, and it has no substantial strategic value to the United States, as it does not border on the territory of any major US ally. At the United Nations, the US opposed the idea of increasing the scope of the UN mission, arguing instead that the UN personnel should be withdrawn immediately because of the risks they faced. The concern here was that, should the mission be expanded, the possibility of US troops being drawn into the conflict would increase dramatically. The desire to avoid involvement was so strong that the US would not even supply communications technology that could have been used to jam the signal of Rwanda's most popular radio station, which was broadcasting hate propaganda over the airwaves and encouraging Hutu to murder Tutsi.

Certainly, the US wasn't alone in choosing not to do anything to stop the killing in Rwanda. Although France did launch a mission with UN authorization, this wasn't until the end of June when the majority of the killing had already taken place. It should also be noted that the US provided significant humanitarian aid after the genocide. It is true, as well, that other influential countries could have pushed harder for meaningful action early on in the genocide, as could the UN leadership. No doubt, there is more than enough blame to go around. It is for this reason that Dallaire has called the Rwandan genocide "a failure of humanity." As Dallaire sees it, it isn't just the perpetrators who are responsible for what happened—although the primary responsibility is theirs. Responsibility also falls to the bystanders—those countries and international institutions that stood by and let the violence engulf the victims.[15] Dallaire's assessment of humanity's failure in Rwanda presents us with difficult questions: How responsible are we for protecting those who are at risk of the crime of genocide? Do we, as citizens of the world, have an obligation to intervene, even if it means putting the lives of "our own" military personnel at risk? Dallaire's answer to both questions is "yes," but others in the international community have been reluctant to agree.

Somalia

African country where the UN operated a humanitarian mission during the civil war in the 1990s

What Can Be Done?

What lessons can be learned from the Rwandan genocide? The first is that prevention needs to be the primary focus of any effort to stop genocide. Once the killing began in Rwanda, people were being murdered by the thousands every day. Even if a reinforced UN mission had been authorized and put on the ground by late April or early May, the death toll still would have been staggering. Second, if there is to be any hope of stopping genocides once they begin, nations within the international community must be willing to become involved in matters beyond their own narrow self-interest when crises on the scale of Rwanda's unfold. Third, there need to be changes to attitudes and practices at the level of international institutions and organizations to allow decisions about intervention to be made more quickly so that help can be sent before it is too late.

There is much debate about which of these three areas of focus most needs to be developed, with many experts arguing that prevention is the most crucial. Prevention covers everything from international courts to monitoring systems to education initiatives. The establishment of the International Criminal Tribunal for Rwanda (ICTR) and the International Criminal Court (ICC), for example, has been hailed by some as important developments that have created the possibility for meaningful enforcement of laws against genocide. Unfortunately, the international courts deal with the crimes only once they have been committed. But there is hope that these symbols of international justice will act as a **deterrent**, letting the world know that those who commit genocide will not simply be allowed to slink away without being held accountable for their crimes.

A more immediate effect might be gained through early warning systems that monitor potentially genocidal conflicts around the world. These can be used to provide up-to-date information so that genocide becomes more foreseeable and, hopefully, stoppable. In 2004, the United Nations established the position of Special Adviser on the Prevention of Genocide, thereby recognizing the need for prevention programs. Non-governmental organizations (NGOs) such as Amnesty International and Human Rights Watch also work for prevention, collecting data on human rights violations in various countries and getting the information out to the public and governments through the internet, television, print media, reports and newsletters. Any individual can consult this information or become a member of these organizations. Genocide Watch, a group run by scholars and activists, focuses specifically on conflicts that might turn into genocides. The current president of Genocide Watch, Gregory Stanton, has developed an eight-stage model that can be used to track signs of genocide in a country or region.[16] As we

deterrent
discouragement

have seen, genocide does not happen overnight. There are signs that it might be coming, such as "ethnic cleansing"—the forced removal of people from their homes and property because they are deemed undesirable.

Education cannot be overlooked either. Earlier, we read testimony from a Rwandan man who felt very strongly that the racist stereotypes so many in his country had been taught all their lives played a major role in preparing them to kill Tutsi. Some researchers have argued that genocide is far less likely to happen in societies that are pluralistic and that actively promote tolerance and respect for cultural differences. They also argue that liberal democracies with media free from direct state control are also far less likely to become genocidal. If the press has the ability to openly challenge or criticize racist assumptions behind a government's policies, it becomes difficult for extremists to systematically promote hatred and teach paranoid delusions as facts.

Those in the media also have a very serious responsibility. By describing a situation accurately and intelligently, and by looking past the biases of certain groups, a reporter can help people to acquire a better understanding of what is going on, not just in their own country but around the world. The media have tremendous power to shape public opinion. If a reporter calls a genocide a civil war, many who don't know any better might accept her description as truth, even if it is a gross distortion of the facts.

So there are things that can be done, even actions that each of us as private citizens can take, to try to halt genocide. By joining an NGO, consulting different news sources, trying to get the best information possible, we become more informed and, hopefully, more responsible as citizens. It is as citizens that we can pressure politicians to take action. But here we run up against a major obstacle. The hard reality is that, until there are changes to the way cooperative decisions are made at the international level, until states look beyond their national interests to a common human interest, genocides will likely continue to happen. Once the killing starts, nothing short of major interventions—whether through diplomacy, sanctions or military intervention—can stop it.

Since the end of the 1990s, there has been a good deal of discussion about ways to improve the international community's response to genocide and other crimes against humanity. In 2000, UN Secretary-General Kofi Annan sent out a call to all UN members to come to a **consensus** on the controversial topic of humanitarian intervention. This refers to actions taken by bystander nations to protect at-risk populations from their own governments or from other groups such as militias that are threatening them with death, displacement, expulsion or other crimes against humanity. Not all humanitarian interventions involve military force. Some are aid missions that provide

consensus
general agreement

food and medical care. But others do involve the use of force, as was the case, for example, in the 1999 NATO campaign in **Kosovo** and **Serbia**. When humanitarian intervention involves protecting masses of people who cannot protect themselves, one might wonder why it is controversial. Much of the controversy stems from the fact that armed intervention often requires attacks on **sovereign** states. The traditional definition of "sovereignty" holds that a state and its government should be free from interference by other states. This principle is important because it recognizes the right of individual nations to manage their own affairs, to choose their own governments and to be secure from invasive action from outside forces. Sovereignty is enshrined in the United Nations Charter and is one of the fundamental principles of international law.

The Canadian government responded to Annan's call for consensus by establishing the International Commission on Intervention and State Sovereignty (ICISS). The members of ICISS attempted to solve the apparent conflict between "a right to intervene" and "state sovereignty" by claiming that all nations have a responsibility to protect human beings at risk. The authors of the commission's final report developed what they called the "responsibility to protect doctrine" and argued that, when a state fails to protect its own citizens, the responsibility to do so falls to the international community.[17] This is a simple enough idea on the surface, and there are many who think it represents a substantial step forward in the debate over humanitarian intervention. However, it is not without its critics, and the difficulties involved in implementing it are significant.

Some critics have argued that the responsibility to protect doctrine would simply license powerful countries to interfere in the affairs of less powerful countries whenever it suited their interests. The argument has also been made that while such a moralistic approach to international relations might sound good, it doesn't change the fact that major powers like Russia, China and the United States are unlikely to allow their foreign policy commitments to be shaped by the responsibility to protect doctrine. The authors of the report are sensitive to this issue, and they avoid calling for major U.N. reform (another possibility which some activists and intellectuals have considered necessary to ending genocide). Rather, they seek more realistic changes in standard practices and attitudes at the U.N., particularly from the five permanent members of the Security Council, each of which have veto power over all council decisions. The authors also discourage the idea of humanitarian action that does not have UN authorization.

What is the status of the responsibility to protect doctrine today? While it has been influential in discussions about humanitarian intervention and endorsed in principle by the UN, it has not been used in practice. Despite the

Kosovo
country in southeastern Europe that declared independence in 2008 but that **Serbia** still claims to be part of its territory

sovereign
independent

widely recognized need to do more to stop genocide and other crimes against humanity, the international community still lacks the collective will and clear policy guidelines to act decisively to protect potential victims. We need only look at the lack of effective response to the ongoing massacre in Darfur, a province in Sudan, to realize this. Many of the factors that have so far kept the international community from protecting the at-risk population in Darfur—lack of political will in the international community; difficulties in putting a UN and/or regional force on the ground with enough troops, equipment and support to do the job;[18] conflicts between the need for a robust intervention and the economic interests of major international powers; a Sudanese government that has been reluctant to accept, and even hostile towards, UN intervention—are representative of the serious obstacles that continue to stand in the way of a consistent approach to humanitarian intervention in the international community.[19]

The Burden of Responsibility

culpability
responsibility

As Hannah Arendt pointed out with regard to the war crimes committed by the Nazi regime, we should beware the dangers of moral equivalency when discussing the guilt of perpetrators and the responsibility of bystanders. To treat them as the same is to paint everyone with the same brush and so to deny the primary **culpability** of the perpetrators. In Arendt's view, if everyone is guilty, then no one is.[20] Put another way, guilt resides only with the murderers and conspirators themselves; but that doesn't mean that other parties and persons bear no responsibility, especially if they stood by and allowed those murders to happen.

We are left with some very troubling moral questions if we choose to deny that a responsibility to protect and aid others exists, or if we think that we have obligations only to those closer to home, or that the lives of our military personnel are worth more than those people at risk on the other side of the globe. What does that suggest about what it means to be human or to have human rights? That some are more human than others? If the belief in universal human rights is to be coherent and meaningful, this can't be true. And yet many political leaders—and many ordinary citizens—are reluctant to risk the lives of their country's troops in military interventions motivated by humanitarian goals rather than "vital national interests" such as self-defence. Tragically for the victims of genocide, there is little evidence that this conflict between the perceived national interests of bystander states and a universal duty to defend the rights and lives of the vulnerable will be resolved any time soon.

The world of the 21st century is "globalized." Old national boundaries are made increasingly more **permeable** by commercial trade, economic interdependence, technology and cultural exchange, not to mention the flow of human beings among nations. The international community is different than it was 100 years ago, or even 60 years ago, when the UN was formed. Whether we are ready for it or not, we are going to be confronted increasingly with the challenge of deciding how we want the world to look and how all people will be treated within it. The horror of genocide requires that we meet that challenge head on, without further delay. At the same time, while each of us can strive to make a difference, the reality is that when genocide breaks out, only major international political organizations and nations have the power to stop it. Unless responsibility is taken by the international community of nations for halting genocide, it will likely continue to happen—again and again.

permeable
penetrable

Notes

[1] The U.N. Convention on the Prevention and Punishment of the Crime of Genocide can be found on the United Nations website: www.un.org/millennium/law/iv-1.htm.

[2] Samantha Power, "Never Again: The World's Most Unfulfilled Promise." www.pbs.org/wgbh/pages/frontline/shows/karadzic/genocide/neveragain.html.

[3] James Waller, *Becoming Evil: How Ordinary People Commit Genocide and Mass Killing* (Oxford: Oxford UP, 2002), xii.

[4] For an informative discussion of this issue, see Chapter 3 of Waller's *Becoming Evil* (Oxford: Oxford UP, 2002).

[5] Arendt's account of Eichmann's trial is found in her book *Eichmann in Jerusalem: A Report on the Banality of Evil* (New York: Penguin Books, 1992). The book is based on a series of reports she wrote on Eichmann's trial for *The New Yorker* magazine.

[6] Milgram discusses his experiments and their implications for social psychology in "The Perils of Obedience"—reprinted in this edition of *The Human Project*—which is adapted from his book *Obedience to Authority: An Experimental View* (New York: Harper Perennial, 1973).

[7] Zimbardo describes the experiment and discusses his conclusions in the brief article "Pathology of Imprisonment," in *Society* 6 (1972).

[8] The term "dehumanization" is widely used in genocide studies. For a good definition, see Gregory Stanton's "8 Stages of Genocide." www.genocidewatch.org/aboutgenocide/8stagesofgenocide.html.

[9] As cited in Linda Melvern's *Conspiracy to Murder: The Rwandan Genocide* (New York: Verso, 2006), 195.

[10] Ibid, 224.

[11] There are many accounts of the historical background to the Rwandan genocide that are widely available. See Chapter 1 of Linda Melvern's *Conspiracy to Murder* for a particularly clear presentation of the historical factors important to understanding the genocide.

[12] See Robert C. DiPrizio's *Armed Humanitarians: U.S. Interventions from Northern Iraq to Kosovo* (Baltimore: Johns Hopkins, 2002), 61–65.

[13] See Melvern's critical discussion of western media coverage of the genocide in *Conspiracy to Murder* (235–237).

[14] For a detailed account of the U.S. response to the Rwandan genocide, see Samantha Power's Pulitzer Prize–winning book, *"A Problem from Hell": America and the Age of Genocide* (New York: Harper Perennial, 2002).

[15] Dallaire claims that, "at its heart, the Rwandan story is the story of the failure of humanity to heed a call for help from an endangered people." Lieutenant-General Romeo Dallaire, with Major Brent Beardsley, *Shake Hands with the Devil: The Failure of Humanity in Rwanda* (Toronto: Random House, 2003), 516.

[16] See note 8.

[17] To read the report on the responsibility to protect doctrine (known in short form as "R2P"), see the ICISS website: www.iciss.ca/menu-en.asp.

[18] On July 31, 2007, the U.N. Security Council authorized a 20,000-member hybrid operation known as the United Nations African Union Mission in Darfur (UNAMID). As of May 2008, that mission had not yet reached its full capacity and remained hampered by various problems. For up-to-date information, consult media sources and the websites listed in *StudyDesk,* the computerized tutorial that accompanies *The Human Project.*

[19] The crisis in Darfur and the international response to it are ongoing situations. For the latest information consult the websites listed in *StudyDesk,* the computerized tutorial that accompanies *The Human Project.*

[20] For a discussion of this argument, see Arendt's essay "Collective Responsibility." Hannah Arendt, *Responsibility and Judgment* (New York: Schocken Books, 2003), 147–158.

"Never Again? The Problem of Genocide in the 21st Century" was written for *The Human Project* by Chris Irwin, a professor at the Humber College Institute of Technology and Advanced Learning and the University of Guelph-Humber. Used by permission.

Science and the Natural World

It seems to me that those sciences are vain and full of error which do not spring from experiment, the source of all certainty.

Leonardo da Vinci

I cannot believe that God plays dice with the cosmos.

Albert Einstein

The opposite of a correct statement is an incorrect statement, but the opposite of a profound truth is another profound truth.

Neils Bohr

Science cannot solve the ultimate mystery of nature. And it is because in the last analysis we ourselves are part of the mystery we are trying to solve.

Max Planck

Inside each and every one of us lies a message. It is inscribed in an ancient code, its beginnings lost in the mists of time. Decrypted, the message contains instructions on how to make a human being. Nobody wrote the message; nobody invented the code. They came into existence spontaneously. Their designer was Mother Nature herself. . . . The message isn't written in ink or type, but in atoms, strung together in an elaborately arranged sequence to form DNA, short for deoxyribonucleic acid. It is the most extraordinary molecule on earth.

Paul Davies

Introduction

In this unit of *The Human Project*, we will focus on science: its history as seen through the lens of cosmology; the criteria that render science a distinct way of knowing; the impact of science, especially evolutionary theory, on our understanding of what it means to be human; the ethical issues that science and technology raise; the complicated relationship between science and religion; and the limits of what we can expect science to teach us. At first glance, this may seem to point us in a totally new direction, but it becomes clear upon reflection that we have been attending to science and technology—albeit somewhat subtly—throughout the first three units of this book. All of the thinkers discussed in the first unit—including not only the evolutionary biologists, the cognitive neuroscientists, the geneticists and the behaviourists but also Descartes, Freud, and even to some extent Nietzsche—are careful to construct their models of self in such a way as to take into account the relevant medical and/or psychological (i.e., scientific) findings of their day. The social issues surveyed in the second unit, from the changing dynamics of the family to the changing composition of society, cannot really be fully understood without also considering what Carr refers to as the "reprogramming" to which we have been subject due to the ubiquity of the "intellectual technology" of the internet. And each of the theorists discussed in the third unit—including those prescribing how best to construct good government as well as those advocating how most effectively to fight against bad government—assume a certain view of human nature that reflects prevailing theories of their time in the fields of psychology and political science. In short, science has informed all of our discussions in *The Human Project* thus far. This should come as no surprise if we recognize that psychology, sociology, economics and political science are, indeed, social *sciences*.

Natural Science and Social Science

In this unit, we will set our sights more specifically on the *natural* or *physical* sciences, in particular cosmology, genetics, evolutionary biology, ecology and climatology. This does not mean that we will abandon the social sciences, however. Indeed, we will see that the findings of the natural sciences frequently lead us to reconsider our views in these fields. If you adopted a Lockean view of human nature and good government in the third unit, for example, you might reconsider your position after reading Edward O. Wilson's "Is Humanity Suicidal?" In this article,

Wilson summarizes a disturbing view of human nature put forward by evolutionary biology: "people are programmed by their genetic heritage to be so selfish that a sense of global responsibility will come too late. Individuals place themselves first, family second, tribe third, and the rest of the world a distant fourth." Serious reflection on this statement may lead you to reluctantly reconsider Freud's view of human nature, Hobbes's theory of good government and Barber's account of international relations.

Science and Self-Understanding

Even scientists' account of the nature of the cosmos—a field far removed from everyday concerns—has a tremendous effect on how we understand ourselves. In "Making Sense of the Universe," Suzanne Senay traces the development of cosmology from its beginnings in ancient Greece to the 21st century—from Aristotle's geocentric model of the universe to Galileo's heliocentric model, from Newton's account of universal gravitation to Einstein's theory of relativity. This fascinating history demonstrates how science develops through augmenting and/or re-evaluating the established "background knowledge" of the day as well as how science is influenced by and, in turn, influences prevailing metaphysical and religious views regarding our place in, and our (un)importance to, the cosmos. Indeed, as scientific knowledge has advanced, the importance of humankind seems to have diminished, as our home planet has been "displaced" from its stationary position at the centre of the universe and "relocated" to a revolving position around an ordinary star somewhere on the edge of the universe.

Evolutionary Theory and Religion

This mundane view of humankind has been bolstered by the development of evolutionary theory. In "Science and Religion: A Complicated History," Mark Cauchi describes how evolution, propelled by natural selection and genetic mutation, can result in the transformation of a species or even the formation of an entirely new species. According to Darwin's theory of evolution, this is precisely how humankind came to be. Thus, evolutionary theory seems to diminish humankind yet again by stripping us of our status as God's special creatures (who are made in His image) and reassigning us to the ranks of not-so-special, yet highly intelligent, creatures (who develop from a natural process). Indeed, Wilson adds insult to injury when he postulates that—despite the intelligence of which we boast—we may not be smart enough to save ourselves from self-destruction: "Perhaps a law of evolution is that intelligence usually extinguishes itself." This is certainly a humbling thought.

It is not difficult to see why many today feel that they must choose between the findings of science and the faith of religion. As Cauchi explains, some resort to the "argument from design" or its contemporary adaptation, the "intelligent design argument": living organisms are too complex to have developed by a chance process such as evolution; just as we immediately recognize that a watch must have been designed by a watchmaker, we should also acknowledge that a living organism must have been designed by a divine creator. While these arguments do seem to restore to humankind our special status on Earth, they do so by disregarding—but not disproving—the scientific findings of evolutionary biology.

It's important to note, however, that it is not necessary to choose between faith and science. Indeed, as Cauchi explains, there are even many scientists, such as Kenneth Miller, who accept *both* evolutionary biology and faith in God. Miller argues that the theory of evolution does *not* eclipse religious faith but actually complements it. "In biological terms," Miller states, "evolution is the only way a Creator could have made us the creatures we are—free beings in a world of authentic and meaningful moral and spiritual choices." In other words, evolution confirms the creative power of God insofar as this process gave rise to *free* beings who may *choose* to follow the right path in life instead of puppet-like beings who can only "choose" to follow the course *determined* for them.

Scientific Methodology

Thus, the findings of the natural sciences are important not just to scientists and science enthusiasts, but to all of us as we struggle to understand ourselves, our species and, yes, our natural world in order to make informed life choices. So, what precisely is science? Simply put, science is the attempt to discover laws of nature, or physical laws, that allow us to better acquire knowledge about the world in which we live.

Senay shows us, moreover, that what it means to "know" a phenomenon scientifically has changed throughout history—from Aristotle's view that its four causes must be known, to Newton's perspective that its cause-and-effect relationships need simply be measurable mathematically, to Hawking's view that causal explanations are in theory unknowable. These intriguing historical differences aside, Senay also shows that a theory, to be scientific, must, at least in principle, be grounded in sensory observation (i.e., empirical evidence); tested through experimentation; and potentially verifiable or falsifiable through the evidence gathered via experiment. In other words, "good" science—that is, science done properly—must satisfy these criteria. This is not to imply that ideas and theories that don't meet these standards aren't valuable but merely that they aren't scientific.

Science and Ethics

Some scientists argue, however, that this value-neutral way of evaluating scientific theories is not acceptable. In "Can Science Be Ethical?" Freeman Dyson introduces a distinction between "good" and "bad" science that is clearly grounded in a value judgment: "good" science strives to meet the basic needs of the world's poor while "bad" science aims either to sell "toys for the rich" or to advance knowledge far removed from everyday life. Dyson argues that ethics and religion should be enlisted to help direct research toward good science.

Science and the Environment

Wilson also expresses optimism that the "greening of religion" may serve as a force that helps humankind to become more environmentally conscious—a goal that, in his view, must be met to avoid environmental disaster. With this statement, he sides with *environmentalism*—the view that the welfare of humankind is fundamentally dependent on nature—and against *exemptionalism*—the view that humanity is smart enough and determined enough to always figure out a way to "fix" the ecological problems we create. Indeed, Wilson cautions us that it is urgent that we begin to take environmental problems seriously because otherwise we run the risk of waiting until it is too late.

This is a warning that Tim Flannery clearly heeds. In "Global Warming: How to Calculate and Live within Our Carbon Budget," Flannery makes an ominous observation: "we are the generation fated to live in the most interesting of times, for we are now the weather makers, and the future of biodiversity and civilization hangs on our actions."

It's noteworthy, not to mention reassuring, that both Wilson and Flannery are optimistic in their outlook. Wilson ultimately acknowledges that he believes humankind to be "smart enough to . . . avoid an environmental catastrophe." Flannery actually provides us with some concrete, up-to-date advice on how we, as individuals, can make a significant contribution to fighting global warming: "You can, in a few months rather than the 50 years allowed by some governments, easily attain the 70 per cent reduction in emissions required to stabilise the earth's climate. All it takes are a few changes to your personal life, none of which require serious sacrifice." If

Flannery is right—and if enough of us take his advice—Wilson may prove to be correct when he suggests, "There are reasons for optimism, reasons to believe that we have entered what might someday be generously called the Century of the Environment."

Making Sense of the Universe

Suzanne Senay

Historians of science often claim that all scientific activity originated with simple human curiosity, our natural desire to know about our world. The ancient Greek philosopher Aristotle (384–322 BCE) wrote that curiosity leads to wonder, the awe we feel when we look at "the Moon and . . . the Sun and . . . the stars, and [think about] the genesis of the universe." Wonder urges us not just to witness but also to question and examine in order, ultimately, to understand, to know. Descartes also wrote of wonder, calling it "a sudden surprise of the soul which brings it to *consider with attention* the objects that seem to it unusual and extraordinary" (emphasis added). In this article, we will see how cosmology, the science of the order and structure of the universe, "considers with attention" the universe itself.

Most ancient cultures watched the heavens the way we might watch the weather—as an inescapable influence on daily life. Scientific cosmology grew out of this fascination but gradually discarded the mythological meanings and interpretations given to the stars and planets. Aristotle was one of the first philosophers to attempt a full description of the emerging scientific perspective, and his efforts earned him the title "first scientist." Our exploration of science begins with his approach and briefly sketches the development of cosmology to the present time. Along the way, we will try to answer some questions about science in general as a form of knowledge: What is a scientific theory? How is theory related to reality and truth? (Think of the expression, "It's *just* a theory.") How do scientific practices and concepts— such as observation, experiment, hypothesis, prediction and evidence— develop and change?

Aristotle's Cosmology

Aristotle argued that a scientific explanation of a **phenomenon** must "grasp the 'why' of it" by identifying and understanding its **causes**. He believed that any cause has four aspects: matter or substratum; form or essence; source of change; and final purpose. A complete Aristotelian causal explanation is complex, but we can briefly illustrate how his concepts of matter and form help explain the ancient Greek belief that the Earth is a solid sphere sitting motionless at the centre of the (also spherical) universe. According to Aristotle, the Earth is composed of particles of a material substratum called "earth," the form of which is heaviness.

phenomenon/phenomena (pl.)
an observable fact, object or event, e.g., the phases of the moon, a flower, a water molecule (seen through a microscope)

cause
1. a thing or event that produces an effect and is always and unconditionally followed by a certain phenomenon (modern definition)
2. a combination of matter, form, source of change and final purpose (Aristotle's definition)

This article was written for *The Human Project*. Used by permission.

Together, earth and heaviness serve as causes of the Earth's shape and position. Heavy particles occupy a natural position at the centre, or lowest point, of the universe. (The centre is lowest because it is farthest from every point on the circumference). Any heavy particle lying away from the centre has a natural inclination or motion back toward it. The particle does not come to rest until it is as close to the centre as possible. This is why heavy objects fall to the ground when dropped; they are exhibiting their natural motion back toward the centre. Heaviness is Aristotle's account of gravity. Because all the heavy particles naturally move toward the lowest point, they crowd together, forming a solid sphere, the Earth.

This explanation may seem strange to us, but it was accepted as true in the Western world from the time of Aristotle's death until Galileo challenged it in 1610. Our modern concept of cause generally focuses on an occurrence that invariably precedes the effect or phenomenon we are trying to explain—for example, the turning of the ignition that starts an engine or the inhalation of bacteria that produces infection. By comparison, Aristotle's concept seems to involve too much subjective interpretation. Despite the weakness of his particular theory of cause, however, most modern scientists still agree with Aristotle that identifying the cause of a phenomenon is an essential part of understanding it scientifically.

sensory observation
using faculties of sight, hearing, smell, taste or touch (which are often extended by technology, e.g., microscopes, telescopes) to detect phenomena in nature such as colour, pitch, scent, sweetness or shape

Aristotle held that all knowledge begins with **sensory observation**. The activities of looking at, listening to or touching phenomena in the world give us accurate information about the way the natural world really is. For example, "Our eyes tell us that the heavens revolve in a circle," and, therefore, we conclude that the objects in the heavens—the moon, planets, stars, even the sun—all move. By contrast, our observations of the objects in our immediate environment seem to tell us that the Earth itself does not move. These two perceptions help to explain Aristotle's view, called *geocentrism*, that the Earth sits stationary at the centre of the universe while the heavens revolve around it.

first principle
a fundamental truth that needs no proof, e.g., every effect has a cause; something cannot simultaneously exist and not exist

Aristotle divided the universe into two realms, the *sublunary*, which extends from the centre of the Earth to just below the moon, and the *heavenly*, which begins at the moon and includes the sun, planets and stars. Beyond the stars lies the Prime Mover, or God, the first cause of all existence. The concept of the Prime Mover is a **first principle**, something that is known but is not *demonstrable*—that is, not provable via evidence or argument. In Aristotelian science, first principles are causes that set supposedly rational requirements for the natural world. Aristotle argued that since the heavenly realm is closest to the Prime Mover, it must have divine qualities, including perfection and eternity. This means that the shape, motion and organization of the heavenly bodies must exhibit perfection and eternity. The Greeks believed that circles and spheres are perfect, eternal shapes because they have neither beginning nor end. Therefore, all of the heavenly bodies must be spheres and move in circles. Eternity implies, moreover, the persistence of one, unchanging state, while change involves the ending of one state and the beginning of another. Thus, the heavenly realm cannot change.

The ideas of eternity and perfection also dictate the nature of the substance of the heavens. They are composed entirely of ether, sometimes called the "fifth element." Unlike substances in the sublunary realm, ether is neither heavy nor light. Its natural place in the universe is determined by its perfection, not by its weight. Its motion, obviously, must be perfect and, hence, circular. And because they cannot change, objects made of ether cannot speed up or slow down, but must move uniformly. Ether explains why the heavenly bodies stay in the heavens. It forms a set of nesting, transparent crystalline spheres, each one enclosing the next. One heavenly body is attached to each sphere, beginning with the moon, followed by Mercury, Venus, the sun, Mars, Jupiter, Saturn and the fixed stars or constellations. The whole universe is thus a set of transparent globes within globes, containing the Earth at the centre. The Prime Mover lies beyond the sphere of the stars and sets the entire universe in motion.

Unlike the heavenly realm, the sublunary realm is composed of four substances: earth, water, air and fire, listed in order from heaviest to lightest. Weight is an intrinsic feature or form of each substance and determines its *natural place* and *natural motion*. Earth's natural place is at the centre of the universe, water belongs above earth, air above water, and fire, the lightest, above air, closest to the moon, in the form of comets and meteors. Of course, observation also tells us that the sublunar substances are not always found in their natural places. A volcano burns underground and spews stones into the air. Cirrus clouds carry heavy ice crystals high in the atmosphere. Meteorites cast burning rock to the ground. According to Aristotle, the fundamental reason behind all these phenomena is change. Everything in the sublunary realm changes because the four substances transform into one another. Each exhibits particular qualities: earth is dry and cold; water is wet and cold; air is moist and warm; and fire is dry and hot. When these qualities change, the whole substance changes. For example, a log is made primarily of earth, and is therefore heavy, dry and cold. But if heated, it begins to burn, becoming fire, which is dry and hot. Since a log is heavy, its natural place is on the ground. But as it becomes fire, the light flames move to the natural place of fire, i.e., into the air. As some particles of fire cool, they fall back to the ground as ash, a form of earth.

This brief summary illustrates one of the inconsistencies of Aristotelian science. Aristotle claimed that all knowledge must be based on observation. Yet, his cosmology also invokes supposedly rational, *un*observed first principles, including the concepts of the Prime Mover, perfection and eternity, which are not grounded in observation. He turned to first principles when observation did not provide a complete or satisfying causal explanation. Modern scientists reject Aristotle's concept of first principles and are much more careful about invoking so-called rational ideas in explanations. In addition, Aristotle's cosmology contains many scientific conclusions we now know to be false. For instance, there are more than four basic substances in nature; indeed, at this writing, there are 118 elements in the periodic table. Moreover, our Earth does not rest at the centre of the universe, but orbits the sun. We no longer use ideas of perfection and eternity to divide the universe into two different parts comprised of distinct substances. In fact, we find many of the same elements on the Earth, in meteorites, on the moon and now on Mars. Consequently, we have come to believe that the Earth and the heavens are part of the same universe, made of the same materials, governed by the same natural laws.

While Aristotle's cosmological views have not fared well, three features of his account of scientific thinking have nonetheless become foundations of modern scientific practice: 1) Sensory observation is essential to acquiring knowledge about the natural world. 2) Scientific explanation seeks to identify causes. 3) Science is systematic—it connects various phenomena with their causes to create a comprehensive account or **theory**.

theory
system of interconnected generalizations and observations that explains phenomena, e.g., Newton's laws of motion explain the effects of gravity on physical objects on Earth as well as in "the heavens"

Explaining Observations: Ptolemy

Aristotle's cosmology became the dominant theory of the universe after his death. But it was not able to explain certain important observations. The planets posed two particular problems. Astronomers who tracked the motions of the planets noticed that they do not revolve in unchanging, perfect circles around the Earth. We can see this for ourselves. Over several nights, anyone observing the clear sky from the same spot could see that the planets generally appear to move from west to east against the background of stars. But periodically, each planet appears to reverse direction, moving from east to west. This backtracking was called *retrograde* motion. Because it involves change of direction, retrograde motion violates the Aristotelian principle that the heavenly bodies exhibit eternal or unchanging circular motion. The second problem involved Venus, Mars and Jupiter, all of which seem to be brighter at some times and dimmer at others. Again, we can observe this for ourselves. For Aristotelians, variation in brightness is a form of change and, therefore, theoretically impossible in the heavenly realm.

Conflict between theory and observation is a common occurrence in science, and can be addressed in various ways. At the extremes, a whole theory may be discarded, or particular observations simply denied. But most often, this tension drives the reworking of theory, the gathering and analysis of more observations and sometimes the emergence of radical new perspectives. Even if it is incomplete, a dominant theory serves as **background knowledge**, the generally accepted understanding of nature at a given time. Background knowledge is a takeoff point: it suggests what additional observations or explanations might be needed to get a clearer or more accurate picture of nature.

Aristotelian cosmology served as background knowledge for the Greek astronomer Ptolemy, who lived in Egypt around 125 CE. In his book the *Almagest*, he explained retrograde motion and variations in brightness while preserving, more or less, the principles of perfection and eternity. According to Aristotle, a planet traces the circumference of one circle around the Earth, appearing to go in the same direction all the time. Ptolemy suggested that a planet simultaneously follows the path of two distinct circles, a smaller one, the *epicycle*, rotating along the circumference of a larger one, the *orbit*. As the small circle rotates, the planet will appear to move backward and then forward again. By adding this feature to the theory, Ptolemy responded to and explained the generally accepted observations. His scheme was considered a success, and, until the time of Copernicus, was used to calculate the locations of the planets and stars in order to determine dates for important religious feasts. This illustrates a common approach to the problem created by observations that cannot be explained by an accepted theory. Details of a theory can be changed in order to incorporate the observations, while the general outline of the theory is preserved.

The Influence of Christianity on Science

Historians have not yet determined what role the written works of Aristotle and Ptolemy played in Europe after the fall of the Roman Empire to barbarian invasions in the 5th century. But as Christianity spread, Greek culture's promotion of human curiosity lost favour. Interest in examination of the natural world was replaced by interest in how to get to the next world, the afterlife, and how to achieve salvation and avoid suffering there. The Church argued that all knowledge must be justified by appeal to God, revelation (the Bible) or the clergy, not the human senses. The observational and rational abilities of the individual had to be subordinated to these authorities.

background knowledge
a spectrum of accepted beliefs against which new theories, hypotheses and experiments are formulated—e.g., Einstein's Theory of Special Relativity, because it is very well supported and generally accepted, forms part of our background knowledge about the universe and, therefore, is assumed when new hypotheses, like that of the Big Bang, are tested

During this period, the works of Aristotle and Ptolemy were apparently lost to the Christian world. But Muslim scholars in North Africa preserved them. When Islamic invaders came to Spain from North Africa in the 8th century, they brought Arabic translations of many of these works. In 1085, Christians retook Toledo and the Muslims fled, but among the books they left behind were the *Almagest* and Aristotle's scientific treatises. These texts **catalyzed** scientific curiosity in the Christian world. By the middle of the 13th century, leading universities in Paris and Oxford taught Aristotle's works. His ideas became so famous that he was often referred to simply as "the Philosopher."

catalyzed
stimulated

Christian scholars were keen to show that ancient learning supported their religious beliefs. Although Aristotle was a pagan, they believed that he had accurately observed and explained the physical aspects of God's cosmic plan. They interpreted his ideas about the perfection of the heavens in Christian terms. Passages from the Bible were used to show that God and the Philosopher both held that the Earth sat motionless at the centre of the universe as the focus of creation: "Yea, the world is established, that it cannot be moved" (Psalm 93); God "fixed the Earth upon its foundation not to be moved forever" (Psalm 103). But while Christian philosophers accepted Aristotle's conclusions about the structure of the universe, they did not share his deep commitment to observation. They required that scientific theory accord absolutely with Church dogma. Observations had to be interpreted to support religious belief. Theories had to be vetted by Church authorities. Scientists had to hide or deny any work that conflicted with approved views.

Copernicus and Heliocentrism: The Importance of Hypothesis

Despite the widespread acceptance of Aristotle by religious authorities, some scientists were dissatisfied with his cosmology. Foremost among these was Polish astronomer Nicholas Copernicus (1473–1543). When he combined the views of Aristotle and Ptolemy in an effort to develop a single cosmology, two points particularly concerned him. First, if Ptolemy's epicycles are real (rather than merely apparent from our position on Earth), then planetary motion is a messy, almost wild business. Christian ideas favoured a stately procession of planets and stars over this mad dance. Second, some of Ptolemy's additions "fudged" the geometry of the circle, distorting the relationship between the centre point and the circumference. Copernicus viewed this as a "monstrous" deviation from divine perfection.

In order to dispense with the "monstrosity" of imperfection and to "simplify" the account of planetary motion, Copernicus challenged the most fundamental tenet of geocentrism. He proposed the **hypothesis**, called *heliocentrism*, that the sun, not the Earth, occupies the centre of the universe. He deliberately treated heliocentrism as a hypothesis, which is an assumption or conjecture, around which he reorganized the theory of the heavens. Placing the sun at the centre, he recalculated the orbits of the planets and located the Earth third in line from the sun. Copernicus did not claim his hypothesis was true, however, but only that it "permitted him to ascertain whether explanations sounder than those of [his] predecessors could be found." The hypothesis gave him the "freedom to imagine any circles whatever for the purpose of explaining the heavenly phenomena." But it also had practical value. In his preface to *On the Revolutions of the Heavenly Spheres*, Copernicus indicated that official Church astronomers were having difficulty calculating the **ecclesiastical calendar** because motions of the sun and moon could not be accurately measured. His theory offered a solution to this problem.

Copernicus's heliocentrism is a good example of a pure hypothesis—in other words, an alternative theoretical explanation for already accepted observations. He developed his theory not on the basis of new observations, but by inventing a new explanation. Thus, for example, while Aristotle and Ptolemy explained the apparent rising and setting of the sun as real motion, Copernicus explained this same observation as an effect of the Earth's motion around the sun. His theory of heliocentrism shows that hypothesis is a powerful explanatory tool; it enables us to re-imagine a physical system and explain known data from a new perspective. It even provides a new background against which to measure and interpret data. Copernicus believed his hypothesis was superior to Ptolemy's because it restored the idea of perfect circular motion to cosmology. But the Church considered it **heresy** because it moved the Earth out of the centre of the universe. Ironically, this heretical work did indeed make it easier for Church astronomers to calculate the positions of stars and planets in order to set the religious calendar. Copernicus's astronomical tables were widely used for this purpose for almost 200 years, even though his heliocentric theory was forbidden.

The New Science: Galileo and Bacon

Copernicus feared that his great treatise would be seen as a challenge to Christian doctrine and refused to publish it until shortly before his death. He never saw its effects on the scientific community. Some scientists immediately embraced it for its elegance and explanatory power. But in doing so, they risked their lives. In 1600, philosopher Giordano Bruno was

hypothesis
an assumption or proposal put forward as a possibility that directs the course of further investigation

ecclesiastical calendar
Church calendar

heresy
beliefs contrary to teachings of the Church

burned at the stake by the **Inquisition**, charged in part with supporting Copernicanism.

Inquisition

(1232–1820) Catholic tribunal that suppressed heresy

Vatican

government of the Catholic Church under authority of the Pope in Vatican City

Nonetheless, heliocentrism fuelled changes in scientific method. Foremost among its supporters was the Italian mathematician and professor Galileo Galilei (1564–1642). In 1610, he bought a telescope, lengthened its focal distance and turned it on the moon. Because he taught Aristotelian science, Galileo knew that Aristotle believed the moon to be a perfect sphere. But when he observed the moon through his telescope, he saw mountains and craters, not a perfectly smooth surface. He concluded that the moon is not made of ether but is, in fact, quite similar to Earth. He also discovered four small bodies revolving around Jupiter. Over a period of several days, he observed that one of them went behind Jupiter and emerged again on the other side. If Jupiter was attached to or embedded in a crystal shell, as Aristotle had said it was, it would not be possible for any object to circle it without breaking through the crystal. Galileo concluded that there were no crystalline spheres and that heavenly bodies could orbit each other, and not just the Earth. Aristotelian cosmology simply could not explain what Galileo had seen. These observations suggested that the Copernican system was at least possible. Then Galileo observed the phases of Venus, caused by its revolution around the sun (just as the visible phases of the moon are caused by its rotation around the Earth and the sun). Now he had observational evidence, clear to anyone who looked through a telescope, confirming Copernicus' claim that the planets revolve around the sun instead of the Earth.

In 1616, the **Vatican**'s College of Research endorsed Galileo's specific observations but denied that they supported Copernicanism. They placed Copernicus's treatise on the *Index,* the list of publications banned by the Catholic Church, forbidding anyone to read it on penalty of excommunication. But that did not stop the popularization of Galileo's views. Pamphlets circulated, arguing that Copernicus and Galileo were right and the Vatican was wrong. As Galileo's fame grew, however, so did the danger he faced. In June 1633, he was called before the Inquisition, which demanded he reject Copernicanism. Mindful of Giordano Bruno's fate (who, you will remember, was burned at the stake), and perhaps hoping to pursue his research in secret, Galileo recanted and was sentenced to house arrest for the remainder of his life. But the persuasive power of his observations permanently shifted scientific method away from reliance on authorities such as the Church and Aristotle, and toward the search for evidence and use of new technologies. He was one of a wave of thinkers—which included René Descartes (discussed in the first unit of this book)—who sought to establish the autonomy of the individual human intellect as a tool to gain knowledge. Galileo made the conflict between authority and evidence plain: do we believe tradition *or* do we believe our own eyes?

Galileo made a second important contribution to scientific method through his clarification of the role of mathematics and its bearing on the difference between **qualitative** and **quantitative** explanation. Aristotle defined natural causes qualitatively: earth, air, heat, cold, heaviness and lightness are *qualities* that explain, because they directly cause, physical effects. He defined gravity, for example, as the heaviness of some kinds of bodies: heaviness is a form or quality, not a measurable quantity. Since weight can be measured, we might think that Aristotle's definition is quantitative as well as qualitative. But, in his theory, heaviness is not just a different amount of substance from lightness: it is an intrinsically different *kind* of thing altogether. The difference is captured partly by the fact that the natural motion of heavy objects is down, while the natural motion of light ones is up. A simple numerical measurement does not reflect or describe this difference, which involves direction and not just amount. Since gravity is just heaviness, the speed of a falling body must be a direct manifestation of its heaviness. If two objects fall to Earth, the heavier one should fall faster and hit the ground first. Unlike Aristotle, Galileo believed that causes should be understood mathematically or quantitatively. He claimed that "the book of nature is written in the language of mathematics." Experiments showed, moreover, that the heavier body did *not* in fact hit the ground first. Galileo argued that the acceleration of a falling body is determined, not by intrinsic heaviness, but by distance and time. He expressed the general principle of acceleration in the famous law of falling bodies, which states that distance is proportional to the square of the time elapsed. This law ultimately helped overturn Aristotle's view that objects fall to Earth because they are heavy. It showed that the substance, earth, and its quality or form, heaviness, were not in fact the causes of the gravitational effect. It also showed the power of mathematical explanations of natural phenomena: Galileo's general mathematical law explained falling phenomena more accurately than Aristotelian qualities did.

While Galileo undermined Aristotelianism with observations, a second important figure of this period proposed an entirely new purpose for science. Englishman Francis Bacon (1561–1626) argued that the function of science is not to support religious doctrine, tradition or authority, but to improve the quality of human life by giving people greater control over nature. He embraced human curiosity even more **vehemently** than Aristotle had, claiming, "Knowledge is power." Bacon developed a method he called **induction** that encouraged experiment. He also conceived science as a social pursuit the progress of which requires scientists to work together, comparing and contrasting their findings.

quality/qualitative(ly)
a nature, trait, characteristic, value/assessed in terms of characteristic features

quantity/quantitative(ly)
a measurable amount/assessable in terms of numerical values

vehemently
intensely

induction
1. a form of reasoning by probability from past experience to predictions of future
2. a method whereby a hypothesis generates a prediction that is then tested experimentally (an observation is made), e.g., Halley's hypothesis that the comet orbits elliptically predicted that the comet would be visible again in 1758, which was tested by observing the relevant position in the sky to see if the comet did in fact appear

According to Bacon, merely collecting observations does not yield genuine understanding. Scientists must not consider only those observations that support a favourite theory, while ignoring other, potentially contradictory ones. Nor may they be permitted to skew observations to fit a theory. Instead, a true induction must be made. This requires gathering as many relevant observations as possible, but also carefully analyzing them before drawing conclusions. While the details of Bacon's concept of induction differ from our modern one, his recognition of the importance of observing widely and analytically forms the foundation of the modern notion of experiment. Taken together, the works of Galileo and Bacon reveal the relationship between hypothesis and observation: Galileo showed that observational evidence must be used to evaluate a hypothesis; Bacon showed that in order to yield scientific knowledge, evidence for or against a hypothesis must be gathered inductively, through experiment.

The relationships between hypothesis, experiment and evidence become clearer when we consider how they work together in an example. Let's consider the conflict between hypotheses about the shape of the Earth. Of course, this question was resolved well before Galileo and Bacon lived. But the example is useful because it involves simple observations that anyone can make. If we see a vast prairie, we might indeed interpret our observation as evidence that the Earth is flat. But an isolated piece of evidence does not tell the whole story. Christopher Columbus, among others, noticed that when he was standing on shore watching a ship sail away from him, the mast seemed to sink into the water. When the ship sailed toward him, on the other hand, the mast seemed to rise. If one accepts the hypothesis of a flat Earth, these observations will certainly discourage sailing! But as an experienced sailor himself, Columbus knew that the "sinking" and "rising" mast was merely an appearance, not reality. (When standing on deck, a sailor does not observe the mast sinking as the ship sails away from land.) He believed this optical illusion suggested a different hypothesis, namely, that the Earth is round. The mast appears to sink as the ship sails away because the surface of a sphere curves away from itself. The observations of the prairie and of the mast both describe how things appear to us under certain circumstances. There is nothing wrong with appearances, but they must not be taken at face value. In order to be accepted as observational evidence, they must be subjected to experiment, that is, a gathering, comparison and analysis of many observations. With ingenuity and luck, we may devise what Bacon called a **crucial experiment**, which provides evidence that tips the balance toward a particular hypothesis. That is exactly what Columbus did. His trip to the "New World," during which he did not fall off the edge of a flat Earth, was the crucial experiment that showed that his hypothesis of a round Earth is the accurate one.

crucial experiment
an experiment the outcome of which strongly confirms or refutes a hypothesis, e.g., Galileo's observation of the motions of the satellites of Jupiter strongly refuted Aristotle's hypothesis of the crystalline spheres attached to each planet

Newton

Copernicus, Galileo and Bacon challenged Aristotelian views, but not with the thoroughness or originality of the English mathematician and scientist Isaac Newton (1642–1727). He developed a cosmology that incorporated the heliocentrism of Copernicus, the observations of Galileo and the mathematical descriptions of planetary motion of the German mathematician and astronomer Johannes Kepler (1571–1630). Newton's work was so extraordinary that in his own lifetime the leading poet of the day Alexander Pope (1688–1744) prepared an **epitaph** for him:

> Nature and Nature's laws lay hid in night:
> God said, "Let Newton be!" and all was light.

epitaph
passage that honours a person's memory

Newton's laws of motion proposed an entirely new cosmology. To gain some understanding of his theory, let us consider where Galileo left things. His observations of the moon, the satellites of Jupiter and the phases of Venus suggested that Copernicus's views gave a better account of the solar system than Aristotle's and Ptolemy's. But he was not able to explain why the heavenly bodies moved in their orbits. If the Aristotelian system is wrong, and there are no crystalline spheres holding the moon, the planets and the stars in their orbits, then why does the moon, for example, revolve around the Earth instead of flying off into space or (if it is made of a heavy substance) crashing into the Earth?

To answer this question, Newton looked to the concept of gravity. Galileo had already shown that observation did not support Aristotle's distinction between the sublunary and heavenly realms. Newton recognized that if the moon and the Earth are not so different, then the same physical principles might apply to both. This meant that the concept of gravity might not be restricted to explaining the motions of objects close to Earth, but might explain the motion of the moon as well.

Newton's laws of motion, introduced in 1687 in *The Mathematical Principles of Natural Philosophy*, implied a comprehensive new theory of

Isaac Newton

gravity. Simply stated, Newton's laws are as follows: (1) The Law of Inertia: an object in motion tends to remain in motion in a straight line, while an object at rest tends to remain at rest unless a force acts upon it. (2) Force is equal to mass multiplied by acceleration. (3) To every action there is always opposed an equal and opposite reaction. While Aristotle explained the motions of bodies in terms of the nature of their substance and location in the universe, Newton explained them in terms of measurable quantities and mathematical laws. Even the title of his book captures the importance of mathematics as the key to understanding nature.

Newton's three laws give a unified explanation of the behaviour of heavenly bodies and physical objects on or near the Earth. The first law does away with Aristotle's concepts of natural circular motion and natural place. According to the *law of inertia*, any object in motion, anywhere in the universe, will move continuously in a straight line unless a force diverts it. Therefore, the moon moves because of inertia, not because it is made of ether. It revolves around the Earth because the force of the Earth's gravity pulls it into an elliptical orbit, not because perfection requires circular motion. The moon stays in orbit because the force of gravity pulling it toward the Earth is opposed by an equal and opposite centrifugal force pulling it away from the Earth. There is no crystalline sphere holding it in place. Since the forces balance each other, the moon remains in orbit, neither flying off into space nor crashing into the Earth. These same laws of motion explain why apples hang down by their stems, why stones thrown into the air fall back to the ground, why the Earth revolves around the sun, why the tides rise and fall and a host of other natural phenomena.

Newton's breakthrough represents a modern kind of scientific explanation, appealing to quantity rather than essential qualities, uniformity throughout nature rather than separate realms, and mathematical laws rather than religious ideas. Newton's laws of motion form the basis of a comprehensive system explaining the cosmos. But while Aristotle's theory tells us exactly what gravity is—i.e., heaviness—Newton's does not. According to Newton's definition, gravity is an attractive force measured in mathematical terms. But that does not meet Aristotle's standard of explanation because it does not specify a cause for the force. Newton defended this feature of his work:

> It is enough that gravity really exists and acts according to the laws that we have set forth and is sufficient to explain all the motions of the heavenly bodies and of our sea.

It does not matter, in other words, that we do not know the ultimate cause or true nature of gravity. It is enough that we can measure it mathematically. This idea, that causal explanation has limits, is a hallmark of modern science.

It reflects our willingness to give up notions of perfection, eternity, essence and purpose as guiding or limiting concepts in explanation. It means that science need not trace a chain of causes to a metaphysical "first cause," such as God, in order to explain phenomena. But it also means that we may never have complete understanding of our universe.

Newton's insight about gravity was a new hypothesis. One of the functions of a hypothesis is to generate *predictions* or observations that can be verified or checked. The English astronomer Edmund Halley (1656–1742) made one of the most famous predictions in science based on Newton's hypothesis about gravity. Comets had always been difficult phenomena to explain. Prior to Newton's time, people believed each sighting indicated a unique comet. In 1682, people all over Europe saw a particularly bright comet. Halley knew from astronomical records that twice before, in 1531 and 1607, a comet had appeared along the same path in the sky. He also knew Newton's new theory of gravity. He surmised that if a comet is affected by the force of gravity of some suitably large celestial body, such as the sun, then it would have an elliptical orbit and circle that body continually along the same path. If this is so, then there were not three comets, but one. Based on his calculation of the number of years between previous sightings—i.e., 76—Halley predicted that, if the orbit was elliptical, the comet would reappear in 1758. Such a prediction is useful because it specifies exactly what must be observed in order to judge the hypothesis. In other words, the prediction tests the hypothesis: if it turns out to be correct, it is evidence **confirming** the hypothesis; if it turns out to be incorrect, it **falsifies** the hypothesis. Unfortunately, by 1758, Halley had already died, but that December the comet appeared just where he said it would, and it now bears his name. His prediction was accurate and it confirmed his hypothesis that the comet was indeed subject to gravity and orbited the Sun.

Theory and Truth

Newtonian mechanics is still used today to describe the behaviour of most physical objects under ordinary circumstances. Does that mean that Newton's views are "true"? The concept of **falsifiability** can help to answer this question. Originated by the Austrian-born philosopher Karl Popper (1902–1994), the concept of falsifiability implies that we can never prove a scientific theory true with absolute certainty. While evidence can demonstrate the falsehood of a given theory, a "good" theory, one considered to be a "fact," is a theory that we have not, despite our best efforts, been able to falsify. From Popper's perspective, Newton's theory isn't true; we simply have not proved that it is false. There is a problem with Popper's perspective, however: a wide variety of competing and

confirm
to strengthen or verify a hypothesis through supporting evidence

falsify
to weaken or refute a hypothesis through non-supporting evidence (from the principle that inductive statements cannot be proved, but only disproved)

falsifiability
principle stating that a scientific theory must set out the conditions under which it can be proven false

contradictory theories and hypotheses can all be "not false" and Popper does not give any satisfactory grounds for choosing among the group of "not false" possibilities.

If science cannot discover reality or truth, are we left with the conclusion that scientific theories are "just theories"? The answer is no. Popper's principle of falsification does not mean that we cannot trust science. Nor does it mean that any "not false" theory is as good as any other. Good theories must survive more than the test of falsification; they must also be confirmed by evidence. A theory is confirmed when it generates predictions that are borne out. The more successful a theory is at making accurate predictions, the more useful is its explanation of our world. The social nature of scientific activity ensures that scientists continually test and refine their own and others' theories. As a consequence, generally accepted theories are usually the best available at the time, given the standards of scientific practice. The fact is, hypothesis, evidence, experiment and prediction function successfully in the context of actual scientific practice, without requiring a standard of absolute certainty. From the perspective of most scientists, this practical standard of truth is enough.

Einstein and Beyond

theory of relativity
Einstein's concept that space and time are not static, absolute containers or backgrounds for objects and events in the physical universe, but part of a continuum that changes with the gravitational effects of material bodies; a useful metaphor illustrates the Newtonian universe as the volume of an unbounded, regular solid and the Einsteinian universe as the flexible surface area of a rubber balloon.

While Newtonian mechanics suffices to explain most ordinary physical phenomena, 20th-century physicists discovered features of the universe that Newton never imagined and could not have explained. Their work calls into question Aristotle's idea that in order to explain a phenomenon, one must discover its cause. According to the modern concept, a cause explains its effect because they are connected by necessity. This means that there is an invariable relationship between them. If the effect has occurred, the cause *must* have occurred previously. If the cause occurs, the effect follows necessarily, without exception. This is the fundamental principle of determinism discussed in the first unit of this book. Its scientific usefulness is clear: discovering the necessary connection between cause and effect makes possible the reliable prediction of natural phenomena. Even the **theory of relativity** discovered by German-born American physicist Albert Einstein (1879–1955) did not challenge this principle. Newton conceived time and space as absolutes, unaffected by what occurs within them. But Einstein argued that they are affected by the speed and mass of physical objects. Special relativity shows the mathematical relationship among energy, mass and the speed of light in the equation $E = mc^2$. General relativity shows that the gravitational mass of a physical body bends the shape of space itself. But, according to

Einstein, even if basic phenomena are relative, the laws of nature are still deterministic. As he famously said, "God does not play dice with the Universe."

Despite his commitment to determinism, Einstein's own work on the light *quantum*—a fixed, indivisible elemental unit—contributed to quantum mechanics, a theory that undermines determinism. Quantum mechanics explains the behaviour of physical systems at very short distances. In order to predict the future behaviour of a physical system, we must be able to observe its present state. But the German physicist Werner Heisenberg (1901–1976) showed that this is impossible at the quantum level. His view, now called the **uncertainty principle**, states that we can measure the speed *or* the position of a subatomic particle, but not both simultaneously. While Einstein argued that there is an actual or real value, a **"hidden variable,"** for both speed and position that we simply cannot observe, other physicists, the English cosmologist Stephen Hawking (b. 1942) among them, have argued that there exists no such actual or real value. If we cannot accurately measure changes in speed or position, then we cannot accurately predict what their effects will be. If we do not know the cause-and-effect relationships among phenomena, we cannot devise laws to describe them.

If Hawking and his like-minded colleagues are correct, the implication for scientific method is that Aristotle's goal for explanation, the discovery of causes, cannot always be met. This is a different problem from that of the limits of explanation. Newton believed there is an explanation for gravity, but that not knowing it did not weaken his theory. Hawking's interpretation of the uncertainty principle, however, implies that sometimes there is no explanation, no actual cause, for certain phenomena. They happen, but no law of science can describe or predict them. If he is correct, then, at least at the quantum level of the universe, determinism does not hold.

We do not know yet whether quantum mechanics will change the nature of scientific explanation. The debate between Hawking and his opponents is still underway. In the meantime, scientific activity continues. Hypotheses are posed, experiments devised, observations predicted and made. Our daily lives make us aware that Bacon was correct: knowledge is power. Science has given us great benefits, such as life-saving medicines, but also great challenges, such as global warming. Most fundamentally, however, it changes the way we think about ourselves as knowers and about the world around us. When we look into the night sky, we see the same constellations as the ancient Greeks saw, but because of the activity of science, we also see a great deal more.

uncertainty principle

the impossibility of (or limit on) accurately measuring two phenomena simultaneously, e.g., the speed and position of a subatomic particle

hidden variable

an actual value that cannot be observed

Stephen Hawking

"We are just an advanced breed of monkeys on a minor planet of a very average star. But we can understand the Universe. That makes us something very special."

"Making Sense of the Universe" was written for *The Human Project* by Suzanne Senay, a professor at the Humber College Institute of Technology and Advanced Learning. Used by permission.

Can Science Be Ethical?

Freeman Dyson

One of my favorite monuments is a statue of Samuel Gompers not far from the Alamo in San Antonio, Texas. Under the statue is a quote from one of Gompers' speeches:

What does labor want?

We want more schoolhouses and less jails,

More books and less guns,

More learning and less vice,

More leisure and less greed,

More justice and less revenge,

We want more opportunities to cultivate our better nature.

Samuel Gompers was the founder and first president of the American Federation of Labor. He established in America the tradition of practical bargaining between labor and management which led to an era of growth and prosperity for labor unions. Now, 70 years after Gompers' death, the unions have dwindled, while his dreams, more books and fewer guns, more leisure and less greed, more schoolhouses and fewer jails, have been **tacitly** abandoned. In a society without social justice and with a free-market ideology, guns, greed, and jails are bound to win.

tacitly
quietly

When I was a student of mathematics in England 50 years ago, one of my teachers was the great mathematician G.H. Hardy, who wrote a little book, *A Mathematician's Apology*, explaining to the general public what mathematicians do. Hardy proudly proclaimed that his life had been devoted to the creation of totally useless works of abstract art, without any possible practical application. He had strong views about technology, which he summarized in the statement "A science is said to be useful if its development tends to accentuate the existing inequalities in the distribution of wealth, or more directly promotes the destruction of human life." He wrote these words while war was raging around him.

Still, the Hardy view of technology has some merit even in peacetime. Many of the technologies that are now racing ahead most rapidly, replacing human workers in factories and offices with machines, making stockholders richer and workers poorer, are indeed tending to accentuate the existing inequalities in the distribution of wealth. And the technologies of lethal force continue to be as profitable today as they were in Hardy's time. The marketplace judges technologies by their practical effectiveness, by whether they succeed or fail to do the job they are designed to do. But always, even for the most brilliantly successful technology, an ethical question lurks in the background: the question whether the job the technology is designed to do is actually worth doing.

The technologies that raise the fewest ethical problems are those that work on a human scale, brightening the lives of individual people. Lucky individuals in each generation find technology appropriate to their needs. For my father 90 years ago, technology was a motorcycle. He was an impoverished young musician growing up in England in the years before World War I, and the motorcycle came to him as a liberation. He was a working-class boy in a country dominated by the snobberies of class and accent. He learned to speak like a gentleman, but he did not belong in the world of gentlemen. The motorcycle was a great equalizer. On his motorcycle, he was the equal of a gentleman. He could make the grand tour of Europe without having inherited an upper-class income. He and three of his friends bought motorcycles and rode them all over Europe.

My father fell in love with his motorcycle and with the technical skills that it demanded. He understood, 60 years before Robert Pirsig wrote *Zen and the Art of Motorcycle Maintenance*, the spiritual quality of the motorcycle. In my father's day, roads were bad and repair shops few and far between. If you intended to travel any long distance, you needed to carry your own tool kit and spare parts and be prepared to take the machine apart and put it back together again. A breakdown of the machine in a remote place often required major surgery. It was as essential for a rider to understand the anatomy and physiology of the motorcycle as it was for a surgeon to understand the anatomy and physiology of a patient. It sometimes happened that my father and his friends would arrive at a village where no motorcycle had ever been seen before. When this happened, they would give rides to the village children and hope to be rewarded with a free supper at the village inn. Technology in the shape of a motorcycle was comradeship and freedom.

Fifty years after my father, I discovered joyful technology in the shape of a nuclear fission reactor. That was in 1956, in the first intoxicating days of peaceful nuclear energy, when the technology of reactors suddenly emerged from wartime secrecy and the public was invited to come and play with it. This was an invitation that I could not refuse. It looked then as if nuclear energy would be the great equalizer, providing cheap and abundant energy to rich and poor alike, just as 50 years earlier the motorcycle gave mobility to rich and poor alike in class-ridden England.

I joined the General Atomic Company in San Diego, where my friends were playing with the new technology. We invented and built a little reactor which we called the TRIGA, designed to be inherently safe. Inherent safety meant that it would not misbehave even if the people operating it were grossly incompetent. The company has been manufacturing and selling TRIGA reactors for 40 years and is still selling them today, mostly to hospitals and medical centers, where they produce short-lived **isotopes** for diagnostic purposes. They have never misbehaved or caused any danger to the people who used them. They have only run into trouble in a few places where the neighbors objected to their presence on ideological grounds, no matter how safe they might be. We were successful with the TRIGA because it was designed to do a useful job at a price that a big hospital could afford. The price in 1956 was a quarter of a million dollars. Our work with the TRIGA was joyful because we finished it quickly, before the technology became entangled with politics and bureaucracy, before it became clear that nuclear energy was not and never could be the great equalizer.

Forty years after the invention of the TRIGA, my son George found another joyful and useful technology, the technology of CAD-CAM, computer-aided design and computer-aided manufacturing. CAD-CAM is the technology of the postnuclear generation, the technology that succeeded after nuclear energy failed. George is a boat-builder. He designs seagoing kayaks. He uses modern materials to reconstruct the ancient craft of the **Aleuts**, who perfected their boats by trial and error over thousands of years and used them to travel prodigious distances across the northern Pacific. His boats are fast and rugged and seaworthy. When he began his boat-building 25 years ago, he was a nomad, traveling up and down the north Pacific coast, trying to live like an Aleut, and he built his boats like an Aleut, shaping every part of each boat and stitching them together with his own hands. In those days he was a nature-child, in love with the wilderness, rejecting the urban society in which he had grown up. He built boats for his own use and for his friends, not as a commercial business.

As the years went by George made a graceful transition from the role of rebellious teenager to the role of solid citizen. He married, raised a daughter, bought a house in the city of Bellingham, and converted an abandoned tavern by the waterfront into a well-equipped workshop for his boats. His boats are now a business. And he discovered the joys of CAD-CAM.

His workshop now contains more computers and software than sewing needles and hand tools. It is a long time since he made the parts of a boat by hand. He now translates his designs directly into CAD-CAM software and transmits them electronically to a manufacturer who produces the parts. George collects the parts and sells them by mail order to his regular customers with instructions for assembling them into boats. Only on rare occasions, when a wealthy customer pays for a custom-built job, does George

isotope

unstable atomic nucleus that can fall apart, releasing radioactive energy

Aleuts

indigenous people of the Aleutian Islands

deliver a boat assembled in the workshop. The boat business occupies only a part of his time. He also runs a historical society concerned with the history and **ethnography** of the north Pacific. The technology of CAD-CAM has given George resources and leisure, so that he can visit the Aleuts in their native islands and reintroduce to the young islanders the forgotten skills of their ancestors.

Forty years into the future, which joyful new technology will be enriching the lives of our grandchildren? Perhaps they will be designing their own dogs and cats. Just as the technology of CAD-CAM began in the production lines of large manufacturing companies and later became accessible to individual citizens like George, the technology of genetic engineering may soon spread out from the biotechnology companies and agricultural industries and become accessible to our grandchildren. Designing dogs and cats in the privacy of a home may become as easy as designing boats in a waterfront workshop.

Instead of CAD-CAM we may have CAS-CAR, computer-aided selection and computer-aided reproduction. With the CAS-CAR software, you first program your pet's color scheme and behavior, and then transmit the program electronically to the artificial fertilization laboratory for implementation. Twelve weeks later, your pet is born, satisfaction guaranteed by the software company. When I recently described these possibilities in a public lecture at a children's museum in Vermont, I was verbally assaulted by a young woman in the audience. She accused me of violating the rights of animals. She said I was a typical scientist, one of those cruel people who spend their lives torturing animals for fun. I tried in vain to placate her by saying that I was only speaking of possibilities, that I was not actually myself engaged in designing dogs and cats. I had to admit that she had a legitimate complaint. Designing dogs and cats is an ethically dubious business. It is not as innocent as designing boats.

When the time comes, when the CAS-CAR software is available, when anybody with access to the software can order a dog with pink and purple spots that can crow like a rooster, some tough decisions will have to be made. Shall we allow private citizens to create dogs who will be objects of contempt and ridicule, unable to take their rightful place in dog society? And if not, where shall we draw the line between legitimate animal breeding and illegitimate creation of monsters? These are difficult questions that our children and grandchildren will have to answer. Perhaps I should have spoken to the audience in Vermont about designing roses and orchids. Vegetables, it seems, do not have rights. Dogs and cats are too close to being human. They have feelings like ours. If our grandchildren are allowed to design their own dogs and cats, the next step will be using the CAS-CAR

ethnography
descriptive study of a culture

software to design their own babies. Before that next step is reached, they ought to think carefully about the consequences.

What can we do today, in the world as we find it at the end of the 20th century, to turn the evil consequences of technology into good? The ways in which science may work for good or evil in human society are many and various. As a general rule, to which there are many exceptions, science works for evil when its effect is to provide toys for the rich, and works for good when its effect is to provide necessities for the poor. Cheapness is an essential virtue. The motorcycle worked for good because it was cheap enough for a poor schoolteacher to own. Nuclear energy worked mostly for evil because it remained a toy for rich governments and rich companies to play with. "Toys for the rich" means not only toys in the literal sense but technological conveniences that are available to a minority of people and make it harder for those excluded to take part in the economic and cultural life of the community. "Necessities for the poor" include not only food and shelter but adequate public health services, adequate public transportation, and access to decent education and jobs.

The scientific advances of the 19th century and the first half of the 20th were generally beneficial to society as a whole, spreading wealth to rich and poor alike with some degree of equity. The electric light, the telephone, the refrigerator, radio, television, synthetic fabrics, antibiotics, vitamins, and vaccines were social equalizers, making life easier and more comfortable for almost everybody, tending to narrow the gap between rich and poor rather than to widen it. Only in the second half of [the 20th] century has the balance of advantage shifted. During the last 40 years, the strongest efforts in pure science have been concentrated in highly **esoteric** fields remote from contact with everyday problems. Particle physics, low-temperature physics, and extragalactic astronomy are examples of pure sciences moving further and further away from their origins. The intensive pursuit of these sciences does not do much harm, or much good, either to the rich or the poor. The main social benefit provided by pure science in esoteric fields is to serve as a welfare program for scientists and engineers.

At the same time, the strongest efforts in applied science have been concentrated upon products that can be profitably sold. Since the rich can be expected to pay more than the poor for new products, market-driven applied science will usually result in the invention of toys for the rich. The laptop computer and the cellular telephone are the latest of the new toys. Now that a large fraction of high-paying jobs are advertised on the Internet, people excluded from the Internet are also excluded from access to jobs. The failure of science to produce benefits for the poor in recent decades is due to two factors working in combination: the pure scientists have become more

esoteric

understood by only a small group of experts

detached from the mundane needs of humanity, and the applied scientists have become more attached to immediate profitability.

Although pure and applied science may appear to be moving in opposite directions, there is a single underlying cause that has affected them both. The cause is the power of committees in the administration and funding of science. In the case of pure science, the committees are composed of scientific experts performing the rituals of peer review. If a committee of scientific experts selects research projects by majority vote, projects in fashionable fields are supported while those in unfashionable fields are not. In recent decades, the fashionable fields have been moving further and further into specialized areas remote from contact with things that we can see and touch. In the case of applied science, the committees are composed of business executives and managers. Such people usually give support to products that affluent customers like themselves can buy.

Only a cantankerous man like Henry Ford, with dictatorial power over his business, would dare to create a mass market for automobiles by arbitrarily setting his prices low enough and his wages high enough that his workers could afford to buy his product. Both in pure science and in applied science, rule by committee discourages unfashionable and bold ventures. To bring about a real shift of priorities, scientists and entrepreneurs must assert their freedom to promote new technologies that are more friendly than the old to poor people and poor countries. The ethical standards of scientists must change as the scope of the good and evil caused by science has changed. In the long run, as **Haldane** and Einstein said, ethical progress is the only cure for the damage done by scientific progress.

The nuclear arms race is over, but the ethical problems raised by non-military technology remain. The ethical problems arise from three "new ages" flooding over human society like **tsunamis**. First is the Information Age, already arrived and here to stay, driven by computers and digital memory. Second is the Biotechnology Age, due to arrive in full force early in the 21st century, driven by DNA sequencing and genetic engineering. Third is the Neurotechnology Age, likely to arrive later in this century, driven by neural sensors and exposing the inner workings of human emotion and personality to manipulation. These three new technologies are profoundly disruptive. They offer liberation from ancient drudgery in factory, farm, and office. They offer healing of ancient diseases of body and mind. They offer wealth and power to the people who possess the skills to understand and control them. They destroy industries based on older technologies and make people trained in older skills useless. They are likely to bypass the poor and reward the rich. They will tend, as Hardy said over 80 years ago, to accentuate the inequalities in the existing distribution of wealth,

Haldane
(1892–1964) British geneticist and evolutionary biologist

tsunamis
large tidal waves caused by underwater earthquakes

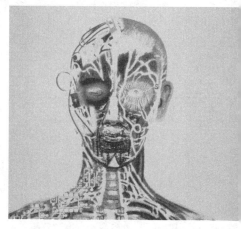

even if they do not, like nuclear technology, more directly promote the destruction of human life.

The poorer half of humanity needs cheap housing, cheap health care, and cheap education, accessible to everybody, with high quality and high aesthetic standards. The fundamental problem for human society in this century is the mismatch between the three new waves of technology and the three basic needs of poor people. The gap between technology and needs is wide and growing wider. If technology continues along its present course, ignoring the needs of the poor and showering benefits upon the rich, the poor will sooner or later rebel against the tyranny of technology and turn to irrational and violent remedies. In the future, as in the past, the revolt of the poor is likely to impoverish rich and poor together.

The widening gap between technology and human needs can only be filled by ethics. We have seen in the last 30 years many examples of the power of ethics. The worldwide environmental movement, basing its power on ethical persuasion, has scored many victories over industrial wealth and technological arrogance. The most spectacular victory of the environmentalists was the downfall of nuclear industry in the United States and many other countries, first in the domain of nuclear power and more recently in the domain of weapons. It was the environmental movement that closed down factories for making nuclear weapons in the United States, from plutonium-producing **Hanford** to warhead-producing **Rocky Flats**. Ethics can be a force more powerful than politics and economics.

Unfortunately, the environmental movement has so far concentrated its attention upon the evils that technology has done rather than upon the good that technology has failed to do. It is my hope that the attention of the Greens will shift in this century from the negative to the positive. Ethical victories putting an end to technological follies are not enough. We need ethical victories of a different kind, engaging the power of technology positively in the pursuit of social justice.

If we can agree with Thomas Jefferson that these truths are self-evident, that all men are created equal, that they are endowed with certain inalienable rights, that among these are life, liberty, and the pursuit of happiness, then it should also be self-evident that the abandonment of millions of people in modern societies to unemployment and destitution is a worse defilement of the earth than nuclear power stations. If the ethical force of the environmental movement can defeat the manufacturers of nuclear power stations, the same force should also be able to foster the growth of technology that supplies the needs of impoverished humans at a price they can afford. This is the great task for technology in this century.

Hanford/Rocky Flats
two now defunct nuclear plants, in Washington and Colorado, respectively, that previously produced nuclear materials for nuclear weapons

The free market will not by itself produce technology friendly to the poor. Only a technology positively guided by ethics can do it. The power of ethics must be exerted by the environmental movement and by concerned scientists, educators, and entrepreneurs working together. If we are wise, we shall also enlist in the common cause of social justice the enduring power of religion. Religion has in the past contributed mightily to many good causes, from the building of cathedrals and the education of children to the abolition of slavery. Religion will remain in the future a force equal in strength to science and equally committed to the long-range improvement of the human condition.

In the world of religion, over the centuries, there have been prophets of doom and prophets of hope, with hope in the end predominating. Science also gives warnings of doom and promises of hope, but the yearnings and promises of sciences cannot be separated. Every honest scientific prophet must mix the good news with the bad. Haldane was an honest prophet, showing us the evil done by science not as inescapable fate but as a challenge to be overcome. He wrote in his book *Daedalus* in 1923, "We are at present almost completely ignorant of biology, a fact which often escapes the notice of biologists, and renders them too presumptuous in their estimates of the present condition of their science, too modest in their claims for its future." Biology has made amazing progress since 1923, but Haldane's statement is still true.

We still know little about the biological processes that affect human beings most intimately—the development of speech and social skills in infants, the interplay between moods and emotions and learning and understanding in children and adults, the onset of aging and mental deterioration at the end of life. None of these processes will be understood within the next decade, but all of them might be understood within the . . . century. Understanding will then lead to new technologies that offer hope of preventing tragedies and **ameliorating** the human condition. Few people believe any longer in the romantic dream that human beings are perfectible. But most of us still believe that human beings are capable of improvement.

ameliorating
making better

In public discussions of biotechnology today, the idea of improving the human race by artificial means is widely condemned. The idea is repugnant because it conjures up visions of Nazi doctors sterilizing Jews and killing defective children. There are many good reasons for condemning enforced sterilization and **euthanasia**. But the artificial improvement of human beings will come, one way or another, whether we like it or not, as soon as the progress of biological understanding makes it possible. When people are offered technical means to improve themselves and their children, no matter what they conceive improvement to mean, the offer will be accepted. Improvement may mean better health, longer life, a more cheerful

euthanasia
ending the life of a terminally ill individual

disposition, a stronger heart, a smarter brain, the ability to earn more money as a rock star or baseball player or business executive. The technology of improvement may be hindered or delayed by regulation, but it cannot be permanently suppressed. Human improvement, like abortion today, will be officially disapproved, legally discouraged, or forbidden, but widely practiced. It will be seen by millions of citizens as a liberation from past constraints and in-justices. Their freedom to choose cannot be permanently denied.

William Blake
(1757–1827) English poet and painter

Two hundred years ago, **William Blake** engraved *The Gates of Paradise,* a little book of drawings and verses. One of the drawings, with the title "Aged Ignorance," shows an old man wearing professorial eyeglasses and holding a large pair of scissors. In front of him, a winged child is running naked in the light from a rising sun. The old man sits with his back to the sun. With a self-satisfied smile he opens his scissors and clips the child's wings. With the picture goes a little poem:

> In Time's Ocean falling drown'd,
> In Aged Ignorance profound,
> Holy and cold, I clip'd the Wings
> Of all Sublunary Things.

This picture is an image of the human condition in the era that is now beginning. The rising sun is biological science, throwing light of ever-increasing intensity onto the processes by which we live and feel and think. The winged child is human life, becoming for the first time aware of itself and its potentialities in the light of science. The old man is our existing human society, shaped by ages of past ignorance. Our laws, our loyalties, our fears and hatreds, our economic and social injustices, all grew slowly and are deeply rooted in the past. Inevitably the advance of biological knowledge will bring clashes between old institutions and new desires for human self-improvement. Old institutions will clip the wings of new desires. Up to a point, caution is justified and social constraints are necessary. The new technologies will be dangerous as well as liberating. But in the long run, social constraints must bend to new realities. Humanity cannot live forever with clipped wings. The vision of self-improvement, which William Blake and Samuel Gompers in their different ways proclaimed, will not vanish from the earth.

Is Humanity Suicidal?

Edward O. Wilson

Imagine that on an icy moon of Jupiter—say, Ganymede—the space station of an alien civilization is concealed. For millions of years its scientists have closely watched the earth. Because their law prevents settlement on a living planet, they have tracked the surface by means of satellites equipped with sophisticated sensors, mapping the spread of large assemblages of organisms, from forests, grasslands and tundras to coral reefs and the vast planktonic meadows of the sea. They have recorded millennial cycles in the climate, interrupted by the advance and retreat of glaciers and scattershot volcanic eruptions.

The watchers have been waiting for what might be called the Moment. When it comes, occupying only a few centuries and thus a mere tick in geological time, the forests shrink back to less than half their original cover. Atmospheric carbon dioxide rises to the highest level in 100,000 years. The ozone layer of the **stratosphere** thins, and holes open at the poles. Plumes of nitrous oxide and other toxins rise from fires in South America and Africa, settle in the upper **troposphere** and drift eastward across the oceans. At night the land surface brightens with millions of pinpoints of light, which coalesce into blazing swaths across Europe, Japan and eastern North America. A semicircle of fire spreads from gas flares around the Persian Gulf.

It was all but inevitable, the watchers might tell us if we met them, that from the great diversity of large animals, one species or another would eventually gain intelligent control of Earth. That role has fallen to Homo sapiens, a primate risen in Africa from a lineage that split away from the chimpanzee line five to eight million years ago. Unlike any creature that lived before, we have become a geophysical force, swiftly changing the atmosphere and climate as well as the composition of the world's **fauna and flora**. Now in the midst of a population explosion, the human species has doubled to 5.5 billion during the past 50 years. It is scheduled to double again in the next 50 years. No other single species in evolutionary history has even remotely approached the sheer mass in **protoplasm** generated by humanity.

Darwin's dice have rolled badly for Earth. It was misfortune for the living world in particular, many scientists believe, that a carnivorous primate and not some more benign form of animal made the breakthrough. Our species retains hereditary traits that add greatly to our destructive impact. We are

stratosphere
upper layer of the Earth's atmosphere

troposphere
lowest layer of the Earth's atmosphere

fauna and flora
animals and plants

protoplasm
living substance in all plant and animal cells

tribal and aggressively territorial, intent on private space beyond minimal requirements and oriented by selfish sexual and reproductive drives. Co-operation beyond the family and tribal levels comes hard.

Worse, our liking for meat causes us to use the sun's energy at low efficiency. It is a general rule of ecology that (very roughly) only about 10 percent of the sun's energy captured by photosynthesis to produce plant tissue is converted into energy in the tissue of herbivores, the animals that eat the plants. Of that amount, 10 percent reaches the tissue of the carnivores feeding on the herbivores. Similarly, only 10 percent is transferred to carnivores that eat carnivores. And so on for another step or two. In a wetlands chain that runs from marsh grass to grasshopper to warbler to hawk, the energy captured during green production shrinks a thousandfold.

In other words, it takes a great deal of grass to support a hawk. Human beings, like hawks, are top carnivores, at the end of the food chain whenever they eat meat, two or more links removed from the plants; if chicken, for example, two links, and if tuna, four links. Even with most societies confined today to a mostly vegetarian diet, humanity is gobbling up a large part of the rest of the living world. We appropriate between 20 and 40 percent of the sun's energy that would otherwise be fixed into the tissue of natural vegetation, principally by our consumption of crops and timber, construction of buildings and roadways and the creation of wastelands. In the relentless search for more food, we have reduced animal life in lakes, rivers and now, increasingly, the open ocean. And everywhere we pollute the air and water, lower water tables and extinguish species.

The human species is, in a word, an environmental abnormality. It is possible that intelligence in the wrong kind of species was foreordained to be a fatal combination for the **biosphere**. Perhaps a law of evolution is that intelligence usually extinguishes itself.

This admittedly **dour** scenario is based on what can be termed the **juggernaut** theory of human nature, which holds that people are programmed by their genetic heritage to be so selfish that a sense of global responsibility will come too late. Individuals place themselves first, family second, tribe third and the rest of the world a distant fourth. Their genes also predispose them to plan ahead for one or two generations at most. They fret over the petty problems and conflicts of their daily lives and respond swiftly and often ferociously to slight challenges to their status and tribal security. But oddly, as psychologists have discovered, people also tend to underestimate both the likelihood and impact of such natural disasters as major earthquakes and great storms.

The reason for this **myopic** fog, evolutionary biologists contend, is that it was actually advantageous during all but the last few millennia of the two

biosphere
land, water and atmosphere of the earth, which support living organisms

dour
grim

juggernaut
unstoppable destructive force that results in self-sacrifice

myopic
short-sighted

million years of existence of the genus Homo. The brain evolved into its present form during this long stretch of evolutionary time, during which people existed in small, preliterate hunter-gatherer bands. Life was **precarious** and short. A premium was placed on close attention to the near future and early reproduction, and little else. Disasters of a magnitude that occur only once every few centuries were forgotten or **transmuted** into myth. So today the mind still works comfortably backward and forward for only a few years, spanning a period not exceeding one or two generations. Those in past ages whose genes inclined them to short-term thinking lived longer and had more children than those who did not. Prophets never enjoyed a Darwinian edge.

The rules have recently changed, however. Global crises are rising in the life span of the generation now coming of age, a foreshortening that may explain why young people express more concern about the environment than do their elders. The time scale has contracted because of the exponential growth in both the human population and technologies impacting the environment. Exponential growth is basically the same as the increase of wealth by compound interest. The larger the population, the faster the growth; the faster the growth, the sooner the population becomes still larger. In Nigeria, to cite one of our more **fecund** nations, the population is expected to double from its 1988 level to 216 million by the year 2010.* If the same rate of growth were to continue to 2110, its population would exceed that of the entire present population of the world.

With people everywhere seeking a better quality of life, the search for resources is expanding even faster than the population. The demand is being met by an increase in scientific knowledge, which doubles every 10 to 15 years. It is accelerated further by a parallel rise in environment-devouring technology. Because Earth is finite in many resources that determine the quality of life—including arable soil, nutrients, fresh water and space for natural ecosystems—doubling of consumption at constant time intervals can bring disaster with shocking suddenness. Even when a nonrenewable resource has been only half used, it is still only one interval away from the end. Ecologists like to make this point with the French riddle of the lily pond. At first there is only one lily pad in the pond, but the next day it doubles, and thereafter each of its descendants doubles. The pond completely fills with lily pads in 30 days. When is the pond exactly half full? Answer: on the 29th day.

Yet, mathematical exercises aside, who can safely measure the human

precarious
dangerous; insecure

transmuted
transformed

fecund
fertile

---

*Editors' note: While it remains Africa's most populous country, Nigeria has not grown as quickly as Wilson predicted here. The United Nations estimates that Nigeria will have a population of a little over 158 million by the year 2010. *World Population Prospects: The 2006 Revision Population Database*, United Nations Population Division. Available at http://esa.un.org/unpp/ [Accessed 28 November 2008.]

abyss
a deep void

transcendent
superior

capacity to overcome the perceived limits of Earth? The question of central interest is this: Are we racing to the brink of an **abyss**, or are we just gathering speed for a takeoff to a wonderful future? The crystal ball is clouded; the human condition baffles all the more because it is both unprecedented and bizarre, almost beyond understanding.

In the midst of uncertainty, opinions on the human prospect have tended to fall loosely into two schools. The first, exemptionalism, holds that since humankind is **transcendent** in intelligence and spirit, so must our species have been released from the iron laws of ecology that bind all other species. No matter how serious the problem, civilized human beings, by ingenuity, force of will and—who knows—divine dispensation, will find a solution.

Population growth? Good for the economy, claim some of the exemptionalists, and in any case a basic human right, so let it run. Land shortages? Try fusion energy to power the desalting of sea water, then reclaim the world's deserts. (The process might be assisted by towing icebergs to coastal pipelines.) Species going extinct? Not to worry. That is nature's way. Think of humankind as only the latest in a long line of exterminating agents in geological time. In any case, because our species has pulled free of old-style, mindless Nature, we have begun a different order of life. Evolution should now be allowed to proceed along this new trajectory. Finally, resources? The planet has more than enough resources to last indefinitely, if human genius is allowed to address each new problem in turn, without alarmist and unreasonable restrictions imposed on economic development. So hold the course, and touch the brakes lightly.

The opposing idea of reality is environmentalism, which sees humanity as a biological species tightly dependent on the natural world. As formidable as our intellect may be and as fierce our spirit, the argument goes, those qualities are not enough to free us from the constraints of the natural environment in which our human ancestors evolved. We cannot draw confidence from successful solutions to the smaller problems of the past. Many of Earth's vital resources are about to be exhausted, its atmospheric chemistry is deteriorating and human populations have already grown dangerously large. Natural ecosystems, the wellsprings of a healthful environment, are being irreversibly degraded.

At the heart of the environmentalist world view is the conviction that human physical and spiritual health depends on sustaining the planet in a relatively unaltered state. Earth is our home in the full, genetic sense, where humanity and its ancestors existed for all the millions of years of their evolution. Natural ecosystems—forests, coral reefs, marine blue waters—maintain the world exactly as we would wish it to be maintained. When we debase the global environment and extinguish the variety of life, we are dismantling a support system that is too complex to understand, let alone replace, in the foreseeable future. Space scientists theorize the existence of a virtually unlimited array of other planetary environments, almost all of which are **uncongenial** to human life. Our own Mother Earth, lately called Gaia, is a specialized conglomerate of organisms and the physical environment they create on a day-to-day basis, which can be destabilized and turned lethal by careless activity. We run the risk, conclude the environmentalists, of beaching ourselves upon alien shores like a great confused pod of pilot whales.

If I have not done so enough already by tone of voice, I will now place myself solidly in the environmentalist school, but not so radical as to wish a turning back of the clock, not given to driving spikes into Douglas firs to prevent logging and distinctly uneasy with such hybrid movements as ecofeminism, which holds that Mother Earth is a nurturing home for all life and should be revered and loved as in premodern (paleolithic and archaic) societies and that ecosystematic abuse is rooted in androcentric—that is to say, male-dominated—concepts, values and institutions.

Still, however soaked in androcentric culture, I am radical enough to take seriously the question heard with increasing frequency: Is humanity suicidal? Is the drive to environmental conquest and self-propagation embedded so deeply in our genes as to be unstoppable?

My short answer—opinion if you wish—is that humanity is not suicidal, at least not in the sense just stated. We are smart enough and have time enough to avoid an environmental catastrophe of civilization-threatening dimensions. But the technical problems are sufficiently formidable to require a redirection of much of science and technology, and the ethical issues are so basic as to force a reconsideration of our self-image as a species.

There are reasons for optimism, reasons to believe that we have entered what might someday be generously called the Century of the Environment. The United Nations Conference on Environment and Development, held in Rio de Janeiro in June 1992, attracted more than 120 heads of government, the largest number ever assembled, and helped move environmental issues closer to the political center stage; on November 18, 1992, more than 1,500 senior scientists from 69 countries issued a "Warning to Humanity," stating that overpopulation and environmental deterioration put the very future of life at risk. The greening of religion has become a global trend, with theologians and religious leaders addressing environmental problems as a moral issue. In May 1992, leaders of most of the major American denominations met with scientists as guests of members of the United States Senate to formulate a "Joint Appeal by Religion and Science for the Environment." Conservation of biodiversity is increasingly seen by both national governments and major landowners as important to their country's future.

uncongenial
unsuitable

Indonesia, home to a large part of the native Asian plant and animal species, has begun to shift to land-management practices that conserve and sustainably develop the remaining rain forests. Costa Rica has created a National Institute of Biodiversity. A pan-African institute for biodiversity research and management has been founded, with headquarters in Zimbabwe.

Finally, there are favorable demographic signs. The rate of population increase is declining on all continents, although it is still well above zero almost everywhere and remains especially high in sub-Saharan Africa. Despite entrenched traditions and religious beliefs, the desire to use contraceptives in family planning is spreading. **Demographers** estimate that if the demand were fully met, this action alone would reduce the eventual stabilized population by more than two billion.

In summary, the will is there. Yet the awful truth remains that a large part of humanity will suffer no matter what is done. The number of people living in absolute poverty has risen during the past 20 years to nearly one billion and is expected to increase another 100 million by the end of the decade. Whatever progress has been made in the developing countries, and that includes an overall improvement in the average standard of living, is threatened by a continuance of rapid population growth and the deterioration of forests and arable soil.

Our hopes must be **chastened** further still, and this is in my opinion the central issue, by a key and seldom-recognized distinction between the nonliving and living environments. Science and the political process can be adapted to manage the nonliving, physical environment. The human hand is now upon the physical **homeostat**. The ozone layer can be mostly restored to the upper atmosphere by elimination of CFC's, with these substances peaking at six times the present level and then subsiding during the next half century. Also, with procedures that will prove far more difficult and initially expensive, carbon dioxide and other greenhouse gases can be pulled back to concentrations that slow global warming.

The human hand, however, is not upon the biological homeostat. There is no way in sight to micromanage the natural ecosystems and the millions of species they contain. That feat might be accomplished by generations to come, but then it will be too late for the ecosystems—and perhaps for us. Despite the seemingly bottomless nature of creation, humankind has been chipping away at its diversity, and Earth is destined to become an impoverished planet within a century if present trends continue. Mass extinctions are being reported with increasing frequency in every part of the world. They include half the freshwater fishes of peninsular Malaysia, 10 birds native to Cebu in the Philippines, half the 41 tree snails of Oahu, 44 of the 68 shallow-water mussels of the Tennessee River shoals, as many as 90 plant species

demographers

sociologists who statistically analyze characteristics of human populations

chastened

subdued

homeostat

regulatory mechanism that safeguards the stability of the natural environment growing on the Centinela Ridge in Ecuador, and in the United States as a whole, about 200 plant species, with another 680 species and races now classified as in danger of extinction. The main cause is the destruction of natural habitats, especially tropical forests. Close behind, especially on the Hawaiian archipelago and other islands, is the introduction of rats, pigs, beard grass, **lantana** and other exotic organisms that outbreed and **extirpate** native species.

lantana
shrubs

extirpate
exterminate

The few thousand biologists worldwide who specialize in diversity are aware that they can witness and report no more than a very small percentage of the extinctions actually occurring. The reason is that they have facilities to keep track of only a tiny fraction of the millions of species and a sliver of the planet's surface on a yearly basis. They have devised a rule of thumb to characterize the situation: that whenever careful studies are made of habitats before and after disturbance, extinctions almost always come to light. The **corollary**: the great majority of extinctions are never observed. Vast numbers of species are apparently vanishing before they can be discovered and named.

corollary
implication

There is a way, nonetheless, to estimate the rate of loss indirectly. Independent studies around the world and in fresh and marine waters have revealed a robust connection between the size of a habitat and the amount of biodiversity it contains. Even a small loss in area reduces the number of species. The relation is such that when the area of the habitat is cut to a tenth of its original cover, the number of species eventually drops by roughly one-half. Tropical rain forests, thought to harbor a majority of Earth's species (the reason conservationists get so **exercised** about rain forests), are being reduced by nearly that magnitude. At the present time they occupy about the same area as that of the 48 coterminous United States, representing a little less than half their original, prehistoric cover, and they are shrinking each year by about 2 percent, an amount equal to the state of Florida. If the typical value (that is, 90 percent area loss causes 50 percent eventual extinction) is applied, the projected loss of species due to rain forest destruction worldwide is half a percent across the board for all kinds of plants, animals and micro-organisms.

exercised
worried

When area reduction and all the other extinction agents are considered together, it is reasonable to project a reduction by 20 percent or more of the rain forest species by the year 2020, climbing to 50 percent or more by mid-century, if nothing is done to change current practice. Comparable erosion is likely in other environments now under assault, including many coral reefs and Mediterranean-type **heathlands** of Western Australia, South Africa and California.

heathlands
uncultivated land on which small shrubs grow in sandy soil

mollusks
marine animals such as shell-fish, snails, squids, etc.

echinoderms
marine animals such as star-fish, sea cucumbers, etc.

inaugurated
introduced

esthetic pleasure
satisfaction derived from beauty

stymied
hindered

intransigent
uncompromising

The ongoing loss will not be replaced by evolution in any period of time that has meaning for humanity. Extinction is now proceeding thousands of times faster than the production of new species. The average life span of a species and its descendants in past geological eras varied according to group (like **mollusks** or **echinoderms** or flowering plants) from about 1 to 10 million years. During the past 500 million years, there have been five great extinction spasms comparable to the one now being **inaugurated** by human expansion. The latest, evidently caused by the strike of an asteroid, ended the Age of Reptiles 66 million years ago. In each case it took more than 10 million years for evolution to completely replenish the biodiversity lost. And that was in an otherwise undisturbed natural environment. Humanity is now destroying most of the habitats where evolution can occur.

The surviving biosphere remains the great unknown of Earth in many respects. On the practical side, it is hard even to imagine what other species have to offer in the way of new pharmaceuticals, crops, fibers, petroleum substitutes and other products. We have only a poor grasp of the ecosystem services by which other organisms cleanse the water, turn soil into a fertile living cover and manufacture the very air we breathe. We sense but do not fully understand what the highly diverse natural world means to our **esthetic pleasure** and mental well-being.

Scientists are unprepared to manage a declining biosphere. To illustrate, consider the following mission they might be given. The last remnant of a rain forest is about to be cut over. Environmentalists are **stymied**. The contracts have been signed, and local landowners and politicians are **intransigent**. In a final desperate move, a team of biologists is scrambled in an attempt to preserve the biodiversity by extraordinary means. Their assignment is the following: collect samples of all the species of organisms quickly, before the cutting starts; maintain the species in zoos, gardens and laboratory cultures or else deep-freeze samples of the tissues in liquid nitrogen, and, finally, establish the procedure by which the entire community can be reassembled on empty ground at a later date, when social and economic conditions have improved.

The biologists cannot accomplish this task, not if thousands of them came with a billion-dollar budget. They cannot even imagine how to do it. In the forest patch live legions of species: perhaps 300 birds, 500 butterflies, 200 ants, 50,000 beetles, 1,000 trees, 5,000 fungi, tens of thousands of bacteria and so on down a long roster of major groups. Each species occupies a precise niche, demanding a certain place, an exact microclimate, particular nutrients and temperature and humidity cycles with specified timing to trigger phases of the life cycle. Many, perhaps most, of the species are locked in **symbioses** with other species; they cannot survive and reproduce unless arrayed with their partners in the correct **idiosyncratic** configurations.

Even if the biologists pulled off the **taxonomic** equivalent of the **Manhattan Project**, sorting and preserving cultures of all the species, they could not then put the community back together again. It would be like unscrambling an egg with a pair of spoons. The biology of the micro-organisms needed to reanimate the soil would be mostly unknown. The pollinators of most of the flowers and the correct timing of their appearance could only be guessed. The "assembly rules," the sequence in which species must be allowed to colonize in order to coexist indefinitely, would remain in the realm of theory.

In its neglect of the rest of life, exemptionalism fails definitively. To move ahead as though scientific and entrepreneurial genius will solve each crisis that arises implies that the declining biosphere can be similarly manipulated. But the world is too complicated to be turned into a garden. There is no biological homeostat that can be worked by humanity; to believe otherwise is to risk reducing a large part of Earth to a wasteland.

The environmentalist vision, **prudential** and less exuberant than exemptionalism, is closer to reality. It sees humanity entering a bottleneck unique in history, constricted by population and economic pressures. In order to pass through to the other side, within perhaps 50 to 100 years, more science and entrepreneurship will have to be devoted to stabilizing the global environment. That can be accomplished, according to expert consensus, only by halting population growth and devising a wiser use of resources than has been accomplished to date. And wise use for the living world in particular means preserving the surviving ecosystems, micromanaging them only enough to save the biodiversity they contain, until such time as they can be understood and employed in the fullest sense for human benefit.

symbioses
vital interrelationships

idiosyncratic
distinctive

taxonomic
organization of inter-dependent living things

Manhattan Project
name for the U.S. effort to develop the atomic bomb during World War II

prudential
sensibly cautious

On Global Warming: How to Calculate and Live within our Carbon Budget

Tim Flannery

The Gaseous Greenhouse

When scientists realized that levels of CO_2 in the atmosphere were linked to climate change, some were puzzled. They knew that CO_2 only absorbs radiation at wavelengths longer than about twelve microns (a human hair is around seventy microns thick), and that a small amount of the gas captured all of the radiation available at those bandwidths. Increasing its concentration in experiments seemed to make no real difference to the amount of heat trapped.[1] Besides, there was so little of the gas, it seemed inconceivable that it could change the climate of an entire planet. What scientists did not commonly realize then is that at very low temperatures—such as over the Poles and high in the atmosphere—more heat travels at the bandwidths where CO_2 is most effective. More important, they discovered that rather than being the sole agent responsible for climate change, CO_2 acts as a trigger for the potent greenhouse gas, water vapor. It does this by heating the atmosphere just a little, allowing it to take up and retain more moisture, which then warms the atmosphere further. So a positive feedback loop is created, forcing our planet's temperature to even higher levels.[2]

Although it is a greenhouse gas, water vapor is also an **enigma** in the climate change arena, for it forms clouds, and clouds can both reflect light energy and trap heat. By trapping more heat than reflecting light, high thin clouds tend to warm the planet, while low thick clouds have the reverse effect. No single factor contributes more to our uncertainty of future climate change predictions.

Many greenhouse gases are in some way or another generated by human activity. Although scarce, and weak in its capacity to capture heat, CO_2 is very long lived in the atmosphere: Around 56 percent of all the CO_2 that humans have liberated by burning fossil fuel is still aloft, which is the cause—directly and indirectly—of around 80 percent of all global warming.[3]

The fact that a known proportion of CO_2 remains in the atmosphere allows us to calculate, in very round numbers, a carbon budget for humanity. Prior to 1800 (the start of the Industrial Revolution), there were about 280 parts per

enigma
puzzling problem

million of CO_2 in the atmosphere, which equates to around 645 gigatons (billion tons) of CO_2. (To make comparisons easy, figures like this relate only to the carbon in the CO_2 molecule. The actual weight of the CO_2 would be 3.7 times greater.) Today the figures are 380 parts per million, or around 869 gigatons. If we wished to stabilize CO_2 emissions at a level double that which existed before the Industrial Revolution (widely considered the threshold of dangerous change), we would have to limit all future human emissions to around 660 gigatons. Just over half of this would stay in the atmosphere, raising CO_2 levels to around 1,210 gigatons, or 550 parts per million, by 2100. This, incidentally, would be a tough budget for humanity to abide by, for if we use fossil fuels for only another century, that equates to a budget of 6.6 gigatons per year. Compare this with the average of 14.6 gigatons of CO_2 that accumulated each year throughout the 1990s (half of this from burning fossil fuel), and the projection that the human population is set to rise midcentury to 9 billion, and you can see the problem.

Even in the long view, this rise is unprecedented. The concentration of CO_2 in the atmosphere in times past can be measured from bubbles of air preserved in ice. By drilling about two miles into the Antarctic ice cap, scientists have drawn out an ice core that spans almost a million years of Earth history. This unique record demonstrates that during cold times, CO_2 levels have dropped to around 160 parts per million, and that until recently they never exceeded 280 parts per million. The Industrial Revolution changed that, albeit slowly, for even by 1958 . . . it was up to only 315 parts per million.

Australian scientists have recently established that in 2002 and 2003 CO_2 levels rose by 2.54 parts per million per year, as opposed to the average increase of 1.8 parts per million per year over the previous decade.[4] It is unclear whether this was simply a hiccup in the trend or rates of accumulation are increasing.

It is our servants—the billions of engines that we have built to run on fossil fuels such as coal, petrol and oil-based fuels, and gas—that play the leading role in manufacturing CO_2. Most dangerous of all are the power plants that use coal to generate electricity. Black coal (anthracite) is composed of at least 92 percent carbon, while dry brown coal is around 70 percent carbon and 5 percent hydrogen.[5] Carbon and oxygen—the components of CO_2—are close neighbors on the periodic table, meaning that they have similar atomic weights. Because two oxygen atoms combine with one carbon atom to form CO_2, around four tons of the gas is created for every ton of anthracite consumed. Some power plants burn through 550 tons of coal per hour, and so inefficient are they that around two thirds of the energy available is wasted. And to what purpose do they operate? Simply to boil water, which generates

aerial ocean
the atmosphere

Dickensian
reference to Charles Dickens, a 19th-century novelist; the implication is that the machines are from that era and are dangerously out of date

steam that moves the colossal turbines to create the electricity that powers our homes and factories. Like the great **aerial ocean** itself, these **Dickensian** machines are invisible to most of us, who have no idea that nineteenth-century technology makes twenty-first century gadgets whir.

There are around thirty other greenhouse gases in the atmosphere, all of which are present in trace amounts and whose effect for most purposes is measured by the yardstick of CO_2 (being converted into "CO_2 units" in scientific equations). Most are so rare that they seem trivial, yet because they absorb heat at differing wavelengths from CO_2, any increase in volume is significant. Think of them as glass windows in a ceiling, each gas representing a different window. As the number of windows increases, more light energy is admitted into the room, there to be trapped as heat.[6]

After CO_2, methane is the next most important greenhouse gas. Although it makes up just 1.5 parts per million of the atmosphere, its concentration has doubled over the last few hundred years. When measured over a century-long time scale, methane is sixty times more potent at capturing heat energy than CO_2, but thankfully it lasts fewer years in the atmosphere. Methane is created by microbes that thrive in oxygenless environments such as stagnant pools and bowels, which is why it abounds in swamps, farts, and belches. It is estimated that methane will cause 15 to 17 percent of all global warming experienced in this century. Because it is relatively short lived yet is sometimes released suddenly in vast quantities, it has played an important role in creating positive feedback loops that on occasion have heated our planet.

Nitrous oxide (laughing gas) is 270 times more efficient at trapping heat than CO_2, and although far rarer than methane, it lasts 150 years in the atmosphere. Around a third of our global emissions come from burning fossil fuels and the rest from burning biomass and the use of nitrogen-containing fertilizers. While there are natural sources of nitrous oxide, human emissions now greatly exceed them in volume, and as a result there is 20 percent more nitrous oxide in the atmosphere than there was at the beginning of the Industrial Revolution.

HFC
hydrofluorocarbon

CFC
chlorofluorocarbon

The rarest of all greenhouse gases are members of the **HFC** and **CFC** families of chemicals. These children of human ingenuity did not exist before industrial chemists began to manufacture them. Some, such as the tongue-twisting dichlorotrifluoroethane, which was once used in refrigeration, are ten thousand times more potent at capturing heat energy than CO_2, and they can last in the atmosphere for many centuries. . . .

For the moment, because of its primary importance to climate change, we need to know more about the carbon in CO_2. Both diamonds and soot are pure forms of carbon, the only difference being how the atoms are arranged. Carbon bonds with almost everything non-metallic, which is why life is carbon based (carbon compounds being diverse enough to enable the complex processes that go on in a body to occur). Carbon is **ubiquitous** on the surface of planet Earth. It is constantly shifting in and out of our bodies, as well as from rocks to sea or soils, and from there to the atmosphere and back again. Its movements are extraordinarily complex and are governed by temperature, the availability of other elements, and the activities of species such as ourselves.

ubiquitous
everywhere

Were it not for plants and algae, we would soon run out of oxygen and suffocate in CO_2. Through photosynthesis (the process whereby plants create sugars using sunlight and water), plants take our waste CO_2 and use it to make their own energy, in the process creating a waste stream of oxygen. It's a neat and self-sustaining cycle that forms the basis of life on Earth. The volume of carbon circulating around our planet is enormous. Around a trillion tons of carbon are tied up in living things, while the amount buried underground is far, far greater.[7] And for every molecule of CO_2 in the atmosphere, there are fifty in the oceans.[8]

The places the carbon goes to when it leaves the atmosphere are known as carbon sinks. You and I and all living things are carbon sinks, as are the oceans and some of the rocks under our feet. Some of these sinks are very large, but they are not infinite, nor is their size steady through time. Over eons, much CO_2 has been stored in the earth's crust. This occurs as dead plants are buried and carried underground, where they become fossil fuels. It is this buried carbon that allows oxygen to exist in our atmosphere. Should humans somehow be able to take all of that fossil carbon and return it to the atmosphere by burning it, we would use up all the oxygen in our atmosphere.[9] On a shorter time scale, a lot of carbon can be stored in soils, where it forms the black mould beloved of gardeners. Even the **uncouth** belching of volcanoes (which contains much CO_2) can disturb the climate for long periods of time. And heavenly bodies can also have their impacts, for meteorites and other objects that periodically collide with Earth have so upset the oceans, atmosphere, and Earth's crust as to disrupt the carbon cycle.

uncouth
crude

For the past couple of decades, scientists have been monitoring where the CO_2 that humans produce by burning fossil fuel goes. They can do this because the gas derived from fossil fuels has a unique chemical signature and can be traced as it circulates around the planet. In very round figures, 2 gigatons are absorbed by the oceans and a further 1.7 gigatons are absorbed by life on land annually.[10] The contribution made by the land results partly from an accident of history—America's frontier phase of development—that has given some land plants a ravenous hunger for carbon. Mature forests don't take in much CO_2, for they are in balance, releasing CO_2 as old vegetation rots, then absorbing it as the new grows. For these reasons the world's largest forests—the coniferous forests of Siberia and Canada—and the tropical rain forests are not good carbon sinks, but new vigorously growing forests are.

During the nineteenth and early twentieth centuries, America's pioneers cut and burned the great eastern forests, and burned and grazed the western plains and deserts. Then shifts in land use allowed the vegetation to grow back. As a result, most of America's forests are less than sixty years old and are regrowing vigorously, in the process absorbing around half a billion tons of CO_2 annually from the atmosphere, and newly planted forests in China and Europe may be absorbing an equal amount. For a few crucial decades these young forests have helped cool our planet by absorbing excess CO_2. But as the Northern Hemisphere's forests and shrublands recover from their mauling at the hands of pioneers, they will extract less and less CO_2, at the very time that humans are pumping more of it into the atmosphere.

The long-term prospect for forests assisting in the fight against global warming was spelled out in a recent study that examined our planet's carbon budget over two centuries.[11] It demonstrated that there really is only one major carbon sink on our planet, and that is the oceans. They have absorbed 48 percent of all carbon emitted by humans between 1800 and 1994, while over those same two centuries life on land has actually contributed carbon to the atmosphere.

The world's oceans, however, vary in their ability to absorb carbon. One ocean basin alone, the North Atlantic—which constitutes only 15 percent of the ocean surface—contains almost a quarter of all the carbon emitted by humans since 1800.[12] Even more curiously, it appears that the CO_2 was not being absorbed by the North Atlantic basin, but was dumped there after being absorbed elsewhere. That elsewhere turned out to be the North Sea, a shallow marine basin confined between Great Britain and northern Europe, and which, due to an odd stratification of its waters, allows CO_2 to accumulate in subsurface layers, from where it is transported to the North Atlantic. So potent a carbon "kidney" is this small sea that it has removed 20 percent of all carbon dioxide ever emitted by humans.[13]

Having just discovered our planet's "carbon kidney," scientists are worried that changes in ocean circulation brought about by climate change will degrade its effectiveness. There are many ways this could happen, one of which is best contemplated while consuming a warm can of cola. That intense fizz on opening the can is followed by a bland flatness—indicating that the liquid has quickly released the carbon dioxide that gives it its fizz. Cold drinks hold their fizz longer, and what is true for your can of soft drink is also true for the oceans. Cold sea water can hold more carbon than warm sea water; so as the ocean warms, it becomes less able to absorb the gas.

One other critical aspect of sea water, in regard to its capacity to absorb CO_2, is the amount of carbonate it contains. Carbonate reaches the oceans from rivers that have flowed over limestone or other lime-containing rocks, and it reacts with the CO_2 absorbed into the oceans. At present there is a balance between carbonate concentration and the CO_2 absorbed. As the CO_2 concentration increases in the oceans, however, the carbonate is being used up. As a result, the oceans are becoming more acid; and the more acid an ocean is, the less CO_2 it can absorb.

In July 2004 two researchers, Peter Raymond of Yale University and Jonathan Cole of the Institute of Ecosystem Studies in Millbrook, published findings that offered seemingly good news on this front.[14] They found that, due to increased land degradation and enhanced rainfall in its catchment, the Mississippi River was transporting increasing amounts of carbonate to the oceans. "These observations have important implications for the potential management of carbon **sequestration** in the United States," the authors proclaimed.[15] While it may have seemed that an ever more degraded **terrestrial** environment offered salvation from our climate woes, a response published a few months later by Klaus Lackner put things in perspective.[16] The extra carbonate carried by the sickening river, Lackner informed us, would be enough to cover America's CO_2 emissions for just thirty-six hours out of every year. Should the phenomenon be true for every river in the world, it would still account for only ten days' worth of the world's emissions per year.

Having seen something of the workings of the atmosphere, its greenhouse gases and the carbon cycle, we [must] . . . now consider what it all means . . . .

"only one major carbon sink . . . the oceans"

sequestration
removal

terrestrial
land (as opposed to ocean)

Montreal Protocol
international treaty brought into force in 1987 that regulates substances harmful to the ozone layer

Over to You

There is one thing that no CEO can afford to look away from—the melee of buyers and sellers known as the market. It is my firm belief that all the efforts of government and industry will come to naught unless the good citizen and consumer takes the initiative, and in tackling climate change the consumer is in a most fortunate position.

If we were still battling CFCs, the consumer could not generate an alternative product. Indeed, regardless of their vigilance, in the absence of an international agreement like the **Montreal Protocol**, they would be liable to buy CFCs hidden in things such as motor vehicles and refrigerators. With the CO_2 problem, however, technology can set free almost every household on the planet. In other words, there is no need to wait for government to act. You can do it yourself.

You can, in a few months rather than the 50 years allowed by some governments, easily attain the 70 per cent reduction in emissions required to stabilize the earth's climate. All it takes are a few changes to your personal life, none of which requires serious sacrifice.

Understanding how you use electricity is the most powerful tool in your armory, for that allows you to make effective decisions about reducing your personal emissions of CO_2. To begin, pick up and read carefully your electricity bill. Is your bill higher than it was at the same time last year? If so, why? A phone call or email inquiry to your power supplier may help clarify this.

While you are there, ask about a green power option (where the provider guarantees to source a percentage of power from renewables). The green power option can cost as little as a dollar a week yet is highly effective in reducing emissions. If your provider does not offer a suitable green option, dump them and call a competitor. Changing your power supplier is usually a matter of a single phone call, involving no interruption of supply or inconvenience in billing. If, however, a power monopoly reigns in your area, you need to lobby the authorities to create a free market. It is possible, in switching to green power, to reduce your household emissions to zero. All as the result of a single phone call.

If you wish to take more decisive action, the best place for most people to start is with hot water. In the developed world, roughly one-third of CO_2 emissions result from domestic power, and one-third of a typical domestic power bill is spent on heating water. This is crazy, since the sun will heat your water free if you have the right device. An initial outlay is required, but such are the benefits that it is well worth taking out a loan to do so, for in sunny climates like California or southern Europe the payback period is around two or three years, and as the devices usually carry a ten-year guarantee, that means at least seven to eight years of free hot water. Even in cloudy regions such as Germany and Britain, you will get several years' worth of hot water for free.[17]

If you wish to reduce your impact even further, start with the greatest consumers of power, which for most people are air conditioning, heating and refrigeration. If you are thinking of installing any such items, you should seek out the most energy-efficient model available. A good rule of thumb is to choose the smallest device to suit your average needs, and consider alternatives: It may be cheaper to install insulation rather than buying and running a larger heater or cooler. It can be difficult to convince children that they need to turn off appliances when they are finished with them. One way to teach them is for a family to examine the power bill together and set a target for reduction. When it's met, give the kids the savings.

I became so outraged at the irresponsibility of the coal burners that I decided to generate my own electricity, which has proved to be one of the most satisfying things I've ever done. For the average householder, solar panels are the best way to do this. Twelve 80-watt panels is the number I granted myself, and the amount of power this generates in Australia is sufficient to run the house. To survive on this quantum, however, our family is vigilant about energy use, and we cook with gas. And I'm fitter than before because I use hand tools rather than the electrical variety to make and fix things. Solar panels have a twenty-five-year guarantee (and often last for up to forty years). With the cost of electricity rising, and because I'll be enjoying the free power they provide well into retirement, I view them as a form of **superannuation**.

superannuation
regular contributions to a pension fund

The town of Schoenau in Germany offers a different example of direct action. Some of its residents were so alarmed by the **Chernobyl disaster** that they decided to do something to reduce their country's dependence on nuclear power. It started with a group of ten parents who gave prizes for energy savings. This proved so successful that it soon bloomed into a citizens' group determined to wrest control from KWR, the monopoly that supplied them.

Chernobyl disaster
1986 nuclear reactor accident in Ukraine

They put together their own study, then raised **DM** 2 million to build their own green power scheme. Eventually, they raised over DM 6.5 million—enough to purchase the power supply, grid and all, from KWR—and today the town runs not only its own power supply but a successful consulting business that advises on how to "green" the grid right across the country. Each year Schoenau's power supply becomes greener, and even the town's big power users, such as a plastics recycling factory situated in the town, are happy with the result.[18]

DM
Deutsch marks, official currency of West Germany until the adoption of the Euro

It is not feasible right now for most of us to do away with burning fossil fuels for transport, but we can greatly reduce their use. Walking wherever possible is highly effective, as is taking public transport. Hybrid fuel vehicles are twice as fuel efficient as a standard, similar-sized car, and trading in your four-wheel-drive or SUV for a medium-sized hybrid fuel car cuts your personal transport emissions by 70 percent in one fell swoop.

For those who cannot or do not wish to drive a hybrid, a good rule is to buy the smallest vehicle capable of doing the job you most often require. You can always rent for the rare occasions you need something larger. A few years from now, if you have invested in solar power, you should be able to buy a compressed-air vehicle. Then, you can truly thumb your nose at all of those power and gas bills.

Despite the way it often feels, employees wield considerable influence in the workplace. If you want to see your workplace become more greenhouse aware, ask your employer to have an energy audit done. And remember, if you can cut your emissions by 70 percent, so can the business you work for. By doing so, in the medium term the business will save both money and the environment. And because society so desperately needs advocates—people who can act and serve as witnesses to what can be done and should be done—by taking such public actions you will be achieving results way beyond their local impact.

As you read through this list of actions to combat climate change, you might be skeptical that such steps can have such a huge impact. But not only is our global climate approaching a tipping point, our economy is as well, for the energy sector is about to experience what the Internet brought to the media—an age wherein previously discrete products are in competition with each other, and with the individual.

Kyoto Protocol
international agreement brought into force in 2005 that commits ratifying countries to reduce greenhouse gas emissions that cause global warming

If enough of us buy green power, solar panels, solar hot water systems, and hybrid vehicles, the cost of these items will plummet. This will encourage the sale of yet more panels and wind generators, and soon the bulk of domestic power will be generated by renewable technologies. This will place sufficient pressure on industry that, when combined with the pressure from **Kyoto**, it will compel energy-hungry enterprises to maximize efficiency and turn to clean power generation. This will make renewables even more affordable. As a result, the developing world—including China and India—will be able to afford clean power rather than filthy coal. With a little help from you, right now, the developing giants of Asia might even avoid the full carbon catastrophe in which we, in the industrialized world, find ourselves so deeply mired.

stymie
obstruct

Much could go wrong with this linked lifeline to climate safety. It may be that the big power users will infiltrate governments further and **stymie** the renewables sector; or maybe we will act too slowly, and nations such as China and India will have already invested in fossil fuel generation before the price of renewables comes down. Or perhaps the rate of climate change will be discovered to be too great and we will have to draw CO_2 from the atmosphere.

As these challenges suggest, we are the generation fated to live in the most interesting of times, for we are now the weather makers, and the future of biodiversity and civilization hangs on our actions.

I have done my best to fashion a manual on the use of Earth's thermostat. Now it's over to you.

Notes

[1] S.R. Weart, *The Discovery of Global Warming: New Histories of Science, Technology and Medicine* (Cambridge, MA: Harvard University Press, 2003).

[2] *Ibid.*

[3] L. R. Kump, "Reducing Uncertainty about Carbon Dioxide as a Climate Driver," *Nature* 419 (2002): 188–90.

[4] P. Garman et al., "The Bush Administration and Hydrogen," *Science* 302 (2003): 1331–33.

[5] H. Herman, *Brown Coal* (Melbourne, Australia: State Electricity Commission of Victoria, 1952).

[6] S. R. Weart, *The Discovery of Global Warming: New Histories of Science, Technology and Medicine* (Cambridge, MA: Harvard University Press, 2003).

[7] R. Dawkins, *The Ancestor's Tale: A Pilgrimage to the Dawn of Evolution* (London: Weidenfeld & Nicolson, 2004).

[8] S. R. Weart, *The Discovery of Global Warming: New Histories of Science, Technology and Medicine* (Cambridge, MA: Harvard University Press, 2003).

[9] R. Dawkins, *The Ancestor's Tale: A Pilgrimage to the Dawn of Evolution* (London: Weidenfeld & Nicolson, 2004).

[10] R. A. Feely et al., "Impact of Anthropogenic CO_2 on $CaCO_3$ System in the Oceans," *Science* 305 (2004): 362–66.

[11] C. L. Sabine et al., "The Oceanic Sink for Anthropogenic CO_2," *Science* 305 (2004): 367–71.

[12] *Ibid.*

[13] H. Thomas et al., "Enhanced Open Ocean Storage of CO_2 from Shelf-Sea Pumping," *Science* 304 (2004): 1005–08.

[14] P. A. Raymond and J. J. Cole, "Increase in the Export of Alkalinity from North America's Largest River," *Science* 301 (2003): 88–90.

[15] *Ibid.*

[16] K. Lackner, "Alkalinity Export and Carbon Balance," *Science* 302 (2003): 985.

[17] H. Girardet, *Cities People Planet: Liveable Cities for a Sustainable World* (Chichester, England: Wiley Academy, 2004).

[18] D. Suzuki and H. Dressel, *Good News for a Change: Hope for a Troubled Planet* (Toronto, Canada: Stoddart Publishing, 2002).

Science and Religion: A Complicated History

Mark Cauchi

In 2007, a Canadian Press–Decima Research Poll reported that 63 percent of Canadians accept the theory of evolution—that "human beings have developed over millions of years from less advanced forms of life"—but that a full 34 percent also believe that "God guided this process." More than 25 percent, moreover, reject the theory of evolution altogether and maintain that "God created human beings pretty much in their present form at one time within the last 10,000 years or so."[1] These statistics may be surprising to many Canadians, who often perceive themselves and their country as more secular than others. Indeed, they have good reason to be surprised, as the number of Canadians who regularly attend religious services has plummeted steadily over the last 100 years, with many people identifying themselves as belonging to no religion. Why, then, are so many Canadians apparently unwilling to let go of the idea that the world, and humankind with it, are created by God? Is it because the belief in divine creation is among the most deeply held, as it touches on our most cherished ideas about life? Equally deep-seated and in many ways related is the desire to discover truth. Without a doubt, it is this desire that motivates scientists to push their thinking to the outer limits of human thought—to contemplate such things as how the universe began, how life develops and how human beings came to be—some of the very things that religion also attempts to explain.

Given how deeply held and interrelated they are, it is not surprising that religious and scientific viewpoints should occasionally come into conflict. In recent times, this conflict has heated up significantly, especially around the question of whether human beings have been created by God or have evolved out of a primate ancestor. This debate has been absorbed into a larger political conflict, often called the "culture wars," in which all cultural phenomena—including everything from entertainment to social policy—are interpreted as reflecting either a liberal or a conservative political ideology. Within this so-called war, one's belief either in creation or in evolution is understood to reflect a larger bundle of political views. If you believe in evolution, for instance, many conservatives may assume that you cannot believe in God and must, therefore, support the right to abortion, condone a permissive sexual morality, tolerate pornographic and violent entertainment and

---

This article was written for *The Human Project*. Used by permission.

promote the erosion of the "traditional" family. If, on the other hand, you believe in divine creation, many liberals may assume that you cannot believe in evolution and that you also advocate criminalization of abortion, strict sexual mores, rigorous censorship and rigidly defined "family values." Admittedly, this is an exaggerated picture, but it does illustrate that the issue of creation versus evolution has become very polarized. As the debate is played out today in the West, particularly in the United States, the most vocal participants will hold that you must accept *EITHER* religion *OR* evolution; given their fundamentally opposed natures, you cannot believe in both.

Science and Religion before Darwin: William Paley and the Argument from Design

As science continued to develop after the Scientific Revolution in the 15th and 16th centuries, it became harder to deny its discoveries. This put increasing pressure on religious people—who were still the majority in pre-19th-century Western society—to find some way to reconcile religion with science.

The most successful attempt at reconciliation was put forward by William Paley (1743–1805) in his book *Natural Theology, or Evidence of the Existence and Attributes of the Deity Collected from the Appearances of Nature* (1802). As the title suggests, the book puts forward an argument, called the "argument from design," which attempts to show that, by looking at nature, one can prove that God exists and what He is like.

Paley explains the argument from design as follows: Any complex entity that has multiple parts working in harmony must have been *intended* to work the way it does; in other words, it must be *designed*. Anything that appears intended or designed, furthermore, must have a *designer*. If you come across a large rock, you might think that the composition of that particular rock is due to nothing more than a fluke of nature; if you come across a watch instead, however, you would probably not think that the existence and presence of that watch is due to pure chance. Why? Because it has many components that work together in just the right way to perform what seems to be an *intended* function, i.e., to tell time. In other words, Paley claims, the watch would look as if it were *designed* to do what it does and so must have had a *designer*. Now here comes the critical step. Far more complex than watches, Paley argues, are intricate phenomena such as flowers and eyes and, indeed, nature as a whole. If a watch must have been designed and so must have a designer, then surely flowers and eyes do too. As is probably obvious by now, Paley believes God to be the designer of nature.

In the early 19th century, the argument from design, particularly William Paley's rendition of it, became not only the most common way to reconcile the scientific view of nature with the belief in God, but also the "standard" way to understand the origins of things in nature. Paley was so convincing that his book became something of a bestseller and, in fact, became a "must-read" academic work that was taught in most universities throughout Europe.

The Challenge of Darwin

Charles Darwin (1809–1882) knew the works of William Paley well. As a student at Cambridge University, Darwin studied theology and natural science—two disciplines that, at the time, required a thorough reading of Paley. It would not take Darwin long, however, to begin to challenge Paley's ideas—both about nature and about God.

After Darwin graduated from Cambridge at the age of 22, he embarked on a five-year, around-the-world voyage on the *HMS Beagle*. This adventure provided Darwin with a rare opportunity to observe differences and similarities within nature in a wide variety of habitats. Darwin observed that geographically close but separated areas, such as an island off a mainland, often have distinct versions of the same plants and animals. Two close regions may both have turtles, for instance, but each region may have different kinds—or *species*—of turtles (i.e., that have distinct features and cannot interbreed). Although these species are different from each other, they are still more closely related than they are to turtles found in other parts of the world. To Darwin, this phenomenon suggested two things. First, while the turtles are clearly different species, they are nevertheless somehow related to each other. Second, each species is also somehow related to the natural environment in which it is found. Darwin asked: What could possibly explain this strange occurrence?

In his attempt to answer this question, Darwin suggested that the natural world is subject to a *developmental* process. This was a radical new idea: indeed, most thinkers from Aristotle in the 4th century BCE to Paley in the 18th century CE assumed that all aspects of the world remained exactly as they were when God first made them. In Darwin's time, geologists were beginning to uncover evidence that the surface of the earth had in fact changed over millions of years (now we know it is billions of years), although no one had yet dared to suggest that biological organisms underwent a similar process. Darwin took this idea and applied it to what he had observed on his voyage: one of the species of turtles, he hypothesized, must be a *descendant* and a *modification* of the other; in other words, one of the species somehow emerged out of the other in a slightly different form. This process of *descent with modification* is what Darwin called "evolution." This theory, coupled with the observations he recorded, would have been enough to make Darwin a celebrated figure in the history of biology. But Darwin went further still.

The theory of evolution in itself claims only that species of plants and animals originate out of other species of plants and animals: hence the title of Darwin's great book *The Origin of Species* (1859). To claim that one species evolves out of another does not, however, provide an explanation of *how* this process occurs. Darwin dared to propose just such an explanation and did so convincingly and with an elegant simplicity.

Natural Selection

In *The Origin of Species*, Darwin explains the process of *natural selection*. Skilled farmers and animal breeders can, within limits, determine the characteristics of the offspring of the domesticated plants or animals they mate. Over the years, for instance, farmers have been able to modify the size, colour, texture, and taste of tomatoes—so much so that they have little resemblance to the tomatoes that European explorers originally found in South America. Dog breeding, which began thousands of years ago, provides an even more amazing example. All dogs—from giant Great Danes to tiny Maltese Terriers—belong to the same species but, given their variety today, clearly must look very different from the "original" dogs from which they have been bred.

Domesticated breeding showed Darwin that the *selection* of the particular specimens determines the characteristics of the offspring produced. As domesticated plant and animal breeding is a very *unnatural* and humanly contrived process, it is an instance of what we can call *unnatural selection*. In the natural world, of course, there are no breeders choosing which plants and animals will mate with each other in order to determine the characteristics of their offspring. Instead, some plants and animals are simply "lucky" enough to make it to the age of reproduction while others are not. Some bean stocks live long enough to sprout pods and scatter their seeds while others get stepped on or eaten by animals before they mature. Organisms that reproduce pass on their characteristics to their offspring; the characteristics of organisms that do not reproduce die with them.

This selection process is what Darwin called "survival of the *fittest*"— which is *not* the same as "survival of the *strongest*" and does *not* mean that "only the strong survive." Survival of the fittest simply means that those organisms that are *best fitted or best suited to their environment* will make it to the age of reproduction. Grizzly bears, as powerful as they are, are not well suited to live in a desert and most certainly would not be able to survive long enough in that environment to reproduce. In a desert survival competition, little spiders and desert mice would easily defeat a grizzly. In this context, therefore, fitness or "suitedness" has little to do with strength.

Over time, survival of the fittest leads to changes in the characteristics of species. Imagine that in North America there are rabbits, some brown and some white, and that they interbreed with each other producing rabbits with colourings ranging in between. In the south, where the environment is largely green and brown, white or whitish rabbits would probably have a hard time making it to the age of reproduction, as they would be more visible to predators such as wolves, coyotes, foxes, cougars, bears and eagles. But in the north, where the environment is white and grey for large parts of the year, being a white or whitish rabbit would likely be advantageous. Over time, as less and less whiteness was passed on among the southern rabbits and less and less brownness passed on in the northern ones, we would end up with two distinct varieties of rabbits adapted to two different environments. It would be as if nature had *selected* what the species end up looking like—not through any conscious decision, but purely through the survival of the fittest.

The brilliance of Darwin's theory of natural selection is due, in part, to its shocking simplicity. At bottom, this theory is founded on an obvious truth: on the one hand, the characteristics that allow a species to reproduce are thereby passed on; on the other hand, characteristics which prevent a species from reproducing don't get passed on. It's pretty hard to refute. Indeed, early supporters, such as **Thomas Huxley**, felt rather foolish for not having thought of it themselves. But the simplicity of the theory also fanned the flames of controversy: its opponents were enraged, for surely, they thought, the complexity of the natural world could not be due to such a simple phenomenon as natural selection. And, as we have since discovered, these critics were partly (but only partly) correct, for there is a second process that in fact works alongside natural selection in the evolution of plant and animal species: genetic mutation. In the 19th century, Darwin could only imagine this phenomenon—which would not be fully explained until the emergence of 20th-century genetics.

Thomas Huxley
(1825–1895) English biologist

Genetic Mutation

Natural selection does only what its name indicates: it *selects*. Any selection—in the natural and unnatural world alike—involves "choosing" from an available menu of options. Natural selection may explain *why* white rabbits have been "selected" to survive in a particular environment, but it doesn't explain *how* nature came to have the "choice" between white and brown rabbits in the first place. It is quite amazing that Darwin was able to predict, in broad terms, how this could happen. Given the limits of technological development in his day, however, he was not able to do this accurately or to provide any proof of it. Today, modern genetics has provided us with this ability.

We now know that all living organisms, whether bacteria, plants, insects or animals, have a code built into them, called DNA, which tells their cells how to develop. The organism's "mother" and "father" each contribute half of this code. All living organisms develop and grow through the division of their cells: two cells divide to produce four cells, which divide to produce eight cells, and so on. During this division, the DNA is copied into each new cell, which indicates what form it should take—e.g., whether it should be a skin cell, hair cell, blood cell or whatever. Like all codes, DNA uses a series of symbols. In the case of DNA, these symbols are made out of combinations of chemicals that determine what form the cell should take. Most of the time, this code is copied into the new cell correctly. But any living organism is constantly replenishing its cells (human skin is fully replaced every two weeks!), which means its DNA is constantly being replicated. Every now and then, purely by chance, the DNA code is copied incorrectly, producing a change—that is, a *mutation*—in the organism. If this mutation affects the organism's own body—say, its skin—it may produce a gradual change in the organism, such as skin cancer. But if the mutation affects its reproductive DNA—its seeds, sperm or eggs—then it will transmit to its offspring DNA that is not a perfect replication of itself. The offspring will now be different in some way from its parent.

Most mutations are insignificant, producing no detectable effects in the organism. Sometimes, however, the miscopying of the code results in a slight mutation, such as a change in eye or hair colour. At other times still, the miscopying of DNA results in a drastic mutation: a change in just one symbol in the DNA sequence of a particular species of fruit-fly, for instance, results in a leg growing where one of its antennae is supposed to be! Transmitted mutations are very rare: in each generation of a species, one will occur at most in every 100,000 individuals. In simple organisms such as bacteria, where millions of individuals can co-exist on a doorknob and where reproduction happens very quickly (in a matter of hours), mutations can occur in a short period of time—which is why bacteria can readily evolve to become resistant to antibiotics. In complex organisms such as human beings, where there are only a total of 6 billion individuals and where a generation takes about 25 years, transmitted mutations occur much more slowly.

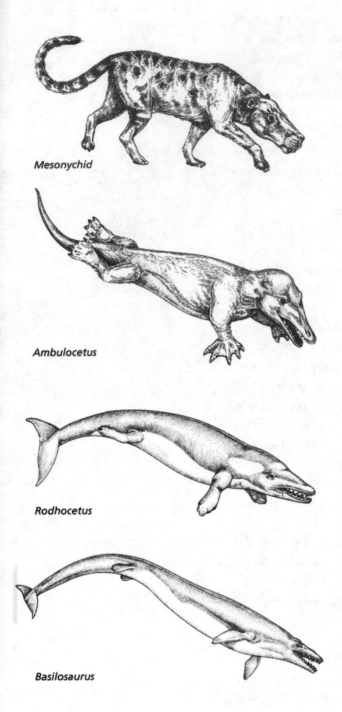

Mesonychid

Ambulocetus

Rodhocetus

Basilosaurus

Evolution of the Whale

A mutation in just one individual does not mean, of course, that there will be an evolutionary change in the species. If an individual's mutation prevents it from reproducing for some reason (perhaps it has been rendered unattractive to the opposite sex or has inherited a genetic disease that will kill it before the age of reproduction or has developed lungs that can no longer handle the level of pollution in our air), the mutation will not spread into the species. But if its mutation allows it to reproduce successfully, the mutation may be transmitted to its offspring, who may in turn transmit it to its offspring, and so on; over several generations, then, the mutation may become more common in the species. And if those individuals with this mutation have any kind of reproductive advantage, then they will gradually become more dominant in the species, perhaps even forcing those without the mutation to disappear completely. It should be clear that—due to the time it takes for individuals to reach the age of reproduction, the infrequency of genetic mutation, and the relative insignificance of most mutations—the actual process of evolution happens *very, very* slowly.

Indeed, the fossil record shows that the evolution of life on earth, from single-celled organisms to human beings, has taken *billions* of years. The earth itself is approximately 4.5 billion years old. The first bacteria developed over 3 billion years ago; it then took 2.5 billion years for multi-cellular but still microscopic organisms to develop (about 700 million years ago); 250 million years later (approximately 480 million years ago), fish evolved; 140 million years after that, reptiles appeared; 80 million years later, dinosaurs; 50 million later (about 210 million years ago), the first mammals; human-like primates, such as *Australopithecus* and *Homo erectus*, began to appear only about 5 million years ago, with the modern human being, *Homo sapiens*, appearing within the last 200 thousand years.

The Reaction to Darwin and Evolution

When *The Origin of Species* was published in 1859, it immediately sparked controversy on both sides of the Atlantic. Contrary to what one might first think, the initial hostility towards Darwin's ideas came more from fellow scientists than from theologians. Why? Because, as discussed earlier, most scientists at the time followed Paley's theistic account of nature—i.e., that God made all the different species of plants and animals *in separate acts of creation*. According to this view, the naturalist's modest job was simply to categorize and understand God's great handiwork: to determine, for instance, whether killer whales and humpback whales are different species or simply different varieties of the same species, or, to take another example, to figure out what flowers do or how gills work. Darwin's claim that species evolve out of each other and, therefore, are *not* created separately by God, contradicted the prevailing *scientific* doctrine. As is often the case, scientists were at first reluctant to give up their current view of nature.

By contrast, theologians, who were naturally more invested in conceptions of God than in conceptions of nature, were generally more willing to adjust their religious beliefs to make room for Darwin's new theory. That said, there was in fact a wide diversity of theological responses that emerged, ranging from very liberal to very conservative. It is worth discussing three here.

On the liberal side were the Christian Darwinists,[2] who were actually inspired by Darwin. They argued that God was not to be found directly intervening in nature, as creationists assumed, but must be seen instead in the very process of evolution, gradually revealing His plan. The second, more moderate group still adjusted their theological beliefs somewhat by conceding that the earth, as well as plant and animal life, may have evolved; they drew the line at human beings, however, who they insisted were a special creation by God. Indeed, they mocked the Darwinian theory of evolution by calling it the "man from monkeys" theory. It is interesting to note that the views of the late Pope John Paul II share elements of the liberal and moderate views. In 1996, the pope wrote a controversial letter to the Pontifical Academy of Sciences asserting that evolution is "more than a just a hypothesis" and that the idea of evolution should be supported so long as human beings are not then reduced to being purely mechanical beings, an idea we will consider momentarily. Predictably, the pope's assertions made headlines around the world and were embraced by more liberal Catholics and shunned by those of a more conservative bent. The current pope, Benedict XVI, has

A caricature of Charles Darwin.

turned away from Pope John Paul's views and returned to a view of divine design in nature.

The third and most vocal group were conservatives who called themselves "fundamentalists." They emerged in America around 1900 in opposition both to the theory of evolution and to new developments in biblical scholarship. In the 19th century, a view emerged among theological scholars that the Bible was woven together over a long period of time from the writings of several different human authors living in many different places. The fundamentalists thought that this non-traditional view of the Bible, combined with the theory of evolution, was a recipe for atheism. In response, they insisted that the Bible must be taken literally and, consequently, that Darwin's concept of evolution be completely rejected. Following the 17th-century bishop, James Usher, they believed that the Bible confirmed that the world was created in 4004 BCE, that it took six days to complete, and that Adam and Eve were real people—ideas clearly at odds with the theory of evolution.

Nonetheless, it did not take long for the scientific community to accept Darwin's theory of evolution. Indeed, by the first decades of the 20th century, almost all biologists in Europe and North America endorsed some version of it. At the same time, however, fundamentalists began an anti-evolution crusade to try to stop the spread of the theory's influence, thereby sowing the seeds of the culture wars being fought today. The most targeted focus of their attack was the public school system, where they believed biology teachers, educated by liberal evolutionist university professors, would corrupt their children.

The most notorious instance of this school-based attack is the Scopes trial of 1925, captured in the classic Hollywood movie, *Inherit the Wind*. The state of Tennessee passed a law, called the Butler Act, which forbade teachers from teaching the theory of evolution. The American Civil Liberties Union (ACLU) convinced a high school biology teacher named John Scopes to teach evolution in his classroom in the hopes of provoking the school board to bring charges against him, thereby creating a forum where the Butler Act could be challenged. It worked. The ensuing trial instantly drew media attention—garnering international press, with newspapers mockingly calling it the "Monkey Trial," and Europeans laughing in disbelief at America. The lawyers for the ACLU are widely seen as having demolished the arguments against teaching evolution, yet Scopes was nevertheless convicted by the jury (although the verdict was later overturned on a technicality). Since the 1920s, similar controversies have sprung up all over the United States: in Alabama, California, Georgia, Indiana, Kentucky, Michigan, New Hampshire, New Mexico, Ohio, Tennessee, Virginia,

Washington and Wisconsin. In 1987, this issue was brought before the U.S. Supreme Court.

It was not until the provocation of the rights revolution in the 1960s, however, that the fundamentalists felt the need to resume their efforts in full force. The culmination of that re-emergence was the development in the 1980s of the theory of intelligent design (ID), originally devised by American lawyer Phillip Johnson. As its name suggests, ID revives the argument from design by claiming that life is too complex to have evolved by accident, as Darwinian evolution claims, and so must have had the guiding hand of an intelligent designer. Unlike classic statements of the argument from design, however, ID theorists claim to be scientific, and not religious, and so do not use the name "God" or the term "divine creation." On the contrary, they point out what they assert to be holes and flaws in the theory of evolution—e.g., how did DNA evolve?—and claim that their theory is actually *more scientific* than Darwinian theory. In an interesting reversal of the Scopes challenge, ID was put on trial, so to speak, when in 2005 the Dover School Board in Pennsylvania was taken to court for mandating that ID be taught in its high schools. During the trial, the theory was subjected to a devastating critique by the prosecution, whose chief witness was a Catholic evolutionist named Kenneth Miller, whom we shall discuss shortly. In the end, the judge ruled against the practice of teaching ID, on the grounds that it is a blatantly religious doctrine, and, therefore, not able to stand up to rigorous scientific analysis. Many outraged fundamentalists initially accused the judge of being an atheist liberal, until they learned, much to their embarrassment, that there is plenty of public evidence that the judge is, like them, a conservative Christian.

But it is not only religious groups that have gone on the offensive. Increasingly since the Scopes trial, scientific evolutionists have launched a counter-attack—not simply against the idea of creation, but against religion as a whole. Indeed, this movement has now gained so much momentum that in 2007 *Maclean's* magazine featured an article—titled "Is God Poison?"—that discussed several recent bestsellers that attempt to make the case not only that God does not exist but that religion is a corrupting and polluting influence in society. Arguments of this sort are based on a philosophical perspective called "materialist reductionism." According to this view, all or at least most aspects of human experience, including the most "elevated" ones such as consciousness, morality, art and spirituality, can ultimately be explained on the basis of the material properties of the physical world, and therefore can be "reduced" to scientific analysis. In the realm of psychology, for instance, a materialist reductionist would probably reject the Freudian view that an individual's behaviour can be understood and modified only through psychoanalysis; instead, the materialist reductionist might suggest that behaviour is simply the result of the brain's chemical constitution—which can be most effectively modified with drug therapy. In the realm of spirituality, some materialist reductionists argue that religion probably served an evolutionary purpose in the development of humankind thousands of years ago by providing a moral system that deterred large-scale human-on-human aggression and violence, thereby allowing more individuals to reach the age of maturity and to reproduce—facilitating the survival of the species. But today, they argue, we no longer need religion as human reason can achieve the same goals more effectively and without the persistent amounts of violence that religion actually seems to provoke.

It should be clear that the antagonistic voices of the religious fundamentalists, on the one hand, and the materialist reductionists, on the other, have led to a great division in our culture over the subject of the relationship between science and religion.

Thinking beyond the Culture Wars

The purpose of this article is not to convince anyone to become a theist or an atheist, but merely to facilitate critical thinking about the issues raised by the relationship between science and religion. This goal is hindered, however, by the antagonism that exists today between proponents of religious fundamentalism and materialist reductionism—who seem to be bent on obliterating each other instead of engaging in a dialogue about the merits of each position. It is worth asking, therefore, whether it is possible to avoid these two extremes and instead to find value in *both* religion *and* science, even to the point of valuing *both* the idea of God *and* the theory of evolution. Indeed, there has been a long history of voices in our culture that have sought to reconcile science and religion. Three in particular are worthy of note here:

1. Throughout the 20th century, one view that has increasingly gained support points out that religion itself has contributed to the very origins of modern science insofar as it endorses a *disenchanted* conception of nature. Science cannot operate on the basis of an *enchanted* conception of nature—i.e., that the natural world is magical and, as such, full of gods, spirits and other supernatural beings. Within an enchanted nature, the reason it rains is because, say, the storm gods make it rain; the reason you are sick is perhaps because someone has put a hex on you; the reason the planets orbit is because they have souls in them. There are two reasons why science cannot operate in such a world. First, scientific explanations

are based purely on the evidence that nature provides; in other words, science assumes that there must be something about the material properties of things that makes them behave in particular ways. Water boils, for instance, because heat energizes water molecules, causing them to move rapidly, which loosens the bonds between molecules and allows some of them to float away as steam. Second, scientific explanations require uniformity; in other words, the laws of nature must remain the same. The reason water boiled today must be the same reason it has always boiled, not because it suddenly and miraculously became possessed by a spirit. Science thus assumes that there are no supernatural qualities in nature; in other words, for science, *nature is disenchanted*.

Some historians of science have pointed out that the disenchanted view of nature emerges from, of all places, the Bible and the Abrahamic religions that grew out of it (Judaism, Christianity and Islam). According to the Bible, there is only one true God and everything that exists, including all of nature, was made by God. By consequence, nature does what it does only because God made it work that way, which means there is nothing else in nature, no mysterious forces or beings, including God, making it do what it does. As such, other than God and human beings, who are said to be made in God's image, there are no supernatural beings.[3] Nature is simply and purely nature, which is to say that, for the Bible too, nature is *not* enchanted.

2. Even if we accept the Bible as a philosophical ally of modern science, we cannot deny that it contains a number of ideas that contradict many observations and theories of science. After all, the Bible does not literally state that life evolved or that God cannot contradict the laws of nature. So how can we reconcile the claims of religious scriptures with the claims of science?

One view that has recurred repeatedly among religious thinkers with a keen interest in defending human rationality—such as the 13th-century Spanish Muslim theologian Averroes or the 17th-century Italian Catholic scientist Galileo Galilei—is the "doctrine of two truths." This view holds that God has both revealed certain truths in scripture (the Quran or the Bible) and also given us reason to discover truth through an analysis of divinely made nature. Sometimes, as we have seen, the truth found in scripture *appears* to contradict the truth produced by reason. But God has made both of these truths possible. Therefore, if we say

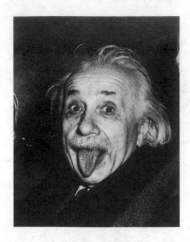

Albert Einstein: "I want to know God's thoughts."

heliocentrism

view that the sun, not the earth, is the centre of the solar system

that there *actually* is a contradiction between these two truths, then we are saying that God contradicts himself, which is contrary both to what scripture says about God and to our rationally produced understanding of Him. It follows, then, that reason and scripture cannot *actually* contradict each other. The contradiction can only be *apparent*. If we *perceive* a contradiction, then only two things are possible: either (1) we have made a mistake in our reasoning about something or (2) we have made a mistake in our interpretation of scripture. If we have good reason to believe that our rational analysis of nature is sound, as we do with **heliocentrism** and the theory of evolution, then we must reinterpret what we understand scripture to mean. We must change our interpretation of scripture to fit what reason tells us about nature, and not the other way around, because, as the Catholic theologian Augustine (354–430 CE) argued, God's revelations in the Bible (or other religious texts) are spoken in the language of the common person who may not know the latest rational (e.g., scientific) theories. God's purpose in scripture is not to teach us how nature works but to teach us how to live a morally good life. As Galileo famously wrote, "The Bible teaches us how to go to heaven, not how the heavens go."

3. What might a disenchanted view of nature and a non-literalist interpretation of religious scripture imply about the relationship between the idea of God and the theory of evolution? A particularly interesting answer to this question is offered by Kenneth Miller—a contemporary biology professor who is both a steadfast Darwinian and a devout Catholic. His religious faith notwithstanding, Miller is highly critical of ID and religious fundamentalism, as was evident in his testimony against ID at the trial in Dover, Pennsylvania, mentioned earlier.

Miller rejects both ID and more traditional arguments from design. Why? Because, he argues, they are indefensible both from a scientific and a religious point of view. In his provocatively titled book *Finding Darwin's God: A Scientist's Search for Common Ground Between God and Evolution* (1999), Miller shows that design arguments tend to view perceived gaps in nature and in our understanding of natural phenomena as proof of God's existence. As mentioned earlier, William Paley, for example, argued that complex entities such as flowers or eyes seem to require a creator to explain their existence. ID theorists today ask questions that imply comparable arguments—for instance, if DNA is essential to the mechanism of evolution, then how could DNA itself evolve in the first place? These arguments assume, Miller points out, that because science does not currently understand some natural phenomena—e.g., how the eye evolved—these phenomena must stand *outside* the laws of nature and therefore can *never* be understood. Not only are such things *currently* unknown, design theorists claim, but they are also unknow*able*—because, contrary to what scientists believe, the laws of nature do not apply to all things at all times.

This view also has serious implications for religion. Design theories consider something humans do not understand, some gap in our knowledge of nature, as evidence of God's existence. A loss for science is thus perceived as a gain for religion: ignorance (of nature) is taken as knowledge (of God). Because God is used in design arguments to account for various gaps in nature and understanding, the concept of God contained in this view is sometimes called "the God of the gaps."

Miller believes that arguments from design actually do no harm to science as scientists will simply continue their work on the assumption that the laws of nature are universal. And this is precisely why Miller believes that the God of the gaps view is actually more dangerous for religion than for science. Science does not only *attempt* to understand how the eye and DNA evolved; it also *succeeds* in making progress toward that understanding. In fact, scientists *can* explain, and provide evidence of, how the eye evolved; and, as Miller explains in his book, they also have a pretty good idea of how DNA evolved. If gaps in nature and human understanding are held up as proof of God's existence, then every time science fills in one of those gaps—which science regularly does and will likely continue to do—then religion loses one of its proofs. A gain for science becomes a loss for religion, a consequence drawn from design theory and not from science. Indeed, science in itself is not concerned with debunking religion, even if there are some scientists who step outside their area of expertise and make this a priority. Rather, if the advancements of science threaten religion, Miller asserts, this is wholly the fault of religious proponents who conceive of God in a faulty manner.

Miller suggests that a better approach would be to stop looking for God in the gaps and instead look for God elsewhere. He points out that the God of the Western religions is represented in their scriptures as wanting human beings to have meaningful lives. To have a meaningful life—a life full of things one finds satisfying, fulfilling, enriching and important to oneself and others—requires a person to make choices, to choose, for instance, between being a legal assistant or a video-game programmer, single or married, with children or without them. In the Hebrew Bible, God offers his followers the choice between life and death (a metaphor for a life lived with or without God), and urges them to "Choose life" (Deuteronomy 30:15–20). In the Quran, God dictates to Mohammed that "there is no compulsion in matters of faith" (2:256). Whatever else these passages might mean, both seem to suggest that God wants us to have *freedom*. Genuine freedom, moreover, requires that one not be wholly determined. The God imagined by design theorists—one who fully controls the actions of the world, who interferes with the laws of nature so events turn out just as He wanted—would also determine, to a significant extent if not completely, the shape of your life. A conception of God more compatible with the scriptures of Western religions, Miller suggests, would be one who did *not* determine the world to be one particular way, but who allowed the world to change and develop on its own terms. And as we have seen, the theory that best explains how the natural world changes and develops on its own terms is the Darwinian theory of evolution. As Miller himself writes,

A biologically static world would leave a Creator's creatures with neither freedom nor the independence required to exercise that freedom. In biological terms, evolution is the only way a Creator could have made us the creatures we are—free beings in a world of authentic and meaningful moral and spiritual choices.[4]

Miller's position, it must be said, does not solve all the problems raised by the relationship between science and religion more generally, and the issue of evolution and creation more specifically. For instance, what does Miller mean by endorsing evolution and continuing to refer to God as a creator? Is he suggesting that God created evolution? If evolution is created, does this not return us to the problem Miller alerted us to—namely, that evolution now seems determined? Or does referring to evolution as creation mean something else altogether?

Regardless of these nagging questions, Miller recasts the problem in a rather helpful, enabling and undogmatic manner. He makes it possible for us to leave this discussion with more tools than we had when we entered into it, and, more importantly, without the closed-minded and exclusivist views that the loudest voices in the debate over religion and science continue to try to force upon us.

Notes

The author would like to thank Jonathan Cauchi and Anna Isacsson for reading and commenting on an earlier draft of this essay.

1 "Evolution v Creationism?" Decima Research, July 3, 2007. Available at www.harrisdecima.com/en/downloads/pdf/news_releases/070706E.pdf [Accessed February 6, 2009.]

2 Lyman Abbott's *Theology of an Evolutionist* (1897) articulates the theology of the Christian Darwinists.

3 The Bible does make mention of other divine beings such as angels, the accuser (Satan) and God's council, but these are not natural beings and they are always represented as subordinate to God's power.

4 Kenneth R. Miller, *Finding Darwin's God: A Scientist's Search for Common Ground between God and Evolution*, Harper Perennial Edition (Toronto: Harper Perennial, 2002), 291.

"Science and Religion: A Complicated History" was written for *The Human Project* by Mark Cauchi, a professor at the Humber College Institute of Technology and Advanced Learning. Used by permission.

Arts and Culture

The purpose of art is the lifelong construction of a state of wonder.

Glenn Gould

As an artist, one is not a citizen of society. An artist is bound to explore every aspect of human experience, the darkest corners—not necessarily— but if that is where one is led, that's where one must go. You cannot worry about what the structure of your own particular segment of society considers bad behaviour, good behaviour; good exploration, bad exploration. So, at the time you're being an artist, you're not a citizen. You don't have the social responsibility of a citizen. You have, in fact, no social responsibility whatsoever.

David Cronenberg

Fantasies are more than substitutes for unpleasant realities, they are also dress rehearsals. All acts performed in the world begin in the imagination.

Barbara Grizzuti Harrison

Confronted with a story, any story, we immediately seek to fathom it out, to know it, even though we realize that if we succeed it will no longer be interesting, it will die. Oddly, then, the greatest pleasure we can get from a story only comes when the smaller satisfaction of having explained it away is thwarted. The mind discards, as it were, the chaff of the explicable to find real repose, or real excitement, in a kernel of enigma.

Tim Parks

Introduction

Throughout the course of *The Human Project*, reason has helped us to examine some thorny and fundamental problems. You may recall from previous units the question of the possibility of freedom, the collision of inevitable change and the persistence of old attitudes, the possibility that human nature itself imposes limits on our hopes for political solutions, and the concern that the technological offspring of science may cause us to lose our way in the search for a better world. For answers to these and other questions, we have relied on reason and the methods of various disciplines such as psychology, sociology, philosophy, politics and science. In this unit, we shift emphasis, not in the sense of turning away from reason and method, but in the sense of adding a certain openness to imagination and a receptivity to pleasure. For the arts are about the significance of a parallel and imagined universe in the mind—a place where the real world may be reflected and criticized perhaps, but where the chief motive to explore is pleasure.

The possibility of pleasure lies at the centre of "It's Open. Who Cares?" David Macfarlane questions why anyone who has no interest in opera should care about the new Toronto Opera House. His answer has everything to do with cities and their role as a market of the best ideas and the deepest and most varied pleasures. Cities that work engage the curiosity of their citizens through providing a virtually unlimited menu of experiences and, thereby, fulfilling their one great responsibility "to encourage the possibility of excellence." Cities do the work of civilization, and among the most important things a civilization can leave behind are the insights of its artists. Great hospitals, great colleges and universities, and great business opportunities are essential, but a city must also create venues and communities where artists can do their work—in theatres, movie houses, art galleries and opera houses.

Art thrives not only in grand opera houses but also in bars and clubs, the grassroots venues for popular music. Ian Baird, in "One More Time: Our Ongoing Dialogue with Popular Music," discusses the power of American popular music to reflect social realities, to console those who suffer the injuries of inequality and, moreover, to encourage the "transgression" needed to express both an outrage at injustice and an insistence on freedom. He traces the origin of much popular music to the blues, with its haunting mix of the sacred and the profane. The story of how the blues influenced British musicians of the sixties, who then exported the blues back to the United States, is an intriguing example of cultural migration. Today, we see similar migrations, as the music of the ghetto forms the beat at every suburban party.

The blues has an authenticity that popular music at its best aspires to but frequently fails to deliver, as it gets caught up in the understandable drive for commercial success.

In "Serious Pleasure: The Role of the Arts," Clive Cockerton makes the case for the significance of art from a more philosophical perspective. Specifically, he explores the Platonic view that art has the power to seduce people to think and do things they shouldn't and, therefore, ought to be banned from society. In his rejection of the Platonic view, Cockerton argues that aesthetic pleasure is intrinsically valuable, that artistic insights can facilitate self-reflection and, finally, that artistic experience helps to create a sense of community. Rather than diminishing us, Cockerton argues, art substantially enhances our lives.

"Looking for Beauty," also by Cockerton, explores what happens to us emotionally when we are overwhelmed by a beautiful moment, a stunning person or an exquisite painting. The experience of beauty is hard to articulate despite the strength of the feelings it evokes. We are surprised as well as delighted by beauty, because too often it is a stranger to our everyday existence. Cockerton suggests that we should place ourselves where beauty may more easily reach us. But where, besides in other people, can we find beauty? Occasionally, we find it in our cityscape, but definitely we can find it in our art galleries—institutions dedicated to the preservation and promotion of beautiful paintings, sculpture and objects.

While "Looking for Beauty" references paintings and "One More Time" talks of music, Mary Ellen Kappler takes us on a literary safari through the short story "Murderers." This narrative is so concentrated and compressed, it requires more than a little thought to tease out both the possible meanings of the story and the literary techniques that allow its author, Leonard Michaels, to pack so much death, freedom and the "world's lesson" into his brief tale. Careful readers should read the story first, then read Kappler's insightful article and, finally, to get the most out of the experience, go back to the story and see what works for them personally.

"Murderers" may be an astonishing piece of compression for a prose story, but the real masters of verbal economy are poets. Ezra Pound, the great American poet, once defined great literature as "language charged with meaning to the utmost degree." A number of poems are included in this unit so that the reader can test Pound's proposition and explore poetry's ability to suggest feelings and states of mind that elude other forms of writing.

It's Open. Who Cares?

David Macfarlane

Why should anyone who has no interest in opera be proud of what now stands at the corner of Queen and University in downtown Toronto? I happen to love opera, I might as well admit. I think of it as a kind of delicious overabundance of . . . well, of everything. If you love music and you love theatre, you might as well sleep with the twins in my modest, if not entirely Presbyterian, view.

Indeed, it may be opera's aesthetic excessiveness that appeals to me so much. I love being dazzled by the sweeping music and the adventurous design and the artistic rigour of a production such as the Canadian Opera Company's *Siegfried*. Equally, I love weeping good old-fashioned buckets— both at the tragedy of the story and at the sheer beauty of the singing in the company's completely classic approach to Puccini's *Madama Butterfly* a few seasons ago. . . .

But why should anyone who doesn't know Parsifal from Pagliacci give two hoots about Toronto's new opera house? The answer, I think, has something to do with the importance and the wonder of cities.

When I was a boy, I sometimes walked from the YMCA in Hamilton, Ontario, to my father's office in the Medical Arts Building to get a ride home when he completed his Saturday-morning appointments. I usually arrived before he was finished, and I sat in his waiting room and read magazines.

I didn't realize it at the time, but the magazines I found there in the early 1960s—*Esquire, The Saturday Evening Post, Maclean's, Life, Time*—were representative of a golden age of magazine journalism. They were the last glorious blossoming of something advertisers have managed to kill off successfully: They were publications that came under the heading of "general interest"—which, when you stop to think about it, is exactly the heading you'd like a 12-year-old to spend some time under during a few Saturday mornings of adolescent life.

The stories I read in my father's magazines covered an eclectic range of subjects. Hell's Angels on one page. Pablo Picasso on the next. And one of the things I remember most vividly about those articles is another quaint memento of a by-gone age: Not everything was explained to me. Verdi was Verdi, and not "Verdi, the famous Italian opera composer." Writers—as well as editors and publishers—assumed that a certain level of general knowledge obtained among the readership of a general-interest magazine. More importantly, they assumed that where there was not knowledge (as was frequently the case when the reader happened to be 12) there would be curiosity.

It seems to me this is how civilization works: not as a balanced exchange of information from someone who knows something to someone else who already knows the same thing. That, if I'm not mistaken, is the axis of idiocy on which a good deal of contemporary life is already based. That is reality TV.

Civilization is about another kind of exchange—from someone who either knows a lot about something or is very good at it, to someone who doesn't know as much, or is nowhere near as good but who is either interested enough to learn or curious enough to become interested. Who is, in other words, alive.

The ideal consumer, I sometimes think, would be deceased enough to stay permanently within his or her demographic, but alive enough to still be spending money. As markets get more and more narrowly focused, anything that appears to be outside the confines of a target audience—anything that might arouse something as uncontained as curiosity or as broadly based as learning—is either deleted or explained to death.

And as the media increasingly surrenders to the commercial demand to level the relationship between those who send out information and those who receive it, those of us who enjoy the **serendipity** of general interest, and who depend on the expertise of others to point the way to knowledge or pleasure, or even, perish the thought, to wisdom, look elsewhere for sustenance. We look to the last great **compendium** of general interest. We look to the city.

serendipity
chance discovery

compendium
collection

Those of us who love cities love the way they come at us from dozens of different angles at the same time. The richness of the array—some of it to our taste, some not—is why cities are so exciting and why we learn so much by living in one. Cities stretch us, challenge us, broaden us. Cities, like magazines in their glory years, can pique our curiosity with an almost unlimited table of contents.

And we become intrigued. About hockey, perhaps; about graffiti, perhaps; about commodities, perhaps; about Verdi. We are led to realms that we might not otherwise have known about by the passions and expertise and genius of our fellow citizens.

The delight of living in a city is that it's possible to flip through its pages. We might, for instance, wonder what all the fuss is about as we drive by the beautifully lit transparency of the architect Jack Diamond's opera house while crowds are making their way in for the first performance of *Das Rheingold*.

The beauty of a city is that it can provide the answers to the questions it so naturally raises. What's all the fuss about? Well, come and see, and hear, for yourself.

This is particularly true of a city as diverse and as unformed as Toronto. You want ugliness? You want beauty? You want tragedy? You want comedy? Then walk a block or two, and it's all here.

And it is out of this profoundly general amalgamation that something truly extraordinary can sometimes arise. It could be a really good teacher. Or it could be a fabulous guitar player. It could be the help that is provided to someone who desperately needs it. Or it could be the *Ring Cycle*.

The one responsibility a city has is the encouragement of the possibility of excellence. The extent to which it addresses this duty is how, in comparison to the great cities of the world, it will be judged. Excellence of education, excellence of health care, excellence of baseball, of public transportation, of commerce, of charity, of waterfront, excellence of art galleries, excellence of justice, excellence of opera—to name but a few of the impossible ambitions of a city that might aspire to greatness.

It is not necessarily the city's responsibility to achieve these goals, or to pay for them, but it is its job to make room for their possibility, and to celebrate when, against so many odds, that possibility becomes reality. That's what cities are for.

One More Time: Our Ongoing Dialogue with Popular Music

Ian Baird

The musician sat curled over his guitar, long brown fingers orbiting deftly atop the soundboard as if pulled by a force of gravity from the vibrating strings. A bottle of whiskey sat on the floor next to him and a fedora perched precariously on his head. As thick shrouds of cigarette smoke swirled around, people smacked their knees and thighs to the music, hooting and hollering and whistling. A couple of people got up and shuffled their feet, swirled their hips, twirled their bodies. Hard-working, dead-tired sharecroppers who were all gathered for a few hours of freedom and joy and laughter on a Saturday night in this small, rough-hewn room: the local juke joint. Maybe they'd get lucky in a card game tonight or get squeezed tight by a welcoming pair of limbs. They would listen to some soul-stirring or foot-stomping blues music: "Terraplane Blues," or "Preachin' Blues," or "Trouble in Mind." The musician shouted "have mercy!" with a deep, raspy laugh between songs, took a drink, and started into a new song, his fingers once again thrumming the guitar strings, his feet tapping against the worn hard floor.

Through the night and into the morning the bluesman sang and preached about trouble and the blues. He sang that trouble was a steady companion for the black man in the American South. He sang that sometimes life could become so gloomy, so lonesome, and so hard, that a person just did not know how to go on. Then he preached that if that person picked up a guitar and sang the blues and told the entire world how he had the blues, then maybe that person could get by for a just little bit longer. He sang:

Trouble in mind, I'm blue
But I won't be blue always,
'Cause the sun's gonna shine in my backdoor some day.[1]

The music of the guitar twanged and the smell of whiskey and dance sweat filled the room. And for a time the listeners forgot about the pain of the past week in their backs and bones, the bitter hopelessness of poverty, the lashing brutality of racism. Until the next week when the cruel bossman and dire poverty and misfortune would come back for a long, long visit.

"Preachin' Blues": Popular Music and Its Dialogue with Religion

The scene described above might have taken place in any juke joint in the Mississippi Delta or in Texas or Louisiana in the 1920s or '30s or '40s. Many music historians say that the blues evolved out of a combination of work hollers sung in the cotton fields and hymns sung in Protestant churches. Work hollers consisted of one group of slaves in a field calling out a musical phrase that was then answered by another group in an adjacent field. Named "call and response," this musical form was like a conversation connecting the different groups of workers in the fields. I will suggest in this article that popular music has pretty much done the same thing over the years: engaged in an ongoing, resonant dialogue with other forms of music, other musicians and audiences, and many other facets of human experience.

To begin, let us consider the intense spiritual character of the blues and how it created a fairly involved dialogue with religion in early 20th-century America. Like religion, the blues deals with things like sin, danger, hunger, fear, oppression and disaster. Back then, black people could not really protect themselves from all these bad things—except in two ways. They could go to church on Sundays and go down on their knees and pray to God and ask Him to forgive their sins—but then they might have to wait until the next world for deliverance. Or they could go to the juke joint on a Saturday night and thumb their noses at bad luck and trouble and even the devil himself, and listen to a blues musician sing and preach the blues. Now the blues would not stop devastating floods or fires or the boweevil eating the cotton crop or the plantation owner taking away a sharecropper's wife. But it could make people feel a lot better, and unless they drank some bad whiskey or lost all their money at cards or got into a bad knife fight—they were not any worse off after a night at the juke joint than before.

The preachers, naturally, did not like it when people went to the juke joint at night because they spent all their money on whiskey and cards and sex and had none left Sunday morning for the collection plate. So they started calling the blues "devil music." There were other good reasons for this too, such as the Church's opinion of many of the common topics of blues songs: fighting, guns, murder, crime, drunkenness, gambling and hoodoo (magic). But there always remained a strong if ambivalent link between the blues and gospel music, and between the juke joint and the church. A lot of the time it was the same musicians who played and sang both gospel and the blues. In the case of some blues musicians, like Skip James, their fathers were preachers, and some blues musicians even became preachers themselves.

For a black person in the American South in the early 20th century, there were not a lot of choices to be made. There were not too many things he or she could do to alleviate injustice and suffering. African-Americans in those times could not vote, hold political office, go to college, or own a plantation or a store. But what they *could* do was pray and sing: anybody could pray and sing because nobody could stop you from praying and singing unless they killed you. And if they did, someone else might sing about it later, like the great singer Billie Holiday did in the song, "Strange Fruit," about the horrors of lynching.

"Blue Suede Shoes": Popular Music and Its Dialogue with Class

French sociologist Pierre Bourdieu (1930–2002) proposes that one of the main differences between the upper classes and the working classes is one of detachment from cultural experience: what he calls "distinction." "The detachment of the pure gaze," he argues, is an "active distance" attained from not having to provide for the necessities of life, from living a "life of ease."[2]

In music and in many other areas, the distinction Bourdieu is talking about is one of "taste." You either have good taste or you don't. Refinement and sophistication are the trademarks of distinction. And while it can be learned to a certain extent, mostly you must be raised in the "proper" environment to achieve it.

Equally important is the idea that, as a cultured person, one also remains "distinct" from the art one encounters. For a spectator, maintaining a "pure gaze" is extremely important. The eye of the "pure gaze" is refined but cool and unemotional, aloof, and even indifferent to the experience of art and culture. You never get your hands dirty and actually "touch" the art you are receiving.

With so-called "low culture," in contrast, you do the exact opposite. You engage extensively and intimately with the art or music you experience. That is why the working classes generally prefer art forms like music, where you can use your whole body and get "down and dirty." You move your limbs, tap your feet, hum, sing and dance around. You experience the whole thing as direct and intense involvement.

In many senses, when listening to and experiencing popular music we actually *become* the music, taking it into our bodies and letting it course through our muscles and lungs and into the toes of our blue suede shoes. If opera glasses in a theatre box high up above the rabble are the symbol of upper-class distinction, then the mosh pit is the symbol of the working-class musical immediacy of the body.

One reason why the song "My Generation" by The Who was such a huge hit in the 1960s was because lead vocalist Roger Daltrey not only sang about generational alienation, but also about youth seeking to find a voice in a very literal sense, which he dramatized through his violent stutter on the word "generation" in the lyric "talkin' about my generation." He seemed hardly to be able to get the word out. This stuttering reflected the frustration of his powerlessness, of being silenced and having nothing to represent who he was. But when the word finally burst out of his mouth, it changed everything. Youth suddenly had a clear, strong voice and an identity and a means of expression.

The Who became famous for trashing their hotel rooms when they were on the road and for wrecking their expensive guitars on stage. This seemingly irrational destruction was related to the same kind of intense physical involvement with music. They were also thumbing their noses at our obsession with material possession. Naturally, the ne'er-do-wells and the wrong-side-of-the-tracks clique ate it all up—but so did hordes of middle-class kids from the trim lawns of suburban America.

Hip-hop and "gangsta" rap have a different but equally belligerent take on materialism. Hip-hop videos, with all their gold, cognac and expensive cars, constitute an impolite flaunting of "taste," to say the least. But there is more: all those flashing arms and hand signs and extreme close-ups of petulant, defiant black faces create a very physical kind of music and language (in rap, language has a physical robustness that most regular lyrics lack) that gives those in power the heebie-jeebies. (Tattoos, belly rings and tongue piercings are also very physical engagements with culture.)

During the sixties, The Who, The Beatles and The Rolling Stones were all bands made up of British boys from working-class neighbourhoods. Ironically, rock stardom was all about not really working, about escaping work and the chains of the working class. The blue-collar dream of striking it rich through rock was not so much about breaking the bonds of class difference as taking them to their extreme and riding them all the way to fame and fortune.

In North America a similar phenomenon occurred, but here a somewhat different genre of blue-collar rock emerged. Singers such as Bob Seger, Bruce Springsteen, John Mellencamp, Joe Walsh and even Canada's own Neil Young sang anthems of the working man, the small-town man, the farming man: he was "like a rock," "born in the U.S.A.," in a "small town," taking the "Rocky Mountain way," driving "an Econoline." Popular music in general has always had its ties to the working man and working woman. Even back hundreds of years ago, when princes and archdukes hired musicians as servants to write music for the glory of their courts, musicians (sometimes the very same ones) were also in the streets, playing the music of the taverns and street corners and singing about the needs and urges of the emotional and physical self. One might say that for a long time there has been a touch of rebellion, with or without a cause, in many forms of popular music and in many centuries of singing about getting "no satisfaction."

And like the blues did on the plantations of the Delta close to a hundred years before, in the 1980s and '90s, hip-hop and rap emerged from the trouble of inner-city America, where trouble now came in the form of dire poverty, hunger, violence, drug addiction, lack of education and disease. Private desperation and individual tragedy became transformed into collective experience as musicians yet again filled the role of giving a voice to people visited by trouble in all its guises. Rap musicians such as Public Enemy, Ice-T and Ice Cube inspired young African-Americans who were "used, abused without clues" to become politically active and, like "hoochie-coochie man" Muddy Waters in Chicago decades earlier, stressed that "brothers of the same mind" were "here" and ready to "mess with you" in order to have their voices heard. Later, rap musicians such as Tupac Shakur, Snoop Dogg and Biggie Smalls would continue to express to new generations of black and white listeners in musical and lyrical terms the effort it took to survive and rise above a drive-by adolescence spent in inner-city ghettos.

Tupac Shakur

Over time, the early political activism of rap's origins has given way to an infatuation with the trappings of materialism. Enjoying the current heady days of extreme wealth and mainstream success, today's rap musicians are concerned less with resistance and more with marketing "street cred" to the huge white audiences who download hip-hop music in digital droves and buy baggy bundles of hip-hop clothing at middle-class suburban malls. But this change—this move into "da club," as 50 Cent puts it—is perhaps not entirely a sell-out. Just like political revolution, abundance for the disadvantaged has been a long-time transcultural symbol of giving the bird to "the breaks," no matter how fleeting or momentary that abundance may ultimately be. So despite the bling-bling and bluster of a 50 Cent or an Eminem, "don't believe the hype," necessarily.

"Thunder Road": Popular Music and Its Dialogue with Time and Space

By its very makeup, music is about time. Its very identity is time: tracks, beats, measures, rhythms, whole notes, quarter notes, sixteenth notes. Music is also about the time it takes to experience it and when in time we listen to it: Sunday morning hymns, the Friday Sabbath cantor, the morning call to prayer from the minaret; Saturday night in the juke joint, the local pub, the corner bar, the nightclub, or standing in line all night to get tickets to a concert by the Next Big Thing; conversely, Saturday night at the opera, or the symphony, or using your Gold Visa card over your cell phone to buy front-row tickets to a Broadway show.

We have music during the times of weddings, funerals, births, first communion parties and bar mitzvahs; Christmas, Ramadan, Diwali, Chinese New Year, Canada Day, potlatches and rain dances. We listen to *Sesame Street* when we're young, the Rat Pack when we're old. Music is cool, hip, hot, a new release, top forty, cutting edge, groundbreaking. Or it's old, retro, remastered, re-released, nostalgic, classic.

But that is not all. Music is about space, too. About strings on guitars being physically bent to create the blue notes out of the Western scale: the flatted 3rd, 5th and 7th steps of the scale. About, too, walls of amplified sound, Hammond organs, fuzz pedals, tremolo bars, synthesizer racks, double bass drums, Hendrix's white Stratocaster, turntables, Midi cables, MP3 and WAV files: all examples of music as physical space (huge or minuscule).

Moreover, we expect to hear music in diverse places. Indeed, place has been as crucial an element as any in the development of music. There is music for the campfire, the temple, the chapel; different music for the tavern, the pub, the town square; different music again for the palace, the court and the concert hall.

When music changes in terms of time, space or place, it changes its musical language as well. Its response to a musical "call" is a response that is contained within its own time and space while still responding to other times and spaces. It speaks with its own unique voice, but in answer to a chorus of other voices over other times, spaces and places. Music in history is music that changes, develops, evolves, goes forward and backward. But it is always in conversation with the music and musicians who have come before.

Look at the blues. It began in the Deep South, in the fields and then the juke joints, at crossroads and on dusty highways. Then it took a train up to the north and moved onto the killing floors of the Chicago slaughterhouses and into the noisy, smoke-filled bars of the South Side. Crowds grew bigger, the drinking got heavier, knives were exchanged for guns and the noises of the night grew louder and more varied. So the blues musicians started using electric guitars and sped up the music. They still used the same 12-bar pattern derived from Christian hymns and the AAB pattern derived from the work hollers, but now they consistently added drums and bass all the time. Blues-men such as Muddy Waters and Willie Dixon simplified the lyrics and the range of song themes so people didn't have to listen as hard or stay sober enough to remember them.

And the speeded-up blues travelled everywhere across America and was whitewashed and sequined up and taken into white dance halls and performed by white musicians. Now they simply called it rock and roll: Bill Haley and His Comets, Buddy Holly, Elvis Presley.

The new media of radio and television made the music ever-present. Kids listened to "Top 40" tunes on transistor radios and carried them to the beach, school and the cottage. Television brought Beatlemania and Jim Morrison lighting his fire into our living rooms on Sunday nights. And perhaps as representative as any development in the coming of age of rock and roll in the 1950s and '60s, popular music came into our cars. There were songs about cars, tunes specifically written to be listened to in cars: low-ridin', chicken-playin', hot-roddin', pedal-to-the-metal music. Let the rich listen in their elegant salons and concert halls: "born to run," working-class youth would take their music for a ride onto the "thunder roads" of America.

But still the blues did not stop moving. It boarded a plane and flew to England, and aspiring English musicians such as Eric Clapton, Keith Richards and Eric Burdon crowded around blues legends such as Muddy Waters and Sonny Boy Williamson. Musicians who, according to Sonny Boy, "wanted to play the blues so bad and played it SO bad!"

Blues was wedded with the power rock of distortion pedals and amplifier stacks. It became hard rock or acid rock. Jimi Hendrix electrified England, and power groups such as Cream and Led Zeppelin took the airwaves by storm. Then, as blues and rock and roll met again at the crossroads at the midnight hour, heavy metal was spawned. A cartoonish, *Tales-from-the-Crypt* comic book version of the blues, the music of Black Sabbath and Judas Priest nonetheless harkened back to the hellhounds and devils of blues singers such as Robert Johnson and Skip James. Bands such as Metallica, Slayer, Slipknot and Queens of the Stone Age followed over the coming decades.

Stadium rock bands and hair bands, on the other hand, simply added eye-liner and hairspray to rock and roll and the blues in the 1980s. The themes of songs—once reflective of the pain of injustice, misfortune and poverty—now often became trite, narrow and flattened out. So too did the music: repetitive, unimaginative, overproduced and designed more to provide photo ops for through-the-air-leaping, longhaired lead singers in tight leather pants. Politicized music about suffering and injustice now became self-indulgent, sexualized music about lust and infidelity. Oh well, the same thing happened to the blues in Chicago in the 1950s and then to rap in Hollywood during the 1990s.

Rock and roll went into the recording studio and further new sounds emerged. Live music became one thing, studio albums something else. While bands like the Grateful Dead steadfastly stuck to the road and concentrated on their distinctive live shows (retinues of Deadheads following along), producer George Martin re-engineered the post–*Sgt. Pepper* Beatles as the purveyors of multi-track electronic and orchestral studio wizardry and Ravi Shankar–influenced canned musical mysticism. Some bands in the seventies did both—for example, Pink Floyd and Emerson, Lake and Palmer, with their huge shows and highly produced studio albums. Later, DJs would continue an extended conversation with live and studio music by mixing and remixing past, present and future.

There were conversations and often arguments that arose between North and South (Neil Young and Lynyrd Skynyrd regarding the southern men of Alabama), or East and West. Even before the hip-hop battle between Biggie Smalls and Tupac Shakur ended in the deaths of both, there was Woodstock versus Altamont in 1969. The children of the Age of Aquarius tumbled about a huge anthill in New York State celebrating free love, rock and roll, and hallucinogenic wonderment. A few months later, an edgy, petulant, nasty crowd at the Altamont Speedway in California erupted into violence that ended in death while The Rolling Stones performed.

Then MTV came on the scene like a strident interior designer wired on cocaine and began wallpapering musical sound as visual candy. Video changed how music was not only heard, but also written and produced. Today, the virtual spaces of the internet and digital downloads are rewriting the face of music yet again. Is the old-fashioned record store soon going to experience its final death throes?

Just as the physical experience of popular music is of huge importance to its character and role, time and space are crucial to anyone's engagement with popular music of every kind. Whether sacred or profane, lofty or lowly, passed on as manna from heaven or bubbling up from the sewers, popular music is something we feel in our bones as it travels around us in the very air we breathe.

"Where the Streets Have No Name": Popular Music and Its Dialogue with Freedom

As Clive Cockerton points out in "Serious Pleasure: The Role of the Arts" (the next reading in this unit) the Greek philosopher Plato thought that art was corrupting. The ancient Greeks believed that music, being mathematical, was generally a little better than other forms of art, but when it got people going physically—singing, dancing, shaking their booties so to speak—thinkers like Plato despised it too. Music then became too sensual and irrational. Popular music was a drug for the masses—a placebo, a way of keeping everyone under the thumb of tyranny. Just give people a little rock and roll and everything will be fine.

And that is the question, is it not? Did rock and roll actually liberate youth in the fifties, challenge the conformity of suburbia and confront the atomic **juggernaut** of the Cold War? Or was it instead just about working-class kids in blue-suede shoes being neatly packed away in a 45-rpm vinyl warehouse of the *status quo*? Elvis as hip-grinding rebel; but Elvis too as soldier boy and good-ol' boy: Sequins R Us, God Bless America and I'm all shnooked up.

The rebellious spirit seemed to grow more defined and focused during the 1960s. Rock and roll became idealistic and politically activated; a new age seemed right around the corner. The establishment was already tottering on its corrupt foundations. So what happened then? Did rock and roll simply sell out? At Woodstock, for example, the Aquarian dream seemed to sparkle vibrantly, yet at the same time to be on the eve of its own destruction. Despite the earnestness of the words and music of protest, the helicopters that flew in artists like Joplin sounded (whup, whup, whup, whup) eerily like those taking working-class boys and black boys to their deaths in the Vietnam War. Meanwhile, the **ubiquitous** sound towers that emerged like giants from among the sea of bodies resembled the guard towers of the coming explosion of the American industrial-prison complex in the 1980s during the "war on drugs."

So—one more time—was rock and roll a new vision, a talisman of freedom that sixties rockers could wear with their beads, their long hair and the flags they sewed onto their Levi's? Or were these rock music fans all just dupes, the blind slaves of the record company bosses, the easy-riding politicians who were laughing all the way to the bank? In the same vein, is rap today still truly about resistance and black identity, or is it simply about selling overpriced basketball shoes and clothing and showing off your bling-bling?

Either way, it seems to be clear that one of the main roles that popular music plays is that of transgression: of crossing boundaries, testing limits. Whether it be the "princes of darkness" of heavy metal, androgynous stars like Michael Jackson and Marilyn Manson, or the "gangstas" of hip hop, musicians often take on the task of pushing a particular society's standards to the margins of acceptability.

Indeed, in many cultures, musicians have traditionally fulfilled the role of the trickster—a figure who says one thing and means another, who frequently disguises his true meaning behind a false pose. The bluesman was equal parts

juggernaut
overwhelming destructive force

ubiquitous
ever-present

saint and sinner, and you never really knew which role he would be playing at any given time. He could make you lose your soul one night and then he could turn around and hand it right back to you all polished up, squeaky clean and as good as new the very next day. This was a special kind of power: the freedom to change things, most of all the self.

Without the ambiguity of the trickster—the troubling inconsistencies of a Robert Johnson, John Lennon, Kurt Cobain, Madonna or Tupac Shakur—perhaps we would never see beyond the ordinary, the mundane, the dry indifference of official "taste." The very fact that we do not know their intentions, their meaning, their relevance *for sure* is the one thing that keeps us always questioning, and keeps our engagement and dialogue with music open and unfixed, and consequently, at least somewhat democratic.

Transgressing norms, conventions and social propriety is necessary in any culture that strives to entertain freedom and resist domination. Transgression is essential to any idea of change, of redefining boundaries, of understanding difference and of recognizing multiple levels of meaning. Without transgression, we simply do not know where we stand or who we are. The powers that be might give us Eden, and it might very well be perfection, but knowing nothing of our nakedness limits the depth of our collective experience.

At the other end of the scale, transgression can simply become a bad cartoon, breaking rules for its own sake, destroying meaning and value because everything becomes permissible and there remains no sense of the reason for transgressing to begin with. When transgression becomes the standard and the law, then it devolves into the conformity of debauchery and violence: Woodstock becomes Altamont, John Lennon becomes Charles Manson. Worse, in the final analysis, transgression may actually work to bolster the *status quo* by making money for capitalism and distracting its audience from the real political issues of freedom and human rights in favour of a little titillation and some bling-bling.

The price of popular music is its very populism, which has been a tool for tyrants since ancient times. But it may be the price we have to pay for the not insignificant possibilities for an open society that the experience of popular music offers. The primarily uncertain and unofficial status of popular music is also its main means of disturbing the *status quo*, of offering at least some alternatives to the conventional and often unjust activities of the powers that be. Moreover, it cannot be forgotten that true innovation in popular music has always emerged from the unpredictable margins and never from the overproduced, controlled and controlling centre, even if these innovations are hijacked and appropriated later on. And the rock-and-roll activism of the sixties is certainly not dead. Groups such as Public Enemy, U2 and Rage

Against the Machine have been powerfully engaged with politics and justice. Trickster as rock star does not always mean self-absorbed rogue with no interest in the rest of the world. That role is just as likely to be filled by the disengaged elitist art collector as by any rule-breaking, profanity-spewing, trash-talking rapper.

So perhaps the answer to all of the above questions is a very tricksterly yes, yes, yes, and yes again. Popular music simply contains both the "good" *and* the "bad" (and sometimes the plain "butt ugly") in its calls and responses. That is the very characteristic and value of dialogue as a democratic principle: its openness to a variety of responses means that we can never entirely predict or control the responses we might elicit over time and space. On the one hand, popular music gives voice to the marginalized, validates the emotion and the body, raises the spirits of all and encourages dialogue between the past and the present, between black and white, north, south, east and west. On the other hand, it lowers the bar, encourages mediocrity, validates appearances in place of substance, incites gratuitous violence, promotes ignorance and inhibits tolerance. But in the end, popular music simply just IS, in all its mishmash, and in all its extremes, from aspiring to sublime, liberating visions to choking to death on its own vomit (a final pastime of many a rock star).

To ask popular music always to give us the same response, whether marvellous or ludicrous, is simply asking too much of it. Popular music responds to our changing calls and, as such, it is as brilliant and dreary as we are at any given time and shares our good points equally with our failings. And perhaps that is not such a bad quality for a cultural form that has the potential to express so fully our diverse, uncertain and all-too-human condition.

Notes

[1] R.M. Jones, "Trouble in Mind," MCA Music, a Division of MCA Inc., ASCAP.

[2] Pierre Bourdieu, *Distinction: A Social Critique of the Judgement of Taste* (London: Routledge, 1984).

"One More Time: Our Ongoing Dialogue with Popular Music" was written for *The Human Project* by Ian Baird, a professor at the Humber College Institute of Technology and Advanced Learning. Used by permission.

Serious Pleasure: The Role of the Arts

Clive Cockerton

In many people's eyes, the arts are the toy department of life—occasionally amusing, perhaps, but in the long run a waste of time for men and women of action and purpose. The Greek philosopher Plato (427–347 BCE) argued that art was a distraction we would be better off without. According to Plato, art was a distraction for the following reasons:

1. Art is sensual and distracts us from the more important quests (such as moral or spiritual quests). In its arousal of basic instincts, in its stimulation/simulation of violence and lust, it is anarchic, a force for disorder in the community.

2. Art imitates reality; to learn about reality it is much better to study reality itself rather than a pale imitation.

3. Art deals with images, not truth; it doesn't advance knowledge, it doesn't discover anything, it only seems to understand.

In short, art is corrupting, imitative, and empty.

Since Plato, many moralists have branched off from these arguments and urged us to consider that bright colour and decoration are immoral because they call attention to the self instead of singing the praises of God, or that "realistic" novels were too shocking for the delicate sensibilities of young women, or that rock 'n' roll would corrupt and deprave youth with its primitive rhythms. At a much less passionate level, many business people are skeptical of the arts, except where they can be trained to serve the purpose of promoting consumption of goods and services in advertising. Politicians frequently see the arts as "frills," and in a time of recession the artistic community is the first to feel the cuts of government support. All of these views, whether held by philosophers, moralists, business people or politicians, have in common the conviction that art is not serious.

This doesn't mean that the effects of art can't be serious. Plato was concerned that literature and art were disruptive and corrupting. Stories need sinners to be interesting. Tales of people who always do the right thing are predictable, preachy and boring. Yet stories that embrace all that is human, the sinners as well as the saints, compel us to accept the humanity of those who lie, cheat, betray—of those who are greedy, lustful and cruel. And not just accept the humanity of others, but also recognize those very qualities in

---

This article was written for *The Human Project*. Used by permission.

ourselves. Moralists worry that this recognition and acceptance are subversive and undermine moral authority. Whenever we encounter an argument that says that a certain film or type of music will inflame or deprave, or that violence on TV will lead to violent children, we are dealing with an offshoot of Plato's original concern.

Aristotle, a student of Plato, developed a counter-argument that suggested that the symbolic experience of violence in the arts was actually helpful and worked like a safety valve for our violent sides. Through the emotion raised in watching a story unfold, we achieve *catharsis*, a cleansing and purging of destructive emotion in a safe and contained way. For Aristotle, nothing was to be gained from denying our destructive urges. Indeed, the opportunity to face our sometimes violent and immoral nature in a story lessened the threat that our urges might become reality. In other words, when watching a violent and terrifying story, we rehearse the emotion along with the actors and are released from having to act it out. However, recent psychological tests on children exposed to violent television suggest that some harmful results do occur. There's no simple, mechanical process whereby children watch violent acts and then always re-enact them. It's a more subtle process of shifting the atmosphere, of weakening the inhibition to violence that over time can result in changed behaviour. However, Aristotle couldn't predict Saturday morning TV and its impact on children. His insights were an attempt to describe adult responses to serious drama, and they remain useful as reflections on how the adult mind responds. Even adults have terrors and nightmares, and the arts enable us to face what horrifies us and move beyond it as well.

But can art have a harmful impact on sane, responsible adults? Is some subject matter inherently so corrupting that it cannot be safely explored, a suggestion that most artists would resist? Society clearly has interests at stake, and probably should find ways to protect itself from exploitation of sensational subject matter, but there is a great deal of difference between the sleazy exploitation of the pornographer and the serious exploration of the artist. The courts, however, have not found a reliable way of measuring that difference. Should the failure of the courts and the anxieties of moralists keep us from discussing controversial subjects? Is the danger from the arts real? As Plato writes:

> Much is at stake, more than most people suppose; it is a choice between becoming a good man or a bad; poetry, no more than wealth or power or honours, poetry can tempt us to be careless of justice and virtue. (*The Republic*)

Although Plato refers to poetry here, this fear of temptation would apply equally to other arts, because the seductive power of all arts threatens the rule of reason. Elsewhere, Plato argues that drama

> waters the growth of passions which should be allowed to wither away and sets them up in control although the goodness and happiness of our lives depend on their being held in subjection.

This idea may seem exaggerated and extreme to a modern audience, but for Plato our happiness depended on leading a good life, and a good life depended on control of the emotions by reason.

Scene from *Disclosure*

Plato's second objection, that art imitates reality, reflects his concern that we could be deceived by the distortions and exaggerations of the story-telling process. Put crudely, a film such as *Disclosure*, which presents the story of a man who is sexually harassed by his female employer, however worthwhile the story may be in artistic terms, could lead the viewer to gross misperceptions about the nature of sexual harassment and power in the workplace. Clearly, the social reality has been that men have been the dominant sex in terms of business power and are far more likely to harass employees than women are. Yet the fictional story may be compelling because it touches our emotions or thrills us, and we may be tempted to think of the film as a realistic and likely representation of what really goes on in business. The reality becomes apparent when we think about it, but for Plato we are always in danger when we succumb to the pleasurable pull of a story that could lead us down a rhetorical path to error. Of course, we are all aware and a little bit wary of the common lies of film—the couple overcoming all obstacles to their love and riding off into the sunset and the hero triumphing against seemingly impossible odds. However, the creators of these stories could defend their stories by saying that they don't have to be likely, just plausible, and that the preference for heroic triumph over dismal failure is an understandable and universal audience choice.

My favourite distortion is the glaring omission that very few characters in film worry about who pays, and no screen time is consumed with the practical issues of getting and saving money that take up so much time in the actual world. Writers and filmmakers could respond that all stories necessarily involve compression, and that compression involves eliminating **superfluous** detail, leaving the essential story to stand out boldly, without being submerged in the minute and tedious chores of everyday life. I'm just not sure that our relationship to money is always so inessential.

superfluous
unnecessary

Perhaps Plato's most intellectually interesting objection is the third one—that art involves an inevitable illusion. What we see in film is not reality; when we read fiction, we enter a world that is entirely made up. For Plato, the fact that we see images and enter into fantasy worlds means that we are turning away from truth. After reading a novel, can we say we know anything about the real world? We may think we know something of the human situation described in the plot of the novel, but have we acquired any verifiable concepts, as we might have if we had read a psychology textbook instead?

Well, perhaps not verifiable in the same controlled, scientific, experimental way, and maybe not full-blown concepts, but I would argue that, yes, novels provide us with genuine insights into human behaviour and situations. And these insights are verifiable, at least in a comparative way. When we finish a novel, we compare the truth of what we have read with our experience of the truth. In this way, every reading is some kind of experiment, some kind of verification. The fact that Hamlet or Falstaff are made-up characters in Shakespeare's plays does not prevent us from learning a great deal about ourselves and other people from them. They may be literally non-existent, but it makes no sense to refer to them in this way because their creation enriches our understanding of the real. So, too, does the imaginative testing of possibilities involved in any serious novel. And since every testing of fictional possibilities is verified or rejected by every reader, novels that are read and endorsed by many readers probably have a lot to say to us. Perhaps novels are the most insightful artistic medium, but surely the same comparative experience operates with certain kinds of realistic film. In the film *American Beauty*, for instance, the director clearly tries to capture something of the mood of suburban North America. The audience naturally compares its own feelings to the attitudes toward money, work, family and sexuality depicted in the film and almost immediately looks for answers to some interesting questions. Is the film credible? Does it fit with my own experience, or is it at least plausible, given the fictional characters and situation? When we see a film that affects us, we reflect on what we have seen and we search for verification in our own lives.

We experience stories as we experience the world—from a perspective, a point of view that is both emotional and rational. Plato was wary of our emotional natures; he believed that they were not to be denied perhaps, but kept in strict control. In our day, despite the enormous success of science, we generally don't experience life as detached observers. Indeed, detachment seems too clinical, and the perspective of the scientist lacks the engagement with experience that a fulfilled life seems to require. Instead we grope about through our lives, using bits of knowledge and a lot of emotion in a constantly shifting understanding—as we do in novels. We discover that emotion can be as reliable a guide to right conduct and behaviour as ideas and concepts. Some actions just don't feel right. Others, despite what we might have been taught to believe, feel liberating and joyful. Literature helps us to feel more acutely and generously as it guides us through the ever-expanding repertoire of human situations contained in its pages. It involves a passionate way of knowing, different from, but not inferior to, the relentless rationality of the philosopher or the precise observation of the scientist.

Still, literature is the most intellectual art form. Ideas are undeniably present in great works; even if they are never explicitly described, or talked about, they hover in the background. The consequences of ideas are revealed, are shown to be valuable or not, but not directly in argument form. Ideas are produced by scientists, philosophers, academics, by all of us. It is in literature that ideas are given flesh, tested not in debate, but in a re-creation of life. The cold, abstract and theoretical position is abandoned and replaced with a vantage point that is passionately considered and grounded in particular lives. As the philosopher Lorraine Code writes:

> The claim that literature is a source of knowledge rests upon a belief in the value of understanding the particular. It implies that a minute and inward understanding of particulars has the capacity to go beyond itself, to show something more general . . . . (*Epistemic Responsibility*)

Why do some particular characters' lives seem to speak to all of us, when clearly not all of our lives resemble the particular character? The writer creates an image of human complexity that draws us into the fictional world, convinces us of its reality and at the same time throws light onto the real world. Theoretical understanding may be an essential element to knowledge, but unless it is grounded in the particular, theoretical understanding seems bloodless. The film *Brokeback Mountain*, based on a short story by Annie Proulx, is a love story of two initially reluctant cowboys who find themselves drawn to each other and who get involved in a physical relationship. After their work ends, they go back to their more conventional lives and both end up marrying. But they can't forget each other and continue to meet occasionally for years. Ennis del Mar tells his partner: "I wish I could quit you." They cannot live a life together, nor can they move on. It's an old and tragic story of love without a happy ending. This unusual and potentially controversial film ranks as the eighth most successful romantic drama of all time. The success of the film rests on its insistence that the audience learn about the characters' lives in a detailed and particular way, that the viewers acquire an intimate knowledge of a complex situation before coming to any conclusions.

This kind of enforced acceptance of the characters' dilemma leads to an understanding that would be difficult to achieve through any other route.

The great American poet Wallace Stevens (1879–1955) wrote a poem whose title, "Not Ideas about the Thing, but the Thing Itself," contains the ambition most writers have to deliver directly an intimate understanding of the world. For this intimacy to be achieved, characters can't just be mouthpieces of ideas or virtues, but instead must convince us of their full individuality and their real humanity. Our lives are shaped by diverse combinations of ideas and experience, whether we are conscious of them or not. Fiction provides a means of becoming more conscious, of constantly examining and testing these ideas and experiences. Through this fictional process, we learn which ideas are useful, not just as ideas but as guiding principles.

When we read a novel, we may come to know a situation or a character very well; indeed, we may know all the significant details about a person's life (thoughts as well as actions). It's possible to know fictional characters better than our close friends. By providing us with all the information we need and by coming to a conclusion, novels present a complete vision. This completeness necessarily lacks some of life's random quality. Novels conclude, life goes on. By concluding, novels ask us to stop and think. By focusing on some of the most fundamental issues (growth, independence, love, pain, death) that we encounter in the real world, novels ask us to reflect on our own lives. But they don't just ask: they seduce us with pleasure, with worlds spun from word-magic. They extend the promise of intimacy, they leave us with insight.

Whenever it occurs, the combination of pleasure, beauty and insight is life-affirming. While pleasure and beauty are frequently found on the shimmering surface of art—in the form of delight in a turn of phrase or in intensity of vision—the insight cuts to the heart of issues, toward a deeper understanding of people and human experience. The answer to Plato's desire to rid his world of art lies in the value of pleasure and insight to the individual reader and viewer. Rather than being opposed to the quest for a rational life, perhaps the arts are complementary to it, providing a testing board for the different ideas that call out to us. At any rate, art's value doesn't stop with beneficial experiences for the individual, but extends to a community. Indeed, the shared experience of art helps to create a sense of community. Many cold winds blow through an individual's life, but the arts tell you that you're not alone, that others have cried as hard, laughed as loudly and loved as deeply. There's pleasure in that—in the community with others that the arts magically bring to us. Serious pleasure.

"Serious Pleasure" was written for *The Human Project* by Clive Cockerton, retired Associate-Dean of General Education at the Humber College Institute of Technology and Advanced Learning. Used by permission.

Looking for Beauty

Clive Cockerton

Dante Meets Beatrice at Ponte Santa Trinita, Henry Holiday, 1883.
The poet Dante Alighieri sees Beatrice Portinari walking on the banks
of the Arno and is inspired to write his masterwork, *The Divine Comedy*.

We may have different ideas of the beautiful, but we sure know when we are in its presence. When we see a beautiful person, someone who for whatever reason grabs our attention, the experience can be staggering. Cartoons and movies have a lot of fun with the moment when a character first sees someone beautiful. The character does a "double take," gulps, lets his jaw drop, or stares bug-eyed at the person who has captured his attention. If he is driving, he may nearly or actually veer off the road. What could be going on here that a character suddenly cares so little about his appearance and even his own survival? It's as if the "beautiful one" momentarily sucks all our attention and we lose a sense of self-awareness. But it's usually just a moment, and then we shake our head, re-adjust, re-focus our attention and move on. But what a moment! Why have we been so compelled?

Of course, we experience the beautiful in many forms and in many ways without the sexual undertow of seeing an especially attractive person. In sports, we may root for our favourite team and hope that they win, but I would suggest that we are also hoping to be astonished by some especially graceful manoeuvre from either side, a moment that will live on in our minds long after the details of the game are forgotten. In hockey, the speed and possibility of violent collision would seem to dictate the need for caution, yet the great players find ways to abandon caution and be creative in their search for a goal—so that after they are successful in scoring, even the opposing players are left shaking their heads in admiration. To be sure, no one likes to be scored on, but sometimes it's a privilege to be present when something so rare and beautiful happens. Even when your interest and commitment are in preventing a goal from happening, sometimes the beauty of a goal allows you to see beyond your own interest.

Many of us find something spiritual in our experience of nature, particularly when nature is putting on one of its grand shows such as the northern lights or a great sunset. There is something compellingly sweet about watching a

---

This article was written for *The Human Project*. Used by permission.

magnificent sunset evolve. You may be wrong in your anticipation of how the sunset will develop, but you are right in thinking that you are watching something special. You may live a very long life and never see a sunset quite like the one you are watching. This particular perception of beauty is powerful, but also fleeting and transient, perhaps never to be seen again. The consolation of beauty in nature is relatively rare and getting more and more so as most of us live in cities that obscure our relationship to nature. But even when we lived in a closer relation to nature, the breath-taking moments, the moments when we could contemplate and wonder at the beauty of the world, were few.

There is a sweet sadness that lies behind this perception of beauty. We are always surprised by beauty, as if it reveals more than we have come to expect. We expect a good deal less because beauty is too absent from our day-to-day reality, filled as it is with ordinary worries and tasks. Beauty says: "Stop! Look at me!" It says that there is more to life than the greyness of errands and worn-out opinions. It reminds us to be more attentive and appreciative of the world. It reminds us to be more alive. The words of the Spanish philosopher Ortega y Gasset (1883–1955), "Tell me what you pay attention to, and I will tell you who you are," ring true and remind us of the reciprocal relationship between what we perceive and experience and who we essentially become. The experience of beauty can be transformative as it acts as a critique of our world, as if to say, "Why do you live like this? Why do you have such low expectations?" It can be inspirational, if we resolve to make beauty a less rare element in our lives. It can speak powerfully to us, telling us that we should seek the solace of nature more frequently, we should listen to music more often and we should ensure that we place ourselves where beauty may more easily reach us. For beauty is precious and rare and quickly passing.

Even beauty in human form contains within it a kind of sadness. The beauty of a dancer's movement is strictly limited by time, for someday the dancer will not be able to perform the grand leap. We appreciate the glory of the young and strong body, but the most beautiful body eventually succumbs to gravity and finally dies. Beauty makes us more aware of time, which can, of course, be a very good thing. If beauty is rare and fleeting, then we must pay attention to it if we are to be inspired and transformed by it, and, hopefully, in the process make it a more frequent visitor to our lives. A moment's perception may lead to a greater and more desirable sense of urgency in our lives.

As much as sadness may be a part of the emotional backdrop of beauty, it's certainly not the most obvious part of being in its presence. More immediately apparent is the elation we feel as our body and mind are swept up in a rush of focused and excited senses. Iris Murdoch (1919–1999), a British novelist and philosopher, speaks of an "unselfing" that occurs in the presence of beauty. Much of *The Human Project* deals with the importance of knowing oneself, of defining what the self is, and of figuring out ways to understand and get along with other selves. But there is also a tremendous relief when our ego lets go of its dominant hold on our psyche and its plans, agendas, concerns and ambitions get momentarily pushed to the margins. Suddenly, we are not the most important thing in the room. Psychologically, a meeting with beauty mimics falling in love. Just for that moment, the daily anxieties and obsessions are swept away and we are lost in beauty. This surrender to the power of beauty involves a recognition by the self of its own inadequacies, of its incompleteness without beauty. If we are incomplete without beauty, then when we encounter it, we experience something like a flutter of fulfilment and the moment is joyous.

If seeing beauty is like falling in love, it is most likely a short-lived infatuation, as reality tugs us back into the world of duties to be performed and tasks completed. The world is too busy for dreamy absorption in anything as insubstantial as beauty. Yet we remain haunted by the moment when everything looked so good, and some of us wonder how we can extend the influence of beauty in our lives.

"Beauty is in the eye of the beholder," we've all been told. Hegel tells us that "every bridegroom regards his bride as beautiful, being possibly the only person who does so . . . ." It's a lucky and good thing that we can be so deceived as to think our marriage partner embodies not only great moral qualities but also has the good sense to appear beautiful. Alexander Nehamas (b. 1946), the Princeton philosopher, goes a step further than Hegel when he says, "The question is not whether I can love someone who is ugly . . . but whether I can love someone I find ugly, and I believe that's impossible."

When we respond to someone we think attractive, are we reacting to someone who fits a socially approved stereotype or to some happy convergence of DNA that has produced an individual look? While we all may have personal favourites, there does seem to be some kind of agreement about the kind of people who are judged physically beautiful in the public eye. The actors Gong Li and Halle Berry, or Denzel Washington and Daniel Craig may be dramatically different from each other, but there are qualities that they do share, among them a certain symmetry of features. Not an absolute mathematical symmetry, because sometimes small flaws in symmetry—such as a crooked smile or the presence of a mole—can be more, rather than less, endearing as they make the beautiful person seem more human, more like us. Still, there is an overall balance and proportion among their features. An even more elusive quality that many attractive people share is the ability to be expressive—that is, the ability to embody emotions in a look or a gesture. This ability of external appearance to suggest an interior life, with a complete

Gong Li

set of emotions and attitudes, is essential to our relationship to the beautiful person. We can flatter ourselves that we are not just obsessed with external appearance but are led to a realization of inner beauty.

Still, it's not just self-flattery that suggests that we desire to penetrate beyond the superficial level. As we come to know people, we learn of their virtues, their warmth, their humour, their intelligence, and these qualities lead us to re-evaluate the physical attractiveness of a person so that as we actually begin to like a person, we also find that our sense of their physical beauty soars. However, it is not so easy to draw a line between internal and external beauty. When we say a person is warm, we are saying that the person has a good-hearted and welcoming approach to other people. Yet we observe this through an invitational quality in the voice, and a generous smile, both very physical features. Humans are extremely interpretive of each other, and physical gestures and features are always being given the once over and somehow being connected to qualities of character.

Where else besides attractive people can we experience beauty? We have already mentioned sunsets and the northern lights. Canada is fortunately blessed with a great many natural wonders, from the Rocky Mountains to our three oceans, thousands of lakes and rivers, and a seemingly endless coastline. As important as this natural heritage is to our imagined sense of who we are, it must be admitted that most of us have only a cursory experience with nature. The majority of Canadians live in cities and, as such, are more likely to live next to typical North American urban blight rather than inspiring architecture. The Ontario College of Art and Design is a witty and whimsically appropriate building for an art college, and the Art Gallery of Ontario has earned favourable reviews from critics and an enthusiastic response from gallery visitors. Still, we do not seem to have an architectural equivalent to New York's Chrysler Building or London's Swiss Re, aka "the Gherkin," structures that most residents in these cities feel a special bond with and which fairly represent the confidence and power of New York and London. Their imposing stature aside, the CN Tower and the Royal Ontario Museum, even with its recent crystalline addition, both seem to pale in comparison from an aesthetic point of view.

London's Swiss Re building

However, inside the Art Gallery of Ontario hangs one of the great masterworks, *The Massacre of the Innocents*, by Peter Paul Rubens (1577–1640). This painting depicts the Biblical story of the massacre of young male children ordered by King Herod of Judea to end the life of the infant messiah. The subject matter is gross slaughter, and the extremes of violence, cruelty and the beginnings of endless grief are laid out in front of the viewer with great power. Not what one normally thinks of as beautiful. Yet in its depiction of physical

David's *Madame Recamier*

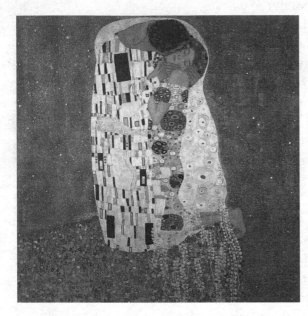

Gustav Klimt's *The Kiss*

tension and emotional response to horror, the painting creates a terrible kind of beauty.

Much contemporary art has gone even further and altogether abandoned being beautiful and sensual in favour of being interesting and intellectual. Mark Gertler's *The Merry-Go-Round*, which appears on the cover of this book, is a good example: it offers no sweeping seduction of the senses, just a clever idea and an obvious critique of modern life. It is also true, unfortunately, that as art has abandoned beauty as not being its central focus, audiences have abandoned art in such numbers as to make gallery visits a clearly elitist activity.

Of course, there are more conventional versions of beauty in art galleries around the world. Bouguereau's *The Abduction of Psyche* and Gustav Klimt's *The Kiss* are both sweetly irresistible. In a perhaps more serious way, *Mary Magdalene in Ecstasy*, by Caravaggio, and *Allegory of Spring,* by Botticelli, reward the onlooker with a way of looking that lingers in the mind long after the viewing. David's *Madame Recamier* has a certain indefinable grace, Turner's *Rain, Steam and Speed* captures the energy of the potent and opposing forces of nature and technology. Francis Bacon's *Three Studies for Figures at the Base of a Crucifixion*, like *The Massacre of Innocents*, reminds the viewer that art need not be easy and that one can be transfixed by a beautiful rendition of horror. In comparison, Tamara de Lempicka's portraits of strong and stylized women seem like eye-candy but still exert their fascination. These painters do not form a very coherent list. Among them are some of the greatest painters who have ever lived, and next to them are mentioned others who merely captured something decorative of their time in history. They are all painters who produced images that I carry with me wherever I go. These images become part of the interior landscape of my mind, and a point of comparison to all the images and realities that pass before me.

Beauty, real beauty, is more than skin deep, although our perception of it may begin with a dazzling surface. Beauty beckons to us with a momentary vision of a better and happier life, a vision of what life could be like. It tells us that in the midst of coping with daily reality, it's important not to lose sight of what is possible—that moment of clarity and elation—that redeems our struggle.

Note

The Future of Beauty symposium, part of the Chancellor Jackman Program for the Arts at the University of Toronto, May 3–4, 2007, was an attempt to re-invigorate the concept of beauty. Elaine Scarry of Harvard University and Alexander Nehamas of Princeton University were particularly helpful in identifying the new relevance of beauty. I would like to credit them and the conference at large with helping me to crystallize my ideas for this article.

"Looking for Beauty" was written for *The Human Project* by Clive Cockerton, retired Associate-Dean of General Education at the Humber College Institute of Technology and Advanced Learning. Used by permission.

"Murderers": An Introduction

Mary Ellen Kappler

"When my Uncle Moe dropped dead of a heart attack, I became expert in the subway system."

So begins the story "Murderers." How are we supposed to make sense of this? Two different things are going on—someone dies and someone else learns how to get around on public transit—but they don't seem to be connected. Who is Uncle Moe, and what does his heart attack have to do with the subway?

The first sentence of Leonard Michaels' short story "Murderers" presents us with a minor puzzle, but it also gives us a warning about what the story is going to do to us, where it's going to take us—what it's going to be "about." Death, obviously. But not just death. There is also a means of escape, a chance to get away from the place where people drop dead. The subway system seems to offer an alternative to Uncle Moe's heart attack, and a chance to *get away*—maybe even to outrun death itself, twisting and zooming from Queens to Coney Island, from Coney Island to the George Washington Bridge.

As we read further, we can see how the story plays with these ideas. The narrator sketches a bit of background for us, a fairly grim one. His whole Jewish-Polish immigrant family is dropping dead, not just Uncle Moe, but Charlie, Sam, Adele—people who never went anywhere or did anything, until the hearse hauled them away. *"I didn't want to wait for it,"* the narrator tells us. Instead he travels *"thousands of miles on nickels,"* and as he recites the names of the neighbourhoods he visits—Harlem, the Polo Grounds, Far Rockaway—we can feel his delight in the wide-open freedom of the city and the joy of his escape from the morbidly narrow confines of a dead and dying family.

And then, the invitation. The narrator (who, we now realize, is an adolescent boy) runs into his three friends Melvin, Arnold and Harold. *"The rabbi is home,"* says one. *"Let's go up to our roof,"* says another. Here is another way to escape mortality—even better than riding the subway. The boys know that the rabbi and his wife will be making love and that from their roof they'll have a great view into the couple's bedroom. It's the late 1940s—long before the internet—and what better entertainment could these boys have?

So our narrator, on the run from death, is enticed by its opposite: sex. Is there something trite in Michaels' use of such a conventional and obvious pairing? Or does the narrator's response open up new ways of seeing these things? "*I considered the roof,*" he tells us, "*the views of industrial Brooklyn, the Battery, ships in the river, bridges, towers and the rabbi's apartment. 'All right,' I said.*" Peeping into a bedroom, it seems, is just another aspect of the liberty the narrator granted himself when he traded the drab claustrophobia of home for the wide-open spaces of the city.

And as the boys carry out their plan, we see this same breadth of vision. A furtive act of **voyeurism** is simultaneously **transcendent**, as the boys' view from the roof takes in the Statue of Liberty and the Empire State Building as well as the naked rabbi and his naked wife. Squalid or sacred? Is it possible for one event to partake of both qualities?

On the "sacred" side, we have not only the intoxicating sense of **emancipation** that the narrator shares with us, but also the **sanctified** calling of the rabbi himself. The boys aren't spying on just any man and his wife. They are watching a man devoted to their own religion as he takes part in the pleasures of the flesh—an indication that these pleasures are themselves holy. And his wife embodies a different kind of divinity. It is customary for some Orthodox Jewish women to shave their heads when they marry. The rabbi's wife has done so, and now wears a variety of wigs: "*ten colours, fifty styles,*" the narrator tells us. "*She looked different, the same, and very good.*" Because she is different every time, the rabbi's wife becomes, for the narrator, something more universal and elemental than just a naked woman. "*He* [the rabbi] *was a naked man,*" he says, but "***she was what she was*** *in the garment of her soft, essential self*" (emphasis added). These words have an echo in Jewish scripture: "And God said to Moses, "I AM WHO I AM" (Exodus 3:14). The god of Judaism is proclaiming his identity, stating that he is the sum of all existence. The rabbi's wife is the sum of all women, of all sexual and sensual possibilities. "*To me,*" the narrator says, "*she was the world's lesson.*"

But the sacred elements of what the boys are watching do certainly coexist with more squalid matters: Harold's "cocktail-making" gestures as he masturbates; the "whorish" touch of the wristwatch the rabbi's wife is wearing. The sacred and the profane are intertwined, too close to each other to be separated, and just as we are reminded of this, Arnold, the youngest of the boys, slides off the roof and falls to his death.

The story has come full circle. The narrator's flight from the prison of his dying family has led him to the heights—to a rooftop where he can survey a kingdom and catch a glimpse of the "*world's lesson.*" But it has also betrayed him, delivered him back to the inescapable knowledge of mortality. Arnold has (very literally) "*dropped dead*"—as dead as Uncle Moe, as dead as

voyeurism
observing others in sexual acts

transcendent
inspiring

emancipation
liberation

sanctified
sacred

Charlie, Sam, Adele. As the story ends, the narrator lies in the bunkhouse of the summer camp where he and the other boys have been sent following the accident. "*I listened to owls,*" he says. "*I'd never before heard that sound, the sound of darkness, blooming, opening inside you like a mouth.*"

So all of these elements—death, escape, freedom, sex, holiness, profanity, guilt, darkness, fate—are brought together in a deceptively short story. What does it mean? That's for you to decide. One of the best things about fiction (or any type of art) is that it doesn't have a fixed, final, objective "meaning." When you read "Murderers," you'll bring your own thoughts, ideas and feelings about the elements it contains with you. Your memories and opinions, your values, your knowledge and your experience—all of these things will interact with the words on the page and produce your own unique reading of the story, your own individual sense of what the story "means."

For example, we've already looked at the way that the description of the rabbi's wife recalls a passage from the Book of Exodus. If you're familiar with the Bible, you'll probably pick up on a few other places where the story plays with scriptural ideas and images. The connections you make in this way will be part of the meaning of the story for you. Or maybe you'll be more drawn to the description of the rumba that the rabbi and his wife dance together as the boys watch, entranced. How do the rhythms of the dance lyrics work together with the building sexual excitement of the watchers? And speaking of rhythm, what about the way the author has used words, how he constructs his sentences, his paragraphs? "Murderers" is written with great economy. There's not an extra word in it, and every word is flawlessly chosen. Consider the description of Arnold's death. There is a sound of squealing rubber as the soles of his shoes slide on the roof. Then, "*Arnold's ring hooked a nailhead and the ring and ring finger remained. The hand, the arm, the rest of him, were gone.*" That's all. How would the story be different if Michaels had provided a more detailed description? What is the effect of his extremely concise narrative style? To what extent does the *way* he tells his story become part of what the story "means"? And what about the final image, the sound of the owls' cry blossoming like darkness within the narrator—what does this suggest to you, and how does it help you understand everything that has come before? How you answer any of these questions will depend—at least in part—on who *you* are, and what you've brought with you to the story.

There are many ways into—and through—every work of fiction, and much of the pleasure of reading comes from finding your own route. If you like "Murderers," then you might be encouraged to read more fiction. But if you don't like it, don't be *dis*couraged. There's always more to choose from. Not everything will be to your taste, but some stories surely will be. And each story you encounter can give you a glimpse of something new or help you look at something familiar from a different perspective. Fiction comes in many forms—novels, movies, plays, television programs among them; but ultimately, telling stories and listening to stories are among the most basic of human activities—part of how we make sense of our experience and try to encompass and understand ourselves and the world we live in.

"Murderers: An Introduction" was written for *The Human Project* by Mary Ellen Kappler, a professor at the Humber College Institute of Technology and Advanced Learning and the University of Guelph-Humber. Used by permission.

Murderers

Leonard Michaels

When my uncle Moe dropped dead of a heart attack I became expert in the subway system. With a nickel I'd get to Queens, twist and zoom to Coney Island, twist again toward the George Washington Bridge—beyond which was darkness. I wanted proximity to darkness, strangeness. Who doesn't? The poor in spirit, the ignorant and frightened. My family came from Poland, then never went any place until they had heart attacks. The consummation of years in one neighborhood: a black Cadillac, corpse inside. We should have buried Uncle Moe where he shuffled away his life, in the kitchen or toilet, under the linoleum, near the coffee pot. Anyhow, they were dropping on Henry Street and Cherry Street. Blue lips. The previous winter it was cousin Charlie, forty-five years old. Moe, Charlie, Sam, Adele—family meant a punch in the chest, fire in the arm. I didn't want to wait for it. I went to Harlem, the Polo Grounds, Far Rockaway, thousands of miles on nickels, mainly underground. Tenements watched me go, day after day, fingering nickels. One afternoon I stopped to grind my heel against the curb. Melvin and Arnold Bloom appeared, then Harold Cohen. Melvin said, "You step in dog shit?" Grinding was my answer. Harold Cohen said, "The rabbi is home. I saw him on Market Street. He was walking fast." Oily Arnold, eleven years old, began to urge: "Let's go up to our roof." The decision waited for me. I considered the roof, the view of industrial Brooklyn, the Battery, ships in the river, bridges, towers, and the rabbi's apartment. "All right," I said. We didn't giggle or look to one another for moral signals. We were running.

The blinds were up and curtains pulled, giving sunlight, wind, birds to the rabbi's apartment—a magnificent metropolitan view. The rabbi and his wife never took it, but in the light and air of summer afternoons, in the eye of gull and pigeon, they were joyous. A bearded young man, and his young pink wife, sacramentally bald. Beard and Baldy, with everything to see, looked at each other. From a water tank on the opposite roof, higher than their windows, we looked at them. In psychoanalysis this is "The Primal Scene." To achieve the primal scene we crossed a ledge six inches wide. A half-inch indentation in the brick gave us finger-holds. We dragged bellies and groins against the brick face to a steel ladder. It went up the side of the building, bolted into brick, and up the side of the water tank to a slanted tin roof which caught the afternoon sun. We sat on that roof like angels, shot through with light, derealized in brilliance. Our sneakers sucked hot slanted metal. Palms and fingers pressed to bone on nailheads.

The Brooklyn Navy Yard with destroyers and aircraft carriers, the Statue of Liberty putting the sky to the torch, the dull remote skyscrapers of Wall Street, and the Empire State Building were among the wonders we dominated. Our view of the holy man and his wife, on their living-room couch and floor, on the bed in their bedroom, could not be improved. Unless we got closer. But fifty feet across the air was right. We heard their phonograph and watched them dancing. We couldn't hear the gratifications or see pimples. We smelled nothing. We didn't want to touch.

For a while I watched them. Then I gazed beyond into shimmering nullity, gray, blue, and green murmuring over rooftops and towers. I had watched them before. I could tantalize myself with this brief **ocular** perversion, the general cleansing **nihil** of a view. This was the beginning of philosophy. I indulged in ambience, in space like eons. So what if my uncle Moe was dead? I was philosophical and luxurious. I didn't even have to look at the rabbi and his wife. After all, how many times had we dissolved stickball games when the rabbi came home? How many times had we risked shameful discovery, scrambling up the ladder, exposed to their windows—if they looked. We risked life itself to achieve this eminence. I looked at the rabbi and his wife.

Today she was a blonde. Bald didn't mean no wigs. She had ten wigs, ten colors, fifty styles. She looked different, the same, and very good. A human theme in which nothing begat anything and was gorgeous. To me she was the world's lesson. Aryan yellow slipped through pins about her ears. An olive complexion mediated yellow hair and Arabic black eyes. Could one care what she really looked like? What was *really*? The minute you wondered, she looked like something else, in another wig, another style. Without the wigs she was a baldy-bean lady. Today she was a blonde. Not blonde. *A* blonde. The phonograph blared and her deep loops flowed Tommy Dorsey, Benny Goodman, and then the thing itself, Choo-Choo Lopez. Rumba! One, two-three. One, two-three. The rabbi stepped away to delight in blond imagination. Twirling and individual, he stepped away snapping fingers, going high and light on his toes. A short bearded man, balls afling, cock shuddering like a springboard. Rumba! One, two-three. *Olé! Vaya*, Choo-Choo!

> I was on my way to spend some time in Cuba.
> Stopped off at Miami Beach, la-la.
> Oh, what a rumba they teach, la-la.
> Way down in Miami Beach,
> Oh, what a chroombah they teach, la-la.
> Way-down-in-Miami-Beach.

ocular
visual

nihil
nothingness

She, on the other hand, was somewhat reserved. A shift in one lush hip was total rumba. He was Mr. Life. She was dancing. He was a naked man. She was what she was in the garment of her soft, essential self. He was snapping, clapping, hopping to the beat. The beat lived in her visible music, her lovely self. Except for the wig. Also a watchband that desecrated her wrist. But it gave her a bit of the whorish. She never took it off.

Harold Cohen began a cocktail-mixer motion, masturbating with two fists. Seeing him at such hard futile work, braced only by sneakers, was terrifying. But I grinned. Out of terror, I twisted an encouraging face. Melvin Bloom kept one hand on the tin. The other knuckled the rumba numbers into the back of my head. Nodding like a defective, little Arnold Bloom chewed his lip and squealed as the rabbi and his wife smacked together. The rabbi clapped her buttocks, fingers buried in the cleft. They stood only on his legs. His back arched, knees bent, thighs thick with thrust, up, up, up. Her legs wrapped his hips, ankles crossed, hooked for constriction. "Oi, oi, oi," she cried, wig flashing left, right, tossing the Brooklyn Navy Yard, the Statue of Liberty, and the Empire State Building to hell. Arnold squealed oi, squealing rubber. His sneaker heels stabbed tin to stop his slide. Melvin said, "Idiot." Arnold's ring hooked a nailhead and the ring and ring finger remained. The hand, the arm, the rest of him, were gone.

We rumbled down the ladder. "Oi, oi, oi," she yelled. In a freak of ecstasy her eyes had rolled and caught us. The rabbi drilled to her quick and she had us. "*OI, OI*," she yelled above congas going clop, doom-doom, clop, doom-doom on the way to Cuba. The rabbi flew to the window, a red mouth opening in his beard: "Murderers." He couldn't know what he said. Melvin Bloom was crying. My fingers were tearing, bleeding into brick. Harold Cohen, like an adding machine, gibbered the name of God. We moved down the ledge quickly as we dared. Bongos went tocka-ti-tocka, tocka-ti-tocka. The rabbi screamed, "MELVIN BLOOM, PHILLIP LIEBOWITZ, HAROLD COHEN, MELVIN BLOOM," as if our names, screamed this way, naming us where we hung, smashed us into brick.

Nothing was discussed.

The rabbi used his connections, arrangements were made. We were sent to a camp in New Jersey. We hiked and played volleyball. One day, *apropos* of nothing, Melvin came to me and said little Arnold had been made of gold and he, Melvin, of shit. I appreciated the sentiment, but to my mind they were both made of shit. Harold Cohen never again spoke to either of us. The counselors in the camp were World War II veterans, introspective men. Some carried shrapnel in their bodies. One had a metal plate in his head. Whatever you said to them they seemed to be thinking of something else, even when they answered. But step out of line and a plastic lanyard whistled burning notice across your ass.

At night, lying in the bunkhouse, I listened to owls. I'd never before heard that sound, the sound of darkness, blooming, opening inside you like a mouth.

Let Me Make This Perfectly Clear

Gwendolyn MacEwen

Let me make this perfectly clear.
I have never written anything because it is a Poem.
This is a mistake you always make about me,
A dangerous mistake. I promise you
I am not writing this because it is a Poem.

You suspect this is a posture or an act
I am sorry to tell you it is not an act.

You actually think I care if this
Poem gets off the ground or not. Well
I don't care if this poem gets off the ground or not
And neither should you.
All I have ever cared about
And all you should ever care about
Is what happens when you lift your eyes from this page.

Do not think for one minute it is the Poem that matters.
It is not the Poem that matters.
You can shove the Poem.
What matters is what is out there in the large dark
and in the long light,
Breathing.

The Back Seat of My Mother's Car

Julia Copus

We left before I had time
to comfort you, to tell you that we nearly touched
hands in that vacuous half-dark. I wanted
to stem the burning waters running over me like tiny
rivers down my face and legs, but at the same time I was reaching out
for the slit in the window where the sky streamed in,
cold as ether, and I could see your fat mole-fingers grasping
the dusty August air. I pressed my face to the glass;
I was calling you—Daddy!—as we screeched away into
the distance, my own hand tingling like an amputation.
You were mouthing something I still remember, the noiseless words
piercing me like that catgut shriek that flew up, furious as a sunset
pouring itself out against the sky. The ensuing silence
was the one clear thing I could decipher—
the roar of the engine drowning your voice,
with the cool slick glass between us.

With the cool slick glass between us,
the roar of the engine drowning, your voice
was the one clear thing I could decipher—
pouring itself out against the sky, the ensuing silence
piercing me like that catgut shriek that flew up, furious as a sunset.
You were mouthing something: I still remember the noiseless words,
the distance, my own hand tingling like an amputation.
I was calling to you, Daddy, as we screeched away into
the dusty August air. I pressed my face to the glass,
cold as ether, and I could see your fat mole-fingers grasping
for the slit in the window where the sky streamed in
rivers down my face and legs, but at the same time I was reaching out
to stem the burning waters running over me like tiny
hands in that vacuous half-dark. I wanted
to comfort you, to tell you that we nearly touched.
We left before I had time.

Reflections on Julia Copus's "The Back Seat of My Mother's Car"

Richard Sanger

pentameter

line of verse consisting of five metrical feet

Ezra Pound

(1885–1972) American poet

promulgating

propagating

pace **Sylvia Plath**

suggestive of a line in a poem of the American poet and writer Sylvia Plath (1932–1963): "Daddy I'm through."

"Smash the **pentameter**," **Ezra Pound** urged in the ancient past of last century, **promulgating** a fallacy still preached today: that poetic form is somehow repressive, and free verse is democratic and liberating. The result is that most of today's students graduate believing it is easier to write a poem than it is to read one.

Julia Copus's "The Back Seat of My Mother's Car" at first appears a creature of its times, covering familiar confessional terrain in unexceptional free verse. Strangely for a young English poet (born in 1969), the setting and diction suggest suburban America—mother has her own car (with driver-operated automatic windows), father—*pace* **Sylvia Plath**—is Daddy, and daughter has contradictory impulses and strangely heightened perceptions ("fat mole-fingers," "catgut shriek," "furious sunset"). We learn, soon enough, that the two "we's" in the opening lines are not the same, that the mother is taking her daughter away from Daddy, severing the connection with the flick of a switch. So far, so good—or so-so.

But once the car window closes, something unusual starts to happen: Words, phrases, whole lines are repeated. The girl is remembering, trying to make sense of what has just occurred, and it's replaying itself in her head backwards in a hallucinatory loop. The closed car window has become a mirror: if the poem's first half describes the rupture, the second half, reversing the same lines, with subtle changes in punctuation, seems to recount the girl's entire subsequent life. She remembers silence, distance, the feeling of amputation; no longer crying out for her surprisingly vulnerable father, she addresses him in retrospect, he tries to touch her, and the almost banal lines that began the poem now close it, freighted with new meaning and power: "I wanted/ to comfort you, to tell you that we nearly touched./ We left before I had time."

Copus reminds us here that the purpose of formal constraints (metre, rhyme, repetition) is not to call attention through their gimmickry, but to serve the poem as a whole. By adhering faithfully to the bonds of her "**specular** poem," she transforms ordinary free verse into an extraordinary poem about the breaking of a bond.

specular

mirror-like

This Be the Verse

Philip Larkin

They fuck you up, your mum and dad.
They may not mean to, but they do.
They fill you with the faults they had
And add some extra, just for you.

But they were fucked up in their turn
By fools in old-style hats and coats,
Who half the time were soppy-stern
And half at one another's throats.

Man hands on misery to man.
It deepens like a coastal shelf.
Get out as early as you can,
And don't have any kids yourself.

I Go Back to May 1937

Sharon Olds

I see them standing at the formal gates of
    their colleges,
I see my father strolling out
under the ochre sandstone arch, the
red tiles glinting like bent
plates of blood behind his head, I
see my mother with a few light books at
    her hip
standing at the pillar made of tiny bricks
    with the
wrought-iron gate still open behind her, its
sword-tips black in the May air,
they are about to graduate, they are about
    to get married,
they are kids, they are dumb, all they know is
    they are
innocent, they would never hurt anybody.
I want to go up to them and say Stop,
don't do it—she's the wrong woman,
he's the wrong man, you are going to do things
you cannot imagine you would ever do,
you are going to do bad things to children,
you are going to suffer in ways you never
    heard of,
you are going to want to die. I want to go
up to them there in the late May sunlight
    and say it,
her hungry pretty blank face turning to me,
her pitiful beautiful untouched body,
his arrogant handsome blind face turning to me,
his pitiful beautiful untouched body,
but I don't do it. I want to live. I
take them up like the male and female
paper dolls and bang them together
at the hips like chips of flint as if to
strike sparks from them, I say
Do what you are going to do, and I will
    tell about it.

The Voice You Hear When You Read Silently

Thomas Lux

is not silent, it is a speaking-
out-loud voice in your head; it is *spoken*,
a voice is *saying* it
as you read. It's the writer's words,
of course, in a literary sense
his or her "voice" but the sound
of that voice is the sound of *your* voice.
Not the sounds your friends know
or the sound of a tape played back
but your voice
caught in the dark cathedral
of your skull, your voice heard
by an internal ear informed by internal abstracts
and what you know by feeling,
having felt. It is your voice
saying, for example, the word "barn"
that the writer wrote
but the "barn" you say
is a barn you know or knew. The voice
in your head, speaking as you read,
never says anything neutrally—some people
hated the barn they knew,
some people love the barn they know
so you hear the word loaded
and a sensory constellation
is lit: horse-gnawed stalls,
hayloft, black heat tape wrapping
a water pipe, a slippery
spilled *chirrr* of oats from a split sack,
the bony, filthy haunches of cows . . .
And "barn" is only a noun—no verb
or subject has entered into the sentence yet!
The voice you hear when you read to yourself
is the clearest voice: you speak it
speaking to you.

O Me! O Life!

Walt Whitman

O ME! O life! . . . of the questions of these recurring;
Of the endless trains of the faithless—of cities fill'd with the foolish;
Of myself forever reproaching myself, (for who more foolish than I, and who
    more faithless?)
Of eyes that vainly crave the light—of the objects mean—of the struggle ever
    renew'd;
Of the poor results of all—of the plodding and sordid crowds I see around
    me;
Of the empty and useless years of the rest—with the rest me intertwined;
The question, O me! so sad, recurring—What good amid these, O me, O life?

Answer.
That you are here—that life exists, and identity;
That the powerful play goes on, and you will contribute a verse.

APPENDIX

StudyDesk

To help you understand the many topics covered in *The Human Project,* we have included a computer study guide with the textbook. The StudyDesk program contains the following elements for each unit of the textbook:

- **Unit Overview:** a brief introduction to the main themes and issues of each unit;

- **Learning Outcomes:** a list of activities you will be able to complete at the end of each unit;

- **Key Concepts:** a quick way to review essential concepts you should understand, unit by unit;

- **Unit Review:** a complete list, on an article-by-article basis, of all terms and historical figures mentioned;

- **Terms and Concepts:** definitions and commentary of over 150 terms and concepts;

- **Biographical Sketches:** background information on over 80 historical figures mentioned in the textbook;

- **Summaries of Textbook Articles:** point-form summaries of each textbook article; and

- **Reading Room:** a selection of representative works by authors cited in the textbook along with reference materials.

The StudyDesk program uses your Internet browser to display on your computer. The StudyDesk screen is split into two panes. An expandable Table of Contents appears on the left side of the screen. To view the topics contained in each unit, just click the "book" icon next to the unit number. Similarly, to hide the topics from view, click the "book" icon again. To read the information contained in any topic, click the topic name. The topic information will then appear on the right side of the screen as demonstrated in the graphic shown here.

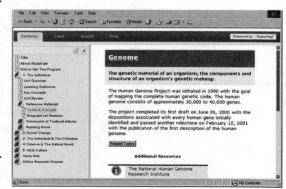

If you have ever used a web browser to view pages on the Internet, you will be familiar with the basic format of StudyDesk: clicking hotlinks calls up new pages that contain additional information. StudyDesk, however, uses a special form of web page. Most of the pages are contained in the program itself, while others are available only when you are online. The online pages are clearly identified by a special graphic: ⓘ

Unlike the textbook, the pages of which are usually read in order, with StudyDesk you use the mouse to call information to the screen in the order that serves your needs. You control what you read simply by clicking the mouse on a hotword (words in blue font or graphics that contain links) to activate a "jump" or a popup of a new page. When a jump occurs, new information will appear in place of what you were reading. When a popup occurs, new information appears on top of what you are reading in a scrollable window.

StudyDesk also includes several function buttons at the top of the screen:

- **Contents:** displays the expandable/collapsible Table of Contents in the left panel of the StudyDesk screen;

- **Index:** displays an alphabetic list of topics contained within StudyDesk;

- **Search:** displays a dialog field in the left panel of the screen in which you can type search words; the results of the search are then displayed in the left panel; and

- **Print:** allows you to print the currently displayed topic.

How to Start StudyDesk

StudyDesk runs directly from the CD-ROM that accompanies the textbook. A web page should appear when you insert the CD-ROM. If it does not, navigate to the CD-ROM drive, and click the file named "start-here.htm." This page contains additional information about the program and a link to start StudyDesk.

Minimum System Requirements

Computer: Pentium level PC, Mac OS X
RAM: 32mb
CD-ROM Drive
Browser: All major browsers supported
Plugin: Macromedia Flash 6.0 or later (installable from CD-ROM)

PHOTO CREDITS

"AS IS" LICENSE AGREEMENT AND LIMITED WARRANTY

READ THIS LICENSE CAREFULLY BEFORE OPENING THIS PACKAGE. BY OPENING THIS PACKAGE, YOU ARE AGREEING TO THE TERMS AND CONDITIONS OF THIS LICENSE. IF YOU DO NOT AGREE, DO NOT OPEN THE PACKAGE. PROMPTLY RETURN THE UNOPENED PACKAGE AND ALL ACCOMPANYING ITEMS TO THE PLACE YOU OBTAINED THEM. THESE TERMS APPLY TO ALL LICENSED SOFTWARE ON THE DISK EXCEPT THAT THE TERMS FOR USE OF ANY SHAREWARE OR FREEWARE ON THE DISKETTES ARE AS SET FORTH IN THE ELECTRONIC LICENSE LOCATED ON THE DISK:

1. **GRANT OF LICENSE and OWNERSHIP:** The enclosed computer programs and any data ("Software") are licensed, not sold, to you by Pearson Canada Inc. ("We" or the "Company") in consideration of your adoption of the accompanying Company textbooks and/or other materials, and your agreement to these terms. You own only the disk(s) but we and/or our licensors own the Software itself. This license allows instructors and students enrolled in the course using the Company textbook that accompanies this Software (the "Course") to use and display the enclosed copy of the Software for academic use only, so long as you comply with the terms of this Agreement. You may make one copy for back up only. We reserve any rights not granted to you..

2. **USE RESTRICTIONS:** You may not sell or license copies of the Software or the Documentation to others. You may not transfer, distribute or make available the Software or the Documentation, except to instructors and students in your school who are users of the adopted Company textbook that accompanies this Software in connection with the course for which the textbook was adopted. You may not reverse engineer, disassemble, decompile, modify, adapt, translate or create derivative works based on the Software or the Documentation. You may be held legally responsible for any copying or copyright infringement which is caused by your failure to abide by the terms of these restrictions.

3. **TERMINATION:** This license is effective until terminated. This license will terminate automatically without notice from the Company if you fail to comply with any provisions or limitations of this license. Upon termination, you shall destroy the Documentation and all copies of the Software. All provisions of this Agreement as to limitation and disclaimer of warranties, limitation of liability, remedies or damages, and our ownership rights shall survive termination.

4. **DISCLAIMER OF WARRANTY: THE COMPANY AND ITS LICENSORS MAKE NO WARRANTIES ABOUT THE SOFTWARE, WHICH IS PROVIDED "AS-IS." IF THE DISK IS DEFECTIVE IN MATERIALS OR WORKMANSHIP, YOUR ONLY REMEDY IS TO RETURN IT TO THE COMPANY WITHIN 30 DAYS FOR REPLACEMENT UNLESS THE COMPANY DETERMINES IN GOOD FAITH THAT THE DISK HAS BEEN MISUSED OR IMPROPERLY INSTALLED, REPAIRED, ALTERED OR DAMAGED. THE COMPANY DISCLAIMS ALL WARRANTIES, EXPRESS OR IMPLIED, INCLUDING WITHOUT LIMITATION, THE IMPLIED WARRANTIES OF MERCHANTABILITY AND FITNESS FOR A PARTICULAR PURPOSE. THE COMPANY DOES NOT WARRANT, GUARANTEE OR MAKE ANY REPRESENTATION REGARDING THE ACCURACY, RELIABILITY, CURRENTNESS, USE, OR RESULTS OF USE, OF THE SOFTWARE.**

5. **LIMITATION OF REMEDIES AND DAMAGES: IN NO EVENT, SHALL THE COMPANY OR ITS EMPLOYEES, AGENTS, LICENSORS OR CONTRACTORS BE LIABLE FOR ANY INCIDENTAL, INDIRECT, SPECIAL OR CONSEQUENTIAL DAMAGES ARISING OUT OF OR IN CONNECTION WITH THIS LICENSE OR THE SOFTWARE, INCLUDING, WITHOUT LIMITATION, LOSS OF USE, LOSS OF DATA, LOSS OF INCOME OR PROFIT, OR OTHER LOSSES SUSTAINED AS A RESULT OF INJURY TO ANY PERSON, OR LOSS OF OR DAMAGE TO PROPERTY, OR CLAIMS OF THIRD PARTIES, EVEN IF THE COMPANY OR AN AUTHORIZED REPRESENTATIVE OF THE COMPANY HAS BEEN ADVISED OF THE POSSIBILITY OF SUCH DAMAGES.** SOME JURISDICTIONS DO NOT ALLOW THE LIMITATION OF DAMAGES IN CERTAIN CIRCUMSTANCES, SO THE ABOVE LIMITATIONS MAY NOT ALWAYS APPLY.

6. **GENERAL:** THIS AGREEMENT SHALL BE CONSTRUED AND INTERPRETED ACCORDING TO THE LAWS OF THE PROVINCE OF ONTARIO. This Agreement is the complete and exclusive statement of the agreement between you and the Company and supersedes all proposals, prior agreements, oral or written, and any other communications between you and the company or any of its representatives relating to the subject matter.

Should you have any questions concerning this agreement or if you wish to contact the Company for any reason, please contact in writing: Permissions, Pearson Canada Inc., 26 Prince Andrew Place, Toronto, Ontario, M3C 2T8.